REALITY

A Sweeping New Vision of
the Unity of Existence,
Physical Reality, Information,
Consciousness, Mind and Time

Edgar L. Owen

Edgar L. Owen

First Edition, Version 1.0, August 1, 2013

Library of Congress Cataloging-in-Publication Data

Owen, Edgar L.
Reality: A sweeping new vision of the unity of existence, physical
reality, information, consciousness, mind and time / Edgar L. Owen –
first ed.
p. cm.
Includes biographical references.

ISBN-13: 978-0615869452 (Edgar L. Owen)

ISBN-10: 0615869459 (Pbk.)

EdgarLOwen.info

Self-published on CreateSpace.com

Printed in the United States of America

To my secret muse

PREFACE

I was born April 1st, 1941 and my life has been one big wonderful April Fools' joke ever since. Nothing is ever as it first appears and that is especially true of reality itself, the nature of which has been the central interest of my life for as long as I can remember even back to the revelations of my early childhood. But it is only now after a lifetime of study that this has coalesced into a clear and comprehensive vision of the deep structure of reality as I believe it actually is. I'm convinced the legacy of my brief time in reality is to realize and record its true nature as clearly as possible both for myself and the others who seek it.

Though it is completely novel, this vision of reality did not originate with me *ab initio* but is a continuation of the work of the many others who have sought it since ancient times. Whatever value my work has is only because it is supported by the noble efforts of all those who have come before in the long struggle to understand the ultimate nature of reality. And rather than taking personal credit for the theories in this book I feel that I am blessed to have received them from reality itself simply revealing itself to a diligent and careful observer. Who can ever know the ultimate origin of an idea! So this is only peripherally the author's work. It is more accurately reality in the continuing process of revealing itself to itself through its observers which the author has just been enormously privileged to realize and record.

Finally I wish to thank all those close personal friends who have been so tolerant and supportive of my unusual hermetic life style for all these years. You know who you are! Thank you, thank you, thank you!

CONTENTS

III: ELEMENTALS

IV: MIND AND REALITY

V: THE WORLD OF FORMS

VI: REALIZATION

VII: THE FUNDAMENTAL PRINCIPLES OF REALITY

EPILOGUE

NOTES

BIBLIOGRAPHY

INTRODUCTION

This book is a search for the true nature of reality. It attempts to reveal the most fundamental secrets of reality and by doing so to invoke the direct experience of reality as it actually is. It presents an entirely new vision of the deep structure of reality including the roles of mind and consciousness. It's a comprehensive and self-consistent vision that I believe seamlessly integrates new interpretations of accepted principles of modern physical, cognitive and information science with many completely new insights enriched by careful objective internal analysis of consciousness, mind and direct experience.

It is also informed by and consistent with some of the most profound of ancient philosophical insights. The result is a single comprehensive theory of enormous explanatory power that unifies and illuminates all the fundamental aspects of reality. It is an entirely new and truly revolutionary view of reality which I believe provides convincing answers to many of the great scientific and philosophical questions.

Though this theory relies only on natural mechanisms it goes far beyond the standard insights of modern science to explain such apparent enigmas as the origin of existence; the nature of consciousness, time and the present moment; the resolution of quantum paradox and the conceptual unity of quantum theory and relativity; the information structure of reality; the integral role of the observer, and even the nature of realization defined as experiencing reality as it actually is. These are all subjects about which neither the usual interpretations of modern science nor the many non-scientific metaphysical theories have had much meaningful to say.

Some may view this as a mystical vision of reality but if so it's a mysticism based in a deep understanding and direct experience of reality as it actually is as revealed by science and reason with no hint of the supernatural or metaphysical. By revealing the illusions inherent in the way reality is usually experienced and conceptualized by mind, reality itself is revealed as it actually is. This is not another 'New Age' feel good book designed to provide comfort (and income!) at the expense of objectivity but rather a serious attempt to reveal the eternal truths hidden within the habitual workings of mind and nature.

The underlying assumption of this book is that reality is accessible to direct experience and the logic of the human mind but only when very carefully analyzed with exacting care given to the hidden assumptions of language and deeply imbedded human thought patterns which evolved to describe a much more simplistic view of reality. However the very fact of our existence demonstrates that human logic and experience does have at least sufficient correspondence with actual reality to allow us to function with reasonable effectiveness within it. Thus by exploring how this comes to be we are set on the right path. The reality ultimately revealed is amazingly exciting and incredibly rich and beautiful.

No doubt there will be naïve criticisms from some scientists that the theories presented here are of no value because they are not mathematical, but the notion that all of reality is mathematical is a major impediment to its complete understanding. The truth is that all of reality is logical (in the sense that the laws of nature follow consistent rules, not that all actors are themselves logical) but only part of that logical structure is mathematical.

Certainly traditional science in its insistence that only mathematical theories can be real has had nothing meaningful to say about consciousness and the present moment which are the two most important aspects of reality in all our lives. And it is important to recognize that even the mathematical equations of science have meaning only by being imbedded in an overall logical context. Without that supporting logical structure they are meaningless. I believe the theories presented here do constitute a consistent logical structure which is also consistent with the mathematical theories of modern science, though not generally with the usual *interpretations* of those theories.

This book presents the latest and greatly expanded and updated version of the complete theory parts of which can be found in previous works by the author. A familiarity with the concepts of modern science and the major issues of philosophy at least at the popular level is assumed. This book is not another wordy popularized recapitulation of modern science, nor a mishmash of metaphysical speculation but immediately cuts right to the chase to grapple with the most fundamental questions of reality.

The structure of every theory emerges from its definitions which affect its logical form. Sub-optimal definitions lead to many unnecessary complexities of structure. Thus an essential part of our theory is the definitions it's based upon. We define some terms slightly differently than normal usage and introduce new terminology as needed to describe concepts novel to conventional ways of thinking. Rather than prejudging these I urge the reader to have patience until the overall structure to which they lead becomes clear. Finally I hope the reader will recognize a much simpler, clearer, and more elegant model of reality in which many important questions have immediate answers and others simply disappear.

The problem the author has faced in this book is how best to present the theory to the reader in as self-evident manner as possible. The theory stands as a complete fairly complex whole in which each part is consistent with and supported by the others but ultimately understood only in terms of the whole. However it is obviously impossible to present the whole theory all at once. Though supporting arguments are given throughout, in the end the approach taken was just to jump right in and begin with the fundamentals of the theory and then in the subsequent parts to integrate the other essential aspects of reality so that the unity of the whole model gradually emerges in a comprehensive and hopefully convincing manner.

Thus the author urges the reader to have a little patience and keep an open mind until the whole theory begins to emerge. When all the pieces begin to fall into place the author believes the reader will be convinced this is the best model of reality that currently exists and that it unifies all aspects of reality in a single self-consistent structure of great elegance, depth and scope.

Reality is the most difficult of subjects and it is hoped that the serious reader will recognize that and approach this work objectively and not prejudge its individual points out of hand on the basis of the very outmoded paradigms that the book seeks to replace. The author understands that the presentation of the book is not yet as clear and concise as it could be and begs the reader's patience in that respect. The author welcomes all serious questions, suggestions and comments which should be directed to EdgarOwen@att.net.

Part I: FUNDAMENTALS

REALITY

We define reality as the 'true' nature of the totality of everything that actually exists. It is clear that many things are not as they initially appear to us. We typically see only the surfaces of things rather than the hidden mechanisms which underlie them. The world has a deeper more fundamental reality that is often obscured by appearances. These illusory appearances of things are due partly to their representation in mind and partly due to the hierarchical complexity of reality itself. This book explores the hidden structure of external reality and how it is simulated by mind to reveal the true nature of the whole system.

There are three fundamental questions with respect to reality. First why does something exist rather than nothing? Second why does what actually exists exist instead of something else? And third what does actually exist? We will attempt to answer all three of these questions.

EXISTENCE

Something rather than nothing exists because only existence can exist. Nothingness does not exist because nothingness is non-existence thus nothingness cannot exist and can never have existed. Only existence exists or has ever existed or can ever exist. Thus there is not and never was and never could or can be a nothingness out of which something came into being. There is and has always been only existence. There is not even nothing outside of existence, or before or after or beyond existence. There is no outside or before or after or beyond existence. There is only existence and all that exists is part of that existence. This is the fundamental self-validating, self-necessitating axiom of reality upon which all else depends. It is the ultimate turtle upon which all others stand.

At first this may appear to be a mere sophism or tautology but in fact it accurately expresses the actual logic of reality and is the only possible self-contained explanation for the fundamental fact of existence. **Existence exists,** or better still; **Existence!** (Demonstrating its own existence by its existence.) **This is the fundamental axiom of reality**. Because the fact of existence is self-evident the axiom is proven true.

One might try to argue that the argument is circular and of course it is but that is precisely the point since the fundamental axiom must always be circular; but it must also be self-evident and meaningfully so. The fact of existence is self-evident and undeniable. Because existence exists it must exist. Because what exists defines reality as it actually is there is and can be no alternative to existence. There of course can be theoretical (though logically inconsistent) alternatives but there is no actually real alternative.

Because there never was a nothingness out of which something was created there is no need for a creator or creation event. Thus the fundamental question becomes not why something exists, but why what exists *is* what exists. Through this proper self-consistent, self-necessitating definition reality becomes simpler and illogical questions concerning non-existence vanish.

Reality is the existence of what exists, and existence is the manifestation of reality. Reality and existence are different perspectives on the same thing. Thus the only thing that can ever be real is existence and the only thing that can exist is reality.

The question how did existence arise out of non-existence is nonsensical and meaningless. It is based on a misapplication of the logic and language of everyday things where individual things do suddenly appear out of non-existence into existence. But whatever appears always actually appears out of something else, it is always the transformation of things. Nothing ever appears out of nothing at all or nothingness. The forms of reality often transform from one thing to another but since reality itself includes everything there is nothing for reality to transform from or appear out of. The question of how existence arose from non-existence is illogical and should not even be asked.

Of course the physical universe as we know it originated in the big bang some 13.7 billion years ago but this was not the beginning of existence as the universe originated not from the absolute absence of anything but from something similar to the quantum vacuum which contained the unactualized virtual possibilities of all possible actualities. We will call this fundamental virtual state of existence 'ontological energy', that is the energy of being, the energy of being real. We must not mistake the apparent beginning of clock time and the physical universe at the big bang for the beginning of existence itself.

REALITY IS A LOGICAL STRUCTURE

The proof of the existence axiom is a simple logical structure based on the invalidity of contradiction. Thus it requires that reality, the universe, be a logical structure for the proof to hold. This is a basic theorem of reality that itself requires proof. But there is incontrovertible evidence in support of it as we will see.

The structure of reality that will be revealed in this book conclusively demonstrates that reality is self-consistent and thus is a logical system. As we will see reality is a rule based computational system which continually computes its current state of existence. Since it is computational it must be logically self-consistent and complete or it would tear itself apart at the inconsistencies and pause at the incompletenesses and could not exist.

While there are likely some subtle differences between the computational logic of reality and human logic they must share a considerable isomorphism. If they did not then human reason and science based on human logic could not compute effective actions in the real world and we could not function or even exist. The fact of our existence demonstrates that human logic shares sufficient similarities with the logic of reality. Thus it is quite clear that reality must have a logical structure. If it did not it would not even make sense.

THE CONSISTENCY CONJECTURE

The entirety of what actually does exist depends on what we will call the extended fine tuning which is the complete set of seemingly irreducible basic laws and structures of reality that all the rest of reality is a consequence of. Thus the second and third questions of reality are inextricably intertwined. Why the extended fine tuning is the extended fine tuning that actually exists is the second question, and the nature of the totality of what does exist as a consequence of the extended fine tuning is the third.

The nature of what does exist is the subject of this book. As that is gradually revealed so too the extended fine tuning that is ultimately responsible for it will be also. But what is the answer to the second question? Why is the extended fine tuning as it is? The inability to answer this question has led many cosmologists to the assumption that our extended fine tuning must be the result of a random choice between all imagined possible extended fine tunings, and that in turn has led to a proliferation of highly speculative theories assuming multiple universes with all possible extended fine tunings must also exist.

We propose a much simpler and more parsimonious solution to the second question of why our extended fine tuning exists rather than any other. The Consistency Conjecture states that the extended fine tuning is exactly as it is because it is the only extended fine tuning that results in a self-consistent and logically complete world and thus is the only one that can exist because only a self-consistent and logically complete world can exist. Though admittedly unproven, evidence for this will be gradually developed throughout this book.

It is important to note that while the extended fine tuning includes the particular unexplained values of fundamental constants that makes up the usual fine tuning it includes many more unrecognized irreducible structural aspects of reality as well. The traditional fine tuning in itself is clearly not sufficient to generate a logically complete and self-consistent reality in fact it is clearly not even sufficient to generate the complete actual structure of our universe as envisaged by science.

If proven true the Consistency Conjecture would stand with the Existence Axiom as the two necessary axioms of reality upon which all else depends by providing the answers to why something other than nothing exists, and to why what exists is what exists. We now move on to explore what does exist.

ONTOLOGICAL ENERGY

Reality is defined as that which exists, and that which has existence is reality. The existence of reality is a self-evident truth. In human terms reality has several defining characteristics. It is real and actual, it has being and existence. It is absolute in the sense that it is exactly what it currently is in the moment and thus cannot be otherwise. It is present and its presence manifests as the present moment in which all things exist. It is happening; that is change continually occurs and clock time passes within it giving it vitality or life. And it is such that all the individual things of the world can exist within it and by doing so become real themselves.

Thus reality is not an abstraction but must be considered an actual living (in the sense of happening) self-manifesting presence that is actually here right now and in which all the things of the world exist thereby gaining their own individual existence and their reality.

Thus reality is the actual presence of a something which fills and thereby defines or creates a space of existence in which things can exist and be real. It is convenient to have a name for this view of reality as the actual presence of a something which creates or opens the space of reality. 'Ontological energy' is the term we will use to express the self-evident presence and space of reality within which all the things of the world become real.

Ontological energy, the energy or presence of being, is simply a name we give to the self-evident fact of the realness and presence and vitality of existence. It is not to be confused with energy in the physical sense; rather it is the living energy of being, of existence. It is the life force of reality; it is what makes reality real, and thus things real within reality. It can be thought of as an all pervasive energetic non-physical 'medium' or space that pervades all being with reality and manifests in all things thereby giving them their reality.

Thus ontological energy has 'always' existed in the sense that there never was a time in which it did not exist. In its pre big bang state ontological energy would have been originally motionless and formless but at the big bang forms arose within it consistent with its underlying nature. That same underlying nature still exists as the fundamental nature of reality in which all forms manifest today. It is a perfectly still formless 'sea' of virtual being within which forms actualize, interact and evolve and dissipate. It is analogous to a perfectly still ocean of water in which the forms of ripples, waves and currents arise. But the forms that manifest in the universe of ontological energy are all the things of the world. Thus ontological energy is the single fundamental 'state' or 'substance' of reality whether it manifests forms or not.

By our definition ontological energy is the essence of existence, the 'substance' of existence. Only ontological energy exists, has ever existed, or will ever exist because it is just a definition for the very fundamental nature of existence whatever that may be. Thus it has always existed and will always exist. It is the substance of being. It is what exists. It is existence itself. It is simply another more descriptive name for existence. Prior to the big bang ontological energy was virtual, completely still and formless, but at the big bang some of its possibilities actualized creating the universe as we know it. But ontological energy is still all that exists; it just now contains our universe of actualized forms evolving in clock time.

Existence, or ontological energy, can also be thought of by analogy to software. Originally there was code but it was not running. With the big bang the code representing our universe actualized and began running.

THE PRESENT MOMENT

Because ontological energy is real and actual it must be present. Therefore its presence generates a present moment, the present moment in which we and everything exists. Existence exists only in the present moment because the present moment is the presence of existence. Existence creates and is the present moment. Ontological energy exists and if something actually exists it must be present thus existence automatically creates and manifests a present moment. The present moment is the actual presence of existence.

The present moment is a name for one of the aspects of the single reality of ontological energy, reality, or existence. It is the only moment of existence, the only place and time that existence exists. There is nothing outside the present moment. Only the present moment exists, has ever existed or will ever exist. There is no other reality. The past exists only as its traces in the present moment. The future exists only as forward temporal projections in the present moment. Existence exists here and now and envelopes us in the present moment which is all that exists. There is nothing other than the present moment. As an aspect of existence it has no outside.

HAPPENING

Happening, also called change or process, is another fundamental aspect of ontological energy. Because of happening clock time flows and the universe comes to life. Since at least the big bang clock time continually flows through the present moment. Because of happening change occurs and things happen. Clock time is the underlying rate of happening at any relativistic location. Happening has nothing to do with clocks *per se*. Clocks are just standard physical processes that measure its local rate. Happening brings the universe to life and makes experience possible. If there was no happening there could be no experience. Happening occurs so that the universe comes alive, events occur, and the universe opens into an observable reality that is able to be experienced.

TWO KINDS OF TIME

There are two kinds of time. There is the present moment which is universal and absolute and this same present moment is common to everything and shared by all observers throughout the universe. And there is clock time or happening which flows through the present moment at different rates in different relativistic situations. Clock time flows through the present moment at different rates but the present moment remains common to all observers. We will call the time associated with the present moment p-time to distinguish it from clock time.

That there are two kinds of time is conclusively demonstrated by the time traveling twins who always reunite in the exact same present moment even when their clocks read different clock times.

There is no doubt at all that there are two kinds of time and it is totally amazing that no one had recognized this obvious truth before I first pointed it out (Owen, 2007). This serves as an excellent example of the blindness of science and common sense to obvious facts that somehow don't register in the prevailing world view or don't seem to fit mathematically into current theory.

THE LIVING UNIVERSE

The universe is alive in the sense that it is continually happening; that clock time continually flows through it and happening continually happens in every part of it. This is true even when individual forms temporarily happen to stay the same. A form retaining its current form as clock time passes is still happening; if it were not it would vanish from existence. Happening continually re-computes and thus maintains the existence of all forms in the reality of the present moment.

The universe is living in the sense that it is actually here and now and has being and is absolutely real and immanent and continually happening. In this respect the entire universe can be thought of as a single living entity or process. Reality is alive in the sense that it continually replicates and regenerates itself from moment to moment, and as a whole is a self-motivating system with no external causes.

We experience the presence of reality like this because that is its fundamental reality. It is the source of the awesome absoluteness, the awesome realness of reality that always encompasses us here in the present moment. We continually live with the direct and continuous experience of these fundamental aspects of reality because we too are individual things within reality and thus gain our reality from it.

SELF-MANIFESTATION

The single substance or space of existence defined as ontological energy has several essential characteristics. It is real and actual, has being and exists. It is living in the sense that its being is energetic and happening continually occurs and clock time flows through it and all things evolve. It has presence which generates and is the present

26

moment in which all things have their existence. It is absolute in the sense that there is nothing else and it is exactly as it is. And its nature is such that forms arise within it and interact and evolve according to consistent rules intrinsic to it.

What this means is that reality is not just a lifeless mechanical, physical world composed of material bodies but something that is really real and actually here and present in the present moment. Thus reality is not the old passive Newtonian universe that just sits there blindly with its clockwork ticking but a real living presence that *actively self-manifests* itself in all its absolute realness.

Reality, existence, the present moment, happening and ontological energy are all names for different perspectives on the same single fundamental and only 'thing'. Tao, properly understood, is an ancient approach to the same idea. Of course this fundamental substance of reality is itself formless and wordless. We seek to describe it as accurately as possible in an English description of its aspects and characteristics since we must after all use language to speak of it. But as Lao Tzu rightly points out, "The Tao that can be named is not the Tao." (Legge, 2010)

CONSCIOUSNESS

The problem of what consciousness is and how it can arise from a physical world, the so called 'Hard Problem' of consciousness (Chalmers, 1995), has long baffled the greatest minds but we can now provide a simple, obvious and definitive answer. All that is required is to combine the defining characteristics of reality with the notion of an observer as a locus within reality.

To understand the nature of consciousness it is first essential to understand the difference between consciousness *itself* and the contents of consciousness, a distinction confusing to many. Consciousness itself does not consist of its various contents which come and go but *is that in which these contents appear and by so appearing become conscious.*

This becomes clear in the mental exercise of meditation in which as the contents of consciousness diminish consciousness itself becomes clearer. In this state of mind it becomes obvious that consciousness itself is fundamental and that the thoughts and feelings that arise as contents within consciousness become conscious only by arising in consciousness itself.

This distinction is crucial. Consciousness itself is the subject of the Hard Problem of consciousness, while the structural characteristics of the various contents and organization of consciousness are referred to as the 'Easy Problems' of consciousness (Chalmers, 1995).

The simple answer to the Hard Problem, of how consciousness arises from a 'physical' world, is that **consciousness is conscious because reality is real.** The very fact of consciousness itself, as opposed to the Easy Problems of its structural details and individual contents, is simply the direct active self-manifestation of reality itself within the form of an observer. The living presence of reality exists absolutely and thus always self-manifests itself. Consciousness is simply the presence and participation of an observer in this living presence and realness of reality because it is a part of reality and thus is itself self-manifested by reality.

Thus consciousness itself is not something generated by a brain, but the presence of an organism in the self-manifesting presence of reality. However the individual contents of consciousness and their structural details are generated by the brain. Not understanding the distinction is the source of the problem of consciousness.

This is clear because all the defining characteristics usually ascribed to consciousness but one are actually characteristics of reality itself. As we have seen, the here and now presence of it, the aliveness and happening of it, the actual absolute realness of it; these are exactly the characteristics of the actual real living presence of reality itself and not something added to reality by consciousness. Consciousness just opens itself to reality from a particular locus and perspective within it and is filled by the self-manifestation of reality in the form of consciousness itself. Things seem conscious because reality self-manifests their existence within the form of an observer.

Of course the individual forms of the contents and structure of that consciousness are highly dependent on the cognitive structure of the observer, but not the fact that they are conscious which is consciousness itself. At first this is a very subtle distinction that may be difficult to grasp but when it is clearly understood it becomes obvious. However this seems to require a real paradigm shift in the way reality is understood by most.

So consciousness is the actual self-manifestation of reality in which an observer participates according to its location and structure. This is actually quite obvious and consistent with direct experience. We simply open our eyes to the already present fact of the self-manifestation of reality. However our representation of the details of what appears in consciousness and our perspective on them is uniquely our own and dependent on our particular biological and cognitive structures.

Consciousness itself is the actual happening presence of reality self-manifesting through the filters of a particular observer. All that an observer adds to the actual presence of reality as consciousness is a perspective from a particular location and a consequent internal simulation of the details of its form content. All the other defining characteristics usually ascribed to consciousness are actually those of the self-manifested presence of reality instead.

So the defining characteristics of what we call consciousness are actually intrinsic aspects of reality itself, not the unreasonable counterintuitive lifeless passive mechanical reality of the old scientific view of the physical universe, but the living actuality of a reality suffused with ontological energy and an immanent presence. So much of the difficulty in solving the Hard Problem was due to consciousness being thought of as something that arises from a *physical* universe when the universe is not at all physical in the sense assumed.

Consciousness has long been mistakenly sought in the human brain without success. This is a confusion arising from several misunderstandings. First that reality is a passive physical structure rather than an actively self-manifesting dynamic reality that is really here and now exhibiting its presence in the present moment.

The essence of what we call consciousness itself is the actual active self-manifestation of reality. It seems conscious only because it is already actually there; because it is actually real in the sense of actively manifesting itself. The observer mind only opens itself to what is already there being manifested. The observer does not generate consciousness in its brain; it only opens its particular structure to the ongoing manifestation of reality which it experiences in terms of that structure.

Thus consciousness itself, the very fact *of* consciousness, is a receptive rather than an active process, while the mind's generation of the structural details and contents of consciousness is an active computational process of mind. Or more accurately consciousness itself is the participatory process of an observer in an active self-manifesting reality that is already present and manifest.

In fact this is self-evidently obvious when we carefully observe and analyze reality in our own consciousness. Though the manner in which things are represented in consciousness is clearly a function of our brain's cognitive structure *the fact that they are represented at all* is because they are actually present in reality. That aspect of consciousness is clearly an actual manifestation of the presence of reality and not something added by our brain.

So the second source of confusion is because the individual details of the contents of consciousness of various observers really do arise in their brains. They are clearly dependent on the perceptual and cognitive structures of observers. These individual *forms* of consciousness, the Easy Problems of consciousness, clearly vary from observer to observer and this fact then reinforces the mistake that consciousness *itself*, not just the structural details of consciousness, also arises in the brain. Thus it is the inability to distinguish consciousness itself from the structural aspects of its contents that is the second reason why consciousness itself is mistakenly sought in the brain.

The third source of confusion is the absurd prejudice that only humans, and perhaps a few other species, are conscious. This stems from the fundamental error that consciousness refers to self-consciousness, the ability to be conscious of the fact that there is a self that is being conscious, and the notion that only humans have this capacity. But this view is self-contradictory as it requires one to be conscious that one is conscious before one can be conscious! It also assumes the objective existence of a self which as we will see is actually a developed mental construct rather than an innate aspect of reality.

The correct view is that not just humans but all beings are conscious because all beings participate in reality through their sense organs which are windows to the active self-manifestation of reality. Even if an organism is not conscious that it is self-conscious it is still clearly conscious of its interactions with the world whether or not it is conscious of its self in the way humans are.

The fourth source of confusion is the fact that consciousness is seemingly turned on and off at the point of the observer, as during sleep or anesthesia. This is of course true but what is turned on and off is the participation in the manifestation of reality, not that manifestation itself which remains real and present whether or not any particular observer's conscious participation is on or off.

The traditional view of consciousness is that it is an active process that somehow shines a light on a world that waits passively unmanifested and by so doing consciousness manifests that world. One way or another something has to manifest reality. Is it more likely that individual observer consciousnesses manifest reality into existence, or that reality itself self-manifests itself into being? The answer is clear. Reality is the self-manifestation of itself. The consciousnesses of individual observers just come along for the ride.

A fifth source of confusion is the fact that the observer actively directs attention from point to point within reality. But again it is the actual realness of those points of reality that makes them already actively self-manifested and thus amenable to the attention and focus of consciousness. The direction of attention is another aspect of the structural details of consciousness rather than consciousness itself and thus not part of the Hard Problem but one of the Easy Problems. Consciousness itself continues to exist no matter where its attention is focused on what contents.

The truth of the matter is even revealed by the syntactical characteristics of words such as 'consciousness' and 'awareness'. We always say we are aware *of* something or conscious *of* something. This clearly indicates a receptive process because one is aware *of* something implies that something is already there and manifest and in fact the presence of reality is already there manifesting itself. Awareness and consciousness is just an observer opening to that actual pre-existing 'thereness' of reality.

An excellent way to conceptualize this is to imagine observers as windows, each with its own uniquely distorted glass, representing its biological and cognitive structure. Thus each observer views the details of reality distorted in terms of its own glass, but the fact that all observers even have a view of reality at all is because reality is actually out there manifesting itself through all observer windows. Consciousness itself is reality self-manifest. The representations of the contents of consciousness is an active computational process of individual observer minds. But these contents of consciousness become conscious only because they arise in consciousness itself.

In fact the confusion in understanding the true nature of consciousness is exactly analogous to the erroneous ancient extramission theory of vision, espoused by Plato and others, that seeing was the result of the eyes shining light on objects (Cornford, 1997). In the same way many still erroneously believe that brains somehow shine consciousness on things rather than that things have an actual real presence in the reality of the present moment and thus self-manifest *to* observers.

But just as seeing actually involves light from objects actively entering the eyes where the structural details are then organized, so consciousness involves the active manifestation of reality impinging on and manifesting as the consciousness of an observer. It is remarkable that the extramission theory of vision was corrected centuries ago but the structurally identical erroneous theory of consciousness was only first corrected by the author (Owen, 2007).

Every observer is of course a part of reality, and that includes the computational results of its mental processes which are also part of reality. Thus both are necessarily part of reality's self-manifestation. Only thus do cognitive forms themselves self-manifest in consciousness itself.

It is the fact that this process occurs from a particular observer location and the details of the forms involved are interpreted in terms of the observer's cognitive structure that leads to the mistaken belief that the fundamental fact of consciousness itself also emanates from mind rather than just being the manifest presence of reality within mind.

Thus consciousness is the participation of an observer in the actual real and present active manifestation of reality in terms of the observer's own particular structure. Because these two aspects of consciousness occur mixed together in the usual process of awareness they have not been recognized as separate phenomena. But when consciousness itself is carefully examined in meditation devoid of its particular form contents it becomes clear that consciousness itself is not the contents that appear within it but the underlying presence of reality itself in which those individual forms become conscious. This underlying consciousness itself is the actual manifested presence of reality itself to the observer.

Observers are conscious because they are part of reality and reality is actually there actively manifesting its reality and presence. Reality is really really there in the realest sense possible actively manifesting its presence. The actual active living presence of reality itself is what is called consciousness itself when the structure of mind participates in that reality.

In this explanation the actual phenomenon of consciousness does not change and is the same as it always was but there is now a radical paradigm shift in how we understand what consciousness itself truly is. When this is truly grasped it becomes clear that there never actually was a Hard Problem that needed solving. Consciousness itself does not originate in the brain but in the self-manifestation of reality itself.

MIND AND REALITY

This bright, colorful, apparently physical world that we think we live in is entirely a construct of our minds. This construct is very different for different humans and even more different for other species. All organismic observers are characterized by having these internal models of reality which they use to organize their functioning in reality. We will use the terms 'mental model' of reality or 'simulation' of reality interchangeably to describe these internal models of reality of organismic observers.

Thus reality is not at all as we perceive it. The world we think we live in is actually an internal simulation of the actual external reality constructed by our mind and projected into an apparent dimensional space populated by physical things with us at its center. It's an imaginary mapping and fleshing out of an actual world which consists only of information. The actual external world has none of the apparent physicality of this simulation and shares only some similarity of logical structure. Like an intelligent robot's simulation of reality that logical similarity is sufficient to allow us to function in the real world by computing our actions against our simulation but by necessity it captures only a miniscule iota of the actual information in the world around us.

At its fundamental level reality is not actually the physical world it appears to be but a world of evolving information forms that follows consistent basic logical rules called the laws of nature. All organisms flesh out this information world each in their own way according to their own perceptual and cognitive structures into the apparently physical world they experience themselves inhabiting.

There are several convincing lines of reasoning that all lead to this same conclusion which will be explored in detail in this book. But it is worthwhile summarizing them here.

1. The laws of science which best describe reality are themselves logico-mathematical structures. Why would the equations of science be the best description of reality if reality itself did not consist of similar structures? This explains the so called "unreasonable effectiveness of mathematics".

2. By recognizing that reality is a logico-mathematical structure the laws of nature immediately assume a natural place as an intrinsic part of reality. No longer do they somehow stand outside a physical world they miraculously control.

3. Physical mechanisms to produce effects become unnecessary in a purely computational world. It is enough to have a consistent logico-mathematical model that is in accord with experimental evidence.

4. When everything that mind adds to reality is recognized and subtracted from the internal model of reality it creates we find that all that remains is this same information structure.

5. This view of reality is tightly consistent with the other insights of this book which I believe are themselves also consistent with modern science though not with many of its interpretations.

6. This view of reality leads to simple elegant solutions of many of the perennial problems of the fundamental nature of reality and leads directly to many new insights.

7. In particular it leads to a new understanding of spacetime which allows a conceptual unification of quantum theory and general relativity and solves the paradoxical nature of the quantum world.

THE WORLD OF FORMS

In itself ontological energy is perfectly still and formless but forms arise within it as ripples and waves arise in still water. The forms that arise in ontological energy are all the things of the universe. Every discrete namable thing that exists is a form or set of associated forms like a particular standing wave or ripple in the sea of ontological energy.

Every 'thing' that exists is a form and all forms consist entirely of pure in-*form*-ation. Forms in this sense are to be thought of as the total information content of every discrete thing in the universe and every discrete thing in the universe is *only* its information content. At the fundamental level everything is information only.

Forms can be thought of as the information contents of things without their apparent self-substances. But as we will see upon analysis the apparent self-substances of things are themselves additional forms carrying the information of how observers interact with things.

Forms include not just the forms of individual 'things', but of all sub-things and all sets of things. The notion of 'thing' is specific to how organisms extract and categorize forms in their particular cognitive simulations of reality. The notion of thing is not so much intrinsic to reality itself which can be thought of as a single all-encompassing form with no intrinsic divisions from which various observers discriminate particular forms of interest. The world of forms is like the single dynamic form of an ocean in which surfers see waves and oceanographers see currents.

Forms also include all the law of nature rules which govern the dynamic evolution of the thing forms. However the analogy with code and data is likely an artificial distinction in the minds of human observers.

THE EMPTINESS OF FORMS

Just as waves and ripples have no substance other than that of water, all the things of the world, the forms, have no individual self-substances. Their only substance is the common substance of the ontological energy in which they arise that gives them their reality.

The apparent qualities and self-substances of things are additional forms added by observer minds to flesh out their simulations of reality and make them more meaningful to an observer. They are the forms of the *interaction* of an observer form with the forms of external reality. This will be discussed further in Part IV, Mind and Reality. For example the experience of the weight and hardness of a stone is not in the stone but in the observer's interaction with the stone as modeled by the observer's mind.

This experience will be different for every observer. The stone itself has no weight or hardness. It contains the information that produces the experience of weight and hardness in interaction with an observer. Qualities like weight and hardness are all 'qualia' that exist only in the internal reality simulations of observers.

INFORMATION ONLY

Because all forms are empty all individual things in the universe are purely information structures rather than 'physical' structures. The entire universe of things is a dynamic self-computing network of information structures rather than a physical structure.

The things of the universe, the thing forms, are like waves that appear in water. They are the information contents of things without their apparent thingness. Their apparent thingness is just additional information forms encoding how particular observers interact with its intrinsic information. The only actual thingness of forms is ontological energy which is as the water that supports their waves and ripples.

This information structure operates according to logico-mathematical rules called the laws of nature and science is the study of those rules. The logical structure of the world of forms is the universe that science attempts to reveal.

THE LOGIC OF FORMS

The universe is a dynamic logical information structure meaning that it is structured and evolves according to a self-consistent set of rules. These rules are logical in the sense they are internally self-consistent and logically complete in that everything in the system is logically connected. Some of these rules are mathematical since mathematics is a subset of logic in the broader sense. Thus all forms obey logical rules in their structures and interactions and evolution. It is because forms obey logical rules that they constitute information. Just as the forms of the waves that can arise in water are determined by the nature of water and have a logical structure, so the logical structures of the form things that arise in ontological energy are determined by the innate nature of ontological energy.

CONSISTENCY AND COMPLETENESS

The logical structure of reality forms a single self-consistent and logically complete whole. If the laws of nature were not entirely self-consistent a computational reality would tear itself apart at the inconsistencies and could not exist.

Likewise reality is logically complete which means that every event is determined by valid rules from its event history. If this were not true there could be events which had no rules to determine them and the evolution of forms would come to a halt thus bringing some areas of reality to a halt and causing the structure of reality to fragment.

The logical structure of reality is not subject to Gödelian incompleteness because it is entirely computed by rules from prior states. Gödel's Theory applies only to certain human originated logico-mathematical systems which are simplified generalizations of the actual physical logico-mathematical system of reality (Hofstadter, 1980).

The basic principle of the universe of forms is that it is logically consistent and logically complete. This makes the world of forms accessible to reason based on human logic insofar as human logic is isomorphic to the inherent logic of forms. The exact formal structure of reality remains to be discovered but will need to address the lack of infinities and infinitesimals in a granular finite reality. Chaitin and others have made some initial steps in this direction (Chaitin, 2006).

THE LAWS OF NATURE

Forms can be arbitrarily categorized into thing forms and the law of nature forms and programs which compute them. These are both forms and both exist equally as part of reality. The programs and laws of nature are part of the real world of forms just as the thing forms are. As long as science believed that the world was a physical structure it could not understand where the laws of nature might reside and how they could affect a physical universe. But when we realize that the universe is actually a computational information structure then the laws of nature immediately take their rightful place as a natural part of that logical structure. Recognizing that reality is an information structure that naturally incorporates the laws of nature solves one of the major problems in the philosophy of science.

The primary difference between thing forms and law of nature forms is that the thing forms are modeled as things in observer simulations of reality whereas other types of forms are generally modeled as abstractions that are in fact closer to the information forms they actually are.

Just as the computational sequences of a computer program consist of complex sequences of machine language instructions so we can assume that the computational dynamics of reality consist of sequences of the elemental laws of nature. However this may not apply to all 'emergent' processes some of which might involve higher level laws. This question will be explored further in Part V, The World of Forms.

THE UNIVERSE AS COMPUTER

Reality is a computational system by which the universe continually computes its own form state of existence. The world of forms contains both the data and code sequences that define its current state and the programs based on law of nature logic that computes how it evolves with each cycle of clock time. The present moment is the locus of the current processor cycle of happening. The universe continually computes its current state of existence and the results become real and actual because they occur in the ontological reality of the present moment.

Though observers simulate the universe as physical it is actually more analogous to software that continually generates the current purely information state of itself. This state is reality because it runs in reality's computer and its apparent physicality comes only as it is simulated in the minds of observers.

One must be careful not to apply the analogy of universe as computer too exactly. For one thing there is no hardware on which the software of reality runs. In particular no physical processor or set of processors and no electrical current to power it. Instead there is just self-computing information that continually evolves in the ubiquitous presence of happening in the present moment. Happening is the processor that manifests reality as its current computational results but happening is something that is part and parcel of all reality rather than having any particular locus as in a silicon computer.

PROGRAMS

Because the world of forms is a computational structure it can be thought of as consisting of programs. There are multitudes of such programs that can be discriminated from the single universal program. All these programs run simultaneously and seamlessly interact to compute reality in a single self-consistent unified system.

Observers discriminate and conceptually isolate individual programs of interest to their own functioning. And in turn observers themselves can be considered programs. Since the discrimination of individual programs is observer dependent what constitutes a program is subject to redefinition as observer needs and interests change.

Thus the definition of programs is observer dependent as is the definition of individual forms. The important consideration is whether the logical structure of the forms and programs discriminated is consistent with the underlying information structure of reality. To the extent they are they constitute knowledge.

GENERIC OBSERVERS

As a part of reality an observer is any form of whatever type within the world of forms that occupies a singular logical locus in reality. In essence an observer is just a particular locus of reality and thus partakes of all reality's fundamental attributes. It is clear this is a very general definition that essentially defines any thing form in the universe as a generic observer. In this broadest sense a generic observer is any thing form in the universe, however defined.

Human and other biological organisms, organismic observers, are a subset of generic observers. In their case their form structure generally includes some manner of simulation model of their view of the reality of the form environment with which they interact and on the basis of which they compute their interactions with reality. In the case of humans and some other 'higher' organisms this simulation may incorporate an additional degree of recursion in which the simulation model is itself modeled in the simulation.

The only experience, knowledge or consciousness of reality possible is to some observer. Without observers the universe would be completely unexperienced and unknown and there is no way its existence could even be established and nothing it could manifest to. However since every form qualifies as a generic observer there is always experience in our generic sense. We define such generic experience as '*xperience*'.

Because every observer is a form structure and every observer's structural view of reality is only in terms of its own form structure its view of reality is always actually a highly selective simulation of reality rather than reality itself. Every observer's experience of the universe is necessarily always from that particular observer's singular perspective because *it is always an alteration of its **own forms***. Thus it is always in terms of its own particular perceptual and cognitive structure.

Thus there can be no completely objective independent observerless view of reality. We can of course attempt such objective descriptions by combining many sources which is an improvement but the resulting model is always constructed entirely within and experienced only within the mind of some observer. And such models always remain direct experience of the models rather than a direct experience of external reality itself. There is simply no escaping this. Our only experience of reality is of our personal internal simulation of it.

However every observer does directly experience the ontological energy of reality and its fundamental characteristics because that is its substance as well and that is the very living presence of reality. If it did not there would be no experience at all.

XPERIENCE

All experiences of anything, without exception, actually occur as changes to the experiencing forms themselves. There is no direct experience of other things other than in changes to the experiencing form. And it is precisely those alterations to a form that constitute its experience of other forms. For example the experience of an object in the external world actually occurs as changes to forms within the mental model of the world. Thus it is the changes to the forms of the mental model that actually constitutes the experience.

We say we experience objects in the external world but this is actually a deduction rather than a direct experience of those objects. What actually occurs is that our internal forms change in ways that lead us to deduce that certain external forms exist in form states that led to our internal forms changing the way they did through a network of intermediate events involving information transfers. Of course these deductions generally occur automatically below the level of consciousness so that we are fooled into believing that we do directly experience external objects.

Since experience actually consists of changes to forms themselves we can very usefully and importantly generalize the notion of experience to every form in the world of forms and consider the changes to any form whatsoever as a generalized type of experience we will define as 'xperience'. This insight leads to a profound new paradigm of the structure of reality.

Very generally we define xperience as the re-computation of any form whatsoever. If the form stays the same it is the xperience of staying the same. If the form is altered in its re-computation it is the xperience of being altered which in general means it is the xperience of its alteration by computational interaction with another form. In this way all forms xperience other forms in the experiences of their own alterations, and organismic *experience* is seen as a specialized subset of *xperience*.

The continual re-computation of all forms by happening is the re-creation of forms into continuing existence in the present moment. Thus this re-computation of forms constitutes the xperience of the form of its own existence. Thus all forms, without exception continually xperience their existence in their re-computations whatever they may be. This should not be misunderstood in any esoteric sense. All xperience is only what it actually is expressed in its actual form structure. For example elemental forms do not 'know' anything about their xperiences other than their actual xperiences themselves. Unless there are forms that actually encode it there cannot be any conceivable context or interpretation of an xperience. It is exactly the form itself and nothing more. Xperiences are not experiences; they are a generalization of the basic structure and process of experience to all forms.

Because an observer is a form or system of forms that is altered in response to an impinging event all things are effectively generic observers. In general the form of an xperience of a computational interaction of forms depends both on the structure of the interacting form and the xperiencing form. And in fact if two forms computationally interact each can be said to xperience the other in the alterations of their own forms and the forms of both xperiences will depend on the form structures of both forms.

Thus an xperience is any re-computation of a form and computational *changes* of a form generally constitute xperiences of other forms. And every xperience is the resulting information content of the interaction event. In general every event is equivalent to the resulting xperiences of all the forms involved.

This new model leads to an entirely new interpretation of reality as composed entirely of xperience rather than of objects and events. We can say that the reality of the world of forms consists entirely of xperience. This is only a new *interpretation* of reality as things and events remain exactly as they were. The exact same things occur, nothing is changed or left out, reality is just understood from a novel perspective. However this interpretation is superior to the old view of things and events because it automatically incorporates the essential nature of the observer in any description of reality. It also sheds light on the nature of decoherence in quantum theory when that is recognized as an elemental form of xperience as we will see below. And it will lead to a profound understanding of the essential nature of the observer as a necessary part of reality itself.

This concept of xperience is also essential to understanding consciousness from a broader perspective. In the xperience interpretation of reality every interaction of forms that involves alteration of forms is equivalent to an exchange of information and every exchange of information is a sort of proto-conscious occurrence that involves the xperience of one form by another.

Our human *experiences* of things are simply specialized *xperiences* that take place in our mental models of reality. The human consciousness of particular things, the contents of consciousness, is the xperience of alterations to particular forms in our mental models of reality, and these become conscious because they occur as re-computational self-manifestations of reality of those internal forms. The structural aspects are xperiences of changes to human mind form structure while the fact they are conscious derives from the xperience being actualized by occurring in the present moment.

The individual forms of all xperiences are the structural contents of reality while the fact they are real and self-manifest their reality as actual xperience is due to the fact that all xperience is the self-manifestation of reality itself in the continual re-computation of forms into existence in the present moment. The paradigm of xperience unifies the world of forms and the ontological energy they occur within that gives them reality in a single continuously happening process of the self-manifestation of forms into existence in the present moment. It is an entirely new way of looking at reality that incorporates everything and leaves out nothing.

LIFE FORCE

We feel within ourselves the special feeling that we are alive, that we are living beings, that we have a life force that animates us and makes us different from inanimate objects. But what this actually is has long been a mystery. We are now in a position to provide an answer. Our personal life force is the same life force that animates all of reality and thus ourselves as well.

The fact that reality manifests itself in happening in the present moment as an actual real reality is the life force that we feel within us. Our life force is our participation in the real and actual presence of reality as it

43

happens as is our consciousness. We feel ourselves alive simply because we are part of the aliveness of the universe and are continually happening ourselves. There is nothing esoteric or supernatural about this. It is simply the experience of the continual happening of the universe occurring within us.

This life force is the direct experience of happening that animates all reality. What we are referring to here is not the biological definition of a living organism as an autonomous purposeful computational system with environmental inputs that is able to replicate its kind. Rather it is this biological structure that is animated because it shares in the universal life force that animates all things each in their own way. Our feeling of being alive is simply what the life force of the universe feels like inside a biological organism. It is the feeling of happening within us flowing through our form.

So we see that both our consciousness and the life force that animates us are not something unique to us but are due to our participation in the realness of reality because we are a part of reality. Of course the particular ways that we express our lives and consciousnesses as biological organisms are due to our particular form structures but the fact that we are able to be animate and conscious, and our experience of that, is due to the self-manifesting happening of reality itself.

SUMMARY

Existence exists because non-existence cannot exist. This explains why something rather than nothing exists. Thus there was never a nothingness out of which something arose or the universe was created. Thus there is no need for a creator or creation event. This Axiom of Existence is the fundamental self-necessitating axiom of reality upon which all else stands.

Of course the universe itself did originate some 13.7 billion years ago in the big bang but not out of nothing but out of something similar to the quantum vacuum consisting of all virtual possibilities of what could become actualized in the big bang.

Reality is defined as the true nature of the totality of what actually does exist. The existence of reality is self-evident and undeniable.

Reality is known in terms of its self-evident attributes. It is real and actual, it is the locus of all being and existence, it is absolute in the sense that whatever it is it is exactly what it is, and it is such that all the individual things of the world gain their own reality by existing within it.

Reality is also present and the presence of reality manifests as a present moment in which everything exists. Reality is also happening which manifests as the happening of all events that continually occur within it. In this sense reality is a living system because it is self-motivating with no external causes.

The presence of reality also manifests as it's hereness. Its presence defines the logical locus of all of existence. This is not a physical space but a logical space as we will see. It is the space in which all things exist and all events happen.

Reality is also self-manifesting. What this means is that all the attributes of reality actually manifest themselves as experience. They are not theoretical abstractions but are actually observable.

These are the self-evident attributes of reality and we define the term 'ontological energy' to describe them as a single concept that refers to the fundamental nature of reality in terms of these attributes. Ontological energy is nothing esoteric but just a convenient term for the combined attributes of reality that define its nature.

Thus reality consists of its fundamental attributes, its ontological energy, and all the things of the world that are real because they exist within it. This is roughly analogous to how individual waves become real by arising in water and the reality of the ocean consists of the water and all its waves, currents and other forms.

Premise: All the 'things' of the world without exception are pure forms of information that arise in ontological energy. All things without exception are actually only the information of themselves. The totality of the information structure of reality we call 'the world of forms'. Forms and information are two words for the same thing; form from the perspective of structure and information from the perspective of content but these are actually exactly the same. We will use forms and information interchangeably throughout depending on context.

Thus the universe does not consist of physical or material things in the usual sense but of the underlying information content of those things. The universe of what appears to be things is actually a world of empty forms consisting only of information.

The apparent physicality of things is generated in the mental models of organismic observers. It consists of an internal model of the logical structure of external forms and how the observer perceives and interacts with them as will be shown in Part IV. Thus the universe as it is usually conceived as a material structure exists only as a simulation in the minds of observers.

All observers themselves are also entirely the information forms of themselves in the world of forms. Again their apparent physicality is a representation in their mental models of themselves.

There is overwhelming evidence that all things are actually only their information and with practice it is even directly observable. The evidence was summarized above and will be explored in detail throughout the book. We will assume it true for the time being and see where it leads.

The world of forms is a continually evolving computational system in which the current state of reality and thus of the universe is continually re-computed by happening in every moment according to forms called the laws of nature and programs based upon them.

As with ordinary software the world of forms must be logically self-consistent and logically complete. If it were not it would tear itself apart at the inconsistencies and pause at the incompletenesses and could not exist.

Because reality is self-consistent the Axiom of Existence is true as it depends on the impossibility of contradiction.

The internal structure of the world of forms will be explored in much greater detail throughout the book.

The continual re-computation of forms continually re-computes them into existence. If they were not continually re-computed by happening they would be left behind out of the present moment and thus out of existence. Thus, in a generic sense, the re-computation of forms can be considered the 'xperience' of their existence. Nothing esoteric should be read into this, it is just a useful term for exactly what it is, the continual re-computation of form with nothing else implied at all.

It is then clear that our usual *experience* is a special type of *xperience* because all experience also consists of the re-computation of form. All experience is actually the re-computation of some internal form whose re-computation constitutes that experience. The experiences of 'other' things are the internal changes of forms that are altered in either direct or indirect computational interactions with external forms. Thus all xperiences and experiences are actually changes to the xperiencing forms themselves rather than direct experience of external forms which is impossible.

This insight leads to a new paradigm for reality that seamlessly integrates the necessary function of the observer into reality itself. All re-computation of form into continuing existence constitutes xperience. Thus since all that happens is the re-computation of forms, reality can be interpreted as consisting of xperience only. Reality continually self-manifests itself as xperience and all xperience is that of the self-manifestation of reality. The reality of reality is its continual self-manifestation to itself as xperience.

In this new interpretation of reality nothing actually changes and everything goes on as it always did. It is just an entirely new way of looking at reality as a single process of xperience which is how the reality of the universe continually self-manifests itself as the xperience of itself in the continual re-computation of all its forms.

Because this means that reality is an actively self-manifesting process that manifests as xperience rather than a passive structure that waits to be xperienced, this immediately enables a new understanding of consciousness which definitively solves the 'Hard Problem' of how consciousness arises from a 'physical' world. The problem with the Hard Problem is that it assumes a type of physical world that does not exist.

We first need to distinguish consciousness *itself* from the contents of consciousness which become conscious by arising within it. Consciousness itself is the clear formless consciousness that remains when all the individual contents of consciousness vanish. It is this consciousness itself, rather than the details of the contents of consciousness, that is the subject of the Hard Problem. It is this consciousness itself that is what the individual contents of consciousness become conscious by appearing within, just as the individual contents of reality become real by appearing within the ontological energy of reality itself.

When carefully considered it is clear that all the attributes of consciousness but one are actually the attributes of reality itself self-manifesting in the form of an observer. The actuality and realness, the happening and self-manifestation, the presence in a present moment. These are all the attributes of reality itself self-manifesting in the forms of mind rather than something generated by mind. The only thing the observer brings to consciousness is a particular locus in which reality self-manifests, and the individual structural details of the contents of consciousness which are generated by the observer which reality also self-manifests.

Thus consciousness itself is not something that originates in a mind or brain but is the self-manifestation of reality in the continual re-computation of the forms of an organismic observer. The structural details of the experiences of consciousness are those of the observer, but the fact that they are conscious and experienced is because reality actively self-manifests these forms within the mental model of the observer as experience and consciousness. The continual re-computation into existence of the forms of experience in the mental model of an observer automatically manifests as their experience and as consciousness itself.

As seeing is not due to light being radiated on objects from the eyes, so consciousness itself is not due to anything being shown onto reality by a brain. Both seeing and consciousness are receiving and interpreting what is being generated by an actively self-manifesting reality. Consciousness is conscious because reality is real, because reality actively self-manifests its reality as consciousness and experience in the cognitive forms of an observer.

Likewise the fundamental life force that animates a person is the internal presence of happening, the same life force that animates all of reality. It is happening, the underlying life force of the universe, that enables and activates the biological life processes of organisms as it does all other processes.

Thus our experience of consciousness and existence in the present moment is the direct experience of the presence and happening of the fundamental nature of reality itself. We are only and entirely the continually self-manifesting presence of reality in the present moment in the xperiences and experiences of our own form. Our consciousness is our direct participation in the essence of reality itself as an actual living expression of a self-manifesting reality. Reality continually self-manifests us into existence as the xperience and experience of our own forms and thus we directly experience the fundamental nature of reality in the forms of our own experience.

This briefly summarizes a few of the fundamental concepts of the theory but this is just the beginning and we now proceed to explore the details and implications of cosmology, the quantum world, mind and reality, information cosmology and how the true nature of the whole can be directly realized in our own experience.

Part II: SPACETIME

THE UNIVERSE

The universe is defined as the totality of the apparently physical world of our experience. Thus it includes everything that exists from that perspective. It is the way the underlying world of forms appears to human observers. It is the physical aspects of ontological energy and the world of forms that arose within it at the big bang. Infrequently the definition is expanded a little but the context should make the usage clear.

The universe is thus equivalent to reality from that perspective. There is nothing outside, before or after the universe in this definition. Some cosmological theories hypothesize multiverses and pocket or bubble universes (Vilenken, 2006) within a single larger universe however in our definition the universe is whatever largest all inclusive structure exists. Reasons to postulate larger structures than the universe we observe around us, such as the seemingly arbitrary nature of the fine tuning, have other more parsimonious answers as we shall see. Thus at this point there is no reason to consider them.

The universe that actualized in the big bang arose from a formless virtual state of ontological energy, essentially a more generalized quantum vacuum, that contained the possibilities of all possible actualities and perhaps from a previous actualized state as well as we will see. This formless virtual state consists of the same ontological energy that is still the substrate in which all the actualized forms of the universe exist in our current universe.

THROUGH TIME AT THE SPEED OF LIGHT

A fundamental fact of our physical existence is that every one of us continually hurtles through time at the speed of light. We experience this as the passage of clock time as a consequence of happening. Day and night, during every second of our existence we continually advance the spatial equivalent of 186,000 miles through time.

Even though this is a central fact of our existence the fact that it is little recognized or appreciated by physicists is quite surprising. Brian Greene (1999, p. 50), (2005, p. 49) is one of the few authors I'm aware of who even mentions the idea, at least in popular expositions, but he seems to treat it only in passing as something of a curiosity without developing its implications which are quite important.

The reason for our speed of light travel through time is what I call the STc Principle which is the principle underlying the special theory of relativity. A simple mathematical derivation[1] and more detailed discussion of the following sections can be found in the author's work 'Spacetime and Consciousness' (Owen, 2007).

THE STc PRINCIPLE

The STc Principle states that everything continually moves through *spacetime* at the speed of light c. That is the combined velocity through space and through time of anything is always c for all observers. Thus if something has some velocity in space relative to an observer then its apparent speed through time (its clock time rate) to that observer will slow accordingly so that the vector sum of the speeds is always c. Thus since it is impossible for us or anything else to have a velocity in space *relative to itself,* all of our own total spacetime velocity is always only through time and thus we and everything in the universe all travel through time at the speed of light according to our own co-moving clocks.

The STc Principle demonstrates that **the speed of light should actually be called the speed of time for that is what it actually is**. It just so happens that light and other forms of electromagnetic radiation always travel at the speed of time through space because they have no speed at all through time.

Most of special relativity including the Lorentz transform can be derived directly from the STc Principle[1]. Add the conservation of energy and momentum and all of special relativity can be derived (Feynman, 2006, Vol. I, chap. 15). The STc Principle underlies special relativity, clarifies the speed of light as the speed of time, and is also responsible for both the arrow of time and the existence of the present moment. Thus it is clearly a fundamental principle of reality and must be recognized as such.

THE ARROW OF TIME

The STc Principle provides a solution to two fundamental questions of physics. **Since the STc Principle requires that time must continually flow and in a single direction (by convention the positive) it is the source of the arrow of time**, an obvious connection no one else seems to have made prior to my pointing it out (Owen, 2007). For the origin of the phrase 'Arrow of Time' see (Eddington, 1928).

THE PRESENT MOMENT

The STc Principle also requires the existence of a particular privileged moment of time, the present moment, because it requires everything to be at one and only one point in time which is by definition the present moment. Thus the STc Principle conclusively refutes the popular erroneous theory of block time (Price, 1996, 12-13, 14, 15-16), that all moments of time currently exist and have equal existence, and provides a firm physical basis for a present moment that seems to have escaped everyone else (Owen, 2007).

COSMOLOGICAL GEOMETRY

The STc Principle also appears to be consistent with only one possible cosmological geometry for the universe. That geometry is a 4-dimensional hypersphere whose surface is the familiar three spatial dimensions and whose radial dimension is the time dimension originating at the center back in the big bang. The actual universe is just the surface of this hypersphere and does not include the interior because the surface is the present moment and the STc Principle requires everything, including the universe itself, to exist only in the present moment. The interior of the hypersphere corresponds to the past which no longer exists.

Because the universe is a hypersphere its geometry must be closed and finite. It has no edges, it is not 'open', and it is not infinite. (Another reason it cannot be infinite is that nothing physical can be infinite.) The *visible* universe for any observer is a 3-dimensional circle on the surface of this hypersphere with the observer at its center and its circumference at the particle horizon. This part of the theory makes the testable prediction that Ω, the 'flatness' of space will be very slightly greater than 1, the value for a flat universe. This means that the geometry of spacetime will be finite and closed rather than flat or a saddle shaped each of which must either have edges or be infinite both of which are physically impossible. Current measurements suggest space is almost flat within 0.5% of 1 and do not rule out our predicted small >1 value (NASA, 2013).

TWO KINDS OF TIME

Another fundamental principle which no one else seems to have discovered is that **there are two kinds of time, clock time and what I call p-time, which is the time defined by the present moment**. This is quite clear because clock time flows at different rates depending on relativistic situation but no matter how clock time varies on different clocks it always flows only through a common shared universal present moment.

This is conclusively demonstrated by the familiar time traveling twins example (Feynman, 2006, Vol. I, 16-2) in which the twins meet up again with different clock times on their comoving watches *but always in the exact same present moment*. The fact that no one has previously recognized this absolutely requires two different kinds of time is truly amazing (Owen, 2007). A great example of how ingrained modes of thought and interpretations of reality can be blind to the obvious.

That present moment which is common to all observers in the universe is the surface of the cosmic hypersphere within which everything in reality actually exists. **It is crucial to understand that since the**

hypersphere's surface is the present moment, the radial dimension of the cosmological hypersphere is the p-time dimension's past rather than that of clock time.

If the radial dimension of the hypersphere were clock time rather than p-time various inconsistencies would arise such as the apparent variations in the rate of Hubble expansion with clock time. The fact that p-time had not been discovered previously has prevented this quite simple and elegant understanding of cosmological geometry.

So it is the continual extension of the radial p-time dimension of the universe that corresponds to the evolution of the universe and the fact of happening. Clock time progresses at different relativistic rates at different locations as p-time uniformly progresses and the surface of the hypersphere extends.

THE HUBBLE EXPANSION

The Hubble expansion of space is a consequence of the continuing *extension* of the radial p-time dimension which naturally *expands* the surface of the cosmic hypersphere. This provides a means to measure the rate of extension of p-time which seems to have varied over the history of the universe. But this is not a straightforward measurement as all measurements of time are made in clock time and thus the relation between clock time rates and p-time must be very carefully determined.

However the value of Ω does give a measure of elapsed p-time since the big bang since knowing the curvature of the surface of the hypersphere its radius can be calculated. The result would be a distance which would then need to be converted to elapsed p-time however it is not clear what the units of p-time actually are since they are clearly not those of clock time. Current WMAP data give a radius of the universe of at least 150 times that of the visible universe or at least 7 trillion light years (Wikipedia: Wilkinson Microwave Anisotropy Probe).

Since the rate of Hubble expansion seems to have varied over the 14.7 billion year history of clock time it is clear that clock time and p-time rates have varied with respect to each other. For example the period of inflation, in which the universe is thought to have expanded enormously in a small fraction of a second, can be simply explained by the p-time rate being temporarily enormously greater than the clock time rate. Thus the p-time radial dimension of the universe could have expanded enormously in almost no clock time.

Variations in the Hubble expansion rate currently attributed to dark energy must correspond to different rates of p-time extension as well. However the actual apparent *rate* of the passage of time on clocks is that of clock time rather than p-time. P-time seems to stand still as clock time passes through it because everything that exists including observers exists only in the present moment, nevertheless it continually *happens* as the hypersphere extends its radial dimension. Therefore the p-time of the present moment does not appear to move because everything including our experience moves in lock step with it.

Thus it appears that the experience of 'proper time', the intrinsic experienced passage of clock time that remains the same no matter how fast one's relativistic clock rate actually is, is the direct experience of the passage of p-time. It is important to understand this as not the rate of any particular clock time process but the very fact there is a clock rate at all. This is what happening is and the fact of happening, though not its rate, is certainly the direct experience of p-time.

A complicating issue is the difficulty of accurately measuring Hubble expansion rates. The assumed acceleration of expansion is based on near space in the *recent* past expanding faster than distant space in the *distant* past based on red shifts. But we have no actual measurements of the expansion rates at any distance in space other than at the single time in which we observe them and those times are all different. In particular we have no way to measure the actual *current* expansion rates of distant space or even for space at any distance at all for that matter so we can only hypothesize how space is behaving right now and thus how fast the radial p-time dimension is actually extending.

It is also not clear that the hypersphere must be a perfect sphere. It could behave more like a giant soap bubble that wobbles back and forth in p-time. One speculative possibility is that the observed acceleration of the Hubble expansion is actually just one side of such a wobble. If cosmological space is the surface of a hypersphere and all directions eventually meet at the antipodes beyond our particle horizon then if the other side of that hypersphere was progressively expanding or contracting towards its antipodes it would appear to be drawing the edges of our visible universe towards it or pushing them away which with the correct dynamics could appear to us to be an accelerating expansion of our universe when it was actually just a wobble from beyond our particle horizon.

The explanation for the acceleration of the expansion of the universe could then be as simple as p-time pulses or wobbles bouncing from antipodes to antipodes as are seen in the fluctuations of large soap bubbles.

The hypersphere cosmology suggests other interesting though speculative possibilities such as a mirror universe beyond the particle horizon where the clock time direction seems to reverse since things beyond the particle horizon are traveling faster than light with respect to us. The interesting implications of this and other possibilities won't be explored here.

THE DARK MATTER EFFECT

The fact that *intergalactic* space is expanding with the general Hubble expansion but *galactic* space is gravitationally bound and thus does not expand (Misner, et al, 1973, p. 718) suggests a simple mechanism to explain the dark matter effect or at least some of it.

This differential expansion of space necessarily produces distortions in space where galactic meets intergalactic space. By the theory of general relativity all distortions in space produce gravitational effects. Thus the effect of the differential expansion over the life of the universe will be quite significant halos of extra gravitation around galaxies which is precisely the presumed dark matter effect but without the need for any dark matter.

Once these halos of distortion are formed they can take on an independent existence and can detach from their original associations with galaxies and move independently through space as do other gravitational bodies which could explain why dark matter does not always manifest as galactic halos though it often does.

It seems clear from the long history of the universe's expansion that such spatial distortions must necessarily be present and must be having considerable gravitational effects yet to my knowledge no one else has attempted to account for that effect. This differential expansion must certainly produce some gravitational effects though there may well be more involved in the dark matter phenomenon.

TIME TRAVEL

As we have seen all observers continually 'travel' through time at the speed of light so we all are time travelers in that sense. We are all continually traveling in clock time as it flows through the present moment. However we all remain in and share the common present moment which is the only real moment that actually exists. Thus time travel outside the present moment is impossible since it would amount to leaving the surface of the hypersphere which is the entire universe and the only locus of reality.

Due to relativistic effects clock time can pass through the common present moment at different rates for observers in different situations and thus their clocks may read different times if they reunite, but the absolutely crucial point is they always reunite in the same present moment whatever times their clocks read. Thus p-time, the present moment time, is the fundamental *absolute* time and clock time is something *relative* that varies from observer to observer.

Thus observers can travel at different clock time rates relative to each other but only within the same shared present moment and only in that sense is time travel relative to other observers possible. However by the STc principle no observer's clock time direction can go backwards relative to any other observer. The direction of the arrow of time is the same for all observers. So time travel into the past is impossible, or more accurately clocks cannot run backwards in the present moment.

However one observer can travel more slowly through clock time and then arrive back at a location where more clock time has passed. This is often mistakenly said to be traveling to the other location's future but this is not true because it always occurs in the same single shared *present* moment common to all observers even if less clock time has passed. No matter how clock times vary it all occurs in the common shared present moment p-time so there is no real travel to the actual p-time past or future but only reuniting in the present moment with more or less clock time having elapsed.

All observers always experience their own time rate as the same speed of light velocity of time since they do not move relative to their own clocks. This experience is called 'proper time'. So there is no way for an observer to tell if his own clock rate changes since his internal biological clocks, like all comoving clocks, continue to tick in unison at the exact same rate whatever it may be. Only by comparing clocks in the present moment can observers tell how their clock time rates vary from one another.

The very fact of happening experienced as the passage of proper time is the direct experience of the passage of p-time. Happening or proper time is the very fact that time passes at all and seemingly always at the same rate for any observer. On the other hand the actual relative rates of passage between relativistic clocks is what is called clock time. In other words the experience of the passage of time is that of happening or p-time, but any quantifiable relative rate of happening is the measure of clock time.

P-time, the time of the present moment is the real and actual fundamental defining time. It is the absolute common universal time and thus there is no *actual* past or future that exists to be traveled to. Only the present p-time, universal and common to all observers in the universe, exists. Traveling to the past or future is both a logical and physical impossibility. Different observers can travel at different rates in clock time relative to each other but they always do so while staying in the exact same moment of p-time which defines the present. This is the only time travel that is possible.

SEEING ALL 4-DIMENSIONS

Though only the present moment surface of the hypersphere actually exists, the history of the universe forms a 4-dimensional structure consisting of the 3 surface dimensions of space and the radial dimension of p-time. These 4 dimensions can be thought of as a single geometry and we can actually see and confirm this geometry with our own eyes.

Elaborate methods of visualizing 4-dimensional spacetime have been suggested but the truth is we actually already see all 4-dimensions all the time! We see down the radial time dimension with distance in all directions. We see the sun, the stars and other galaxies as they were in the past because we actually do see down the time dimension to where they were in the past. So we really do see all 4-dimensions all the time. They are always right there in front of us – no special technique is needed!

And this actually demonstrates that time is in fact the radial dimension of our hyperspherical universe because we can actually see this with our very own eyes. We actually directly see the hyperspherical geometry of the universe with our own two eyes. The familiar 3-dimensions of space are the surface of the universal hypersphere and everyone sees the radial dimension of time in all directions from his location in space. **The actual 4-dimensional geometry of the universe lies clear before us and all we have to do is look and recognize it for what it is!**

Of course there is a slight catch. This means we don't see all 3-dimensions of space as they currently exist in the present moment at any distance. Instead we see a progressive time slice of those 3 spatial dimensions into the past. This slice of our 4-dimensional universe that we actually see is called our light cone and its geometry is determined by the speed of light. Only if the speed of light, which is really the speed of time, were instantaneous would we actually see just the 3-dimensional spatial world we mistakenly think we see, but then everything would happen all at once and all of clock time and the history of the universe would be over in an instant!

Of course since the actual seeing occurs only where we are located we see the past of the time dimension but only in the present moment and this leads to another insight.

OBSERVER SINGULARITIES

An observer cannot move relative to itself so all its combined spacetime motion takes place only in time. In an observer's experience only it and it alone exists in the present moment. Everything else exists in the past. Our experience of everything at any distance from ourselves is always as it was in the past, even if by the slightest amount because of the time it takes for time and thus for light to reach us. Thus only we ourselves exist in the present moment in our own experience and everything and everyone else exists at least slightly in the past.

Though we all share a common present moment it is impossible to directly experience this because we do not share the exact same p-time with anything or anyone else in our experience. Luckily our internal time sense is not accurate enough to distinguish this time lag for close events so we maintain the illusion that we inhabit the same present moment as the world around us and those we interact with. Another example perhaps of the mysterious fine tunings of the universe since the speed of time relative to that of our internal clocks could in fact be very different and certainly it is somewhat different for other species.

Thus every observer is effectively a singularity through which clock time continually comes into being and the future becomes the present. Every observer is a point into which reality continually comes into being. From every observer singularity there radiates a 4-dimensional time cone out into the past in all directions. The aggregate of all these time cones for all observers represents the entire cosmological geometry of the universe as experienced by observers.

We can imagine the universe as consisting of billions of observers each a singularity through which the flow of clock time continually comes into being in the present moment from a future which has no existence and thus no location and then radiates out into the past in all directions. Of course this whole model of time cones can only be experienced from the time cone singularity of some individual observer.

The radial time dimension continually flows into existence in the present moment at the speed of light though each observer singularity. The singularity is where a nonexistent future which has no spatial location at all even though it seems closer than a hair's breadth emerges from the blackness of nonexistence into existence and expands outward in every spatial direction into the past. No observer can see into the future because there is no direction there for its eyes to point; instead every observer sees only into the past no matter in what direction it looks. Every observer is like someone viewing the landscape continually receding from the back of a speeding train; and it is impossible for him to ever turn around and look where he is going in time!

In the most general sense this applies not just to human observers but to every object in the universe since every object as a generic observer is a spacetime singularity through which clock time continually enters reality in the present moment and flows away in all directions into the past.

ENTROPY

Entropy is not a fundamental characteristic of the universe as often imagined because its expression depends on the prevailing forces. For example in an initially static universe where gravitation was wholly attractive the ultimate entropy state would be a single immense black hole incorporating all matter and time and space as well. However in a universe where gravitation or some equivalent force like dark energy was entirely repulsive the ultimate entropy state would tend towards a less and less dense but uniform distribution of matter throughout an entire perpetually expanding universe.

One also has to consider the electromagnetic, strong and weak forces which in general favor small clumpings of matter at scales below which gravitational effects are felt. And in an expanding universe such as ours which contains an apparent mix of attractive and repulsive gravitation-like forces and their relative strength appears to be changing the ultimate entropy state is not clear though the current long term trend appears to be towards local gravitationally bound clusters collapsing into black holes separated by greater and greater empty interstellar distances. But in all cases the ultimate entropy state depends on the relative strengths and fields of influence of the various forces which seems to vary over time, and if those change so will the entropy.

The point is that entropy is not a fundamental principle but rather the long term result of whatever balance of forces prevail. Thus the notion that entropy is somehow an independent principle is incorrect. And the notion that entropy somehow has anything to do with time, or is the source of clock time is completely off the mark. If that had any validity at all the very fact that entropy states vary wildly across the universe would require that clock time rates also varied with entropy states but there is of course no such correlation at all.

A BIG BOUNCE?

Entropy could well provide clues to the big bang however. Penrose and others claim that the state of the universe at the big bang, where all the 'stuff' of the universe was packed into what amounts to a minute singularity, constituted the most unlikely possible low entropy state imaginable because everything was clumped in one place rather than being equally distributed, and he and others have come up with all sorts of convoluted theories in an attempt to explain how this state might have originated (Penrose, 2005).

First of all if I understand it correctly the whole analysis seems inadequate because if space itself was a minute point there could have been no alternative to packing everything into that small point, so it could be characterized as either maximum or minimum entropy or anything in between. What's the difference if space has no volume to speak of? In any case what Penrose and the others fail to recognize is that there is another simpler explanation.

If there were a previous version of the universe with a state of extreme gravitational attraction prior to the big bang it would naturally result in the packing of all the stuff of the universe into a black hole type singularity which would naturally constitute the most probable *high* entropy state. At that point just a simple reversal of gravitation from attractive to repulsive would automatically reverse the entropy state from maximally high to maximally low and simultaneously produce a big bang with inflation. This would automatically account for the apparent initial low entropy state which now becomes the *most probable* initial state! Thus we have a natural explanation for the initial low entropy state at the big bang.

This is obviously a theory that needs to be fleshed out but it does provide a very simple mechanism for the big bang naturally originating from a prior 'bounce'. The theory is that of a bouncing universe which inflates from a singularity, expands and then gradually collapses into a black hole whose other white hole side is another big bang and so on. Key confirmation would be a mathematical proof that gravitation does indeed reverse from attractive to repulsive through a black hole to white hole singularity event.

This hypothesis suggests a universe in which gravitation in its inflationary stage is initially repulsive, but then becomes partially attractive as matter condenses and galaxies and stars are formed. Finally at some point late in life attractive gravitation overpowers repulsive causing the universe to collapse back into a single massive black hole. However current evidence is that repulsive gravitation is winning out over its attractive counterpart since it appears the universe is expanding at an accelerating rate. So the jury is still out on this one.

CONCLUSION

The most fundamental experience of our human existence, of being conscious in the present moment as happening occurs, is precisely the direct experience of the fundamental cosmological reality, namely the continual extension of the radial p-time dimension of our hyperspherical universe! Because we are part of reality this process continually occurs within us manifesting as our experience of consciousness in a present moment in which reality exists. Our very existence is the actual experience of the fundamental process of the universe. We continually experience it as the very essence of our being.

Our consciousness, and all the xperiences of all generic observers, are singularities through which reality continually flows into existence at the speed of light as we continually travel through time towards the future at the speed of light.

We live in a 4-dimensional hyperspherical universe and we directly confirm that by actually seeing all 4 dimensions all the time. We see the familiar 3 spatial dimensions around us and we see the radial dimension of p-time as distance in all directions from every point in space.

Part III: ELEMENTALS

UNIFYING QUANTUM THEORY AND GENERAL RELATIVITY

This part of the book considers the structure of reality at its smallest scale. It explores how the quantum world emerges from an underlying computational information structure in a manner that conceptually unifies quantum theory and general relativity while resolving quantum paradox.

The primary reason that quantum theory and general relativity have seemed incompatible is that quantum theory treats spacetime as a classical Newtonian or at best only special relativistic framework within which quantum events play out. This view is fundamentally incompatible with general relativity where spacetime and mass-energy are tightly coupled, each affecting the other. In fact, as we will see, they are so tightly coupled that they are effectively two aspects of the same thing.

Our theory resolves this incompatibility and provides a conceptual framework for unifying these two fundamental physical theories. In our theory dimensional spacetime is not a pre-existing fixed background to quantum events, but something that emerges from a purely computational underlying structure. When computational elements interact in certain ways they generate 'decoherences' which produce actual events that establish transient point by point dimensional relationships between the elements involved.

What progressively emerges from this process is a network of dimensional relationships which are effectively individual mini spacetimes. These are sets of observer centered spacetime views, or manifolds, rather than a single fixed all-encompassing Newtonian spacetime shared by all observers and the same for all observers. In addition if we simply take mass-energy as the relative numeric scale of the dimensionalizations that occur in this process the curved spacetime of general relativity naturally emerges.

This model also provides a simple straightforward resolution of all the so called quantum paradoxes. The key insight here is that quantum paradoxes appear paradoxical only with respect to the fixed spacetime background mistakenly assumed. Understood in the light of our theory's dimensionalization process all quantum paradox becomes non-paradoxical, intuitive and natural. Several of the classical quantum paradoxes will be analyzed to illustrate this.

The quantum paradoxes are apparent contradictions that demonstrate quantum theory is incompatible with a fixed background spacetime and that a new theory is needed. When such inconsistencies arise one must always take equations that work at face value as the true description of reality and concentrate on finding a new and more consistent *interpretation*. In this case that means abandoning the naïve view of a pre-existing spacetime and adopting a new model in which general relativistic spacetime emerges naturally as a consequence of quantum events.

This theory and reinterpretation may at first seem counter intuitive and thus difficult to grasp, which no doubt is why it has not been previously discovered. But when it is understood it all becomes simple, natural and intuitively clear and one may wonder why it wasn't obvious from the beginning.

THE ELEMENTAL BITS OF REALITY

The usual interpretation of modern physics is that the elementary particles are the basic components of physical reality but upon consideration the particle *properties* such as mass-energy, charge, and spin that compose these particles are even more elemental. Elementary particles frequently interact and transform into other particles but the total amounts of the particle properties that compose these particles always remains the same through all particle interactions.

[There are some rare exceptions to strict particle property conservation. These can likely be resolved with a better understanding of *what the actual elemental particle properties that are always conserved* are. Whatever the complete list of particle properties are that are sufficient to completely describe the elementary particles and that are actually always conserved will be the actual elemental components of reality.

This discussion pertains to whatever that set turns out to be.]

Unlike elementary particles the total quantities of all particle properties are conserved through all particle interactions. So since the amounts and types of particles change but the amounts of particle properties never do it must be the particle properties rather than the elementary particles that are the actual elemental constituents of the physical universe. The belief that elementary particles conceived as physical objects are elemental is a remnant of the outmoded view that the universe is fundamentally physical in the old Newtonian sense even though elementary particles are clearly not physical at all in that sense.

This situation is exactly analogous to the chemical substances of the world which can be transformed from one to another because they are all actually compounds of more elemental types of atoms. Elementary particles can be transformed from one to another only because they too are composed of more elemental components, the particle properties.

Thus what are referred to as particle properties are not so much *properties* of particles but instead are the actual elemental *components* of reality that when properly combined in valid sets produce or act as elementary particles. Take away all their particle properties and there are no elementary particles remaining. The particle properties are the elemental bits of what it takes to make something physically real in our universe. They are the elemental information structures that in combination make up all the thing forms in the universe.

Only a small set of particle property components are necessary to produce elementary particles. These include type or identity (traditionally misleadingly called 'number' as in lepton and baryon number), the several charges associated with the various forces, spin, intrinsic spatial and temporal handedness, and mass-energy. With the important exception of mass-energy these components come in only a few discrete amounts in exact multiples of a single natural unit value and can be either positive, negative or null in value.

Very few possible combinations of property components form actual elementary particles. Why some combinations form real particles and some don't is a basic aspect of what we call the 'extended fine tuning' of the universe because in general there are no known more underlying reasons for what makes some combinations manifest as actual particles and some not. These are the basic recipes of reality's cookbook, the basic data types of reality.

The quantum vacuum, or more generally ontological energy, which is our term for the locus of reality's presence, is not empty but contains a virtual sea of particle properties only some of which are grouped in the proper combinations to form real elementary particles. The other particle properties exist unassociated or 'virtual' and thus do not manifest as elementary particles or anything at all until they properly associate and by doing so become 'real' particles.

THE ELEMENTARY PARTICLES

According to the Standard Model there are 61 elementary particles that are valid combinations of particle properties that make up what science considers physical reality. This includes the fermions (36 quarks and 12 leptons) that make up physical matter and the 13 gauge bosons that carry the three forces (gravity is not included in the Standard Model) of nature. Tables of these particles and their component particle properties can be found in the standard references (Wikipedia: Elementary particles).

COMPUTING REALITY

The very fact that the universe obeys mathematical and logical rules demonstrates that it must be a computational structure. How else could the laws of nature govern physical events if they were not actually computing them? What other mechanism could possibly produce events that obey laws?

The obvious model is that all the data states of all the particle properties in the universe are continually processed moment by moment by the elemental laws of nature to compute the elemental details of reality.

In this model at the elemental level the universe functions as a computer, or more accurately as a computational system, that continually computes its own state of existence. All discrete entities at this fundamental level exist as abstract computational structures as purely data forms rather than physical things. Every discrete 'thing' in the universe is at its fundamental level entirely an information form. These forms can be thought of as code forms processing data forms in a cosmic computer which continually computes its current form state. This is how happening manifests in the all-encompassing information space of ontological energy, the substrate of reality in which all information forms exist.

The analogy is imperfect. There is of course no physical computer nor is ontological energy a medium in the usual sense. Rather the forms themselves are a sort of self-executing software that simply evolves according to innate logical rules driven by happening. These are abstract purely information forms that continually evolve as a computational whole in interaction with others thereby generating the subsequent states of all.

This information structure has no physical size or location because it does not exist in a dimensionalized space and thus it is has no physical measures or attributes. It is entirely a computational structure like a software program existing not in a physical computer but in the logical medium or space of reality in the present moment. It does however contain logico-mathematical code structures and information which together manifest as physical things and events in the experience of observers to generate what is called 'physical' reality.

The laws of nature are an intrinsic part of this world of forms, information structures just as real as the data structures they operate upon. They are analogous to code and data forms in a computer program. Thus the laws of nature do not stand in some mysterious metaphysical world outside of a physical world they control as the usual interpretation of modern science would have us believe even though that view directly contradicts its own interpretation of reality as an exclusively physical structure.

This understanding of the laws of nature as an integral part of nature is strong evidence for our theory. The laws of nature must exist as actual information forms in the universe itself for nature to know how to act in accordance with them. The computational model of reality is much superior to the old exclusively material model in this respect. This becomes apparent as soon as the ancient paradigm of trying to understand fundamental reality by analogy from the interactions of apparently physical objects is discarded. This will become more and more obvious as the non-materiality of objects becomes clearer under subsequent analysis.

Happening is the fundamental aspect of reality that drives this process. The existence of happening within reality is the processor that drives this computational system and that continually generates subsequent form states from previous ones. This is not analogous to the individually localized processors of silicon computers but is a single process that sweeps through all the code forms of the universe simultaneously in the present moment. Though all happening occurs simultaneously in the common p-time present moment the varying rates at which it runs is the source of local relativistic clock time rates.

THE REALITY OF FORMS

We must abandon the old view that the universe is 'physical'. All the evidence indicates it is not physical in the Newtonian or even the Einsteinian or quantum sense. The only consistent view is that it is a self-executing computational structure consisting of pure information forms, and that its apparent physicality is generated only in its interpretations in the mental world models of organismic observers.

However even though this fundamental information structure is not 'physical' it is absolutely 'real' in the realest sense possible. In fact it is the only thing that is real because it is the actual system that constitutes the fundamental structure of reality.

This is not a 'simulation' of reality in the usual sense of the word. It does not simulate reality but actually *is* reality at its most fundamental level. It is real and absolute because it is takes place in the very substance or space of reality, and is it all that actually exists. It is the actual information components of reality self-computing their ongoing evolution in clock time. And there is just this one single incredibly complex networked program running in reality's computer which contains all the evolving forms of the universe.

Though it might be considered a simulation of reality by reality itself, it is not something that can be turned on or off or its fundamental code reprogrammed and there is no reason to think it is under any sort of external influence or control. There is after all nothing external to it by definition. This is simply reality itself computing itself and its information structure is what organismic observers in turn model to varying degrees of precision as the physical universe in their own cognitive models of reality.

Though it's only abstract information this evolution of forms has real actual effects. Every aspect of the reality of the world emerges from it and it produces real physical effects in the experience of observers. The reality of a bus at this elemental level may be an abstract logical structure but if this structure computationally intersects the logical structure of an observer the forms generated are what are experienced by observers as real injuries.

At the elemental level your leg is an information structure. If that information structure becomes deformed computationally by interacting with the form of a bus, the leg you experience will be a broken leg. Even though the bus hitting an observer is entirely a computation of forms it is real because it occurs in reality's computer. Its resulting forms are interpreted and experienced by observers not as abstract fictions but as real life because they are real life. This is explained further in Part IV, Mind and Reality.

As we will see there are a number of consistent avenues that suggests this is the best model and truest picture of the reality that underlies all things at the most elemental level. It is an entirely abstract non-material computational information structure which evolves according to basic logical rules just as ordinary software does. There is no physicality, materiality or dimensionality to this underlying structure just as there is none to software. But this computational structure carries all the code and data for physicality, materiality and dimensionality. It generates the information that manifests dimensionality, the quantum world, and the curved spacetime of general relativity in one consistent integrated structure in the experience of observers.

At this fundamental level all is information, empty forms in the underlying substrate or space of ontological energy, analogous to how water waves exist and interactively self-compute their forms in otherwise perfectly still water. The water waves themselves are merely energetic information forms arising in the underlying structure of the water. They have no intrinsic physical self-substances other than that of the underlying water in which they exist. Likewise by arising as information wave forms in the underlying sea of ontological energy the information structures of reality take on the underlying reality of being real and actual in the present moment and their computations underlie all the other apparent levels of the reality of our universe.

As with computers many of the computations at the fundamental level are remarkably simple logical operations. None or very little of the usual complexity of quantum theory exists at this fundamental level of logical computation though phenomena of apparently unlimited complexity can be generated by them just as computer software seems to be unlimited in the complexity of programs consisting only of sequences of a small set of elemental 'machine language' operations.

THE PARTICLE PROPERTY CONSERVATION LAW

Because the particle properties are the true elemental components of reality the total amounts of all particle properties are conserved through all interactions and remain constant no matter how they recombine into new particles. In any particle interaction one simply adds the amounts of each of the particle properties and redistributes them in valid combinations among the new particles. This simple arithmetic conservation law of particle property interactions is one of the most fundamental laws of nature, one of the most elemental code sequences of reality's computational structure.

This conservation law requires that the total quantities of all particle properties in any interaction must all be used up to create the resulting particles. None can be left over 'naked' outside of a particle in any interaction. They must all be completely accounted for and used. No event can take place in which this is not true and all events in which it can take place must take place with some degree of probability. In particle physics this is called the 'Totalitarian Principle' which states that all events which can take place according to the conservation law must take place with some probability and as a corollary no event can take place that is not allowed by the conservation law. The Totalitarian Principle was first expressed by Murray Gell-Mann as, "Everything that is not forbidden is compulsory." (Johnson, 2000, p. 224.)

Thus the particle property conservation law is a primary determinant of which events are possible in our universe and which are not. This single simple arithmetic conservation law determines much of the structure and dynamics of our universe.

It is important to understand that this law applies to each type of particle property separately even though it can be considered a single

71

law; namely that **the total amounts of all particle properties always remains the same through all physical events**. This is an extremely powerful law with profound implications for understanding reality.

As noted previously there are a few exceptions in which particular particle properties as currently defined are not exactly conserved but they are an extremely minute percentage of the total number of particle interactions that take place. Examples are CPT invariance where either electromagnetic charge (C), parity (P), or intrinsic time direction (T) may not be individual conserved in certain weak interactions such as neutral kaon decay. However CPT together is always conserved which perhaps suggests that CPT together should be considered as a single always conserved particle property.

It is clearly possible that P and T might best be considered a single particle property since T is intrinsic time handedness and P is spatial handedness and the universe is a single 4-dimensional structure even though the radial time dimension is only a surface without extension. Thus PT together is the complete 4-dimensional handedness of a particle with respect to this 4-dimensional world. How the electromagnetic charge component can be reconciled is more problematic though one recalls that Kaluza-Klein theories explain electromagnetic force as curvature in a fifth dimension in the same way that gravitation is now accepted as curvature in the first 4-dimensions (Halpern & Wesson, 2006, p. 179-181).

Lepton number conservation also seems to be violated by neutrino oscillation in which free neutrinos seem to oscillate between their lepton number levels though this process is not yet completely understood. This quite likely has something to do with the vanishingly small masses of neutrinos and hints at a relationship of mass to particle identity. So though these exceptions need to be reconciled it is quite clear that in general particle properties are almost always conserved and thus certainly more fundamental than the particles they compose.

Every particle that exists can be destroyed or created by interactions with other particles, but with extremely rare possible exceptions no particle properties can be created or destroyed in any way whatsoever.

THE PARTICLE PROPERTIES

The particle properties are the elemental components of reality necessary to make something actual. They are effectively the data building blocks used to construct the information forms that manifest as real physical things. Each of these components contributes an amount of one of the several necessary aspects of reality that makes something real in our universe.

We will briefly examine the most relevant particle properties to explain what they contribute to generate the reality of the physical world in particular the emergence of dimensional spacetime. This is a fascinating story that reveals a new understanding of what dimensional spacetime is and how it arises and that leads naturally to a conceptual synthesis of quantum theory and general relativity and the resolution of quantum paradox.

PARTICLE IDENTITY

The type or identity particle property, traditionally called lepton or baryon (or more accurately quark) 'number' in reference to the several different amounts it comes in for various types of particle, actually designates the type or identity of the particle it creates as well as the amount of that identity. It has been called number because it is usually understood as the numeric amount of lepton or baryon number present. However it is simpler to interpret type as a single identity property that comes in two types and several amounts.

In any case the type particle component is what gives every particle its fundamental identity or suchness and amount of that identity. While we normally think of particles such as electrons as having some mysterious intrinsic electron identity independent of their particle 'properties', in fact the characteristic of its identity is conveyed by the amount of the type component, which is itself a little bit of identity existing in a virtual state until it is combined with the other particle properties necessary to construct an actual particle. This is one reason only certain sets of particle properties result in valid particles; all the components must mesh to form particles that are logically consistent with the extended fine tuning and thus able to exist in our universe.

On consideration it is entirely reasonable that reality requires a little bit of identity to make something really one thing as opposed to something else, but that in itself is not sufficient to produce something actual. It also requires an acceptable amount of each of the other constituents of reality which are supplied by the other particle properties.

Essentially there must be an amount of each of the particle property components so that the underlying structural components of the universe at large can manifest in something real and actual. For example there must be dimensional particle properties for something to manifest in dimensional spacetime with dimensional attributes; charge properties for something to manifest charge or not; spin for something to manifest intrinsic angular momentum in an aligned cosmological geometry or not. All the properties combined give their resultant particles all the necessary characteristics of physical reality in a universe whose overall structure is defined in terms of those same characteristics. Thus the universe itself must also consist of an underlying framework in which those particular particle properties are necessary to manifest all necessary characteristics or components of reality so that something can become real.

Thus the type or identity particle property is a necessary component of having a real identity or suchness with respect to a universe defined in terms of those attributes without which something would have no identity or suchness and thus could not exist within a structure that requires it.

The universe can be thought of as an incipient background structure that must be filled with associated amounts of the basic particle property forms for something to become real and actual in that universe. A good analogy would be to consider the universe as a logical structure defined as a set of empty arrays one corresponding to each particle property, and for something to be real and actual it would have to have an appropriate entry in every array.

SPIN

The spin particle property is reality's basic unit of intrinsic rotation or angular momentum and is also a source of magnetism. For something to be real in our universe it must have some fundamental notational (information) component of intrinsic rotation even if that amount is zero. **Otherwise it can have no alignment within a dimensional reality and thus cannot exist**. Like most particle properties spin comes in only a few discrete amounts which are multiples of the basic unit of spin; but unlike others it also carries an intrinsic 3-dimensional orientation that is responsible for matter's absolute rotational orientation relative to dimensional space.

Spin is also a distinguishing characteristic between the fermions (matter particles) which all have half integral spins and the bosons (force carrying particles) all of which have integral (including 0) spins. The Pauli exclusion principle prevents matter particles from simultaneously occupying the same location but allows the force carrying particles to do so (Smolin, 2007, pp. 67-68). Thus spin is the source of the apparent materiality or substance of matter. Spin is the intrinsic dimensional orientation and angular momentum of the particle itself and is not to be confused with an actual rotation or circular orbit of a particle.

The basic take away is that spin is one of the elemental components of what it takes to make something real in our universe. It generates an intrinsic alignment of its particle with a universe which requires such alignment for something to be real. It is one more of the elemental aspects of reality that are necessary to make something real.

PARITY (P)

The parity particle property is another basic component of reality necessary to make something real. Parity is the intrinsic handedness of a particle relative to its mirror reflection with respect to all 3 spatial dimensions. This is a little different than what regular mirrors do since they reverse only 2 of the 3 spatial dimensions, the side to side and front to back dimensions. Parity would be like looking into a mirror where up and down were also reversed. It is essentially the intrinsic handedness of particles, whether they are like left or right handed gloves but in all 3-dimensions. What the existence of parity tells us is that there is an intrinsic spatial handedness to dimensional reality which seems to be hidden in most classical level phenomena though there may be a trace of that in the left and right isomers of certain molecules essential for biology (Wikipedia: Stereoisomerism).

The exact function of parity is still a mystery, but it is clear that it is an essential component of the dimensionalization of reality. Every elementary particle must have a parity component even if zero to be real. Almost all anti-particles have negative parities and most regular particles have positive parities. Parity reversal is part of what distinguishes particles and their antiparticles.

TIME HANDEDNESS (T)

There is also an analogous particle property called time handedness which is the intrinsic time handedness or time direction of a particle. Everything that is real must have a time handedness relative to the forward direction of clock time just as everything that is real must have a spatial handedness relative to the handedness of our usual 3-dimensional space. Together with parity the time particle property allows for mirror reversal in all 4-dimensions. It is only anti-particles that have negative time handedness or orientation in time. All regular particles have positive time handedness and align with the overall positive flow of clock time.

In fact it is possible that the reason there are so few antiparticles relative to regular particles in the universe is that there is some mechanism by which many of them are left behind in the past due to their reversed temporal orientation with respect to the arrow of time. Because they are going against the flow of time some of them can't keep up and leak out of the present moment. The mechanism controlling this is something that needs to be explored.

ANTIPARTICLES

For every valid set of particle properties that produces a real particle there is another valid set that produces its antiparticle. Antiparticles have the same mass and spin as their regular particles but the signs of all their other particle properties are reversed. They thus have the same energies and momenta as their regular particles assuming they are moving in the same manner. Thus there is an antiparticle corresponding to every regular particle though the massless bosons are effectively their own antiparticles.

To the consternation of physicists, because of their negative time handedness antiparticles can only be understood mathematically as traveling backwards in time. In fact they must be represented as such in Feynman diagrams to obtain valid results for particle interactions (Penrose, 2005, pp. 638-639). Though physicists routinely depend on Feynman diagrams to understand particle interactions they have a mental block about accepting the idea of reversed time orientation as real or even attempting to understand what is really happening here. The question is just ignored.

However when we discuss the genesis of dimensionalization below an answer will become obvious. First everything happens in the present moment so there is no way anything can actually get to or exist in another 'non-present' moment no matter which direction in its own clock time it is pointing so that is not the problem. In our universe clock time in aggregate flows in what we call the positive direction but that may be only because of the continual chorusing of the myriads of regular particles with forward time orientations which greatly outnumber antiparticles.

The existence of the time orientation particle property indicates that each particle carries with it its own intrinsic clock time orientation. It must have an intrinsic clock time orientation to exist in a universe that requires it due to its own time dimensionalization. So long as an antiparticle doesn't interact with a regular particle that negative clock time direction is not patched into the established time manifold formed by the continual interaction of myriads of regular particles. However when it does decohere with a regular particle its backwards time orientation gets patched in negatively which accounts for antiparticle interactions. More on manifold patching shortly.

When a particle and its antiparticle collide they annihilate into energetic photons which conveniently are their own antiparticles thus conserving all particle properties including the T property. Photon T values are zero as a consequence of photons having no time orientation as they do not travel in time at all as a consequence of all their combined spacetime velocity being through space. Clock time does not pass at all in their frames which is why all their spacetime motion is in time and they always travel at the speed of light in all other observer frames as a consequence of the STc Principle.

CHARGE

There are several kinds of charge particle properties each corresponding to one of the three fundamental forces of nature in the Standard Model. There is C, the electromagnetic charge particle property, that is the source of electric charge and the electromagnetic force in the classical world and there are six (plus and minus red, green, and blue) color charges for the strong force, and there is weak isospin which is the equivalent charge for the weak force. Since some particles carry both electric and weak charges these may have to be considered separate particle properties however under the electro-weak theory the electromagnetic and weak forces can be unified and both expressed in terms of what is called weak hypercharge. Again for something to be real everything can be considered to have some amount of each of the various charge particle properties even if that amount is zero.

Since the charge particle properties are scalar properties it might appear that charge has nothing to do with dimensionalization of space but the association of electric charge with parity and time in CPT conservation hints otherwise. So charge may in fact contribute some cryptic aspect to the dimensionalization of space. Some additional evidence this might be true comes from Kaluza Klein theory in which electric charge is effectively modeled as an additional 5th dimension though this theory currently seems incompatible with other accepted theories. Also it should be noted that in string theory other particle properties are associated with up to 11 or more additional compacted dimensions (Greene, 2005).

LOCATION AS A PARTICLE PROPERTY

It makes sense to include spatial location (in a pre-dimensional numeric form) as another particle property. If we do this we have the complete set of components that make up not just all the various types of particles but of all individual particles because the only thing that distinguishes individual particles of the same type are their different spatial locations, energies and momenta.

In this way every individual particle of any type in the universe is completely described by its particle property set because this set includes all the elements of reality it takes to make individual particles real and actual. In this respect numeric location is a necessary component of anything real in a universe in which dimensional relations exist. Without having a relative numeric location particle property nothing can exist in a universe constructed of dimensional relationships.

However at the fundamental computational level spatial location exists as purely relative numeric information in computational space rather than as an actual location in a previously existing dimensional spacetime. This purely numeric information is what is used to generate physical dimensionality.

MASS-ENERGY AND THE GENESIS OF SPACETIME

The mass-energy particle property is the total energy component of a particular particle. It consists of the sum of the intrinsic rest mass of the particle plus its energy of kinetic or wave motion. Both of these components are essentially different forms of energy inter-convertible according to Einstein's $e=mc^2$. It is the sum of these two forms of energy that compose the mass-energy particle property that is conserved in all particle interactions.

Every particle must have some non-zero positive energy to exist as a real particle in our universe. Some mass-energy is necessary to give something a physical reality. Things with no energy have no existence. Energy is necessary for existence and its hidden nature as relative motion will be explored in more detail below.

A unique aspect of mass-energy is it is apparently the only particle property that doesn't come in negative amounts. That in itself is certainly unusual, though it is unclear what the reality of something with negative mass and energy would be or how it would behave; for example whether it would have an attractive or repulsive gravitational effect. Since positive mass-energy is what generates motion in space, particles with negative mass-energy might be expected to move backwards in both time and space whatever that might mean. We can safely assume they don't exist on the basis of the STc Principle.

Mass-energy requires special consideration because it has two components, rest mass and the energy of its motion. In the case of the kinetic energy of motion it is always relative to an observer and thus varies in value from observer to observer so that the conservation law holds only within fixed observer frames. Thus the total mass-energy of a particle will be different for observers in different frames but it is always conserved within any given frame. There is an important insight hidden here vis-à-vis the conservation law, and the nature of energy and relative motion which will be explored shortly.

Because kinetic energy is always relative to some observer and is measured from that observer's frame, mass-energy does not have a single set absolute value common to all observers. This is why all motion is relative because there is nothing in the mass-energy particle property that ties an interaction and its mass-energy conservation to any absolute location or motion in space. Thus all motion and all energy is relative to the observer that measures it.

Most importantly for the current discussion, the values mass-energy can assume are not restricted to a small set of multiples of a unit value. Unlike all other particle properties the amount of energy a particle can have varies almost continuously. Almost, because nothing physical is completely continuous since everything is quantized at the finest scale.

The hidden implications of these simple facts are enormous when it comes to understanding the structure of our universe. For example, it is only the fact that the energy of motion can take on near continuous values, rather than being restricted to a small set, that allows objects to have free movement through space at all velocities and in all directions. The particle property conservation law requires that the total mass-energy component be conserved in particle interactions and this is only possible by sending off particles in the correct directions with the correct velocities.

Because the rest masses of different particles don't come in exact proportions to each other the conservation law would not allow any particle transformations to take place at all if only the rest masses themselves had to be conserved because the masses of particles of different types never exactly add up. So it is only the fact that discrepancies in rest masses can be expressed as relative velocities in space that allows total mass-energy to be conserved and thus makes particle interactions possible at all.

Kinetic energy is rest mass times velocity squared so the mass-energy particle property absolutely requires that there be a dimensional clock time as well as a dimensional space for velocities to exist.

Thus it is clear that the conservation law operating on the mass-energy property is intimately bound up with the dimensional extension of spacetime. It is only the near continuous values mass-energy can take on that enables physical events to have dimensional characteristics and thus to take place at all. Thus it is primarily the conservation of the mass-energy particle property that allows physical particles to assume the dimensional characteristics of position and motion in space and in time that produces the basic event structure of our universe.

Another very important point regarding mass-energy is that it is only these discrete positional values that allows multiple particles to exist at all. If particles could have no positions then there would be nowhere for multiple particles to exist. Thus the details of the mass-energy particle property open up space and time so that matter and the universe as we know it can exist.

Because mass-energies are not restricted to a small set of values like the other particle properties this allows multiple particles to move in a multitude of ways even though they are otherwise identical. It is all a very elegant and precise design nature has come up with to allow our universe to be as immensely rich as it is; again a consequence of the extended fine tuning.

SPACETIME CONSISTS OF DIMENSIONAL EVENTS

We tend to think of space or spacetime, as a single fixed, empty, pre-existing all-encompassing framework within which events play out. This view seems consistent with our common sense experience and is the traditional view of science as well. But under careful analysis there is little evidence to support it.

What we call spacetime actually manifests only as the dimensional characteristics of *actual events*. It is not something that can be observed at all except in the form of the dimensional values of actual events. **Because spacetime itself in the absence of dimensional events**

81

cannot be observed or measured its existence as a ubiquitous pre-existing background cannot be confirmed. Thus the assumption of a fixed, ever present, empty spacetime filling the 'spaces' between events seems to be an imaginary entity with no actual evidence for its existence.

Scientific belief must be observationally confirmable to be accepted. And there simply can be no direct confirmation of empty space. All that is actually measurable is not empty space but the dimensional values and relationships of individual events. Thus the most reasonable interpretation of actual observation is that events occur with certain consistent dimensional values but there is no evidence at all of anything called empty space within which those events occur.

The most reasonable interpretation is that the conventional view of a continuous spacetime is a convenient fiction extrapolated from the dimensional relationships of individual events. We assume events occur within space but in fact this dimensional space is actually just the consistent logico-mathematical relationship among events.

Thus we must conclude that the dimensional space we seem to live within is a convenient mental model arising from the consistency of the dimensional relationships among events. At best spacetime is a purely logico-mathematical structure inherent in the computational realm rather than an actual physical entity that 'fills' the universe between events. Here again is more evidence that reality itself is fundamentally a computational rather than a material structure.

Of course when we look out at the world the illusion of a space filling it is very convincing but what we are actually observing are events, not the space we think they occur within. Every photon striking our retina is such an event so the very density of events is sufficient to establish the illusion of a background spacetime.

This illusion works because of the inherent consistency in the dimensional relationships among events. This dimensional consistency is what is expressed in the dimensional aspects of the laws of physics. All the laws of physics that are interpreted as encoding a physical spacetime are actually encoding the consistent dimensional dynamics of events within what we think of as a physical spacetime but which the evidence suggests is actually just the consistent logico-mathematical structure itself.

In our prejudice that reality must be physical we have projected a purely logico-mathematical structure into the world as an actual physical thing when in fact there is not any way whatsoever to touch, feel or otherwise experimentally confirm its existence as anything physical that actually exists.

Thus there is no evidence at all for an empty space between events within which things exist and events occur. The evidence is that events occur computationally in a purely computational space and that those events include purely numeric dimensional interrelationships among the interacting participants in the events that are imposed by the particle property conservation law. It is the systematically consistent manner in which these interrelationships are imposed that generates a mathematical framework that can be misinterpreted as a fixed ever present empty space in which events take place. Dimensionality, like everything else in the world of forms, is fundamentally computational rather than a physical world existing inside a physical spacetime. Every possible measurement of space is actually an observation not of space itself but of the dimensional relationships among information forms including the measurement devices used and the observers involved.

It is the conservation law acting on the particle properties, most particularly the mass-energy particle property, that is responsible for all the dimensional interrelationships between events. **The inescapable conclusion is that events themselves produce the simulacrum of a dimensional spacetime rather than occurring within an already extant spacetime.**

Since spacetime manifests itself only through dimensional events and events at all scales are aggregate particle interactions the particle property conservation process actually creates what observers experience as dimensional spacetime because it is what imposes dimensional relationships on particle property interactions. It is the particle property conservation law that determines the dimensional relationships between resultant particles and this in aggregate is what is interpreted as the apparent experience of a fixed spacetime background in the mental world models of observers.

Thus the observer experience of a continuous empty pre-extant spacetime is a mental model based on an interpolation between the dimensional relationships of events. Observer minds create the illusion of a physical space-time within which events occur by projecting the purely logico-mathematical dimensional relationships between things out into an internal model of reality which mind places 'out there' in an external physical world. These internal models of a ubiquitous background spacetime are convenient fictions of individual observer minds rather than being an actual aspect of external reality which actually consists just of programs running in information space.

This is one of the most important insights of this book and it has profound implications. It is another fundamental aspect of the extended fine tuning that is absolutely required for our universe to have the apparent dimensionality and structure it does and thus for us to exist. It is one more essential component of the great mystery that is reality.

ALL EVENTS ARE ENTANGLEMENTS

The particle property conservation law imposes necessary relationships between the particle properties of interacting particles. Because the amounts of particle properties must exactly add up to be conserved the amount of any property in one particle determines how much is available to the other particles in the interaction thus establishing a relationship among them.

This interrelationship among the particle properties of particles in an event is called 'entanglement'. The resulting particles are said to be entangled on every particle property specified by the conservation law in the event.

Thus entanglement is nothing mysterious at all. It is just the necessary interrelationships imposed by the particle property conservation law on all particles involved in any interaction. The conservation law entangles the particles with respect to each other on each of the particle properties defined in the event. Entanglements are very simply the particle property relationships generated between interacting particles by the conservation law.

For example in any particle interaction the velocities of outgoing particles must be such as to conserve the total mass-energy and momentum of the incoming particles. Thus the outgoing particles are entangled on their related velocities. Likewise the total spins of outgoing particles must be oriented correctly with respect to each other to conserve (equal) the incoming spins. Thus the spins and the spin orientations of the outgoing particles are also entangled by the conservation law. This is true of all particle properties conserved in any particle interaction without exception.

ENTANGLEMENT NETWORKS

Thus every particle interaction is an entanglement event and the universe consists of myriads of entangled particles and entanglement relationships. While most scientific discussions treat entanglement as something that occurs between a few particles in specific laboratory experiments the truth is that entanglement is a ubiquitous phenomenon that occurs in every event in the universe.

Not only that but when already entangled particles interact they entangle not only themselves and any resulting particles but they also entangle all the particles they were previously entangled with into an entanglement network. This is because all the previous relationships still exist and thus become related to the new relationships.

Consider a network of nodes representing particle interaction events connected by lines representing the particles. Each node produces an entanglement between all the lines entering and leaving it because the particle property values are conserved in that event. Thus if there is a path through the network from any line to any other line those two particles are also entangled because at each intervening node particle property relationships were imposed. This is true no matter how many event nodes separate the two particles.

For example the total mass-energy of particles will be conserved all along a network of events connecting them. At every step in the way particles become entangled with all the other particles they have interacted with in their event histories and with all the other particles those particles have interacted with as well in their event histories. Thus very complex entanglement networks emerge in which the particle properties of every particle in the network are related to all the others.

A good example is the total mass-energy of a system of particles like the molecules of a gas in a container which will be conserved by being continually redistributed among the particles as they continuously collide with each other inside the container. Each collision entangles two particles and all the particles they are already entangled with thus there is a progressive entanglement chain reaction in which all the particles in the container eventually become entangled with each other.

It is important to understand there is a separate entanglement network for each particle property because the particle property conservation law operates on each particle property separately. Therefore the total entanglement network consists of layers, one for each particle property, stacked on top of each other.

Also depending on the type of particle interaction not every particle property is affected in every event. Thus the particle lines of some layers will pass through such nodes unchanged. There will be no node for that layer corresponding to that event. For example two particles that collide and bounce off each but do not interact to produce new particles will leave most of their particle properties unchanged. Such particle scattering typically does not affect spin, charge, or particle identity but only changes the energies and momenta of the particles. The particles do not break apart to redistribute their particle properties among new particles. This means that only the energies and momenta expressed as particle velocities are entangled by that interaction. Those two particles do not become entangled on any of their other particle properties.

The aggregate effect of entanglement is that every particle in the universe is entangled with all the other particles it has interacted with due to the particle property conservation law that governed their interactions. Thus most particles in the universe are entangled with many other particles on most but not necessarily all of their various particle properties and the universe consists of myriads of entanglement networks of entangled particles. These networks are the causal networks that make up reality at the elemental level and all causal networks have this elemental structure.

Thus entanglement is a ubiquitous phenomenon that weaves reality together by interrelating its elemental components into vast entanglement networks that form the computational nexus of the universe. All thanks to the operation of one single very simple but immensely powerful particle property conservation law.

DECOHERENCE AS DIMENSIONAL ENTANGLEMENT

An entanglement of a dimensional particle property is called a 'decoherence', and the dimensional layers of entanglement networks are called decoherence networks. Decoherences and their resulting decoherence networks are dimensional events that lead to the creation of networks of dimensionality between events.

There is an essential difference in the nature of decoherence type entanglements due to the unrestricted values that dimensional particle properties like position, velocity and spin orientation can assume. All the non-dimensional particle properties are restricted to a small set of multiples of a unit value so when they are redistributed the resulting values are very limited and always exact.

However the ways in which dimensional values can be redistributed among particles in an interaction is potentially unlimited. This introduces an element of randomness because there is no law that chooses one redistribution over another. And in nature when there is no determining law nature is forced to choose randomly among the available possibilities.

This is The Law of Random Choice. And this law is the source of all randomness. When there is no law that exactly specifies an outcome nature is forced to choose randomly among the available possibilities based on their probabilities. This principle is the source of all quantum randomness and all classical randomness since all classical randomness is quantum. It is also the source of all free will and all uncertainty and unpredictability. Without this single law the universe would be completely deterministic.

Thus thankfully nature doesn't know exactly what to do in some cases because it has no law telling it exactly what to do. This Law of Equal Choice is another essential component of the extended fine tuning that makes our universe the amazing place that it is.

The result is that the redistribution of dimensional particle properties in a decoherence event is probabilistic. The overall conservation of amounts is exact and deterministic but the particular distribution of those amounts among particles cannot be exactly predicted. Thus the exact directions and speeds and spin orientations of particles issuing from an interaction cannot be exactly predicted and are unknown to outside observers until measured by a subsequent decoherence.

However they are all already specified exactly with respect to each other by the conservation law in the event that produced them.

A decoherence is an elemental event that generates a point of dimensionality *in the frames of the participating particles* by entangling the dimensional particle properties of those particles. While the precise dimensional values of the event are probabilistic to an external observer, they are already exactly interrelated by the particle property conservation law in the frames of the interacting particles. In this way spacetime attributes emerge probabilistically in a manner that satisfies the equations of quantum theory while obeying the determinism of the conservation law.

As with entanglement, decoherence is usually discussed in textbooks in the context of specific laboratory interactions involving a few particles at most but like entanglement decoherence is actually a ubiquitous phenomenon which occurs with every measurable event in the universe. The text book examples are particular instances of a universal process.

Since there are invariably dimensional aspects to every event all events are effectively decoherences. [Though newly emerging experimental evidence indicates that some decoherences can be partial (Aharony, et al, 2012).] Thus decoherence includes every particle interaction of whatever sort including transformations, collisions, scatterings, and absorption or emission of energy as photons by electrons. An event can be defined as any measurable occurrence and to be measured there must be some dimensional characteristics. If something is not measureable or observable it cannot be confirmed to exist or even to have happened.

However this includes all events since even particles themselves act as generic observers because they xperience the events they participate in in the re-computations of their own forms. All events in the universe are 'observed' only by their participants in their own re-computations. A human observer's 'observation' of a particle event is actually a participation in a subsequent measurement event which conveys information about the original particle event being measured and ultimately the computation of the resulting changes to the forms of the observer itself.

All decoherences occur at the elemental level. However in the typical laboratory experiment there will be a measurement device that magnifies the result of the original decoherence up to the classical level of a human observer through a sequence of additional decoherences. At the computational level observers, measuring devices, and everything else are information structures which computationally experience one other at the particle level only through complex sequences of aggregate decoherences.

Every actual event in the universe is a decoherence in which particles effectively 'measure' each other via their dimensional relationships to each other as determined by the conservation law. Every event that occurs in the universe is a decoherence and it is only through decoherences that information forms emerge into observable reality by acquiring dimensional relationships, if even only to particles themselves acting as generic observers.

Every participant in events in the universe acts as a generic observer at the level we have called *xperience*. Thus events are not known to any particular observer until their decoherence network is linked to that of the observer. Until there is some interaction with an observer nothing can be said to have happened from the perspective of that observer since events are defined as re-computations to the states of things and there is no way to verify a change without some observation since an observation actually consists of the computation of some change in the form of the observer.

A decoherence is how a quantum event emerges from the unseen logical world as something that has dimensional attributes and can therefore be observed. It is how the logical substructure of reality begins to become physical in the usual sense of that term. A decoherence is an xperience or an observation in the generic sense *at the elemental level*. So it is the process of xperience or decoherence which begins to generate the appearance of a physical world from the information world that underlies it.

MATTER AS BOUND DECOHERENCE

To complete the picture we must consider not only free particles but particles bound in the atomic and molecular matter that constitutes all the familiar things of the world. It turns out that the bonds that hold matter together can be interpreted as 'bound' decoherences, that is as continuous interactions between particles.

What this means is that some of the particle property relationships between particles bound in matter persist in fixed states rather than occurring transiently in the interactions between free particles. For example the various orbital energies of atomic electrons are fixed and in continuously defined relationships to their nuclear particles. Bohr's discovery that the orbital energies of electrons exist only in certain fixed amounts or quanta was of course the genesis of quantum theory (Penrose, 2005, p. 573).

Besides the particle property conservation law there are additional laws that govern atomic structure. The law of quantum numbers governs the structure of the electron orbitals. There are 4 quantum numbers each of which can have only a small set of values, and this law states that no two electrons in an atom can have identical sets of quantum numbers. This law determines the slots in the orbitals that electrons can occupy and in turn the chemistry and much of the physics of our material world (Wikipedia, Quantum Number).

An additional law is that the number of orbital electrons wants to balance the number of protons in the nucleus to produce an electrically stable atom with equal positive and negative charges (Wikipedia, Atomic number). And there are similar laws that govern the structure of the nucleus (Wikipedia, Atomic nucleus).

All these laws serve to persistently entangle the particle properties of the constituent particles of matter in a state of bound decoherence in which the particle properties have continuous dimensional relationships to each other. However these relationships are only fixed with respect to each other. They are not fixed with respect to the frame of an external observer until they are 'measured' by some decoherence event that relates them to the observer's frame.

Thus the dimensional relationships between orbital electrons and the nucleus have exact fixed quantum values but the locations of those electrons in their orbitals is not exact with respect to an external observer. Likewise the energy of electrons involved in orbital jumps shows that the energies of orbital electrons is exact even though their positions seem fuzzy in the frame of an external observer until actually measured.

Atoms consist of electrons occupying orbitals around a nucleus of protons and neutrons which in turn are composed of up and down quarks bound together by the gluons of the strong force. In turn molecules consist of multiple atoms bound together primarily by the electrical charges of shared electrons. All these relationships between the constituent particles of matter are bound decoherences. And photons are emitted and absorbed by atoms to transfer energy from and to them thus modifying the states of these decoherences.

DECOHERENCE MANIFOLDS

A decoherence manifold is the view of the dimensional aspects of a decoherence network from the perspective of any particular particle or particulate object within it. It is the dimensional frame of reference of that element in the network. It consists of all the dimensional relationships among all elements of a decoherence network relative to the frame of that particular element. The particular element can be any particle, or in a more general sense any observer in the network since all observers are collections of particles.

Of course the manifold of non-organismic observers such as particles themselves is virtual in the sense it is not thought of as such by the particles. It exists only implicitly in the actual relationships between particle properties devoid of any context or conceptualization.

Thus a manifold is any observer's view of spacetime in terms of the actual dimensional measurements (decoherence interactions) it has had with everything else. Thus every particle or other observer in a decoherence network has its own unique manifold which constitutes its entire dimensional (and entanglement) view of reality as a generic observer. This applies to particles acting as generic observers, classical human observers and everything in between.

Since what we call dimensional spacetime actually consists of *the dimensional aspects of events* rather than being a pre-existing empty framework in which events occur, a manifold is the actual spacetime view of an observer, and in fact is its actual individual spacetime. This is not an observer's *view* of a single classical spacetime since that does not in fact exist. Instead it is the actual individual spacetime of that observer which consists entirely of the network of actually observed dimensional relationships between events from its perspective.

Thus we can actually call the manifolds of all observers of whatever type at whatever level their individual spacetimes. Thus every

observer, generic or organismic, has its own individual private spacetime and all these mini-spacetimes are independent structures each incorporating an observer's view of the dimensional relationships between all events in its interaction history.

Thus spacetime actually consists not of a single independent pre-existing structure common to all observers within which all events occur, but of innumerable independent individual spacetimes associated with individual observers. And these mini-spacetimes are not actually physical space-like structures but merely the dimensional interrelationships between experienced events. It is quite clear that this is what spacetime actually is because we have the well-established natural mechanism of the particle property conservation and other elemental laws of nature that clearly produce it!

Thus spacetimes are always private and particular to their participants, each from its own perspective. Objects not involved in events within a network are unknown to the spacetimes within the network and thus not part of the shared dimensionality of its members.

However in general separate spacetimes can be patched together by shared events that connect their networks at those events. Due to the conservation law that governs all events any such shared event will immediately establish dimensional relationships between the participants in the event and thus between the entanglement networks of the objects participating in the event that extend to all relationally connected members.

Spacetime manifolds are not a new concept but are used in general relativity. Penrose discusses how the proper local view of spacetime in general relativity is in terms of individual observer manifolds and that in general it is impossible to simultaneously reconcile all points in the manifolds of relativistic observers (Penrose, 2005, pp. 217-222).

One can always patch spacetime manifolds together at shared individual event nodes but then the dimensional characteristics of other events may not exactly match due to relativistic effects. Because of this large scale relativistic models will always be approximations, no matter how useful. Penrose seems to agree with us that spacetime is a structure known only from the dimensional events that occur within it however he does not seem to grasp that is all that spacetime actually is or that it actually emerges from decoherence events.

This model demonstrates why there can be no single universal pre-existing spacetime framework. What we think of as dimensional spacetime is actually just our individual spacetime manifolds which are extrapolations of the way measurements of individual dimensional points work in our experience of them. It was the fact that in daily life we were effectively non-relativistic observers that led to the illusion of a common pre-existing fixed universal spacetime framework we all shared.

We previously generalized the definition of 'observer' to include everything in the universe including particles as generic observers, since everything effectively *xperiences* other things via shared entanglement and decoherence events and thus everything is embedded in its own effective manifold of dimensional relationships which constitutes its xperience of its world.

Human observers act as observers only because everything that has interactions with other things is effectively an observer of those things. In Part I, Fundamentals, we introduced the concept of xperience defined as the re-computation of a form that may be altered in interaction with another form. Xperience is a functional generalization of decoherence events to events at any level of complexity. Because decoherence occurs at the elemental level all experience, observation or measurement by a human or organismic observer, even at the classical level, ultimately consists of decoherences with what is measured or observed.

So the key to understanding spacetime comes from a deeper understanding of the concept of manifolds in general relativity. In general relativity there is no single absolute observer independent dimensional spacetime (though cosmological scale spacetimes are often usefully approximated in theory). Instead every observer has its own view of dimensionality from its particular relativistic perspective. This is the view used in this book though we take it much further to include the actual generation of spacetime as individual observer manifolds.

All spacetime manifolds are built up entirely of the dimensional attributes of individually observed events, each of which establishes a dimensionalized point in the manifold. The individual spacetimes that emerge are to be understood not so much as spacetimes in the traditional sense but rather as how dimensional type measurements work in that observer's frame. They are simply rules that govern dimensional relationships rather than actual all-encompassing physical spacetimes.

In this view dimensional spacetime is not a single fixed absolute structure that pervades the universe but instead consists of multiple individual mini-spacetimes, one for every observer, each built up from personal observations of participatory events each of which establishes a single point or relationship in that observer's spacetime.

These spacetimes are not just different views of the traditional common spacetime because not only are there relativistic differences but they will invariably include the dimensional characteristics of different sets of events as well. Thus the notion of a single common spacetime shared by all observers is the convenient fiction *of particular individual observers* constructed from mentally interpolating the blanks between measurements rather than an actual physical structure common to all observers.

Because everything in the universe is effectively an observer with its own spacetime manifold, the complete picture of dimensional spacetime is not a single Newtonian structure but consists of the total set of individual spacetimes of everything in the universe. Shared events establish only some common patch points among these spacetimes. The end result is a messy ragged dimensional structure cobbled together from the patched together points of myriads of individual spacetimes and always with plenty of loose ends and unlinked points.

Thus spacetime is not a single continuous all-pervading stable ever present structure but rather a description of the way dimensional measurements work in the views of everything in the universe as represented in their individual and only partially interlinked spacetime manifolds. Even observers that share relativistic conditions will have spacetimes that are not completely isomorphic because the points of actual dimensionalization in their spacetimes will never be identical due to their different event histories.

LINKING AND ALIGNING INDIVIDUAL SPACETIMES

Because of the manner in which they are generated every entanglement network is effectively an independent mini spacetime of its own with no immediate dimensional relationships to any other. What this means is that there is absolutely no way to compare the scales, orientations or any other dimensional characteristics of events or objects within separate spacetimes as long as they remain unlinked.

The only theoretical way to compare them would be with respect to a common background space in which they both existed but that is precisely what does not exist. Thus there is absolutely no way at all to compare the sizes, orientations or states of motions of objects in separate individual spacetimes until they are linked and aligned through shared events. They simply do not have any dimensional relationships to each other no matter how counter intuitive that may seem. Thus for example a spin orientation in one spacetime would have no orientation whatsoever to anything in another independent spacetime.

The critical insight here is that the particle property conservation law dimensionalizes points only with respect to the interacting particles and not with respect to a common spacetime background because no such background spacetime exists. At every decoherence the conservation law establishes a dimensional relationship only between the interacting particles because it governs and computes only that single relationship. That event *in itself* says nothing about how that dimensional relationship is related to those of any other particles or objects in the universe unless they are dimensionally linked through shared decoherence events in the same network.

Because there is no pre-existing universal spacetime the original dimensionalizations that emerge are not with respect to anything at all other than themselves. For example if a spin orientation relationship between two decohering particles is generated it is not oriented with respect to any other spacetime unless linked to it by previous or subsequent decoherences. Thus the manner in which dimensionalizations appear is undefined with respect to anything that is not linked through its decoherence network. The dimensional relationships that arise are entirely independent and isolated from any background spacetime and aligned only with respect to the participating particles and their decoherence networks.

However as more and more particles mutually decohere and link spacetimes they create a growing network of dimensionally aligned connections relative to which they all become oriented and positioned. These interlinked dimensional relationships are all that actually exists of spacetime, and these are all produced by decoherence events.

95

The conservation of mass-energy and spin in decoherence events determines the values of those particle properties among the interacting particles and so establishes a shared dimensional relationship between them. This produces a dimensional frame alignment between the particles and begins the process of dimensionalization; the creation of the individual spacetime fragments in which objects xperience their existence. Dimensionalization is the network of dimensional relationships between particles and particulate objects created by the operation of the conservation and other laws in decoherence events.

Not all particle properties are specified by the conservation law in every event. This means that some of the layers will have gaps at some events where their values were not specified because the event did not involve all particle properties. A gap means that the subsequent values of that particle property in the network will not be related to whatever previous values it may have had. There will be no relationship between before and after values of that particle property.

Spin orientation is of particular note here. All non-zero spins have a dimensional orientation, but if plus and minus spins cancel to zero spin in an event that spin orientation is lost and the spin orientation layer of the network breaks at that event node. Likewise if particles with plus and minus spins are created in an event their orientation will be fixed as opposite to each other by the conservation law but will be undefined with respect to any previous segments of the network and specifically will be undefined with respect to the frame of any outside observer.

To the extent that a particular particle property has been specified through the decoherences in all nodes connecting them then any two particles are entangled with respect to that particle property. If they are not connected on that particle property layer they are not entangled. Since mass-energy is always specified in every entanglement event the mass-energies of all particles in the network will be related. However since spin orientations for zero spin particles are not specified if either of the two particles has zero spin or their event sequence contains a zero spin node the spin orientations of those particles in the network will not be entangled with each other.

This is crucial when it comes to understanding dimensional relationships, in particular the nature of quantum paradox. Since spacetime is created as mini dimensional networks by elemental events, until networks are patched together by a common event there can be no dimensional relationship between them. There simply is no common up or down or scale or any other dimensional comparison possible. In particular the spin orientations of particles in one spacetime will have absolutely no relationship to those of other spacetimes. Because there is no common background space by which to compare their alignments it is utterly impossible to compare them with respect to anything at all.

However when spacetimes share a common event they then get patched together into a single spacetime at that event. Only then do the dimensional attributes of the two spacetimes such as positions, velocities and spins gain alignment and other relationships with respect to each other. **This doesn't mean there is any actual change or reorientation whatsoever within any of the spacetimes; there isn't. It just means that there is now a common frame of reference they both share**, and that their particle properties are constrained in a single self-consistent system determined by the entanglement laws.

Each dimensional network is effectively a spacetime unto itself, and each spacetime is complete in itself. The frame of reference of each spacetime is completely internal and completely arbitrary with respect to anything external because there simply is nothing external that is known to that network until there is some event they both share in which case their spaces merge into a single dimensional network. Other spaces can exist but they are unknowable unless and until they too are patched together by a common decoherence event in which case they merge to become a single dimensionally consistent spacetime.

Though this model of spacetime consisting of manifolds that emerge from entanglement or decoherence events is clearly a paradigm shift it is the natural consequence of the operation of the conservation law when its implications are fully understood. And as we shall see this model of spacetime emerging from quantum events naturally leads to the conceptual unification of quantum theory and general relativity and is the key to understanding the true nature of quantum paradox as well.

THE EMERGENCE OF CLASSICAL SPACETIME

Each decoherence event establishes a single dimensional relationship; in effect a single point of dimensionality shared by two particles and the others they are linked to in their networks. However in the world around us decoherence is ubiquitous and continuous on vast scales both in the form of bound decoherence in matter and in the enormous flux of photons of light. This process of continual myriads of interlinked decoherences is how a seemingly stable dimensionalized physical world appears to emerge from a purely computational substratum.

As these vast dimensional nexuses continually emerge from decoherence events they are interpreted as dimensional spacetime in the minds of classical observers and it is within these dimensional nexuses that a seemingly material world is able to populate itself.

Human observers continually patch their own dimensionalization into that of their environment and so begin to experience themselves in the classical 3-dimensional space we are so familiar with. Human observers patch into this dense network of decoherences via the continuous multitude of their own decoherences with it. In this way the persistent appearance of existing in a physical world in a dimensional spacetime can be fleshed out over its logical structure and simulated by observers. But this always occurs only in the form of individual observer spacetime manifolds whose dimensionality is linked to that of their environments.

Though the manifolds of classical observers such as humans are experienced as classical level events they always have an immensely complex hierarchical fine structure down to the level of individual decoherences at the particle level. It is always these acting in concert that generates the semblance of a physical world within a classical spacetime.

These individual entanglement networks are not little complete classical spaces at all. They are always transient, incomplete, fuzzy and with raggedy edges. The vast majority of events are not part of any particular observer manifold at any given time. Many but not all entanglement relationships are interlinked through past chains of shared events. We assume these events are part of the same spacetime as our manifold but this cannot be confirmed except by linking to current events and extrapolating backwards in our mental model of spacetime. What we are doing here is not linking those original unlinked events directly but linking to current events still linked to them in their past event histories.

Thus classical spacetime is not a common fixed background in which all observers live out their lives, but rather consists of the separate private manifolds of each observer. And the apparently common spacetime they seem to share is an illusion generated by observers sharing multitudes of common decoherence events in their individual spacetimes. It is that multitude of shared events that effectively links the spacetimes of individual observers to produce the illusion of a common classical spacetime by aligning the dimensional characteristics of many of the events in their individual spacetimes in a shared relationship.

Spacetime is never what it seems to be in our mental simulation of it. For example there is the issue of transience. Any memory of past nodes in a manifold exists only in the present states of particles. There is no way a particle can refer back to previous event nodes in its manifold because particles have no memories in the organismic sense. Their memories exist only as their current information states as products of their past interaction histories. Thus since spacetime is produced by events, it properly exists only in the dimensional relationships actually taking place in the present moment. Nevertheless the particle properties of all current particles are interrelated through past entanglement events. In this way the past lives in the information of the present.

Individual spacetimes including dimensional aspects of past events are thus convenient imaginary constructs since only what actually exists in the present moment is real. What is actually real is only the current states of particle properties which themselves carry the information results of all their previous decoherence interactions. The current states of all particle properties, including current position and velocity, are the current information result of all prior events.

In contrast to individual particles and inorganic events, biological organisms construct internal models of their realities which include selected memories of past states. They build an internal recursive simulation model of their reality within that reality. Thus they can conceive of events occurring within an internal spacetime model where previous dimensional events are encoded as elements in the model. Only because of this are organismic beings able to inhabit a much richer conception of spacetime in which causal sequences can be modeled and thus predictive actions become possible. Thus they are able to incorporate a model of their spacetime in memory rather than having it immediately fade away.

As useful as this is, it's an illusion, since the actual individual spacetimes of even human observers consists only of present events even though those present events may include the recall of representations of past events. Thus, in truth, the actual spacetime we exist within consists only of the dimensional characteristics of present moment events, and whatever is not observed cannot be said to actually exist, nor is its dimensionality properly part of our current spacetime. Since reality consists of xperience, what is not observed does not exist in any real sense, and in particular dimensional spacetime immediately fades away unless continually maintained by current decoherence events.

However human sensory perception consists of continual myriads of decoherence events. Every photon that hits someone's retina does so in a decoherence event that helps maintain the dimensionality of spacetime for that person. Close your eyes and not only can't you see objects in space anymore, the space you believe they occupy no longer exists in any real sense except as a recallable construct in your mind. Of course it is maintained to some extent by other sensory cues but when those fade as in deep dreamless sleep so does the actual reality of spacetime itself. Your actual individual spacetime simply shuts down unless it is continually maintained. It is not an actual aspect of external reality itself, but a construct of mind. Of course this refers to the *conscious experience* of the individual spacetime. The actual individual spacetime is largely maintained by the continual multitude of decoherence xperiences of the unconscious processes of the body.

THE CLASSICAL MIRAGE

Manifolds in general relativity are thought of as event networks over some duration of time. However since events are transient, and actually real and present only in the present moment, dimensionality too emerges and is maintained only though the continual occurrence of events. Thus since spacetime is created by events in the form of manifolds it too exists only transiently, maintained only by continuing sequences of decoherence events. Thus dimensional spacetime itself is a mirage that instantly fades in the absence of decoherence events.

This can be imperfectly visualized as a totally dark landscape in which fireflies intermittently flash revealing a point in that landscape. The flashes are analogous to decoherence events which continually generate points of dimensionality. It is only through many continual events that the overall structure of the landscape begins to emerge but it is never complete because as soon as each flash fades its point of dimensionality in the present moment also fades. And it is only when all fireflies flash nearly continuously that the whole landscape comes clearly into view and the appearance of a spacetime populated by events emerges. The standard physical view of a manifold with temporal duration would correspond to the continually open shutter of a camera that combined all flashes of light into one picture, a simulation of a reality which does not actually exist.

The takeaway is that spacetime is a phantom construct that has no real concrete duration or even an actual existence in the usual sense. The actual reality of spacetime is the dimensional information produced by individual decoherence events which mind then places in the context of an internal model of what it thinks spacetime should look like. Though it is entirely a figment of our simulation of reality that internal spacetime model does have some validity when understood for what it is. This is because it is a fairly accurate structural model of what the intrinsic logico-mathematical structure that produces the dimensionality of individual decoherence events would look like if it had actual temporal duration and actually existed everywhere that decoherence events have not yet taken place.

Thus the spacetime in which we believe we experience our existence is a backward projection by mind onto reality of the underlying logico-mathematical structure of individual decoherence events. Mind actively extracts this underlying structure from the dimensional aspects of individual decoherence events and then projects it back onto reality as an opened physical spacetime populated by events. It then gives this whole structure a continuing existence and duration in time which does not actually exist in a reality which actually consists only of what is occurring in the exact microsecond of the present moment, and that only in the form of logical computations.

When we close our eyes we no longer observe events in space around us. Our mind tells us that space is still out there and events are still occurring within it. But in fact it was never there in the first place other than as a mental projection mind produces to provide an apparent world for us to inhabit and feel at home in. In fact the actual dimensional linkages from our manifold have faded away with the loss of visual events and can only be refreshed by opening our eyes. When we close our eyes or otherwise restrict sensory input, we don't just stop sensing an external world that remains as it appeared, the actual dimensionality of that world, which depends on our decoherence interaction with it, vanishes as well. And with that loss of dimensionality the apparent physical and material structure of everything in it vanishes as well. It doesn't vanish in the sense that it was there and now it is gone, it was just never there in the first place other than as a mental construct.

So when we close our eyes, the real logical computational world doesn't vanish. It still continues to compute reality. What continually turns on and off is our mind's lavishly embellished model of that reality which includes not only a greatly simplified information sample of the external form state of reality but the information encoding the forms of our interaction with those external forms as well, all lavishly visualized and given meaning and feeling by our mind in the form of an actual dimensional spacetime populated by physical things centered around ourselves as a living feeling being.

It all seems very very real, and in fact it is real, absolutely real. But its reality is that it is entirely constructed of self-computing information forms real only because they are running in the ontological energy and presence of reality itself. All the apparent meanings and feelings we have for this world are themselves only the information encoding those meanings and feelings. But we are getting ahead of ourselves here.

This may seem counterintuitive and even crazy, but in fact it is the way reality seems to work. The existence of a seemingly dimensional physical world can only be confirmed by again opening our eyes and interacting with it so that it again manifests itself. But again what manifests to us is our mental model of reality, not the actual logico-mathematical reality upon which it is based.

Of course spacetime appears very substantial when maintained by near continuous decoherence events such as the streams of billions of photons impacting our retinas and that substantiality is reinforced by our experience because wherever we seek another point within the manifold we are likely to find it where we expect it if there is something there to decohere with. Our individual spacetimes in aggregate do largely obey the rules of classical spacetime our mind assumes they do but not entirely so.

As interacting particles go their separate ways and undergo additional sequences of decoherence events their original dimensional relationships are gradually submerged in subsequent ones and can even be lost completely if not specified through chains of subsequent decoherences. Though the particle property conservation laws necessitate that the original dimensional relationship is preserved indefinitely new dimensional relationships are established by subsequent interactions and the original relationships become less evident as they are distributed through the network. This is analogous to how a water wave gradually loses its identity in subsequent waves though it is always actually there in its subsequent effects at least down to the level of elemental granularity.

However in the absence of subsequent decoherences the initial dimensional relationship is preserved indefinitely and can be recovered by a subsequent decoherence with a measuring device which reveals its dimensionality by linking it with that of an observer.

A dimensional network is only viewable from the perspective of individual observer manifolds within it. Though we may conceptually imagine it from the outside this is impossible to actually experience. Observers only observe their network by becoming a part of it and viewing it from their perspective within it.

Every observer and more generally every participant in events continually generates its own dimensional perspective in the form of its individual spacetime constructed from the events it participates in and since that is different for every generic observer the view of every generic observer will be different. However these dimensional views of things will be related through the shared interactions of their networks. While shared dimensionality does emerge where sets of generic observers are linked through shared network interactions there will inevitably be unlinked loose ends and dimensional relationships not shared by all observers. Spacetime manifolds will not in general contain all the same events, and even shared events are always xperienced from each participant's individual perspective.

So the classical 3-dimensional space that emerges from the vast network of continual decoherences is always partial and incomplete in that some aspects of some particle properties will not be patched in and aligned with at least some others. Thus there will always be some dimensional alignments that are unrelated to others at any given time.

What this means is that the classical 3-dimensional space we think we live within is not a fixed all-encompassing structure that exhaustively and robustly fills the universe but is instead a point-wise structure in continual flux, always partial and incomplete with plenty of loose ends. Actual dimensionality exists only at points where decoherence events create it.

Thus classical dimensional space is a mirage maintained only by continual myriad decoherences including the decoherences of our

103

sensory organs with events in the external world. The continual flood of photons from external sources decohering with the cells of our retina not only brings us images of the external world but also dimensionalizes what we see with respect to our own internally generated dimensionality thereby maintaining the illusion our brain then further fleshes out as the familiar continuous 3-dimensional space we think we live within.

When a tree falls in a forest its interaction with its environment generates a multitude of decoherences that link the dimensionality of that event into that maintained in the environment. But until an observer links his own dimensionality into that of the tree and environment via decoherence events its dimensionality remains undefined from the perspective of that observer.

Since there is so much happening at the elemental level at any given time there are going to be continuous myriads of decoherence events connecting most but never all events on the planet. But it always takes time for the entanglement relationships of any event to link through the network to any particular observer. And of course the vast majority of events are never linked to the individual spacetime of any particular observer.

Thus the physical dimensional world as we know is a mirage that exists only in our minds, and it must continually be maintained by a huge interconnected network of continual decoherences lest it dissolve back into the unseen logical mist which underlies it.

CONVERGENCE ON COSMOLOGICAL GEOMETRY

Even though the classical spacetime we imagine does not exist, the cumulative aggregate effects of the basic entanglement laws, of decoherences, tend to produce large scale networks whose dimensional structures converge towards the spacetime described by general relativity and thus of our familiar Newtonian spacetime at the usual scales of experience. The dimensional relationships across the nodes of a network will be consistent with and thus describable by the laws of general relativity at the aggregate level. This is why the usual physical laws dealing with the behavior of events in spacetime work even though there is no actual spacetime in the sense they assume.

The overall geometry of the dimensionality that emerges converges towards that of the cosmological hypersphere described in Part I, but instead of it being a common all-pervading pre-existing structure independent of any events, it always emerges as a construct from the various perspectives of the individual spacetimes of individual relativistic observers within their respective decoherence networks. As every individual spacetime grows in extent and inclusion of events it always tends to converge towards this same hyperspherical structure from the perspective of any particular observer even though there may be minor incompatibilities between them. So it is clear that the underlying computational structure itself must contain this hyperspherical geometry in an implicit logical form expressed by how individual dimensional relationships work.

Thus cosmological spacetime itself is best thought of as the purely logico-mathematical framework that dimensionality converges towards in the spacetime manifolds of individual observers as it emerges from myriads of decoherence events. That spacetime itself is actually just a logico-mathematical structure rather than a physical one is convincingly confirmed by the fact that it is best described by human logico-mathematical systems. If reality were not itself a logico-mathematical structure why would human mathematics and logic be its most accurate depiction? This is the explanation for the apparently "unreasonable effectiveness of mathematics" (Wigner, 1960). It turns out not to be unreasonable at all when the fact that reality *is* a logico-mathematical structure is recognized.

In this respect spacetime is clearly a computational information structure rather than a physical 'space' that fills a 'material' universe and within which events occur. This insight represents a major paradigm shift in our understanding of reality. Spacetime is the way dimensional relationships work rather than being something physically real.

However there are always loose ends and glitches in the fine details of this structure. It never converges completely on the canonical ideal because no matter how tightly linked it always consists of individual manifolds with different frames that in general may contain relativistic incompatibilities.

This is why all cosmological spacetime views must be only useful generalizations based on simplifying assumptions. There simply is no actual universal spacetime other than as a mathematical fiction. In actuality spacetime consists of all the incompletely interrelated dimensional manifolds in the universe, each from the perspective of every individual observer down to the particle level, and these are at the fundamental level only computational structures. Taken in aggregate these all converge towards the spacetime equations of general relativity but always with some unresolvable inconsistencies and loose ends.

GENERAL RELATIVITY AS THE SCALE OF SPACETIME EMERGENCE

One of the strengths of our theory is that not just ordinary Newtonian spacetime emerges from decoherence networks but there is a very simple and natural way to get the curved spacetime of general relativity as well. All that is necessary is to take the mass-energy particle property as the relative scales of the spacetime structures that emerge in dimensionalization. Thus as general relativity suggests gravitation is actually a pre-dimensional numeric attribute of the underlying information space rather than a physical attribute though the mathematics works out to be the same.

In this model the purely numeric values of mass-energy in information space are the scales used to produce dimensionalizations by decoherence events. **Thus mass-energy is just numeric values in information space that provide the relative scales of dimensionalizations. This simple assumption correctly reproduces all the effects of general relativity.** (How special relativity works in this context will be discussed at another time).

This relative scale assumption generates individual spacetimes that are naturally dilated around mass-energy concentrations. In effect we have a natural mechanism that creates a geometry analogous to the familiar rubber sheet model traditionally used to illustrate the relativistic curvature of space around massive objects (Wikipedia: Gravity well).

The usual rubber sheet model is illustrative but misleading. It consists of a tautly stretched rubber sheet with a square grid representing a 2-dimensional analogue of 3-dimensional space. A large and a small spherical weight representing the sun and earth are placed on the rubber sheet each depressing it proportionally to their weights. The smaller sphere is then rolled across the sheet and naturally curves in towards the sun due to the surrounding depression the sphere representing the sun makes in the rubber sheet. This illustrates how gravitational attraction is actually the result of the curved space around a massive object rather than being an attractive force.

This traditional rubber sheet model is misleading in several ways but can be refined to accurately model real gravitational curvature. The traditional model depends on an external gravitational field acting on the weights to produce the bulge when what is actually needed is a dilation mechanism within the cells of the rubber sheet itself. In our model the presence of mass-energy in a grid cell is equivalent to a dilation of that cell proportional to the amount of mass-energy and it is this dilation propagating through surrounding cells that causes the sheet to bulge. Thus the curvature is correctly produced by what is *inside* the space rather than by an external force.

This is necessary because since the rubber sheet represents all space there can be nothing external to it. This model demonstrates that mass-energy is a simply a particle property that dimensionalizes grid cells in proportion to its numeric value. This effect *in itself* is sufficient to produce the curved spacetime of general relativity. Thus a second object sliding through the surface of the sheet will automatically curve in towards the mass-energy concentration generating the effect of gravitational attraction due to the curvature produced by the dilation. And in our actual universe objects sliding through the surface of the cosmological hypersphere will follow the dilations within it produced by the dilated dimensionalizations around massive objects.

There is no gravitational force in our rubber sheet model so objects fall along dilations towards massive bodies following what are called geodesics along the slope of dilations. Geodesics are the shortest distances along curved spaces and thus are the inertially straight lines that objects naturally follow in curved spaces (Thorne, 1994, pp. 108-112). This is the standard explanation of gravitational motion in general relativity and it holds in our dilation model as well. Movement along a geodesic minimizes the 'action' of a system defined as energy times time. This can be thought of as following the 'easiest' path in a curved space.

Just as in our 3-dimensional universe, this dilated surface will appear flat in the frames of all observers within it since light itself travels along the surface even where it is dilated. However since the surface is dilated it will take longer for an object to traverse what appears to be the same distance from the perspective of an observer outside the dilation. This will be interpreted as a gravitational time dilation in the frame of that outside observer. Note that the standard term 'time dilation' used in relativity theory even suggests the dilation in our model!

An observer moving along the dilation will notice no time slowdown on his comoving clock since it slows at the same rate his motion does, and thus from his perspective the clock of the outside observer will seem to run faster. Thus the model correctly models gravitational time dilation as the ratio of distance between grids along the slope of a dilation to the same distance between the grids anywhere else on the rubber sheet. This is in fact the accepted explanation of time dilation given by general relativity in our universe.

Actually most of the spacetime curvature around a mass is in time rather than space so we must extend the model by imagining the clock time dimension as a stack of rubber sheets representing slices of clock time. Relativistic time effects can be reproduced in this model with certain assumptions about the relative rates of traversal of the dilated grid cells versus a clock that uses the number of grid cells traversed as ticks of its clock.

So simply taking mass-energy as the relative size of dimensionalizations automatically produces the curved spacetime of general relativity. Thus it appears that mass-energy really is just is a particle property that numerically sets the scale of dimensionalizations in computational space and is not anything 'physical' at all. It is just the information used to scale the relativistic dilations of curved spacetime. In this manner general relativity emerges naturally from our theory as decoherences create dimensionalizations consistent with gravitationally curved spacetime.

Note that there doesn't need to be any physical mechanism to generate this structure since in our model everything is generated computationally. It is enough to have a consistent logical mathematical schema. Another great advantage to a computational view of reality!

THE CONSTRAINED RANDOMNESS OF DIMENSIONALITY

A fundamental characteristic of our universe is that dimensional variables exhibit constrained randomness at the elemental level. Every event at the elemental level occurs somewhat randomly with respect to an external frame so that its dimensional characteristics cannot be precisely determined beforehand in that frame. This randomness occurs only with respect to dimensional variables, and not to other particle property variables such as charge, spin, or identity. This phenomenon lies at the heart of the apparent strangeness of quantum theory.

However in every case this randomness is constrained by precise deterministic equations at the aggregate level. This is a consequence of quantum events being described as *probabilities* of manifesting those classical constraints. The larger the number of particles the more accurately the precision of the dimensional characteristics of their events approaches the classical constraint. For example it is impossible to predict when any one particle will decay but the half-lives of large numbers of particles are very precisely predictable. In aggregate, quantum randomness always converges on its constraint.

In terms of our model this means that when spacetimes link at a decoherence event there is an intrinsic probabilistic fuzziness in the precise dimensional location they might link up at. It could be either this or that within the quantum constraints. This is not unexpected considering that spacetimes are computational constructs in the process of being generated by those decoherences. While the dimensional relationships imposed by the conservation law in decoherence events are precisely fixed once they occur what those fixed values will be is determined probabilistically within their constraints.

Thus the dimensional values of two particles emerging from an interaction are always exactly related by the conservation law. Subsequently when a dimensional property of one of the particles is measured by a subsequent decoherence interaction its precise value will again be determined probabilistically but then if the same observer measures the dimensional value of the other particle it will always be found to exactly conserve that of the initial decoherence. In this way a consistent spacetime structure is always preserved even though the dimensional values of any event are probabilistic.

This is the same computational mechanism that allows the spin orientation of the first particle measured emerging from an event to be probabilistic but the measurement of the spin orientation of the second to always be exactly opposite to that of the first. This same mechanism applies equally to all dimensional particle properties. In this way reality integrates quantum probabilities into the deterministic framework of the networks generated by the particle property conservation law. Reality contains enough deterministic predictability to enable organisms to function but adds enough randomness to make it interesting.

The theory of decoherence upon which our model is based has revolutionized quantum physics by providing a confirmed mathematical theory of how wavefunctions interact that replaces the previous nonsensical theory of wave function 'collapse'.

The standard representations of the dimensional aspects of particles as wavefunctions expresses the probabilities of the dimensional values particles can acquire at any particular time. When wavefunctions interact with sufficient strength they undergo a decoherence which produces a precise value for one of their dimensional characteristics, such as their position or momentum, that both interacting frames share. At that point the dimensional value is randomly 'chosen' on the basis of its probability of occurring and becomes the actual dimensionality of the particle interaction at that moment.

In the standard quantum model wavefunctions interact so that their combined probability amplitude of being at some location is reinforced and effectively isolated at a particular dimensional location or other dimensional variable. It should be noted that this is never a complete total event since the combined wavefunction is never completely isolated to a precise single point. It transiently manifests in a localized form but both wavefunctions still exist and go on their merry ways tending to revert to the form they had prior to the decoherence.

Imagine two water waves approaching each other across a still pond. Where they meet their combined amplitude shoots up as they effectively decohere in a mutual measurement but they then pass through each other and go on their ways. This is a pretty good visualization of how wavefunctions decohere. The waves are amplitudes of the probabilities of being in various particular locations and where they mutually reinforce and peak makes it appear they interact at that precise location.

Though in textbooks decoherence is invariably described as the position of the particle being measured it is actually the position of the measurement, the position where both the particle and measurement wavefunctions interact in a decoherence. A decoherence always involves more than one wavefunction, and the decoherence is always the dimensional localization of the interaction rather than that of a single particle.

Like other aspects of quantum theory, the mathematics of decoherence is quite firmly established. However science has the interpretation of what actually happens here backwards.

REINTERPRETING WAVEFUNCTIONS

In standard quantum theory the dimensional aspects of particles (and by extension all physical objects) are represented by wavefunctions which are equations interpreted as representing the probabilities of where particles could be located (or manifest other dimensional properties) in an assumed pre-existing spacetime. In this interpretation of the equations the particles themselves are imagined to be smeared out in a fixed space and being everywhere at once with some degree of probability.

This is the standard interpretation of what wavefunctions are but it's actually backwards. There is no dispute with the equations of quantum theory; they have been verified to great accuracy. The question is what do they actually represent? What standard science has backwards is the *interpretation* of what wavefunctions actually represent.

Rather than representing actual physical particles spread out as probability waves in a fixed pre-existing spacetime, wavefunctions actually represent the probabilities of how spacetime may become dimensionalized by decoherence events with respect to the spacetime manifold of an external observer.

When an entanglement event occurs the dimensional relationships produced by the conservation law will always be exact *with respect to each other, but not necessarily with respect to an external observer.* To get an exact dimensional value with respect to an external observer that event must subsequently decohere with the observer. Individual particles interact and decohere with each other generating precise points of dimensionality all the time but that precision does not automatically extend to external observers until they measure it with a decoherence of their own.

111

As time elapses from a measured event uncertainty as to the exact dimensional value of the next measurement begins to creep in. When individual dimensional coordinates are measured by subsequent decoherence events their values will be subject to some degree of uncertainty with respect to each other. This intrinsic randomness in the way that dimensionality arises is another intrinsic aspect of the extended fine tuning of our universe and it is this intrinsic randomness in the emergence of dimensionality that is mathematically described by wavefunctions.

This is one more way that our common sense view of spacetime fails. Its elemental dimensional structure does not consist of fixed well determined points but of fuzzy points subject to quantum level uncertainty with respect to each other until actual decoherence measurements occur.

At the fundamental level particle interactions occur in information space and are straightforward computational events involving the simple logic and arithmetic involved in particle property conservation. They have none of the complexity of quantum equations such as wavefunctions which are mathematical descriptions of how spacetime may become dimensionalized through decoherences.

A wavefunction describes not the smeared out location of a particle in a pre-existing space but the range of probabilities of the possible dimensional values of a decoherence event, of where the decoherence will *generate* a point of dimensional spacetime. A wavefunction is not an actual physical entity but an equation in information space expressing the probabilities of the co-ordinates of the spacetime point that will be created. This is exactly the same process as the standard view of decoherence but viewed from a novel more useful perspective.

Actually no physical spacetime points are actually being created by decoherences except in a computational sense. What is actually being created by decoherence events is a consistent information network of dimensional attributes of events and particles, but all at a computational rather than a physical level. Though one can of course quibble about what 'physical' really means in a purely computational universe.

It is primarily only with respect to dimensionality at the quantum level that physical reality appears complex. Basically this complexity enters only when the computational results begin to be interpreted in the context of dimensional spacetime. Mainly here does the mathematics become difficult. At the level of the particle property conservation law most of the mathematics is simple arithmetic and computational logic.

THE RESOLUTION OF QUANTUM PARADOX

Now that we understand how dimensional spacetime emerges from decoherences we are in a position to understand the true nature of the apparent paradoxes of the quantum world. **Upon examination all quantum paradoxes involve apparent inconsistencies with a mistakenly assumed pre-existing classical spacetime.** But this is precisely what we would expect when we understand that quantum processes occur in a pre-dimensional world where such a dimensionalized spacetime does not yet exist! When the manner in which dimensional spacetime arises from quantum decoherence is properly understood the paradoxical nature of quantum processes disappears completely.

The key to understanding the true nature of quantum paradox is the insight that while the conservation law determines exact dimensional relationships between individual particles in their own frames it does not automatically align those frames with those of the outside world including the frames of human observers and their laboratories.

The fixed pre-existing spacetime in which all events occur that quantum theory assumes does not exist. Thus there is no pre-existing all-encompassing frame to which events automatically dimensionally align as they occur. This is why the dimensional characteristics of every event are determined only with respect to the interacting particles. Thus the dimensional frames of all events become aligned with the frame of an observer only when there is an additional decoherence interaction event between them. In this context that will be an event that measures some aspect of the apparent paradox and thus resolves it in the frame of the observer by aligning the frames of original event and observer.

When decoherence events occur the spatial characteristics of the resulting particles are dimensionalized with respect to each other but not necessarily to their surroundings. The degree of dimensional linkage to their surroundings depends to what extent the particles produced by the event were already linked to a common dimensional network and to what extent any previous dimensional linkages were maintained through the event.

We will now examine how this key insight explains some of the classic quantum paradoxes by giving some examples.

RESOLUTION OF THE SPIN ENTANGLEMENT PARADOX

The classic example of quantum paradox and 'nonlocality' is the quantum spin paradox (Wikipedia: Bell's theorem). This involves an event in which two particles with equal and opposite spins are created and fly off in different directions. Due to the conservation law the *amount* of spin of the two particles is equal and opposite as is the dimensional orientation of the spins. Thus the spins are entangled by the event that created the particles. So both their amounts and relative orientations *are already fixed with respect to each other in their own two frames* by the conservation law.

However the conservation law operates only on the particles themselves and does not align their spins with respect to the frame of the laboratory in which they occur. The upshot is that though the relative opposite spin orientation of the two particles is already fixed with respect to one another it is not yet determined *relative to the laboratory* and will not be until it is linked into the spacetime manifold of the laboratory via a decoherence with it.

Until it is linked to the laboratory frame the already fixed spin orientation of the particles with respect to each other could be in any direction at all with equal probability with respect to the laboratory. This situation persists until the spin orientation of either one of the particles is measured in the frame of the laboratory at which time the existing relatively opposite spin orientation of the two particles is linked into the dimensionality of the laboratory. At this point the spin orientations of the two particles will always be measured with equal and opposite spins in the frame of the laboratory.

So the spin entanglement paradox is a consequence of the fact that prior to a measurement the spacetime network of the two particles, specifically its spin orientation component, is unlinked and thus

114

independent and unaligned with the spacetime orientation of the laboratory and since there is no universal reference spacetime there can be no automatic alignment between them.

Thus even though the spin orientation of the particles is already defined relative to each other, it is undefined in the spacetime of the laboratory until a measurement aligns the orientations of the two spacetimes through a decoherence between them. This subsequent decoherence is an event common to both spacetimes and at this point the conservation law establishes dimensional relationships between them and thus aligns their intrinsic orientations and thus the existing spin orientations of the particles resolve and align with respect to the laboratory.

This effect has been termed 'quantum nonlocality' because it has been mistakenly thought to imply the measurement of the spin orientation of the one particle instantaneously determines the spin orientation of the other in a faster than light process. But that is an error that arises from assuming the entire process takes place within a single pre-existing spacetime which it does not. The truth is that all particles carry around with them dimensional relationships only to particles they have interacted with either individually or though interaction networks of linked dimensional relationships.

It is only when dimensional linkages are established via decoherence events that the spacetime manifolds of the interacting particles become linked in a common shared dimensional network with respect to which their dimensional characteristics are mutually aligned. So the so called spin entanglement paradox turns out to be not a paradox at all but a simple example of how the piecewise generation of dimensionality from decoherence events constructs different aspects of spacetime at different times as the dimensional relationships of various particles and objects become progressively linked and aligned.

It is only when a laboratory measurement device decoheres with one of the particles that the already interrelated manifolds of the two particles are patched into the manifold of the laboratory and thence into that of the human observer. At that point the whole two particle, laboratory, and observer system becomes a single consistently dimensionalized spacetime with respect to which the alignments of all components are known.

This all occurs in information space to produce the semblance of a shared dimensional 'physical' space. There is no faster than light communication, there is just aligning various spacetime manifolds with one another via mutual decoherences. Thus there is no paradox because there is no pre-existing common spacetime for there to be a paradox with respect to.

The lesson here is that every event establishes a point of dimensionalization and thus a mini spacetime fragment – but only in the frames of its participants. Any subsequent observation or measurement of that event is itself a decoherence with some component of that event and results in linking and aligning the observer's spacetime to the spacetime of the event.

Prior to a common decoherence event there need be no dimensional correspondence between systems. We humans only seem to live in the same shared dimensional space due to the continual multitude of shared decoherence events each of which establishes a common point of reference between our individual spacetimes. So in our familiar classical world spacetime seems fixed and substantial, but in situations where events are few and far between gaps often arise between individual spacetimes and it is precisely in these gaps between spacetimes that the so called quantum paradoxes appear.

Thus instead of being something mysterious and paradoxical the quantum spin 'paradox' is instead the quite simple and natural consequence of the way dimensional spacetime is generated piecemeal and stepwise by successive decoherence events.

NEWTON'S BUCKET

Though not usually considered a quantum paradox the riddle of Newton's bucket is solved by our theory in a similar manner. Newton's bucket refers to the question of what the seemingly absolute spatial orientation of rotation is relative to (Wikipedia: Bucket argument). Rotating a bucket full of water eventually produces a centrifugal effect where the water climbs higher around the sides of the bucket than the center.

This is because rotation involves acceleration, but rotation and acceleration relative to what? It is not the earth's gravitation because gravity has no such rotational component and the same effect also occurs in weightlessness which is why gyroscopes can guide spacecraft because they maintain an absolute rotational orientation. There is obviously some absolute orientation to the universe with respect to rotation which is closely aligned to the earth and the night sky but what is it?

Ernst Mach proposed what is now known as Mach's Principle (Penrose, 2005, p. 753) which explains the absolute orientation of rotation as relative to the combined inertial effect of all matter in the universe though there is no known gravitational mechanism to account for this.

The actual answer is that the particles that compose matter all have spin alignments which establish alignment networks which in concert establish an intrinsic absolute rotational orientation to the dimensional network of the observed universe which will of course be closely aligned to the cosmological distribution of mass. Myriads of entanglements of spin alignments network to establish an absolute spatial orientation with respect to rotation for the entire universe and that is what the rotation of Newton's bucket is relative to, the aggregate rotational orientation frame of the entire universe established by the entangled spin alignments of its material particles.

This is of course doesn't imply the spin alignments of individual particles are all lined up, they obviously aren't. What it means is that the great majority of decoherence networks are linked in a single (though fragmentary and incomplete) spacetime network with a common background orientation alignment with respect to which individual spins and other rotations find a common background reference to align with respect to. This enables the spins and rotations of most objects in the universe to find a common background reference to align to. But newly created spin systems, as in the spin entanglement paradox example must first decohere with this to become aligned with respect to it.

This explanation is also consistent with the proposed hyperspherical geometry of the universe since rotation is absolute with respect to the surface of a sphere but position and velocity are not due to the fact that a sphere's surface is continuous with no standard point of reference and has symmetry with respect to translation along its surface. But rotation and angular momentum are absolute because they occur with reference to the fixed geometric surface of the hypersphere which is more or less equivalent to the aggregate position of the galaxies which is in fact what is observed. Thus Mach was close but for the wrong reason.

If cosmological geometry has a fixed absolute orientation with respect to which all rotations are relative that will be measurable through those rotations. There are then a number of interesting experiments that could be done to determine exactly what that intrinsic background reference is and to what extent it actually aligns with the distribution of mass in the universe. This should provide information on the large scale decoherence history of the universe and some other interesting information as well.

THE RESOLUTION OF WAVE-PARTICLE DUALITY

Perhaps the fundamental quantum paradox is that quantum processes seem probabilistic with respect to classical spacetime. The standard interpretation is that quantum processes are smeared out over a fixed pre-existing spacetime and that somehow particles are everywhere at once within that area with some finite probability. But this interpretation is a fundamental misunderstanding of elemental reality. What the probabilistic nature of quantum equations is actually describing is not particles with respect to fixed classical spacetime but the probabilistic manner points in spacetime manifolds become dimensionalized with respect to each other through the decoherence interactions of particles. When this is understood the nature of wave-particle duality (Wikipedia: Wave-particle duality) becomes clear.

At the fundamental computational level in information space quantum processes are described by the simple relational and numeric equations of the conservation law. Wavefunctions are equations that describe the wave like probabilities that dimensional variables might take on when they decohere with an individual observer spacetime. **Thus wavefunctions are always descriptions of particles from the perspective of a spacetime manifold they have not yet decohered with**. Prior to a decoherence with another manifold a particle's potential dimensional linking to that network is probabilistic and the particle acts as a probability wave with respect to it. Thus the particle acts as a wave with respect to an observer even though it is acting as a particle in its own decoherence network due to the precise dimensional relationships already established therein.

Then when a particle wavefunction interacts with sufficient strength with a particle wavefunction in another network they decohere and their dimensional probabilities with respect to one another become actualized in the creation of a specific common point of dimensionality. And since the particles now have specific point locations in each other's frames they both appear as point particles rather than waves in each other's frames.

Thus in our usual classical frame of reference an information level particle now manifests specific dimensional values and thus behaves as a particle rather than a wave. This is how particles act both as waves and particles depending on whether they have decohered with an observer's frame of reference or not. Particles behave as dimensional probability waves prior to a decoherence with a measuring frame of reference but as point particles with specific dimensional values when they decohere with a measurement frame. Wave-particle duality is a natural consequence of how spacetime arises from the points of dimensionality generated by decoherence events.

When decoherences occur particles act like particles, but when their dimensional attributes prior to a decoherence are deduced (rather than actually measured) they appear to have acted like waves with respect to a dimensional framework with which they have not yet decohered. The wave behavior of particles is never directly measureable only inferred. It can only be deduced from a pattern of actual measurements of particles acting as particles rather than waves. In their deduced behaviors prior to measurement they seem to have acted as waves because their dimensionality was still probabilistic and wave like with respect to the observer's spacetime. At that point a wavefunction described the wave like probabilities of where and when the particle's spacetime could be patched into the spacetime of the observer.

Though dimensionally they act as both waves and particles, at the fundamental computational level particles are simply information structures consisting of valid combinations of particle properties rather than either physical point particles or waves and at this level they are exact rather than probabilistic. Their probabilistic nature is only with respect to spacetimes with which they have not yet decohered.

Quantum wavefunctions are not actually descriptions of particles but rather of how and where spacetime points may be dimensionalized by particles undergoing mutual decoherence with another particle and by extension a classical observer frame. Thus a particle acts like a particle or a wave depending entirely on where and how it participates in decoherence events. Since all measurements are decoherence events this explains how measurements seem to determine whether wavefunctions act as waves or particles. Measurements just reveal to the human observer a process that continually occurs throughout the universe between particles themselves acting as generic observers as they link their entanglement networks.

So the paradox here if there is one is not that particles act sometimes as particles and sometimes as waves but that decoherence frame linking alignments are inherently probabilistic with respect to dimensional variables. Another way to understand this is that the dimensional spacetime that is generated by decoherence events is fuzzy and probabilistic at the elemental level. Something that quantum theory has been telling us for some time. However this is not because there is an inherently fuzzy cosmological spacetime but because of the way various dimensional decoherence networks, which themselves are precisely determined by the conservation law, link up probabilistically.

The key insight is that when individual spacetimes interlink they must interlink probabilistically. Why? Because there can be no intrinsic alignment between separate spacetimes, and there is no common background frame of reference, therefore the choice must be made on the basis of the probabilities of the possible alignments available. By the very fact that the spacetimes are independent of each other there can be no rule that chooses one possible alignment over another when they do interlink, thus the actual alignment must be probabilistic.

This single insight seems to be the source of the probabilistic nature of all quantum processes and thus of all randomness. Quantum randomness occurs when an event necessitates a decision for which there are no deterministic rules. This is why alignment linking of separate spacetimes must be probabilistic. There simply is no alternative. I call this the Law of Probabilistic Choice.

RESOLUTION OF THE DOUBLE-SLIT PARADOX

The double slit paradox is the classic experiment demonstrating wave particle duality. In the simplest setup a beam of particles passes through a barrier with two parallel slits and produces dots where the particles impact a screen beyond. Each dot represents the decoherence of a particle in the beam with the screen and thus the particle acts as a point particle which hits the screen at some exact location. When particles hit the screen their decoherences establish precise positional relationships with the screen. Every particle hitting the screen acts only as a particle with a precise location at that point (Wikipedia: Double-slit experiment).

Though each dot is clearly the impact of a particle the overall pattern of dots produces an interference pattern as if the particles were acting as waves when they went through the slits just as water waves would interfere with each other. But if one slit is blocked the interference pattern disappears and all particles impact the screen in a direct line with the open slit. Thus the particles seem to be acting like waves when they pass through the slits but particles when they hit the screen. They act as waves before they are measured but as particles when they are measured in a decoherence with the screen. They never act as both waves and particles at the same time.

In the light of our theory the explanation is straightforward. Particles produced by a particle beam are produced with precise dimensional relationships to their source as required by the conservation of energy and momentum and thus are acting as particles with respect to the source at that point. But this precise dimensional relationship is probabilistic with respect to the incompletely linked dimensionality of the laboratory. Thus the particles fly off in the general direction of the slits but their precise location with respect to them is not fixed because they exist as an independent dimensional system. Thus the particles pass through the slits as probability waves and interfere with them to produce a pattern which is then visualized by their decoherences with the screen where they once again behave like particles.

This is functionally equivalent to the standard quantum explanation and the standard wavefunction equations correctly describe the resulting pattern; it is only the interpretation of what happens that is new. The usual interpretation is that the particles are acting as waves in a fixed space common to both them and the laboratory, but in our interpretation there is no such common fixed space. Both the particles and the laboratory have separate unlinked spacetime manifolds and the probabilistic nature of the particles passing through the slits indicates the range of variation in the way those individual spacetimes can link up when they decohere.

And this is in fact visually measured in the pattern the decoherences of the particles make impacting the screen. The interference pattern on the screen is the visual representation of the probabilistic manner in which the particles can decohere with the laboratory and thus how their manifolds can be linked, but it is displaying in the actual decoherences of particles with the screen. The pattern on the screen shows us the actual form of that hidden probabilistic separation between two individual spacetimes in the process of being linked into one.

The double-slit experiment demonstrates that dimensionalization is probabilistic in nature at the quantum level. That is when quantum events occur the dimensional entanglements between the particles *participating in the event* are precisely determined by the conservation law. But in general that precise dimensional relationship will have a degree of constrained randomness with respect to the dimensionality of surrounding systems. This continually interjects a degree of randomness into quantum processes which is well understood. But what is not generally recognized is that this means that spacetime is not a fixed precise common pre-existing structure in which events take place but instead consists of innumerable individual spacetime manifolds created by quantum events which are in general incompletely and imprecisely interlinked.

HALF-LIVES

Half-lives are the prime example of how particles and atoms can exhibit random dimensionality with respect not just to space but also time. Half-lives are an example of the constrained randomness of quantum phenomena. Particles in large aggregates decay in a very precisely constrained pattern over time but the time of decay of individual particles in the aggregate seems totally random within that constraint even when the time scales involved are enormous (Wikipedia: Half-lives).

What is really going on here? It almost seems that a case could be made that there is some precise higher level law that in aggregate governs the behavior of individual elemental level particles. On the face of it, especially in a computational universe, this seems just as reasonable as the current quantum description which describes the process in terms of probabilities of the decay of each individual particle. However there is no known natural mechanism by which such higher level laws could govern the behavior of quantum processes even though in general all quantum processes exhibit a similar phenomenon of constrained randomness.

122

It does seem that the theory of high level laws is functionally equivalent to the accepted theory of the constrained randomness of elementary processes. This question of the existence of higher level laws and emergence is explored further in Part V, The World of Forms.

It is not clear that half-lives are simply a matter of the time dimensionality of the particles not being patched into that of the surroundings since they behave normally with respect to time in other respects within the usual quantum constraints so there must be something else going on here.

Nevertheless our model should be able to shed some light on this phenomenon. What is clear is that decay is the result of probabilistic processes within the dynamics of the nucleus and occurs when some natural variation in these dynamic processes exceeds some threshold. So I think we need to wait until more is known about how that works though the success of our theory likely indicates that it has to do with nuclear level spacetime manifold disparities.

So the explanation of half-lives is probably to be found not so much in any disparity of the atoms with the time manifolds of their surroundings but in manifold disparities within the components of the nucleus itself.

WEAVING THE FABRIC OF REALITY

The cosmological consequence of the way that spacetime becomes dimensionalized is that the evolution of the overall form structure of reality in the present moment is not a single straightforward process that is the same for all observers. While reality seems to evolve as a single computational process at the information level this is not reflected in the dimensional experience of individual observers each of which has a different dimensional perspective.

At the level of observers, recalling that every event is an xperience or decoherence, reality evolves not as a single drama on a single spacetime stage but as innumerable private local spacetimes maintained only by actually xperienced (participated in) events. So while a single information structure evolves below the level of observation the observer views of that process each evolve separately as individual private spacetimes whose emergences are probablistic and are only patched together and aligned at shared events. In this respect the weaving of reality forms an enormously complex and interesting tapestry whose shape shifts from every observer's perspective.

This then is how the appearances of classical worlds emerge from their computational source differently in the frames of various organismic observers. The classical dimensional world in which we believe we live is a transiently dimensionalized fiction very different from those of other observers except as patched together at the shared decoherence events that maintain them.

In Part II, Cosmology, a hyperspherical cosmological geometry was proposed in which the three familiar spatial dimensions of the universe are its surface and the radial dimension is the continually evolving and extending dimension of p-time, the time of the present moment. In this geometry the actual universe that exists in the present moment is analogous to the surface of an expanding soap bubble or balloon. The interior was the now vanished past and there is no future since the surface represents the entirety of the universe and there is nothing either inside it or outside of it.

The surface of this hypersphere was envisioned as a precise well-defined spatial surface with an extremely minimal time thickness corresponding to the duration of the present moment. However it is now clear that the dimensionality of this thin surface is not a single precise fixed cosmological structure but is continually being constructed piecewise and raggedy from myriads of decoherence events as p-time progresses. At the elemental level its extension is literally woven by happening flowing through all decoherence and entanglement events. It can be visualized as a dimensional fabric being continually woven from the threads of these causal networks.

Thus the surface of reality, which had been visualized as the perfect surface of a cosmological hypersphere is now seen to be quite chaotic and fragmentary at the elemental level and even fuzzy, incomplete and transient at the classical level. Instead of being a single well defined very thin surface it consists of churning fragments of transient dimensionalization. And all these dimensional fragments exist as individual spacetimes of varying complexity never fully inter-linked and thus never completely patched together into a single universal dimensional structure.

In particular the thinness of the time surface is not the actual state of the surface but rather an idealized view of it from the frame of a hypothetical omniscient classical observer. In actuality it consists of the continually interacting spacetime networks of innumerable thing forms including all interacting particles in the universe. Many of these fragmentary spacetimes are continually interacting as bound matter to produce higher level froths of networked frames but free particles not currently undergoing decoherence interactions often carry only local spacetime fragments only minimally patched into larger ones.

So the overall view of the continual p-time extension of the cosmological surface of reality can be conceptualized as a continual weaving and unraveling of myriads of fragmentary animated patterns in the fabric of reality. This is reminiscent of the Greek myth of the Fates weaving the lives of men and Gods alike on their looms or especially Indra's web as visualized by Alan Watts (Watts, 2008) as a spider's web full of dewdrops in which each dewdrop reflects all the others including the reflections of all the others in each of them including itself ad infinitum.

As a result the cloth of reality that is woven is imperfect and contains plenty of dimensional loose threads embedded in the fabric which are not patched in to the warp and woof of the whole pattern. And like Penelope's wedding cloak it continually unravels in the night absent the continual decoherences necessary to maintain it. This is a continuous dynamic process in which local manifolds are continuously woven and unwoven from the larger fabric as p-time progresses.

The underlying logical structure implicitly contains computational structures that tend towards the emergence of a cosmic hyperspherical geometry consistent with general relativity, but this actually emerges only in the frames of individual observers each of which approaches the whole from its own individual perspective. They converge towards the whole revealing hints of its large scale cosmological structure only as they network together, but are ultimately constrained by the differing relativistic perspectives of their manifolds and their inevitably incomplete linkages.

This fundamental structure of the world of forms does not exist in a dimensional spacetime or a material universe. It is simply code running against data states, or more accurately self-evolving information forms in the present moment as happening continually occurs in the reality of ontological energy. At this fundamental level all is self-evolving information forms which continually compute their state of existence, and by extension the current state of the universe as dimensionally expressed in the individual spacetime manifolds of all observers at all levels.

MASS AND ENERGY ARE RELATIVE MOTION

At the elemental computational level of particle properties there is a single mass-energy particle property which is conserved through all particle interactions in the frame of any particular generic observer. Because all forms of mass and energy are inter-convertible all the other various forms of energy in the universe must be different manifestations of this one particle property.

It is only because all forms of mass and energy are various forms of relative motion that they can be converted into one another as required by the law of conservation of energy. How else could they be inter-convertible if they were not different forms of the same thing? What is really being conserved when various forms of energy are converted into each other is the amount of relative motion from one form to another. For energy to be conserved no matter what form it takes demonstrates that it is fundamentally one single thing and that single thing is the amount of relative motion at the computational level.

This is another important insight with profound consequences for the nature of reality. It means that when the purely numeric values of mass-energy in information space dimensionalize they always emerge as various forms of relative motion in the resultant spacetime network. And as we have seen they also dilate and thus curve the dimensional structure of the resulting spacetime in a manner consistent with general relativity as they emerge.

This is most obvious in the case of kinetic energy which is clearly defined in terms of the relative motion between a mass and some observer frame. We have previously discussed how conservation of the mass-energy particle property is the source of relative motion and how dimensional space arises to allow this relative motion to manifest itself. So it is quite clear that kinetic energy is just relative motion as standard science agrees.

126

Rest mass is an intrinsic 'frozen' amount of energy that consists entirely of vibratory motion. This is consistent with string theory which views particles as vibrating strings (Susskind, 2006, p. 199). Because the motion of mass is a very high frequency vibration its motion is always identical relative to all other systems and thus appears as a fixed absolute amount of motion and this fixed amount manifests as its mass. So rest mass is the relative motion of vibration which is identical for all observers.

One unexplained problem is why mass as well as kinetic energy increases as velocity approaches the speed of light. If anything the rate of mass vibration should slow down with its time dilation and the mass should become less but of course it increases.

Kinetic energy is linear relative motion and is inter-convertible with rest mass according to $e=mc^2$. The conversion of rest mass to kinetic energy is simply transforming some amount of vibratory motion into an equivalent amount of linear motion. Likewise the conversion of rest mass into electromagnetic energy consists of transforming some amount of vibratory motion into an equivalent amount of wave frequency motion which is the linear vibratory motion that manifests as the energy of photons.

This transformation of the fixed vibratory motion of mass into other forms of relative motion is called atomic energy. The process is reversible since both the linear motion of kinetic energy and the wave frequency motion of electromagnetic energy can be transformed back into an equivalent amount of fixed vibrational motion as mass.

All the other forms of energy are also forms of relative motion. For example it is well known that heat energy is the aggregate kinetic energies of atoms or molecules as they collide and bounce back and forth in a gas or vibrate in place in a solid.

Chemical energy, the energy bound up in atoms and molecules and released in chemical reactions is actually a weak form of atomic energy produced by conversions of minute amounts of the vibratory mass of particles to energy. These are called chemical binding energies. The tensile energy of a spring and the energy of resistance to compression are other forms of binding energies involving interchanges in the relative and vibrational motions of atomic particles.

What is called potential energy is actually the blocked kinetic energy of inertial motion. Take a weight suspended in a gravitational field. It has a natural inertial motion to fall that is blocked by some suspension mechanism. Potential energy is always the blockage of one form of energy by an equivalent amount of some other type of energy. When the suspension energy of the support is released its energy is converted into the kinetic energy of the falling body. So what is called the potential energy of the suspended body is actually the suspension energy of whatever kept it from falling. So what we really have here is conversion of some binding energy in the support into the kinetic energy of the falling body.

Thus potential energy is really an accounting trick and is not really a form of energy at all. It simply makes it easier to understand the behavior of isolated systems by ignoring their surroundings. The equivalent energy involved in potential energy is actually the blocking energy of some peripheral system. But it can be thought of as stored energy blocked by the equivalent energy of another system, e.g. the vibrational matter of the earth's surface supporting a weight, or the tensile energy of the electrical charge of the atoms in a wire suspending a mass in a gravitational field.

Another way to understand potential energy is that it's just a difference in choosing the frame of reference. A suspended weight is in motion and thus does have kinetic energy relative to a free falling frame in a gravitational field. Since energy is relative spatial motion it is always possible to choose the frame of reference the energy is measured relative to. It just must be chosen consistently for conservation of energy to hold.

Since energy is *relative* motion it will be measured differently in different frames of reference. A moving body such as a spacecraft can have enormous kinetic energy relative to the earth but none relative to an astronaut aboard the spacecraft. The reason that energy manifestations such as heat and mass seem absolute rather than relative is because vibrational motions are identical relative to everything else so they are more or less the same relative to all observers. Only when that vibrational motion is transformed into an equivalent amount of linear motion does its relative nature become obvious.

Because mass and energy are not physical in the usual sense but are relative spatial motion the total amount of mass-energy in the universe is a measure of the total computational relative motion of forms. There is no physical energy or mass in the usual sense. There is just the code for relative motion in the world of forms manifesting as actual relative motion as decoherences dimensionalize spacetime. If there were no dimensional particle properties being conserved in events there would be no relative motion in the universe and thus no things and no events and without the consequent xperience the existence of the universe could not be confirmed since it could not manifest.

So at the computational level there is no dimensional space and no matter or energy, it's all just the way information forms move computationally relative to each other. Thus much of apparent physicality reduces to conservation of the mass-energy particle property from the perspective of some particular observer frame.

The effects of relative motion are not actually physical but like all effects are computational results given reality by occurring in the ontological energy of reality. Moving forms de-form each other when interactions are computed. This is experienced by observers as energetic effects when those forms are interpreted in their cognitive models, including for example an injury like a broken leg when the information form of the leg bone interacts computationally with that of a bus in relative motion.

Because the relative motion of mass-energy is fundamentally occurring at the level of computational reality there need be no pre-existing dimensional spacetime for it to occur within. All 'motion' occurs as computational results in information space. It is a computational simulation of physical motion which generates points of spacetime dimensionalization via shared decoherence events in the individual spacetimes of observers. The only 'space' in which this occurs is the computational space of ontological energy which gives it its reality. There is no underlying 'physical' medium and no pre-existing spacetime.

So at base mass and energy, like dimensionality, are computational effects that are not physical in the usual sense but merely calculations that generate the appearances of physical reality in the internal models of reality of observers.

How can the particle property conservation law conserve mass-energy which is motion relative to observer frames? It simply sums the total incoming amount of numeric relative motion in the frame of the event and distributes it all in the outgoing relative motions of the resultant particles. In computational space these are just numeric values but it is these numeric values that define the dimensionality of the events that emerge.

An external observer will observe this from the perspective of its own relative motion via a similar computational interaction. However since an external observer was not a participant in the original event there will be probablistic uncertainties in exactly where one particle from that event will be found in the frame of the observer. However when it decoheres to a precise location with the observer frame so will all the other dimensional attributes of the original event be found to occupy locations that exactly conserve the total relative motion of the event. This is the same mechanism that exactly aligns the spin orientation of the second particle with the first in the spin entanglement experiment once the observer frame decoheres with it.

ACCELERATION

Acceleration is the time rate of change of velocity and velocity is linear motion relative to whatever frame it is measured from. So acceleration is simply the addition or subtraction of relative motion which is consistent with its usual definition. Since an acceleration is not just a change in motion relative to other frames but also to the frame being accelerated it can be felt and thus is absolute. However relative motion itself cannot be felt because it never has a value relative to itself but only to the frames of other observers. This is why all velocity is relative but all the changes in velocity of accelerations are absolute.

We can feel any change of relative motion but we cannot feel relative motion itself. Another way to understand this is because as we have seen there is no intrinsic fixed space for motion to be relative to. All observers define and carry with them their own spacetime manifolds and these are the *only* spacetimes that exist to them. Thus there is no absolute frame of reference for motion to be relative to because there is no fixed common spacetime background. All locations on the surface of the hypersphere are equivalent in this respect and there is no absolute motionless background for there to be any reference to. Thus there is no absolute inertial motion and inertial motion is motionless with respect to itself. It establishes its own frame of reference with respect to itself. One can say that relative motion is absolutely motionless with respect to itself but changes in relative motion are not and thus can be felt as energetic processes.

These insights are consistent with our previously stated views of observers as singularities, the cosmological hypersphere, and that spacetime is created by decoherence events rather than being a pre-existing common background.

One of Einstein's great insights in developing his theory of general relativity was his equivalence principle that states that gravitation is indistinguishable from acceleration (Smolin, 2001, p. 81.). That for example a man in a windowless elevator cannot tell if the elevator is accelerating upward in empty space or whether he is standing in a building under the influence of earth's gravitation. In either case he feels himself pushed against the floor with the same force.

Since acceleration and gravitation are equivalent acceleration curves space just like gravitation. This is because energy is always required to produce an acceleration and thus it is really the energy expended that is producing the curvature since both mass and energy curve spacetime. But since energy is relative spatial motion this is actually just the addition of more relative motion to a relative motion which increases the amount of the relative motion. So acceleration is just a change in the amount of relative motion which is equivalent to an equivalent change in the amount of energy. Acceleration turns out to be a very simple concept indeed.

Take the case of a rocket firing its engines to accelerate. The amount of relative motion stored in the chemical binding energies released in the burning of propellant is converted into the relative motion of the exhaust with respect to the rocket thereby increasing the relative motion of the rocket. Everything all boils down to various manifestations of relative motion. Mass, energy of all types, force and acceleration, are all just the calculus of relative spatial motion. In particular all force is simply the addition of relative motion in one form or another.

What is usually mistakenly called gravitational energy is not really energy at all. The motion of objects in gravitational fields is actually inertial which is why there is no acceleration felt in free fall even though velocity increases relative to the earth. It is actually opposing free fall as we do in standing on the surface of the earth that is an acceleration which is why we do feel the force of gravity in this case.

Thus all the apparent physics of a material world boils down to relative motions between observer frames, and changes in the amounts of those relative motions. And at the fundamental level this is all computations on the data forms that manifest as things in the frames of observers, including every thing form at any level of complexity acting as a generic observer.

SUMMARY

Our theory of reality at the elemental level provides a conceptual unification of quantum theory and general relativity, resolves all quantum paradox, and explains why nature must act randomly at the quantum level when linking and aligning individual spacetimes.

The source of the apparent incompatibility between quantum theory and general relativity is the fixed, pre-existing, classical background spacetime it mistakenly assumes. And all the paradoxical aspects of quantum theory are also paradoxical only with respect to this same non-existent spacetime. Thus when spacetime is understood as something that *emerges from* quantum events rather than being *a background to them* all becomes clear and quantum theory and general relativity are conceptually unified.

The elemental forms of the world of forms consist of the particle properties that combine to compose the elementary particles and the elemental laws of nature that compute them.

Of particular importance is the particle property conservation law that requires that the total amounts of each particle property are conserved in every particle interaction, and the other elemental laws that compute the structures of atoms and molecules.

The operation of the particle property conservation law establishes necessary relationships between the particle properties of all particles in their interactions. These relationships are called entanglements and if they involve dimensional particle properties they are called decoherences.

The aggregate result of the particle property conservation law is to produce large networks of entangled particles with dimensional relationships to each other. This is how individual spacetimes begin to emerge from elemental decoherence interactions.

Spacetime is not the single, fixed pre-existing background structure that all events take place within that it appears to be but the dimensional relationships built up from decoherence events. This becomes clear when it is understood that spacetime is knowable only by observing events 'within' it. There simply is no evidence that the apparent spacetime we believe exists between events does exist since it is impossible to measure spacetime absent events.

What actually exists are the dimensional relationships established by the operation of the particle property conservation law in the form of networks of dimensional relationships, each of which can be considered an individual mini-spacetime.

The crucial insight here is that the dimensional relationships in each one of these individual spacetimes exist only in that spacetime and have no dimensional relationships to those of other spacetimes until the spacetimes are linked by a shared decoherence event in which case the two individual spacetimes become linked as a single shared spacetime.

This insight is the key to understanding the true nature of quantum paradoxes which seem paradoxical only with respect to an assumed fixed common spacetime which does not exist.

Take the spin alignment paradox. In this case two particles with equal and opposite spins are produced by an entanglement event however the entanglement event establishes that relationship only between the two particles in their own mini-spacetime which is not immediately aligned with that of an external observer. Thus with respect to the frame of the external observer the spins are not aligned at all.

However if the observer then measures the spin alignment of one particle that constitutes a decoherence and the spacetime of the particles then becomes aligned with the spacetime of the observer. Thus the alignment of the other particle is now also aligned as well. Nothing actually changes other than the alignment of the two previously unaligned spacetimes into a single spacetime.

So there is no 'non-locality' or anything traveling faster than the speed of light here. There is simply the mandatory random alignment involved in linking two separate spacetime fragments into a single dimensionally consistent spacetime.

This is the principle by which all so called quantum 'paradoxes' resolve. They all become intuitive and natural when the way that dimensional networks are generated by decoherence events is understood, rather than being mistakenly understood as events occurring in a single fixed classical spacetime common to all observers.

Because spacetime arises from decoherence events as many individual spacetimes, one for every separate entanglement network, these individual spacetimes are dimensionally separate and not immediately aligned with each other.

As there can be no rules for how separate spacetimes align nature has to align them randomly (within certain overall constraints). This Principle of Free Choice is the source of all the randomness of reality and thus of all randomness since all randomness occurs at the quantum level *in the linking of separate individual spacetimes*. Nature acts randomly only when it is forced to by lack of any possible rules determining how the dimensionalities of separate spacetimes become aligned when they link.

This process is how spacetime emerges from elemental quantum events rather than being a pre-existing structure in which events play out. The traditional view of spacetime as a pre-existing background to all events is a convenient fiction constructed in our mental models of reality by interpolating an empty space between actual dimensional events it remembers. This spacetime simply does not exist in external reality.

However the intrinsic structure of the elemental laws of nature is such that the individual spacetimes that do emerge tend to converge on the spacetime of general relativity at large scales and thus classical Newtonian spacetime at familiar scales. At the largest scale emergent spacetimes tend to converge on the 4-dimensional cosmological hypersphere described in Part II.

Thus spacetime can be understood as this underlying general logico-mathematical structure of convergence rather than as an actual 'physical' structure that fills the 'space' between events. There simply is no such physical space that fills reality; there is only a consistent gross overall information structure towards which dimensional relationships tend to converge. This is strong additional evidence that reality is entirely a computational information structure rather than an actual physical dimensional structure.

The curved spacetime of general relativity is consistent with this and emerges naturally from our model if we simply take the mass-energy particle property as the scale of dimensionality emerging from decoherence events. When the amount of mass-energy is taken as its scale the spacetime that emerges is dilated proportionately to the presence of mass-energy and this in itself is sufficient to generate the curved spacetime of general relativity.

Thus this part of the theory conceptually unifies quantum theory and general relativity and resolves the apparently paradoxical nature of the quantum world while providing an explanation for why and how quantum processes are random.

In addition it explains that mass and energy are both different forms of computational relative motion between information forms when they are dimensionalized with respect to each other. Thus all mass and other forms of energy are simply various forms of relative motion. Thus mass and energy at the information level is simply numeric information indicating what the relative motion will be between forms as they dimensionalize and this seems to be involved with the resulting dilation of space that emerges.

Acceleration is simply adding or subtracting relative motion. It is absolute and can be felt because it is a change to the relative motion of the observer while relative motion cannot be felt because there is no change with respect to itself for the observer. The nature of force and the other basic quantities of physics follows as all are explained in terms of changes in relative motion or the consequences of relative motion.

Because reality exists only in the present moment and because not all particle property relationships are defined in every event, the spacetime manifolds of observers are always transient and partial. Thus the actual spacetime manifold of any observer is a transient mirage that exists only as its present moment fragment and fades instantly unless it is maintained by continuing present moment decoherence events.

Thus the apparently physical, material, and dimensional world is a fiction emerging from the fundamental level of pure information where it is computed. It exists only as entanglements and decoherence relationship in the individual spacetimes of generic observers and as further fleshed out in the mental models of organismic observers. How this occurs and its further consequences for understanding the nature of reality is the subject of Part IV, Mind and Reality.

Part IV: MIND AND REALITY

INTRODUCTION

This Part of the book explores the intimate relationship between reality and the mind of the human observer and how our perceptual and cognitive structures influence our knowledge of reality. Ultimately all that we can experience and know of reality is through our own biological and cognitive structures and is inevitably formatted and known only in terms of that structure. No matter how elaborate or objective any model of external observer independent reality it is ultimately still known only through our experience and as formatted by our minds. And without an observer there can be no experience of reality at all because all experience comes through observers.

Thus it is reasonable to seek the true nature of the real external world by progressively identifying and subtracting all that mind adds to it in its internal representations of it. When this is done it turns out that almost all of the characteristics usually ascribed to reality are actually characteristics of mind's model of reality instead. This is especially true of all the apparent physicality of reality including the apparent self-substances of things. Carefully analyzed these are all added by mind and do not exist in external reality.

The end result of this process is that all that remains of external reality itself is an abstract information structure with none of the usual characteristics we ascribe to physical reality. External reality is just an information framework that mind uses as a foundation to construct a simulation of the world that is far different from actual reality. And there are several even more interesting final twists to the story!

It should be noted that this discussion applies to all organismic minds, animal as well as human, all of which stand in a similar relationship to a common external reality they model internally in one form or another. This discussion demonstrates the necessity of understanding the relationship between observer and reality to understand the nature of both. A more detailed discussion is to be found in the author's earlier paper 'Mind and Reality' (Owen, 2009).

136

OBSERVER SIMULATIONS OF REALITY

The world that we think we live in exists entirely within our mind. This is clear because if mind disappears so does the experience of the world. It exists as a cognitive simulation or mental model of what we assume is an external reality that exists independent of us. And it is quite easy to prove this internal model is not at all like the real actual world we experience it to be. In the ultimate analysis all our simulation shares in common with the actual external world is some similarity of logical structure and the fact that they both are real and actual by virtue of existing in the reality of the present moment.

We will use the terms 'simulation' and 'mental model' interchangeably. They both refer to the internal model of reality that mind constructs for each living organism in which it actively simulates the processes of reality. These simulations are different for every organism through there are certainly structural similarities between the models of different organisms depending on how closely they are related. And these simulations are private to every organism. Every simulation of every organism constitutes the private reality in which that organism experiences its existence. And in all cases these simulations represent a world that is much different than the actual external world.

Organismic observers are characterized by having these internal computational models of their environments and the execution of purposeful actions computed within them. Living organisms are complex computational systems that execute purposeful actions directed towards instinctual goals that primarily facilitate survival and procreation and actions that provide feedback in the form of feelings experienced as positive rather than negative. To further these instinctual imperatives organisms also have the ability to compute and execute intelligent actions based on learning routines to greater or lesser degrees.

Functionally organisms can be well modeled by intelligent robotic systems even though the ability to completely simulate even the simplest organisms robotically is in its infancy. From this point of view an organism is a computational system with specific instinctual imperatives which provide general direction to its actions.

Organisms have perceptual systems that extract and organize functionally useful information from their environments, internal models of their environments updated against these inputs, and they generate intelligent purposeful goal directed actions computed against these models which are then activated as actions within their environments via internal modeling of synchronous control of their motor abilities. Though they are structurally much different it is the intensive development of intelligent robots that has probably done most to show how living organisms operate from a purely functional perspective.

Just as robotic systems are effective to the extent their internal simulations of reality accurately model the logical structure of external reality so too the fact that living organisms do function effectively in their environments demonstrates that their simulations of reality do accurately model the actual logic of external reality to a sufficient degree. This is turn demonstrates that external reality is in fact a logical structure, and that it is amenable to representation with some sufficient degree of accuracy in its cognitive simulations in the minds of observers. Thus it is inherently possible for human observers to have some knowledge of the true nature of reality based on the accuracy and scope of their simulations and their understanding of the structural nature of those simulations.

THE RETINAL SKY

When we look out into the world we are actually looking into our own minds. Most of the structure we see there is the structure of our own minds. And when we act in the world we are actually acting in the model of that world in our minds. What we are experiencing is the structure of our own perceptual and cognitive systems overlaid on a logical framework consisting of the evolving information systems of external reality.

Thus the world in which we live is a complex mixture of both the structures of our minds and the structures of external reality which we need to carefully tease apart to determine which is which. Essentially this consists of a highly simplified logical structure sampled from external reality and every other aspect of the world we experience is entirely the product of our mind overlaid on that logical structure and fleshed out with all its apparent physicality.

I call this world we see with our eyes, and by extension all of the reality that we experience, the 'retinal sky' because it is clear that when we look up at the sky what we are really seeing is the combined photo chemical state of our two retinas extensively post processed by our visual system. This is not the 'real' external sky as it actually is but our mind's overlay on a sample of its logical structure. What is the 'real' sky and what is the overlay is the question.

Thus both mind and world exist like two sides of a mirror in which mind is coterminous with sky, and by extension with the entire experienced universe. No matter how far out or how close in we look, we are always looking into our own mind and experiencing the structure of our own mind projected onto the logical structure of the actual external sky.

THE GENETIC TRANSMISSION OF ORGANISMIC SOFTWARE

DNA is clearly information encoded in a chemical structure. This information is a program which actually builds new organisms to design. **But what no one seems to have recognized is that DNA must also encode and transmit the actual basic software that controls how that new organism operates.** For a new organism to operate it simply must be loaded with the software to run it and that software can come only from its DNA as well. Therefore DNA encodes and transmits not only the software to build a new organism but to operate it as well.

That the operational software as well as biological hardware must be encoded in DNA is self-evident because there is no other mechanism by which it could be passed from generation to generation even though to my knowledge I'm the first who has recognized and stated this obvious fact (Owen, 2009). That no one currently seeks to understand how and where organismic software is encoded in DNA is an amazing scientific oversight, one of a number pointed out in this book.

This operational software includes the basic logical and computational structure of mind, the instinctual imperatives that provides volitional

139

direction to the organism, and intelligent computational and learning routines.

The instinctual imperatives provide the basic direction to an organism's actions. They include self-preservation and reproduction and in general the valuation of actions in terms of positive versus negative feedback feelings. They also include many specific sub-programs such as various types of bonding, suckling, etc. in specific organisms.

The entire organism, from the cellular level, to individual organs, to organ systems, to mind, is best considered as a single tightly integrated computational system. This computational system consists of great numbers of individual subroutines operating in concert to compute the functioning of the organism as a whole. Mind is not separate from this but tightly integrated with it. The whole organism then can be considered as running software or a program.

It is the top level of mind that computes the overall functioning of the organism in its environment. Functionally mind consists of input routines which continually sample information from the environment, a mental model of the environment which is updated against it, intelligent computational routines which operate against that model, instinctually informed volitional systems which give intelligence direction, and servo-active systems which translate internally computed actions into real actions in the environment.

All of these systems must operate correctly for an organism to function effectively in its environment. Almost all of these computations occur at the unconscious level but there is another system that monitors the operations and provides an overall quality control function called consciousness.

The basic computational software structure that operates the organism is encoded and passed in DNA from generation to generation. What is not transmitted genetically is of course the individually learned information structures that make up the bulk of the internal model of reality and encode data about the individual organism and its particular environment and how to operate effectively within it.

Thus both the hardware and software of all organisms is encoded in their DNA and passed from generation to generation. Organisms are intelligent computational systems that must have both hardware and software to function effectively and survive in their environments. Without the genetic transmission of operational software organisms would be inanimate zombies and unable to survive or function. Thus all the heretofore unrecognized software of organisms is equally as important as the hardware it runs in.

THE NATURE OF ILLUSION

If the true nature of reality is what is really out 'there' in an external world independent of observation then whatever mind adds that obscures its direct experience can be called illusion. This means that most of what we normally think of as reality actually turns out to be illusion, and as we will see there are many layers or 'veils' of illusion.

Thus we define illusion as what mind adds to external reality in its internal model of reality which does not exist in external reality itself. These illusions exist only in the mental representations of reality inside organisms rather than in external reality itself. Illusion is what the observer adds to reality in its internal representation of it.

THE PARADOX OF MIND

The paradox of mind is that while our mind's representation of reality is not at all like actual external observer independent reality, it is the only means by which we experience reality at all. As observers we are both informed and deluded by our minds. The only glimpse we have of reality at all is through the many illusory veils of our mind's simulation.

Most of these veils are inevitable so long as we are in human form because they are consequences of our human biological and cognitive structure. They can be recognized for what they are but we are pretty much stuck with them. The trick is seeing for the first time that what we see is not things as they actually are but as things seen through the various veils of illusion. That entails seeing the veils that we are seeing things through as well as the things that we see through them. It is seeing for the first time the distorting lens as well as what it distorts. This is accomplished by recognizing the distortions in what we experience.

We will briefly examine the major veils of illusion and how each distorts the actual reality behind it. In this way we come to better understand the true nature of the reality beyond our mind's simulation of that reality.

THE PROGRAMMABLE VEILS

The highest level veils of illusion are the results of our personal programming. We all undergo extensive childhood and societal programming that is a major determinant of our individual personalities and world views. Since this programming is learned behavior it is at least theoretically subject to reprogramming.

This programming is a complex mix of accurate and inaccurate information, prejudices and ideologies, emphases and omissions, and attachments and desires. These constitute our personal reality and our personal view of broader reality and our relationships to it. In particular it includes our own personal varieties of the classic Buddhist veils of ignorance, desires and attachments that so often lead to suffering.

There are two kinds of people, those who understand they are programmed and seek to understand, correct and transcend their programming and those who think they are their programming. It is necessary to be the first kind to hope to understand the true nature of reality.

Our programming is learned and thus can be corrected. Mind has the potential power to correct or reprogram itself by right thought and by exposure to the truth. Functionally these are programs running in individual minds rather than basic structural aspects of mind. For example suffering due to not having something one desires unreasonably can be eliminated by simply discarding the unreasonable desire. This enables one to drop a veil that unnecessarily separates oneself from reality and thus see the reality of what is and what is not obtainable more clearly. As a result one begins to see reality not in terms of the forms of one's desires and suffering but to see one's suffering as the result of unrealistic thought sequences that can be reprogrammed.

We then no longer see the world from within the veil of that desire mistaken for a necessity but recognize it as a code sequence we can choose to let run or not. One no longer identifies with the thought sequences that perpetuate the suffering but finds these are only thoughts that one no longer needs to pay attention to. The attachment may still appear but one is no longer attached to the attachment. One no longer identifies with one's desires or attachments. They become personal baggage one can choose to discard or carry as one wishes. Thus they cannot be part of the true external observer independent reality. External reality has no emotional content or valuations, no desires or attachments. Because they do not exist in the real external world, by abandoning them we automatically see that external reality more clearly.

The second category of programmable illusion is the vast category of false beliefs about reality. No matter how trivial, every mistaken thought obscures the true nature of reality and if one is to experience reality must be discarded and replaced by accurate understanding. To understand reality correctly it is self-evident that the logical structure of our internal model of it must be made as accurate and extensive as possible. This is simply a matter of educating ourselves to the true nature of the facts and logical structure of reality insofar as possible. It is refining our internal model of reality so as to more accurately reflect the actual logical structure of reality. Even the most trivial of mistaken beliefs about reality obscure its true nature from us.

Of course human knowledge is an evolving process and even at its best is not a totally accurate or complete understanding of reality, so a totally accurate simulation model of reality is simply not yet possible. There are inevitably many things that no one currently understands. However the important point is that we do correctly understand what is known and so eliminate ignorance and false beliefs insofar as possible as these make it impossible to know reality to the degree that is possible. Delusion is maintaining false beliefs in the face of convincing evidence to the contrary and the deluded mind can never know the true nature of reality.

It is appalling how wide spread clearly delusional beliefs are in the world as a result of being programmed into people's minds beginning as children and then maintained by a host of dysfunctional social memes. Only universal education with broad and accurate knowledge can effectively diminish if not eliminate this aspect of programmed illusion and bring humanity closer to the direct experience of reality as it actually is. It is my hope this book contributes a little to that effort.

Everyone tends to view reality in terms of their own histories, world views, interests and prejudices. This inevitably skews the views of reality that various people and other organisms hold. They are all structures and relationships of interest or usefulness to the observers in question. One observer will think of the world in one way in terms of his beliefs and interests while another will think of the same part of the world in an entirely different way. Both believe their view is how reality actually is but both are inevitably wrong.

Actual external observer independent reality does not contain the relationships observers' mental models impose upon it. These are not aspects of observer independent reality but aspects of the *relationships* various individual and very different observers have to that reality.

Some of these are personal, some cultural, some gender based, and many are species based. The take away is there is an enormous very complex difference in the way various observers view their reality at this level. All of these obscure the true nature of the external observer independent reality we seek.

ILLUSIONS OF LANGUAGE AND MEANING

One level below individual and cultural programmable illusions are illusions of language. The very syntactical structure of the human mind and human language imposes its own structure on the actual structure of reality which there is no reason to believe actually exists at least in the exact same form. For example the grammatical structures of the parts of speech, which vary from language to language, impose a view of reality in terms of objects, subjects, actions, qualities, qualifications and so on which while meaningful in terms of how humans and other organisms relate to reality likely does not exist in external observerless reality itself at least not in the same form.

There is an extensive volume of work on how language structures reality with several basic competing theories (Chomsky, 1965) but it is quite clear that humans do structure their internal views of reality in terms of their languages and thus that the actual structure of external reality itself is likely quite different (Wikipedia: Philosophy of language). And of course other organisms will also structure their

144

internal simulations of reality in their own terms as well (Wikipedia: Animal cognition). Every organism will impose its internal logical structure onto the external reality it experiences.

Human language, and by extension human mathematics and the various forms of media, do not just model reality, they are generalized structures able to model *unreality* as well and they do this with great facility. The various forms of fiction and propaganda bear obvious witness to this, but the truth is that all human expressions are to a great degree fictional in the sense that they impose structures and relationships on reality that are not necessarily there.

The very fact that human language is able to model unreality as well as reality clearly raises well-founded suspicions that it differs from the actual logical structure of reality which obviously expresses only reality.

The actual logical structure of reality then must be sought in specific modifications to human logic and syntax which are able to model only reality and not unreality. This is a necessity in a reality which is apparently a logical structure which can only encode things that are actually able to be real. Gregory Chaitin is one mathematician whose work may be relevant here (Chaitin, 2006).

The study of the fundamental structures of language elucidate the structures in terms of which humans tend to model reality. One must careful examine these structures one by one to determine to what extent they actually exist in external reality itself.

PERCEPTUAL ILLUSIONS

The next level of illusion is illusions of perception; that is how our sensory systems selectively filter and model what we think we perceive. There is a vast body of good research on the many aspects of how perception works from researchers in a variety of fields and popular science channels frequently run programs exploring the nature of perception and how it can be tricked and manipulated.

This type of illusion also includes the fact that our reality appears 3-dimensional when our retinas are 2-dimensional and similarly with regards hearing, and in other species olfaction and infrared reception. Other examples are the perceptual selection of edges and movement at the expense of backgrounds, the eye's blind spot being filled in, the eyes' adjustment to light levels, optical illusions, and so many more perceptual illusions too numerous to list (Wikipedia: Illusion). Even a cursory understanding of the nature of perception convinces us that the perceptual world in which we experience our existence is almost entirely the product of our minds rather than the real world we believe it to be.

Since there is so much information readily available on the many ways our perceptions very selectively sample reality leaving it mostly unregistered and how easily they can be fooled due to their constructing the reality they expect rather than reality as it actually exists, we won't delve into the perceptual illusions here other than to put them into the context of our discussion.

Magic tricks also demonstrate how our mind easily fools itself into false representations of reality. Here the logic of our simulation of reality is misled by event structures in reality outside the normal range of the expected. A usual the mind sees and experiences what it expects to see and experience (Wikipedia: Magic (illusion)).

How the mind is fooled by magic and illusion is well studied and supports the theory that the world we experience ourselves living in is entirely an internal simulation of reality with just enough logical feedback to tie its logic to the actual logic of external reality to enable us to function. Nevertheless almost nothing of how we experience the world actually reflects its true reality which is fundamentally only a computational structure.

Psychedelic drugs such as LSD and belladonna also shed considerable light on how our minds can construct vastly different various realities at will, and thus the very questionable nature of the usual reality it constructs. Once such realities are experienced one is in a position to better understand how our usual everyday reality is also very much a 'made up' construct as well.

Mind's continuous construction of its model of reality is a process that involves both filtering out vast amounts of reality but also the addition of detail which isn't actually there. Our mind continually fills the gaps in the reality it perceives with what it expects to be there. The important example of the illusory continuous space between dimensional events has been previously discussed but mind also constantly fills in expected

146

speech, missing letters in words, hidden motives and nearly every other aspect of reality it can with what it expects. In fact this phenomenon is so pervasive that most of what we think we see and experience in the world around us is actually just what we expect to see unless and until corrected by contradictory input.

The important point to understand is that all the many ways researchers demonstrate that perception can be fooled and go wrong actually expose all the mechanisms that generate an experience of a reality which is not actually there in the external world. The researchers correctly tell us that when the logical structure of illusions contradicts reality that our perceptions have been fooled, but in general they fail to recognize that even when the logical structure of perception is consistent and what we expect, it is still almost entirely a construct of mind and of our sensory-perceptual systems.

SINGULARITY ILLUSIONS

The fact that observers are singularities within reality rather than coterminous with all of reality is responsible for another category of illusion. Every observer, every organismic mind, by definition occupies a particular location in space and thus constitutes a unique experience singularity. By necessity every observer experiences reality only from the perspective of its particular location. But reality itself pervades the whole of itself. It has no particular location but occupies all locations simultaneously.

Because all observers are singularities while reality is the entirety of itself this means that all observer models of reality contain relativities that do not exist in reality. This means that observer models of reality simply cannot correspond to reality itself. This obvious but little appreciated fact has very interesting consequences for the nature of reality.

This means that reality has no location since location is only relative to some frame of reference and there is no single innate frame of reference in reality. Only observers add frames of reference to reality in their simulations of it. Of course things have relative positions in reality but always only with respect to some observer perspective of that reality. **Reality itself has no location, it is not actually anywhere.** And this includes all of the components of reality as well. They simply cannot be said to be anywhere at all except relative to one another and that only in some observer's frame of reference. In themselves in our hypothetical observer independent reality nothing is anywhere at all.

One cannot even conceive of reality except from the frame of reference of some observer but reality itself has no such single frame of reference it exists in terms of. So every view of reality is inherently not a true view of reality as it itself exists. Reality contains all observer frames but it has no single frame itself. This is a very difficult concept for any observer to comprehend. But it gets worse.

Likewise **reality has no orientation**. Orientation is relative again to some observer frame of reference and cannot exist in observer independent reality itself. There is no left or right or up or down to reality as a whole. Orientation is only a characteristic of the relationships between parts of reality from some observer frame of reference. Reality itself as a whole cannot be correctly conceived as having any orientation at all and thus it simply cannot be conceived of at all except as the logico-mathematical structure it actually is.

Orientation is added by the observer and when the observer is subtracted and we try to describe the orientation of reality we cannot. Reality has no up or down or sideways or front or back. These attributes do not apply to actual external reality.

And **reality has no size** either because size again is relative only to some observer scale. There is no innate size to anything in reality because there is no innate scale. Size scales are always relative to some observer's size scale. The world appears much larger to a fly than a human. Different size organisms do not experience the same size world. Thus reality itself cannot be characterized by the attribute of size. Reality itself has no size nor does anything that exists within it.

Likewise **clock time has no intrinsic relative rate in reality** itself since the experience of the passage of clock time varies greatly among species. A second passes much more slowly for a fly than a human. Innate reaction times and internal clocks vary widely among species. So while there is an intrinsic clock time rate for happening at any relativistic location our experience of it is not like anything in reality itself but is completely a comparative experience with our own internal clocks.

Reality itself contains all clocks and so has many different relative clock rates. However there is no single clock against which the rates of all processes are experienced. Thus there can be no sense of passage of clock time in external reality itself without reference to some observer clock. Thus external reality cannot be correctly conceived as having an experienced rate at which events happen.

Happening occurs at local clock time rates, but that rate is not measurable or perceptible except with respect to the clock of some observer. So external observerless reality itself cannot be said to have any clock time rate because it is impossible to measure such a rate except in terms of some observer clock, be it biological or physical. Thus the attribute of clock time rate does not apply to external observerless reality.

As a consequence **reality has no innate velocities or speeds of any kind of physical processes** either since these are observer experiences relative to their internal clock rates and size scales. Things in reality have no such actualization of velocity. Velocity is entirely the experience of some observer and there are no inherent velocities in reality.

So reality itself absent the observer becomes very strange indeed. Reality loses all of its familiar aspects of physicality and dimensionality. Actual reality becomes more and more an abstract logical structure rather than the familiar physical structure it appears to be to human observers. It is only when an observer observes the universe from its singular perspective and measurement frame that these most familiar and necessary aspects of physicality appear. Thus all the familiar basic physical aspects of reality are clearly added by mind in its simulation of reality and are not actually characteristics of external observer independent reality itself.

The human mind may attempt to transcend its own singularity view of reality but it is impossible for the human mind to imagine reality from all positions and orientations at once especially since we would also have to allow for those points to be every size and velocity at once as well. The best we can do is try to imagine some God like perspective but since that too is a single perspective it is completely false and inadequate to capture the true nature of reality. Again reality becomes less and less physical and more and more only an abstract logical structure.

Another approach is to construct an abstract logico-mathematical model of reality, but that is exactly our point, that the true nature of reality must actually be such a logical structure, rather than a physical one, because that is the only structure that can exist absent the physical characteristics we have now subtracted as additions of mind.

The takeaway from this section is that reality itself has none of the most basic attributes of physicality and dimensionality our experiential model of it imbues it with. Therefore reality itself must be an entirely abstract information structure.

The second takeaway is that it appears more and more likely that the only reasonable view of reality must include observers as a necessary and integral component. That the very notion of our sought after external observer independent reality may itself be questionable.

SENSORY ILLUSIONS

The sensory illusions are another class of illusions that arise from the structural nature of the human sense organs and organismic perception in general. For example in actual observerless reality light waves are unfocused and there are no images of things flying through space. Some primitive life forms actually do see the world through light receptors without lenses which do not focus light and this is closer to the structure of actual reality.

Thus reality itself is much closer to frosted glass than as we see it. Images of things at a distance simply do not exist in actual external reality. Reality contains no images of things at all. It contains only the information that can be processed by observer lenses and minds to produce images. So we simply cannot correctly conceive of reality as consisting of the visual images of things we normally imagine it to be. **Reality does not consist of visible things** and does not include them.

We tend to imagine reality as visual things in classical space but both are now recognized as illusions of mind. What then remains of reality 'out there' other than a logical information structure that allows mind to flesh it out into its apparent reality inside our brain?

Also only light in the visible and near visible range can be focused by biological lenses to form images. Reality itself is full of electromagnetic wavelengths of all possible ranges not to mention fluxes of other particles as well but life is sensitive to only a very limited range of these. So our experience of reality again is very little like the whole of reality itself; only a minute spectrum of it even registers.

We imagine reality as a visual world but there is in fact no visible world at all except in the eyes of organismic observers. External observerless reality itself simply is not visible in any wavelength. There is no actual visible world out there at all independent of observers. **Seeing is something added by observers.** It is an interaction between external reality and the observer, not something in reality itself. True external reality itself is blind and invisible, so blind it is not even dark but entirely an abstract logical structure.

Likewise our ears are sensitive to only a small range of sound frequencies. Some other species are sensitive to considerably higher and lower frequencies but even that is but a small fraction of actual sound waves so here again our view of reality is very unlike actual reality. Reality itself contains no sounds. Sounds arise only in the minds of observers. At best reality itself contains only compression waves in an enormous range of frequencies moving through all sorts of media.

The same is true of olfaction and taste and the chemical receptors of other organisms. Humans are sensitive to an extremely limited subset of all possible airborne and tactile chemicals. Thus the actual reality of chemicals in our environment is vastly different than what we perceive. And again reality itself contains only chemical molecular form structures, not odors or tastes which vary widely among species and to some extent even among individuals. For example it is well know that our taste buds are sensitive to only five basic tastes and that all the nuances of taste are actually generated not by the tongue but by the nose. Tastes and odors exist only in mind and not in external reality.

There are no species with unlimited ranges of all inclusive senses and sensitivities; each has only a very limited sampling of the complete richness of actual reality. Reality itself contains no sensations at all. It is not a sensory structure. And even if it were it would have to include all possible sensations and levels of those sensations, at all possible locations in the entire universe to capture the true nature of external observerless reality itself. Once again reality is simply impossible for any localized mind to comprehend much less experience.

ILLUSIONS OF PHYSICS

Even the standard interpretations of modern physical theory demonstrate that the world is nothing at all like we experience it to be. Physics tells us that matter is almost entirely empty even though we see and experience it as solid. Physics also tells us that empty space is filled not with colored images of things but electromagnetic waves. At an even deeper level quantum theory tells us that the entire material world actually consists only of wavefunctions rather than material objects and that these wavefunctions are not actually physical things but only the probabilities of those things and that wavefunctions don't even exist in a real but in an imaginary space. And even these interpretations, as far from our usual experience of reality as they are, don't go far enough.

Properly understood modern physics tells us that everything actually consists of only of logico-mathematical structures because this is precisely how physics describes reality. If logico-mathematical structures are the best description of reality then reality must actually consist of logico-mathematical structures in the external world.

The only possible reason for the apparent "unreasonable effectiveness of mathematics" is that reality itself must be a logico-mathematical structure since it consists of running programs whose functional components share many similarities with the underlying structure of human computer languages.

The takeaway here is that even though modern physics clearly reveals a more accurate view of reality far from our everyday common sense view it is very rare for even scientists to take this to its logical conclusion and understand it demonstrates that the universe must be a logico-mathematical computational structure. But if we are to truly understand the lessons of modern science that is exactly what we must do.

ILLUSIONS OF QUANTITY

In all cases the true nature of external observerless reality itself can never be captured by any individual local observer because no matter how sensitive it is able to experience only that part of reality that impinges on its particular observer location in the present moment, when the actual reality of reality is all possible signals everywhere in the universe all at once in the present moment. Again any observer's view of reality just cannot be a true model of reality itself as it actually exists.

In addition only a minute fraction of the signals that do impinge on the sensory apparatus are passed along to the mind, and even then only as extensively post-processed summaries. Each human retina is equivalent to roughly 200 million pixels capacity but the optical system only passes on a small fraction of that in the form of movements and edges generally near the center of vision. Most of what falls on the retinas is not actually seen in a perceptual sense.

Our mental model of reality is enormously poor and biased compared to the actual reality of the entire universe in the present moment. The reality we see and experience around us, as rich as it seems, is a minute pale shadow of the richness and complexity of actual reality. The illusion that we have an accurate perception of the actual reality around us grows weaker and weaker.

Once again the science is well established but once again the lesson needs to be understood, and that is that the whole notion of an external observer independent reality is not and never can be anything at all like our mind models it. It is simply impossible for any individual observer to ever have an internal model of reality that actually captures anything at all like its true nature. It is beyond the capacity of the human mind or any possible individual mind.

Reality by definition is not some scientific theory or model of reality but the totality of reality itself as it exists in the present moment. Knowing or experiencing reality is not achieved through some set of equations no matter how accurate or comprehensive. Reality is the totality of everything as it currently is but there is no mind that can come close to simulating the entirety of form therefore there is no conceivable way to 'know' reality in the actual sense of knowing it completely. Only reality as a whole can 'know' itself because only it is coterminous with itself and only it can compute itself.

Observers model only the minutest fraction imaginable of the entire reality of the universe which is many many orders of magnitude greater than the capacity of any organism to perceive or comprehend. That is even true for an organism's immediate surroundings in which only the minutest percentage of events even registers, but even more impossible when the entire universe is considered.

ILLLUSIONS OF QUALITY

All the many qualities of objects that give them their apparent self-substances are called qualia and are attributes of mind's simulation of reality rather than of external reality itself. These qualia are all internally generated information forms added to internal representations of external thing forms to help mind discriminate and valuate them with respect to their importance to the personal functioning and survival of the organism in question.

All the experienced colors, sounds, smells, tastes, touches, emotive feelings and meanings of things are types of qualia. Seemingly physical qualities such as hardness and softness, heaviness or lightness, stickiness, roughness; these and every other quality of anything is added by mind and does not exist in external reality. They are information forms produced by the interaction of the organism with external reality. Thus they exist only in an observer's internal simulation of that reality. These apparent characteristics of external things that seem to give them the appearance of physicality are all actually information about how the organism is interacting with the purely information forms of external things as represented in mind.

Qualia are characteristics of the interaction of an observer with external reality, not of external reality itself. External reality itself has no such qualities. External reality itself has no colors, smells, tactile feelings, emotions, or meanings. It is entirely an abstract logical structure consisting of information that produces qualia in its interactions with observers. The qualia exist only in the minds of observers and are observer dependent. Qualia are the information encoding the interactions of observer forms with external forms.

Since qualia are completely observer dependent they vary widely with individual observers and even more across observers of various species. The fact that the experience of reality is so diverse across species demonstrates that no observer captures reality as it itself actually is.

154

It is important to clearly understand that it is qualia which imbue thing forms with their apparent physicality in the mental models of observers and that these qualia are also only information forms. These are internal information forms which encode feelings and meanings in the broadest sense in organisms. These feelings and meanings are internal information forms associated with external forms to help discriminate and valuate them with respect to the functioning of the organism. All feelings and meanings *are only the information* encoding and carrying those feelings and meanings.

ILLUSIONS OF PHYSICALITY

We believe we live in a physical world but this is an illusion generated in our mind's simulation of reality from *associations of qualia* such as texture, hardness, color, touch, weight, temperature etc. which are all added by mind to enhance and make more meaningful those characteristics of reality important to our survival. What appear to be physical objects are actually just associations of qualia in sets representing the apparent characteristics of physical objects. These qualia do not exist in external reality but are only information encoding how an observer interacts with an information structure in external reality.

For example the qualia that associate to generate the appearance of a physical stone don't exist in the stone itself. The stone itself is simply an abstract information structure in the external world that elicits the qualia information structures in its interaction with the form of an organismic observer. All the apparently physical things of the world, and in fact all things without exception, are only associations of information, some external and some internal.

But the actual world that includes both external forms and the observer itself as one of those external forms, consists entirely of running computationally interacting programs that compute the evolution of information forms. Reality is not a physical structure; all the evidence indicates it is composed only of interacting information forms. The apparent material world of our experience exists only in our minds encoded as complex associations and hierarchies of information.

Even the basic attributes that seem to make reality physical in physics turn out to be qualia because all the forces, energy, matter etc. turn out to be known ultimately only by their qualitative effects as experienced in the minds of observers. The so called forces of nature are simply logico-mathematical descriptions of how forms evolve.

All these apparently basic physical attributes such as forces and energies are ultimately experienced as types of qualia such as pushes, resistances, heat, sound, etc., or as perceptual observations of their effects. Even forces and energies strong enough to cause injury are perceived as qualia, as burns, breaks, pain and so forth. The basic concepts of physics are abstract symbolic representations of these qualia and their interactions. But this again demonstrates our point, that reality itself is the symbolic logico-mathematical information 'out there' that produce the qualia of our experiences of them.

Strip away layer after layer and only the logic of forms in a world of pure information remains; a consistent purely computational structure which evolves in clock time according to logical rules called the laws of nature and more specifically in the form of programs composed of those laws of nature. It is the continual computational interaction of all these programs that is the fundamental structure of reality.

The reduction of reality to an abstract logical computational structure does not make reality any less real or rich, not even in the slightest. Things themselves do not change nor does our experience of them. It is only our realization that changes as we recognize this familiar richness is simultaneously within both us and an external reality in their interaction, even as we find ourselves within an ever more fascinating combined reality.

THE ILLUSION OF A VERBAL REALITY

We tend to think of the structure of reality as being largely isomorphic to how we describe it in language but this is far from the truth. When we understand how language encodes meaning this becomes quite clear. Language uses single exact words to stand for form structures that are inherently amorphous even in our own mental models of reality and thus the relationship of the structure of language to that of external reality is even less exact.

156

Information on the structural nature of forms comes from understanding non-verbal forms of meaning. Many animals clearly know many things about their environments including the states, actions and relationships of things in great detail. However since these animals lack the complex symbolic languages of humans how is that knowledge organized and stored since it is clearly not verbally?

Humans tend to think that their knowledge of reality is verbal, or at least primarily verbal, but there are many aspects of human knowledge that are similar to that of other animals which is not surprising since human verbal abilities are add-ons to the more primitive knowledge we share with our animal relatives.

As with animals much of human knowledge is stored as perceptions which are organized sensory memories. Recognition of individual faces is a good example. Humans have the ability to distinguish far more individual faces than they are able to describe verbally and this is true of many other types of knowledge as well. Clearly tagging a face with the name of the person is one type of knowledge but while the name of the person can call up the representation of the face it is clearly not the knowledge of the description of the face which is stored separately and merely labeled with a person's name in a type of identity relationship.

Again it is artificial intelligence that sheds light on how knowledge of this sort is extracted from raw sensory input and stored. Facial recognition systems extract and combine measurements of a number of standard features of human faces deemed most useful in distinguishing individual faces to seek the best match from databases of known faces. Humans no doubt use a functionally similar method to identify faces though they are still much better at it than computers.

The point is that 'Bill's face' is not stored verbally as those two words but as the representations those two words label. The actual stored representation in human memory is an extremely complex set of associated individual data which even includes how Bill's face changes with his various moods and emotions and how it has changed through the time Bill has been known as well.

Thus most of human knowledge consists not of verbal structures but of verbal structures overlaid on very complex representational structures built up from organized perceptual structures. And animal knowledge consists primarily of this though there is certainly a considerably symbolic 'verbal' overlay as well since many animals do associate particular calls with particular representational knowledge.

Many animals express feelings vocally and these vocalizations are the language expressions of those feelings. Such vocalizations also communicate those feelings to other animals quite effectively even to animals of other species. Take the growl of a dog for example. And some feelings arise in response to specific environmental information and are expressed by vocalizations which thus are the words or phrases that communicate that external information as well as the feeling it elicited.

The warning cries of birds of the presence of a specific type of predator for example are effectively the words for the presence of that type of predator in the language of the bird that utters them. And other animals clearly do understand each other's language to a considerable extent, in general much more fluently than most humans do.

Human language is just a further development of this. Early humans would simply have vocalized the feelings elicited by social situations such as hunting or other group activities in more and more detail as they performed them with the meaning reinforced by accompanying body movements as other animals also do. In this way symbolic language would have gradually developed as a natural outgrowth of animal vocalizations.

The point is that knowledge, the structure of the mental models of organisms, is mainly representational. Though it does, especially in humans, partially consist of verbal structures in the form of the syntactical logic of language, its vast substratum consists of very complex representational structures in which each individually verbally labeled 'thing' exists as a convenient label for a complex stored structured set of individual perceptual data.

This is the internal structure of the forms in organisms' mental models of reality, and thus it is this representational form structure which brings us closer to the actual form structure of external reality. The external form structure of reality is clearly not verbal. It does not consist of individual verbally tagged 'things' which stand in English syntactical relationships to each other.

Nor is it representational in the form it exists in animal mental models of reality. These are extractions of emergent structures of their interaction with a reality which consists more of great fluid masses of continuously interacting waveforms which are tuned by organism's interactions with them to extract information useful to their functioning.

Thus the structure of the reality of the world of forms clearly is not at all similar to the human syntactical structures language nor is it representational in the same sense that most human and animal knowledge of the world of forms is. Rather it is an enormously complex continuous interaction of fluid waveforms from which the representational and verbal forms of organismic beings can be extracted. Thus all of the individual things, actions, properties and relationships which make up organismic models of reality are useful artificial internal constructs. Though these all exist only in internal mental models of reality, they tend to be based on natural structural boundaries of various aspects of the world of forms rather than being completely arbitrary.

Take the example of a wave in an ocean. The wave is actually part of the continuous form of the ocean and its precise boundaries and duration of existence are to a great extent arbitrary and observer defined, however there clearly are natural boundaries upon which the discrimination of the wave from the ocean can be based. This is generally true of all of what humans think of as 'things'.

With their technologies humans are able to construct thing forms with sharper than natural boundaries so they more clearly exist as distinguishable individual things with easily identifiable and useful functions. This in fact is the function of technology, the construction of forms with precise specific boundaries in a world consisting primarily of less precise natural forms.

THE ILLUSION OF INDIVIDUAL THINGS

Another level of illusion is revealed by the functional structure of mind's simulation of reality. How the mind's simulation of reality develops in children and is expressed in other species has been extensively studied by cognitive science beginning systematically with Piaget (Piaget, 1956, 1960). Advances in artificial intelligence and robotic perceptual and control systems also shed much light on the fundamental functional structure of mind as they elucidate the mechanisms necessary to effectively model reality.

For example what we experience as a flower is actually an association of qualia forms within our simulation of reality. A flower comes into our awareness not as a flower but as all the many perceptual components of a flower. The flower is actually an dimensional association of certain colors, textures, shapes, fragrances, and behavioral and other forms that tend to maintain that association over time as well as having relational associations with other forms such as those of bees, florists, gardens etc.

These associations can be quite complex and certainly exhibit a very convincing reality of a flower as a physical and biological object. But when one understands how mind works and what is involved in cobbling raw perceptual fluxes together into mental concepts to create 'things' one realizes all these reduce to purely computational structures composed of consistent complexes of information.

Minds tend to model reality in terms of discrete individual things and relationships but this is not the fundamental structure of reality. From the continuous vast flux of sensory information our perceptual and cognitive systems function as antennae tuned by evolution to extract and classify discrete patterns meaningful to our existence and to associate and store them as discrete things and relationships. From this continuous information flux individual things are defined as repeating patterns with similar characteristics which are logically separable from the background flux of sensory information.

For the notion of things defined by attributes and relationships to even arise there must be a pre-existing logical computational structure of mind, the ability to define and distinguish similarity of inputs, and the ability to store and reference similarities. All this is based on an innate notion of equivalence or similarity, an effective computational capacity, and innate formal logical structures in terms of which models of reality can be formulated.

However the logical structure of external reality does not consist of individual things and relationships, these emerge only in the comparative data structures we call memories within our internal models of reality.

As we have seen in Part III, it is clear that at the elemental level the logic of reality consists only of decoherence events with no inherent relationships to classical level things at all. Reality at this level consists only of entanglement decoherence networks among elemental particles rather than any classical level 'things'. Thus even at the classical level reality consists of continuous fluxes of elemental information forms with no classical level 'objects' as these are all aspects of observer models of reality. The question here is whether organismic observers extract high level logical structures such as things and relationships correctly from the flux of elemental reality, or whether these classical level phenomena exist only in the simulations of observers.

Quantum theory agrees in modeling reality as consisting only of interacting wavefunctions which are probabilistic structures rather than physical 'things'. And most certainly the gross things of human experience exist in the quantum world not so much as discrete things as vast fuzzy fluxes of associated probabilities. Quantum theory conceives of external reality as a colorless invisible world of interacting probability waves. This is of course strongly supports the view we arrive at from several different approaches. However we interpret the equations of quantum theory as logico-mathematical rather than physical structures because of course that is what they actually are. Upon consideration the equations of quantum theory are in fact more information structures than physical phenomena as usually conceived.

How much simpler to consider the logico-mathematical structure of modern science to actually *be* the direct representation of a logico-mathematical reality rather than *a representation* of some additional physical structures which cannot even be demonstrated to exist. We must finally discard the ancient delusion of a physical reality. The resulting model is much more parsimonious and convincing.

So the whole idea of 'thingness' at the classical level of human experience seems questionable. It is clear that the discrete things called waves and currents are both parts of a single continuous ocean. Surfers and oceanographers see different things in that same ocean. And frogs and fishes see the same ocean in terms of even different things. So it seems quite clear that individual things are observer constructs.

The actual reality even of human experience is always a continuous complex flow of immediate sensory information. The relationships between portions of this raw xperience, if any, are not immediately apparent from the individual perceptions themselves because they aren't necessarily temporally simultaneous. Thus the relationships between them may be artifacts of the sequences of inputs rather than aspects of reality itself.

The relationships between things become apparent only within mind where raw event sequences from different times are stored as relationships. Thus things and their relationships seem to originate in and become part of the mind's cognitive model of reality rather than existing in external reality itself. While the logical sequences may in fact be part of external reality they are experienced as such not in external reality but in the internal model of reality. Again robotic perceptual software provides great insights into how things and relationships are constructed out of raw sensory data and what a difficult complex and inherently fuzzy process this is (Wikipedia: Outline of object recognition).

When robots extract the same objects that humans do from the flux does that tell us that those things actually exist in the flux or does it just mean we've taught AI systems how the human mind works to construct things that have a questionable existence in reality itself? In any case we know that both humans and robots certainly increase their functionality by organizing their mental models of reality in this manner. Does that indicate these higher level 'emergent' forms exist in external reality or not?

The fact that organisms do model reality effectively in terms of things and relationships does demonstrate that reality is meaningful in those terms even if that is not the only possibility. This can only be the case if the whole underlying structure of reality is simultaneously self-consistent across all levels so that all subsystems and hierarchies within it are also self-consistent. This is what allows an ocean to be simultaneously meaningful in terms of both waves and currents. This *super-consistency* is an important aspect of reality that will be explored further in Part V as will the nature of individual things.

THE ILLUSION OF SELF

One of the most significant 'things' constructed by mind, at least for human observers, is the self. Nevertheless the thing we call our self arises in our reality model like all other things do as consistent fuzzy and flexible associations of similar perceptions. It is constructed from repeating associations of particular categories of perceptions involving proprioceptive feelings, emotive perceptions, spatial associations, perceptions of direct control and so forth.

Only gradually does the division of reality into self and not-self arise in children usually in late infancy (Piaget, 1956, 1960). And only gradually does the realization arise of a self that 'has' perceptions of all the thing constructs that make up both the self and not-self. It is thought that in many other species this process never develops to the extent it does in humans but nevertheless they manage to function quite effectively in their simulations of reality. So the notion of self does not seem to be a necessary or even actual aspect of reality. However it is quite clear that most organisms do computationally categorize their own characteristics separately from those of not-self things on the basis of feelings and meanings. If they did not distinguish self from not-self aspects of reality in some manner they obviously could not survive or function.

In the actual reality of the present moment the flow of raw experience occurs antecedent to its discrimination and categorization into individual things and specifically prior to their super categorization as parts of self, not-self or other individual things. Thus we can reasonably think of all experience without exception as part of a greater or 'true' self consisting of the entirety of an observer's fundamental experience without exception. This is of course obvious when one considers that all experience, even of seemingly 'not-self' things is actually part of the observer.

From this perspective every experience of an observer in its totality is part of that observer and what actually defines that observer. Whether these experiences are then categorized in the internal model as part of self, not-self or simply ignored they are all part of the total observer experience and thus part of the whole observer prior to the division it makes between self and not-self. **Thus every experience in every detail of an observer is properly part of the 'self' of the observer because every bit of it without exception occurs within the observer as part of its model of reality, and thus the entirety of that modeled reality *is the observer itself*.**

This is compatible with the view that consciousness itself rather than the contents of consciousness that may appear within it is one's 'true' self, it is just a matter of perspective. From an external perspective consciousness is reality from the point of view of an individual observer, but from the point of view of that consciousness itself there is no individual observer, there is just consciousness and everything that appears within that consciousness is part of it. This is just the distinction between the self-manifesting presence of formless ontological energy and the forms that may arise within it.

THE ILLUSION OF HISTORICAL TIME

While there is no doubt that categorizations like 'self' and other 'things' helps to organize our models of reality in functionally useful ways they are still an artificial and questionable construct. Since reality actually exists only in the present moment rather than in our cognitive model's historical view of reality all things stored in the simulation must be realized as an illusion because they are not currently extant in external reality. Their reality is not their prior reference but their present moment existence as memory forms within the mental model.

Thus the historical memory of all observers is an illusion if it is taken as moments of a real past since the past is clearly not actually real. And since individual things are only meaningful as historical constructs they must be figments of the historical memory of the simulation rather than actual aspects of external reality. They appear to be only meaningful associations of temporal networks of perceptual data when stored in memory. And we must also conclude that since the simulation is almost entirely a historical structure of memory that it is inherently illusory with respect to a reality that actually exists only in the present moment.

THE PRESENT MOMENT ILLUSION

There is another illusion that is especially interesting and relevant to understanding reality. We seem to exist within a present moment of some short duration that persists as clock time flows through it but this is an illusion. The actual present moment of external reality has almost no duration at all since it is just the time it takes for quantum processes to resolve and weave the fabric of reality. Its duration is far far below the ability of the human mind to detect. And it is intrinsically fuzzy because quantum processes are indeterminate as some are decohering and some are not at any given moment.

There does seem to be a definite p-time processor cycle of happening that defines the local clock time rate. However this is clearly a computational rather than physical process though it manifests as physical clock time in the experience of generic observers as a physical world emerges from the decoherence interactions of the logical.

In contrast the duration of the apparent present moment within human consciousness seems to continually encompass perhaps a second or two depending on how consciousness is focused. In mind's simulation of reality short term memory holds an artificial present moment open long enough for things to be compared which is the only way anything can be made sense of at all by mind.

For example music depends entirely on the relationships of note to note in a sequences of notes. If we had no short term memory that artificially held the present moment open and gave it duration there would be no experience of music. Our only experience of reality would be what was occurring in the exact nanosecond of the actual present moment and without any possible context or reference to anything else at all. This is in fact the nature of the *xperiences* of non-organismic forms. But life for any organism would be impossible because computational thought based on comparisons and relationships would be impossible.

Certainly other organisms' short term memory functions and duration may vary and their perceptions of reality could be much different on this point alone. One might also imagine a being with a much greater short term memory capability than humans which would be able to make enormously greater relational sense of event networks.

There is a useful meditation exercise where one focuses more and more precisely on the exact moment when new events come into being and zeros in on the exact moment of becoming into being while allowing what has already entered the present moment to vanish instantly out of consciousness. This is most effective while listening to smooth continuous music or sound. With practice one can circumvent one's short term memory and let consciousness continually surf the exact moment of becoming into being. It's quite an awesome and enlightening experience as to how very tenuous and fleeting the actual razor's edge of time is! Consciousness is so intensely and extremely near to the nonexistence of the past and future. That continuous durationless nanosecond of real actual existence is truly marvelous!

This is one more way in which the world as we experience it is an illusion generated by mind. The extended present moment as we experience it is entirely an illusion, an elaborate and clearly useful mental construct that does not exist in external reality. Only recognized as such does its reality appear and we experience the amazing reality of the actual nearly dimensionless present moment. This is a basic evolutionary characteristic of mind that seems to be necessary to make life possible even though it does not exist in external reality itself. It seems absolutely necessary for organisms to conceive of a temporal universe with an expanded present moment to make sense of reality.

Another example is the visual trails of moths around lights at night. Looking at the moths we don't see the moth in a single location but as the head of a trail of images. Our visual system and perceptual systems in general are designed to facilitate our short term memory spreading out the present moment to the duration of a second or two so that we have a dynamic context for paths of motion. This occurs with all motions though less obviously and is what enables us to correctly analyze motion paths so as to avoid impacts, catch baseballs, and walk safely down the street, and it is only these perceptual tricks that allow us to synchronize our actions with motions in the external world.

It is well known that the apparent motion of film and TV is an illusion generated by the mind smoothly connecting separate visual frames. But what is not well known is that is equally true for all motion. It is only the ability of short term memory to temporally connect and sequence sensory events that creates the experience of the very passage of clock time including the illusion of motion. All motion is an illusion that exists only as experienced in short term memory. Not that change does not happen in reality, but the experience of it via comparison of before and after states that generates the illusion of things actually changing into other things is entirely a construct of mind. Reality itself consists only of the current instantaneous states of things, the xperience of singular events with no before since there is no before that still actually exists.

THE ILLUSION OF CHANGE

We have previously explained that reality can be interpreted as consisting entirely of xperience defined as the re-computation, including the computational alteration, of any form. And that xperience is how the self-manifestation of reality becomes manifest to a generic observer, and that this is how every form functions as a generic observer of its xperience. Thus the manifestation of reality to a generic observer is an xperience and an xperience is the xperience of a manifestation of reality. Xperience is how the self-manifestation of reality becomes manifest.

This means that only change manifests because all observation, measurement or xperience itself constitutes a change in the form of a generic observer and even a re-computation of the same form is actually a change in the existence state of a form. For example the visual observation of a scene is actually a change in the observer's own visual system. Thus we can say that only change manifests as xperience because only change is xperienced because change in the form of continual re-computation of forms is what xperience is.

But if the duration of the present is vanishingly small and only the present exists then there can be no actual before state to compare the present state to and therefore how can it be said to constitute a change? Before and after comparisons are possible only in organismic mental models of reality rather than in reality itself as xperienced by generic observers. Thus in external observer independent reality how can change actually be change without a previous state for it to be compared to?

We must be careful here to arrive at a correct understanding. The key insight here is that every form is actually changing all the time whether or not its information content changes. This is because reality continually re-computes every form at every moment of happening. All forms that are not recomputed into continuing existence vanish and are gone from reality. Even forms that appear not to change are continually being recreated and their existence refreshed at every moment.

Thus all forms are always in an instantaneous state of change or happening but this is far below the resolution of the human temporal system so that mental models of reality inevitably extract and represent forms as static video frames and sequences of video frames. Thus change as represented in mental models of reality is illusory because it consists of sequences of static video frames rather than the instantaneous happening of the real external world of forms.

The world of forms is a single continuous form that continually computationally evolves due to happening in the present moment. Every bit of it is recomputed at every instant in the present moment. Thus whatever the form of any segment is, whether its information

167

content has changed or not from the perspective of some observer, its existence is entirely new at every instant.

Thus all form states in the present moment without exception are both xperience and manifestation, or more accurately the xperience of manifestation and the manifestation of xperience since both are the same thing from different perspectives. Because they are continually recreated in every instant in the present moment their current form state, whatever it may be, actually is the self-manifestation of reality in the world of forms. And thus it simultaneously constitutes the xperience of that self-manifestation.

Every form state is its xperience of the re-computation that is producing it and the self-manifestation of that form state in the reality of ontological energy in the present moment in the form of that xperience. Every form without exception manifests the ontological energy in which it exists in the continual re-computation of its form. Self-manifestation is xperience and xperience is self-manifestation. Just different organismic observer perspectives on the nature of existence in the present moment.

Recall that individual forms do not have fixed independent existences in the external world of forms which exists as a continuous whole. Every individual form is properly a discrimination in the mental model of some organismic observer of some structural domain within the total form environment. At the level of generic forms themselves, individual forms cannot even be said to exist in their own xperience because they have no mental models of anything, though of course from our perspective their current forms are the information of their computational histories. At that non-organismic level there is only raw xperience devoid of any context or conceptualization. And even this is properly a concept in the mental model of this organismic observer.

So change in the sense it is perceived by organismic observers does seem to be an illusion. This type of change consists only by comparison of before and after states in their present representations and there is no before that actually exists. We must conclude that in actual external observer independent reality change in this sense cannot be said to exist. There is only continuous happening with no comparison of before and after.

Certainly existence exists. That was our fundamental axiom. And the presence of existence manifests as a present moment therefore the present moment must have some duration. Thus happening just happens

168

and the concepts of change and clock time rates and classical durations emerge from this process as conceptualized in the mental models of organismic observers rather than occurring in external reality itself.

All forms without exception in the present moment continually happen as they are in a continual state of re-computation. This continual happening of forms simultaneously constitutes xperience and self-manifestation which are two sides of the same coin. Thus everything that exists without exception self-manifests itself as its xperience of itself, as xperience itself, and by extension xperience of the other forms it shares a computational history with, though this last insight is accessible only to the mental models of organismic observers.

THE PRESENT FUTURE ILLUSION

Our minds constantly anticipate reality and actually construct it momentarily in advance, only correcting it if necessary against inconsistent sensory input. This advance construction of anticipated events gives organisms obvious functional advantages.

So to a significant extent we live in a non-existent future created by temporally projecting our simulations of current trends in advance of actual events. So far as this projection is accurate we are one step ahead of potential prey or predators and relevant events in general, but of course this is not reality and our projection can be wrong in which case we are clearly at a disadvantage. This can be called the Illusion of the Present Future.

REALITY IS INFORMATION ONLY

We have attempted to discover the true nature of external observer independent reality by identifying what mind adds to it in its internal model of that reality. We find that mind adds everything responsible for the appearance of the physicality and materiality of reality. All the attributes of the apparently material things of the world all turn out to be added by mind rather than being intrinsic aspects of external reality.

Every last one of them without exception is part of mind's model of reality rather than of external reality itself.

The inevitable conclusion is that external reality itself consists only of the underlying information structure of what we experience. That is all that remains after all that mind adds is identified and subtracted. This information structure is what is experienced by organismic observers *in their internal representations of their interactions with it* as the apparently physical classical world in which they exist.

Though the external world consist only of information only it is completely real in the realest of senses because it is the actual world of forms that exists in the very substance of being in the present moment.

Individual observers of all species including humans approximate and flesh out this logical structure each in their own way in their simulations of it. Though they are never exact nor complete, it is clear these approximations must have some considerable degree of logical correspondence otherwise organisms could not function in external reality in accordance with its intrinsic logic on the basis of logical computations within their simulations of it. And the fact that we can trust the logic of this assertion also requires a degree of logical correspondence between the logic of reality and the logic of our simulation of it.

There are many other lines of reasoning that lead to this same conclusion. The very fact that reality is best described by the logical rules of science, reason and mathematics is actually telling us that external reality itself must also be a similar computational structure. How else could mathematics and science so accurately describe reality if reality itself was not also similarly computational? As previously mentioned this is the secret behind the so called "unreasonable effectiveness of mathematics". Human mathematics is effective in its descriptions of reality precisely because reality itself *is* a logico-mathematical computational structure which human logic and mathematics approximates. This is one more line of reasoning that leads us to conclude that a computational world of abstract information forms is the fundamental structure of reality.

The forms that constitute external reality clearly must be enormously more complex than their simulations in the minds of any one observer at any particular time because they actually compute the totality of reality down to the finest details. Yet there must also be an extremely dense consistency framework if all observers are able to extract logical snippets at all different levels and use them to express effective functionality back into that shared reality.

KNOWLEDGE IS LOGICAL SELF CONSISTENCY

If our experience of reality is entirely within our own simulation of it then what is knowledge and what is the test of true knowledge? If every view of reality is only a simulation model in some observer mind then why is the theory of reality presented by this author more accurate than all the others (assuming it is)? If all observer views of reality are entirely mental models of actual reality how do we judge among them as to which is the truer representation? How do we decide what is the true test of knowledge? The theory presented here clearly arises in the author's mental model of reality. So how can its correspondence with the reality it attempts to model be tested?

There is one simple test for true and accurate knowledge and one alone. That test *cannot be* the direct correspondence of the mental model with external reality because all that is known is the simulation and not reality itself. Thus that test is simply impossible. **The only valid test of knowledge is the degree of its *internal* logical consistency and completeness across its entire scope.** Insofar as the logic of the mental model is internally self-consistent and complete it does accurately model the actual logic of external reality and thus does constitute true knowledge.

We want to test the consistency of the internal logic of our model of reality against the actual physical logic of reality. But it is impossible to compare them directly because we are always inevitably inside our own model of reality and thus have no direct access to the actual logic of reality.

However just as the inhabitant of a non-Euclidean space can determine the geometry of his world from within by measuring the sums of the angles of triangles so there is a way to determine the accuracy of a mental model of reality from inside that model. Just as it is not necessary to stand outside a space to know it is curved by the presence of matter it is not necessary to stand outside our simulation to know whether it is an accurate depiction of external reality.

171

The internal method of determining the accuracy of our simulation of reality is simply to determine its self-consistency over scope. The greater self-consistency the more accurately it maps the external observer independent reality, and that is true whatever it may be. Whatever is inconsistent with an internally self-consistent theory of sufficient scope will not be true of external reality and whatever is consistent will be true.

This works only because reality itself is a self-consistent and complete logical structure. A computational reality itself must be an entirely self-consistent logical system otherwise it would tear itself apart at the inconsistencies and could not exist. And since a mental model of reality is a part of reality it must also be internally self-consistent to the extent it is a true simulation of external reality. Of course that internal self-consistency must be tested and confirmed across the entire simulation to ensure its completeness.

In this context it is important to understand how inconsistent simulations of reality can exist as parts of an entirely self-consistent encompassing reality. Inconsistent simulations become consistent when considered not as isolated systems but in the broader context of false premises and ignorance of salient facts. Given partial or confusing facts or incorrect data the emergence of an inconsistent simulation may be the logically consistent outcome.

This is how inconsistent belief systems can be part of a fully consistent reality. This includes the illusions and delusions added by the minds of observers to their conceptions of reality which seem consistent to them even though they are not in a broader context. Newtonian theory is consistent across most of our experience. The theory of epicycles was once the most accurate explanation of the movement of the planets. Once a world controlled by gods was the best science of the day.

This is a corollary of the principle that it is the self-consistency of any organism's model of external reality that enables it to function effectively in external reality on the basis of computations within its internal simulation. To the extent the simulated reality was inconsistent with the actual external logical structure the organism will not be able to function effectively within its environment assuming the inconsistencies affect the actual functioning rather than merely being largely irrelevant abstract beliefs.

Thus we can have confidence that our mind's approximations of reality are at least accurate enough for us to enjoy our basic organismic functions. Because we function reasonably effectively based on our internal simulations of reality demonstrates it does actually approximate the logic of external reality at least to that extent. We merely extend this same principle from basic organismic functioning to include our abstract theories of reality.

Any serious inconsistency in an organism's simulation model of reality is likely to lead to serious consequences, and these consequences will manifest in the simulation as inconsistencies with respect to expectations. Thus inconsistencies in the simulation always reveal flawed knowledge.

We must confirm this consistency across the whole range of our simulation to ensure all aspects of theory and experience are self-consistent with the whole. And we also need to broaden our observer perspective as much as possible by including as much new data as possible from scientific instruments, other observers, and shared information sources.

This is precisely what this book attempts to do and I believe the theory presented here is internally self-consistent as well as being consistent with modern science (the observational facts and core theory though not necessarily the interpretations). And I believe it is also consistent with the nature of carefully analyzed direct experience, and thus with the overall corpus of human knowledge. Self-consistency and completeness of the theory will be the only possible ultimate test of its truth. I hope our theory lives up to this test, at least better than any competing theories. I believe it does.

It should be noted that this is a recursive process since the self-consistency test itself is another component of the mental model, and it itself must be self-consistent with the whole. This seems to be as close as we can possibly come to discovering the true logical structure of the reality of the world of forms.

Internal self-consistency is of course the fundamental principle of epistemology and science though not often recognized as such. It is the essence of proof and the scientific method. The notion that knowledge is even possible is based on the assumption that the world is a logical structure and that human logic being part of that world is also valid and thus is capable of eventually accurately mapping the actual logic of reality at least to a considerable degree.

Communication with other observers is an important component of this process. To the extent that other observers in one's simulation agree that your simulation of reality is consistent with their own adds an additional area of consistency to the whole simulation. It is an additional area of overall consistency to have your simulation agree with the simulation of another observer you are simulating.

If an observer's simulation of reality is inaccurate then it will necessarily contain some inconsistency. To the extent one's simulation of reality is inconsistent one is less likely to function effectively in reality. A simulation that contains even a single inconsistency has some inaccuracy somewhere, and it is the discovery of inconsistency that most often leads to improving the accuracy of the simulation's representation of reality. This is standard application of scientific method, criminal investigation and mathematical proof. Popper's insistence that theories must be falsifiable to be meaningful is precisely a test of inconsistency (Popper, 1959).

Self-consistency does not mean trivially commonsensical. The history of modern science provides abundant testimony for that. But there must always be a deep consistency, at the proper level of understanding, with the logic of things by which organisms function. The mountain remains in the same place unless something moves it. Events have causes and causes form a self-consistent natural structure.

Predictability is often considered the proper test of theories of science. But predictability and tests of conformance with predictability are always internal to the model of reality so ultimately they are just another test of self-consistency. So again the only criterion is consistency. The underlying assumption is always that the nature of reality *is* logical consistency and that **reality cannot contain any true inconsistency**. This requires that no internally consistent model of reality of sufficient scope is likely to be a false representation of reality. But to be confirmed it must be consistent over all known data. If there is any internal inconsistency in the model at all there must be some inaccuracy in its representation of reality hidden somewhere within that inconsistency.

It is important to note that even inconsistent false simulations of reality are in fact part of reality and therefore must be consistent with it and therefore must themselves be consistent! Inconsistent simulations are in fact consistent with greater reality but only when recognized as false representations of reality are they also part of a fully consistent reality. This is only possible when the false assumptions they are based upon

174

are included as such. When a false premise or invalid logical form is stated as such the logical structure it engenders can be consistently incorporated within a fully consistent whole. This includes the illusions and delusions added by the minds of observers to their simulations of reality which may seem consistent but are not.

ILLUSION SEEN AS ILLUSION IS REALITY

Reality is defined as the 'true nature' of everything that exists. And most certainly the simulations of all observers exist so they too are part of this same reality. So any theory of reality must also include these simulations of reality and be able to integrate them seamlessly into its logical structure. But this is possible only when they are understood as inexact and illusory models of reality rather than mistaken for the reality they appear to be. The reality of these mental models of reality is that they are mental models rather than the reality they model. But as part of reality the logical information structure of all such models is part of the overall logical information structure of reality. All organismic simulations of reality are part of the reality they simulate.

Because we live inside our simulation of reality we live inside an illusion relative to any actual observer independent reality but that illusion recognized as illusion is reality since the observer simulation is itself a part of reality. In fact that reality of the simulation is the only part of the entire reality we actually experience, but it must be understood as the experience of itself as a simulation rather than the direct experience of external reality for its reality to be realized.

The illusions of the simulations of observers are part of reality, but only when recognized as the illusions they are is their true nature realized. The more we are able to see that we are seeing external reality through the veils of our cognitive model of it the better we are able to glimpse that actual reality and the reality of the various veils of illusion as an entire system. Only in this way are we able to see the entire picture which consists of both our simulation and the reality it simulates. That whole picture is the whole of reality.

Though we can never experience its details directly something out there appears to be the source of the consistent world of our simulation in which we are able to function with some effectiveness. The only alternative would be a complete solipsism in which the entire world existed in our own head (Wikipedia: Solipsism). But solipsism is itself self-contradictory because it assumes a head and by doing so a world in which that head exists. Thus there must in some sense be an external world in which our mental model of that world exists. This view is consistent with both direct experience and with the insights of science but we must be very careful how we interpret it because it stands outside the scope of the usual syntactical constructs of language.

The external world we have arrived at in our search by subtraction is a very strange abstract non-dimensional logical entity most closely analogous to running software programs. And it is clearly our mind and our mind alone that fleshes that running code out into the bright colorful meaningful world in which we appear to live and relate to with all the variety of feeling that we do.

But as we ourselves are also part of external reality then we ourselves must also be just another program running in reality, just another set of computationally evolving forms of information. But this is all absolutely real because all these programs are endowed with the reality of actual being by running in the ontological energy of the present moment. We too are the continual self-manifestation of reality in all the continual re-computations of all the forms of our being which constitutes our experience of the presence of that reality.

REALITY IS XPERIENCE ONLY

We have sought to discover a true observer independent reality by subtracting everything our mind adds to it and found that all that is left 'out there' is an underlying logical structure of pure information analogous to running software programs. But when we take the final step and subtract all observer experience of that reality even that logical structure disappears, *in our experience*. Without our xperience of it reality is no longer able to manifest itself, at least to us.

No doubt one less observer matters very little to the universe as a whole, but when we extend this to all generic observers, then reality is no longer able to manifest at all because all xperience of it has vanished. Of course this can happen only if all forms disappear since every form functions as a generic observer through which reality

176

manifests itself. Thus forms, xperience and manifestation are all different perspectives on the same single fundamental process that is the core of the reality of reality.

From this perspective reality actually exists only as its manifestations as xperiences in the forms of generic observers. Other than as xperience it cannot manifest its existence. This is why at the generic level we must speak of the world of forms as a unified whole rather than consisting of individual forms. In this way the universe self-manifests its entire reality as its entire xperience of itself rather than fragmentarily as individual xperiences. It is only artificially in organismic simulations that individual experiences seem to exist of seemingly individual forms.

This makes sense because if no form exists then reality cannot manifest itself and there is no xperience possible. Obviously if no form exists the universe cannot be said to exist since existence is known only through form. If even a single form exists then reality self-manifests as that form. Forms are how reality manifests itself and it manifests itself as the xperience that is the continual re-computation of that form.

What is always manifested in form is the formless reality in which the form exists and becomes real. This is the originally formless ontological energy, the realness of being actual in a present moment, that is manifested but it must manifest in forms to manifest as xperience and thus appear and be knowable.

Pure formlessness cannot manifest. Even the putative spiritual experience of the formless actually manifests as some minimal forms, as experience itself is form, though those forms are minimal compared to the continuous multitude of forms that usually flow through mind. Without some form reality simply cannot manifest itself and thus its reality cannot be manifested.

If reality consists only of forms xperiencing manifestation then we observers too as parts of that reality are likewise only forms experiencing our own manifestation. Thus the internal simulation of reality we have tried to escape is now recognized as our own form's xperience of the manifestation of reality. Thus we finally arrive back at what we have so diligently tried to escape though we now see it as it actually is. **Reality is our experience of its manifestation in the form of our simulation of its reality** (and of course as the total *xperience* of every molecule and cell of us as well from a broader perspective).

So we are back where we started but now we have a new perspective on its true nature. We understand it from the perspective of the journey as the illusion that it actually is and the reality it actually is. **Our own simulation of reality is the actual 'external' reality we have sought but only when its deep structure is realized.**

We, as all forms, xperience reality only in our own xperience whatever that may be. The totality of our xperience of reality actually is our own simulation of that reality and that is all the reality we can experience. Even the entire theory of this book is inevitably just its experience in our simulation of reality. Thus we are forever trapped within our own simulation experience of reality. So it is inherently impossible to discover the true external reality outside ourselves. We can find it only in the forms of our own experience in our own simulations of reality.

Reality *is* its manifestation in the xperience of observers. It manifests variously in xperiences depending on the structures of the forms of those observers whether generic or organismic. Xperiences are re-computations of the forms of observers and thus highly dependent on the original forms of those observers. Xperiences are not views by observers of an independent external reality, but xperiences of the realities of themselves, of their own structures.

Xperience is always a re-computation of the structure of an observer. By its very nature it has nothing to do with any reality external to that observer except to the extent that the re-computation is due to a computational interaction with other forms that then become observed as their effects on the changes in the form of the observer itself.

We can say that all that exists is *xperience*, and in the case of organismic observers, *experience* as well. But we cannot properly say that xperience is the xperience of an xperiencer of something xperienced. All that properly exists is xperience itself. In the experiences of organismic observers experience is subsequently organized and categorized into an experiencer and what is experienced. But this categorization itself exists only as its experience. Thus there is no way around the fact that pure xperience is all that exists and is antecedent to any dualism of experiencer and experienced.

Bishop Berkeley was correct as far as he went (Berkeley, 1974). Everything does exist as experience but that experience is not properly in one's head because the head is just another experience. There is no real convincing sense in which xperience exists as the xperience *of* generic observers since there is no notion of observers in xperience itself and that is all that actually exists at that level. So at the inorganic level there is just the pure xperience of the re-computation of form itself without any context or conceptualization. All conceptualization and context is added only in the simulations of organismic observers.

So even this model of reality manifesting as the total xperience of the world of forms is itself an experience in the experience of this single observer and hopefully now in the experience of many other observers as well. But again it is always only that experience itself that exists, and to the extent of this concept this observer himself exists only as the experience of that concept.

Thus all is xperience only, and all xperience is the xperience of the self-manifestation of reality. Reality manifests itself as xperience and only thus can it manifest and become real in the ordinary sense rather than virtual. Likewise xperience is only possible because reality manifests as xperience.

But this too, and all such statements, are ultimately only a further internal simulation model of the real thing. In the final analysis reality manifests only in the experience of observers or more generally *in the xperience of all generic observers in the experience of this observer*. Without observers there simply is no manifestation of reality at all. And how can a reality that cannot or does not manifest itself be considered real and in what sense?

Without forms for reality to manifest its reality as xperience in their continual re-computations reality must be considered virtual and that was the state of reality prior to the big bang when forms first appeared and reality was first able to manifest itself as xperience.

So since reality is xperience only it is not the external observer independent reality that we sought out there independent of all observers but instead only the *xperiences* of itself including the *experience* of this observer of its representation in his simulation. And this too is only another experience! Thus the correct view of the true nature of reality always depends on the perspective on it, which is itself a necessary component of that reality. All is xperience only.

This model incorporates both a single all-encompassing reality as a computational structure as well as the notion of reality consisting only of xperiences. It also neatly integrates the notions of happening in the continual re-computations of forms and the observer as integral parts of reality.

Thus the observer no longer stands outside of reality observing it but becomes a necessary integral part of reality since reality manifests only in the xperience of observers and every form in the universe functions as a generic observer. Nevertheless the fact that this whole model, even though wonderfully self-consistent and complete, exists only in the experience of *this* observer (and hopefully a few readers of this book) remains somewhat troubling.

So viewed from the perspective of the mental models of reality, reality itself is a logical computational information structure that manifests entirely as xperience in the most generic sense. In this model the notion of observer arises seamlessly as a necessary and integral part of reality because without the generic observers which constitute it reality could not manifest its presence and as such could not exist in an observable form.

This model is also consistent with the notion of individual observer spacetimes in Part III. It also neatly incorporates the notion of an external observerless reality as a sharable illusion based on commonalities of its logical structure as simulated in the minds of observers of similar structure.

OBSERVERS AS RUNNING PROGRAMS IN REALITY

Since observers are part of reality and reality consists only of forms so all observers, including the author and the reader, must also be computationally evolving information forms, or more concisely running programs. At the most fundamental level all we actually are is enormously complex programs continually computing our own existence in the context of and in interaction with all the other running programs that constitute our environment. All the very real feelings and meanings we experience are the computed information of those things that enables our mental models of reality to simulate them as they actually are experienced.

The program that is us includes not just the computations of our conscious mind but the integrated programs of every organ, every cell and down even to the programs of the elemental chemistry and particle interactions that make up our bodies. An enormously complex system in which our functional consciousness mainly just goes along for the ride exercising a minimal quality control function.

Not only is the reality we simulate only evolving information forms but so are our simulations and so are we. How is it then that we experience reality as the bright meaningful material world in which we believe we exist and that seems and feels so real?

The answer is conceptually quite simple though difficult to grasp. We all live within a simulation of our mind's construction which programs 'us' to experience reality the way we do. We experience ourselves experiencing reality as feeling biological humans in the same way we experience the external world of forms as a bright physical reality. The information of those experiences and feelings actually is those experiences and feelings. Our experiences and feelings, as real as they are, are precisely the information of those things and the information of the reality of those things. The continual re-computation of the experiences of those things actually is the experiences of them.

This is quite clear when it is properly understood though it certainly constitutes a paradigm shift in how we think about feelings and experiences. Everything without exception is information. The feelings and meanings that seem to fill that information and give it life actually are just the information encoding those feelings and meanings. Our experiences are the information of those feelings just as everything without exception is the information of what it is. And all are given reality by arising in the actuality of being in the present moment.

Why the programs that we are feel real in the sense they do can be made clearer when the nature of feelings and meanings is understood. Under careful analysis a feeling is actually just the information of that feeling and a meaning is just the information of that meaning. The feeling and meaning themselves don't change they are just understood for what they really are as types of information. Everything without exception is actually just the information of itself.

For example it is well known that all feelings ultimately exist as electrochemical patterns in the brain, that is as patterns of information. Some of these patterns are generated or informed in response to peripheral nerve signals which are again flows of information and some arise spontaneously. And it is also known that various feelings can be generated by direct electrical stimulation of various parts of the brain.

181

Phantom feelings associated with missing limbs also demonstrate the information nature of feelings since they clearly have no physical basis. So it is clear that all feelings, no matter how real they feel, are ultimately just information signals in the brain. Thus even current biology itself agrees that all feelings are just forms of information, specifically the information of those feelings that encodes those feelings.

Likewise the meaningfulness of reality consists of a particular type of feeling associated with its various meanings. Everyone agrees that meanings are information, and the feelings of meaningfulness associated with those meanings are also just information, so ultimately there is no escaping that we ourselves consist only of the information of ourselves. All the characteristics that we interpret as our realness ultimately all reduce only to the information encoding those things. We are our information only, but that information is very real because its underlying reality is the reality of it existing in the reality of the present moment, and this is what our reality actually is. The pure information of all aspects of ourselves given reality by existing in the actuality and presence of the present moment.

That is precisely what feelings and meanings are after all. They are all just the information encoding those feelings and meanings. What else could they be but the information of what they are? When this is understood and realized it all becomes clear and self-evident.

Thus we have the information and the reality of the information. As with all forms the forms of all aspects of ourselves are the information of themselves given reality by existing in reality itself. And it is this arising in reality that gives all our experience the realness we experience.

The observer simulation is not just a passive independent recipient of xperience but itself part of the reality it simulates. All the many different simulations of reality, whether accurate or inaccurate, are themselves constituent logically integrated parts of the reality they attempt to simulate, and this in turn is simulated in simulations such as the one this book presents. So ultimately any complete simulation must simulate itself simulating itself and all other simulations simulating each other. Our theory succeeds in doing just that.

We exist not just within our simulation of reality but because our simulation is part of reality we also exist in the actual external reality itself. The external reality of our simulation realized as a simulation.

We are part of both external reality and our simulation of it, therefore everything must be taken as the absolute reality of what it is but only when properly and consistently understood for what it actually is. Our simulation, taken as a simulation, is part of external reality itself and thus we are part of the external reality we attempt to simulate.

In the final analysis we can only conclude that reality is everything exactly as it appears at whatever level. But for proper realization it is crucial our understanding of this reality is complete and consistent and therefore true. Everything exactly as it is no matter how inaccurate or mistaken is reality but reality can always be seen more clearly. Our mental model of reality is always exactly reality as it actually is in that moment. Nevertheless it can be made clearer by incorporating the understanding of its deep structure so as to reveal the unified structure of the total reality we seek.

THE UNIVERSE AS OBSERVER OF ITSELF

The entire world of forms, consisting entirely of xperience in the continual re-computation of all its forms, can be considered the xperience of the universe of itself. The entire world of forms taken as a whole can be considered as one immense program simulating its own reality, which because it is running in the substance of reality is reality. This single simulation is the only true and complete simulation of reality because it is the only one that includes everything exactly as it actually is down to the last detail. Thus only the universe as a whole truly xperiences itself as it actually is. The reality of the universe is its continual xperience of itself, and this xperience is simultaneously the self-manifestation of the reality of itself.

It is clear that no individual observer can ever truly 'know' the entire universe of which it is a part. A complete knowledge would consist not just of understanding some general principles by which the universe operates but of every last xperience of its actual operation not only from its own perspective but also from the perspectives of every one of its generic observers which is clearly impossible for any individual observer.

Extending the observer model of reality to its logical conclusion the universe itself must be considered to be the single ultimate observer of its own reality. Only the universe itself considered as a single entity composed of all its constituent forms can completely and accurately 'know' itself because every event in the universe is an xperience, and thus an xperience, metaphorically speaking, in the 'mind' of the universe. The only complete and accurate simulation of reality is reality itself because reality is the simulation of itself in the simulations of all its forms, which include all possible definitions and hierarchies of forms.

The program that is the entire universe is in effect a mind, albeit largely unconscious, that continually computes its own existence and thereby its own xperience of its own existence. It is effectively the simulation of itself. This is because xperience is the xperience of existence. In this way reality continually self-manifests itself into existence as the xperience of itself. In this sense it continually 'knows' itself because xperience is a form of knowledge.

In a sense the universe continually 'thinks' or xperiences itself into existence, and simultaneously self-manifests itself into existence as that xperience. If one wants a God, this self-manifesting self-xperiencing universe, this immanent reality of the present moment, would certainly qualify as the only possible candidate. In this sense God continually creates itself as the xperience of itself. God, or the universe if you prefer, continually re-computes itself into existence and into reality in the present moment, self-manifesting itself as the xperience of itself.

Together the self-manifestation and self-xperience of reality as the continual re-computation of forms are two perspectives on our single original axiom of existence, that existence must exist because non-existence cannot exist. Existence continually self-manifests itself into existence in a continual act of self-creation in the form of xperience. All else follows from this.

So what is the observer independent external reality we have sought? Reality is the xperience of itself; it consists entirely of the xperiences of itself by the generic observers that compose it through which it manifests itself into existence. Thus the observer independent external reality we have sought does not exist because there is no reality independent of observers because everything is an observer in the generic sense and everything is an xperience.

So in that sense our search has been entirely in vain. The external observerless reality we have sought simply does not exist! All that exists is the illusory but real models of that observerless reality in the

184

simulations of observers, and the real but unconscious xperiences of generic observers. And it is only these then, in all their various forms, that constitute the real and actual reality.

So reality consists of everything, and everything consists only of generic observers xperiencing themselves. It is the total xperience of all observers xperiencing themselves, and thus each other in their continual computational interactions. That's the model but the actual experience is always the direct xperience of a single observer, in this case you the reader. So reality consists of all observations being observed by this observer in the experience of this observer in the present moment.

Of course we must not lapse into unwarranted metaphysics. The universe as a single observer is certainly not a consciousness in the same sense that individual organisms are. It is exactly what it is as defined by the actual xperiences of its constituent forms. But on the other hand it does function as a single intelligent system because all the processes of separate observers within it all function as a single computational system.

Information does travel across this network from node to node as forms interact computationally and taken in its entirety it is an entirely consistent logical system. There can be said to be a single self-awareness to it consisting of all the networked xperiences of which it consists. But this is very much different than the consciousnesses of the individual organismic observers which it includes, and it is certainly different than the traditional view of the mind of God as a consciously all-knowing being. If this is God then God is largely unconscious.

If the universe, if reality itself, can be thought of as a single observer, then it is certainly an intelligent observer because it incorporates an intelligence of design and computation many many orders of magnitude greater than that of any individual organismic mind, human or otherwise. The question is not so much as to the intelligence of the entire structure as to whether this intelligence is 'known' in any sense other than in the minds of its individual component observers and whether or not there is any sense in which the universe as a whole can be considered to have any will, volition, consciousness or purpose. We will explore these questions more thoroughly in the upcoming Part V, The World of Forms.

It is clear however that that both generic and organismic observers can be considered the individual sense organs and distributed minds of a single dynamic intelligent logical information network. One can define this as a universal 'mind' if one merely defines that by its actual attributes and imputes nothing more than what can be actually discovered about it. One could then speculate that perhaps the natural evolution of this universal 'mind' is to progress towards greater self-awareness by incorporating more and more interconnected knowledge systems and more and more intelligent beings as more effective sensory organs of itself including of course more readers of this book. ☺. We will discuss this in more detail in Part VI, Realization.

The universe as a whole can also be considered as a living entity because it is self-motivating. Because it moves, and there is nothing external to it that moves it, it moves of itself and can thus be considered a living entity. Thus the universe, or God if one prefers, is a living intelligent entity that continually self-manifests or creates itself as the xperiences of every one of its constituent entities including you and I and every other observer, generic or organismic.

THE REALITY OF THE FORMLESS

Most of the discussions in this part of the book have been concerned with the world of forms, the individual details of reality. The simulations of observers are simulations of the form structure of reality. However both the forms of external reality and their simulations in the forms of observer models of that reality are forms that exist within ontological energy, the formless actuality of being real in the present moment. Thus besides the simulation of its forms there is the direct experience of the underlying formless reality of the ontological energy in which all forms arise.

The closer the formless reality beyond the forms is approached the more direct our experience of reality becomes because it is the forms of our mental model of reality that often obscure the underlying reality of both forms and observer. When forms become clearly recognized for the forms they are their apparent self-substances vanish and the formless appears within them. When the 'things' of the world are recognized as the forms they actually are the formlessness they manifest appears. This is nothing supernatural or metaphysical, this formlessness is simply the self-evident fact of their actual existence that makes them real and actual and present in the present moment. This is simply the realization of the underlying immanent reality of existence

186

self-manifesting itself as the world of forms.

In the previous discussion of consciousness we saw the formlessness of pure consciousness itself is not something that mind adds to reality but the actual presence of reality as participated in by an observer. The observer clearly populates consciousness with the individual forms of its own simulation of reality. But what the observer adds to the underlying consciousness itself within which these forms appear is quite tenuous and subtle and not easy to describe. It is not reality's basic characteristics of presence and actuality *per se*, which are attributes of reality, but the direct participation in those characteristics from the particular locus of the observer.

Of course this does require the actual existence and presence of an observer and certainly even these fundamental characteristics must to some degree be experienced in terms of the structure of the particular observer, but the observer does not add the fundamental characteristics of self-manifestation in the same sense as it adds and interprets forms in its simulation. It merely participates in them at the singularity of itself. Fundamentally we are the self-manifestation of reality in the form of our own form. The totality of our experience and xperience is that self-manifestation of existence as us and that includes our consciousness itself.

From this perspective then what is left when the observer vanishes is not nothingness but the formless ontological energy itself even if it is not experienced and thus does not manifest its existence. The manifestations of forms may vanish with the individual observer but the substance of reality does not vanish because it cannot vanish. Existence must exist because nothingness cannot exist and thus it remains whether manifested or not.

Forms appear out of the formless only as xperience because their continuing presence itself constitutes xperience. But the formless substance of being in which all forms arise can be said to be ever present whether xperienced or not even though this cannot be experienced because it cannot be manifested. When all forms vanish only the formless reality of ontological energy remains, but it remains unmanifested.

So we all do experience reality directly in the reality of all forms. This is how we do directly experience reality's fundamental characteristics such as realness, presence, absoluteness and happening. However the manner in which we experience the formless reality itself, as well as the

187

logical structure of the forms that appear within it, depends heavily on the structures of our own forms. We all live directly in reality and thus must necessarily experience only reality all the time, but how we experience that reality depends heavily on our own form structures since actual experience is always some re-computation of form no matter how subtle.

The fundamental common characteristic of all experience is that it has being and reality, that whatever it is, 'thought' or 'thing', it actually exists. It has presence in the present moment. It is absolute in that it is exactly what it is whatever it is and nothing else. And it manifests happening, the energy and life of continuous creation. Therefore these shared fundamental characteristics must be direct expressions of the actual nature of reality itself, at least as experienced by us.

DREAMS

Our minds continually generate a world of forms irrespective of its connection to external reality. That is what minds do, they continually create the world in which they think they exist. In a waking state there is a quality control process by which these thought forms are continually guided and corrected by reference to incoming forms sampled from the current information state of the environment so that our waking thoughts can deal with the actual ongoing logic of external reality as needed. However this is an iffy process and our minds often drift off into internal forms such as daydreams and other thoughts and feelings not directly tied to the current reality of our environment.

In dreaming sleep the mind still generates thought forms but since our sensory and motor systems are largely shut down there is little of the continual correction and guiding of thoughts back to correspondence with external forms. Thus in dreams the mind generates thought sequences of its own making that are able to wander off where they will according to internal direction only. This enables the mind to organize and refresh its internal model of reality temporarily unhampered by having to deal with ongoing events.

In fact this process also occurs to a much greater extent than recognized during wakefulness. Even when processing external forms the mind tends to look first for what it expects or wants to see and that is only corrected when disparities are recognized. This also is how our minds are so easily fooled by magicians' tricks which typically fool the mind into expecting something other than what actually occurs.

Not only does the mind continually generate its own reality whether corrected by reference to external forms or not, it also tends to generate actions on the basis of these thoughts. This is why the mind's control of bodily motions is shut down during sleep to keep dreams from being acted out. This sleep paralysis is not foolproof however and can fail in either of two ways.

The first is when one wakes and the body remains paralyzed and try as one might one cannot move one's body. It is an open question why one often has a very strong feeling of the presence of some other being in the room just out of sight during these experiences. In earlier times these were described as the presence of various supernatural or malevolent beings and more recently as alien abductions.

The second way the sleep paralysis mechanism can fail is in sleepwalking where the dreamer acts out his dreams with only minimal reference to the actual forms of external reality sometimes with tragic consequences.

Thus an understanding of the dream mechanism provides another example of how mind continually generates its own internal simulation of the reality of the external world and how that simulated reality must be constantly corrected by reference to incoming perceptual forms.

OUT OF BODY EXPERIENCES

Out of body experiences also provide insights into our simulations of reality. **The important insight from OBEs is not to understand how the location of our consciousness could be experienced as outside our body, but to understand why it is normally experienced as located inside our body!** It is only because our mind usually places the location of our experience of our self inside our body as part of its total simulation of reality that we normally experience it there. This again demonstrates another way in which every part of our simulation of the world we live in is a mental construct rather than an intrinsic logical aspect of the reality of the world of forms. The experience of a self with a felt location inside a physical body in a dimensional world is entirely a construct of mind.

Once this is understood it is quite obvious that during times of extreme threat to our physical body the mind might temporarily relocate the simulation of the conscious self to a safer location somewhat removed from the physical body in an attempt to reduce potential trauma. In fact it is theoretically possible for the mind to simulate the conscious self anywhere it likes with reference to its simulation of the physical location of the body but this certainly doesn't mean that actual sensory abilities are relocated as well. If things are seen from a different perspective it is not because the eyes are actually there but because the mind is constructing a view of reality from that perspective. More evidence that the entire dimensional view of reality we seem to inhabit is always only a mental construct.

One can also look at this from another perspective. Every experience always happens inside our own consciousness. So the fact that our mind normally locates all the 'not-self' things outside of ourselves is the real illusion. During OBEs and normal perception as well it is the rest of physical reality that is simulated as located *outside* the experience of a conscious self even though every experience is actually occurring *inside* the brain.

This because it is the direct experience of consciousness itself which is primary since it is direct experience of the actual presence of reality rather than a construct in the simulation. The experience of separate location of 'self' and 'not-selves' is simply another artifact of how our cognitive model represents reality within our minds. Our mind distributes our experiences throughout the various parts of our body and throughout space even though they are all actually occurring in the brain, or more accurately in a single realm of experience that it chooses to organize in this manner.

NEAR DEATH EXPERIENCES

As a complex system the body normally dies gradually as its various systems shut down at different rates. As this occurs consciousness tends to retreat towards its center in the primitive central area of the brain which shuts down last. The forms of the world both internal and external gradually die away and the relatively formless consciousness itself comes more into view. As in dreaming sleep when thought forms are also not continually being corrected by reference to external forms the mind then may generate its own forms representing the passage to the center of one's being.

These experiences are often reported as imagery of passing down a dark tunnel into the light, which is the light of consciousness itself at the center of being. For religious people this is often associated with religious imagery, be it meeting Jesus or angels for Christians or the Bardo Thodol passages of Tibetan Buddhists (Evans-Wentz, 1957), or the passages of the soul through the underworld described in the Egyptian Book of the Dead (Budge, 2008).

There is no evidence these experiences have any objective reality. In fact it is quite clear there can be no consciousness or experience after death since there is no longer an observer to be consciousness or any human forms to have experience. Experience is the re-computation of form and without the living form of an organismic being there are no organismic forms to re-compute and thus no possibility of experience. There is no 'soul' independent of body or mind that can exist after death.

Likewise since there is no consciousness or experience independent of a structure to support it there is no reason to believe that reincarnation has any objective reality though it clearly does have a psychological reality in that people can be regressed to 'experience' past lives.

PARANORMAL PHENOMENA

Mind simulates reality according to its own rules which are not always those of external reality. Thus there are many opportunities for discrepancies between the forms of external reality and the internal cognitive forms which simulate them. Thus it is always possible that form structures may exist in the reality of the external world which are not properly represented in our simulations. That could theoretically include some forms of 'paranormal' experiences.

However it is quite clear that since the form world must be a completely consistent logical structure that if such currently unrecognized phenomena exist they too must be logically consistent with the rest of reality. So far as we know the typically reported paranormal and supernatural experiences are not consistent with the logical structure of reality as we currently understand it.

It is clear that we are surrounded by things and events we know nothing of because we are not tuned to pick them up for what they are and thus they never appear in our simulations of reality even though their forms are an actual part of external reality. We know what many of these are but there could always be others of which we are unaware. These could be as simple as new scientific phenomena, including even dark matter and energy, or as complex as alien beings who understand our simulation structures well enough to trick them into masking their presence. It is quite clear we are able to directly perceive very little of what actually goes on in the world around us with our senses, and that is equally true of our minds as well.

Normally when unexplained phenomena are encountered, and there are many that occur every day, they tend to be ignored or rejected by our simulation as mistaken glitches in our perception of reality and quickly forgotten as irrelevant. This is typical unless they can be reliably reproduced. Thus sufficiently clever technology and slight-of-hand could certainly conceal much of reality from us. I think we all quite often see things out of the corners of our eyes that don't quite register in the ways we ascribe to normal physical objects and so are discounted as unimportant aberrations. Even phenomena as obvious as the ringings in our ears no doubt are conveying plenty of information about something whether or not it's the secret music of the spheres!

CONCLUSION

It is abundantly clear that when everything that mind adds to its internal model of reality is subtracted that all is left is a computational world consisting only of evolving information. The apparently bright colorful, physical, dimensional world we believe we live in is actually entirely a construction of our own mind and not at all the actual external reality we originally sought. It is primarily a highly embellished and fleshed out model of the interactions of our own forms with the forms of external reality rather than the direct representation of the forms of external reality it appears to be. All that it has in common with the actual external reality is enough similarity of logical structure to enable us to function reasonably effectively within external reality.

In addition we ourselves, and all other observers of whatever type down to the elementary particles as generic observers are likewise only evolving information forms or more concisely running programs in that reality. Thus even the bright colorful seemingly physical models of reality in our heads are also only computationally evolving information forms. However all these forms are absolutely real by virtue of existing in reality in the present moment. And all these internal information forms that model our experiences of the world we believe we live in *are precisely those experiences themselves*! All the meanings and feelings we experience that make our world seem so real are actually just the information conveying those meanings and feelings and their reality is due to their occurring in the actual self-manifesting presence of reality in the present moment.

The world of forms is how reality manifests itself, how it self-manifests its existence. It manifests itself as xperience which is the continual re-computation of forms into continuing existence by happening in the present moment of reality. This is the continual self-manifestation of reality into existence as xperience.

All that exists is reality, and thus our mental model of reality, as illusory as it is, is our actual experience of reality and is the actual manifestation of reality in our forms. Thus our illusory mental model of reality is reality as it actually manifests in our forms. It is our experience of reality as an observer. However only when its true nature as empty information and mostly illusory forms becomes clear does its true nature and the formless reality manifested within it appear

Thus all is xperience only. All models and theories of reality, including this one, are all ultimately only the xperiences of those models and theories. All is xperience and self-manifestation only in the continual re-computations of forms.

Thus the true nature of the external observer independent reality we have sought is not actually observer independent after all but actually consists only of the xperience of itself, including our experiences of it in the simulation we hoped to escape. Thus our simulation of reality is itself an integral part of external reality as it is simulated by other observers, and in our own experience is our direct experience of that external reality itself. However its forms are clearly a combination of our own forms with the forms of the external reality it simulates. So the reality we sought is to be found not external to our simulation, but in the true nature of that simulation because it is only in that simulation that we experience reality at all.

So if reality consists only of evolving information forms computed by running programs then what are the deep structures and rules of that world of forms? Does everything occur only at the elemental level or are higher level emergent laws and structures also part of it? In Part V we will explore the amazing hidden mysteries of the world of forms.

PART V: THE WORLD OF FORMS

THE NATURE OF FORMS

What are forms? Forms are all things without exception that have form of whatever type or level. All *individual things that can be discriminated from other things* are forms. Everything that can be discriminated or named is a form. A form is anything that has any shape or individual characteristics that distinguish it from anything else whatsoever. Forms include anything that has any structure at all and all things are their forms. And all forms are information only so that all things are the information of themselves.

The content of a form is always information, and since the structure of a form is identical to its content all forms are information only. Forms are the information contents of all things no matter what their nature; they are the abstract logical structures of things in contrast to how they appear. They are the contents of the formless presence of reality or ontological energy in which they manifest. Forms are all the ways in which that formless ontological energy manifests.

In this respect forms are analogous to the waves and currents that manifest in water. They are entirely pure abstract information and they acquire reality by appearing in ontological energy just as water waves become real by appearing in water. Forms are the shapes and all other informational aspects of things of any type without exception.

Just as water waves take on the particular forms they do in water because of the nature of water, so the forms of ontological energy take on the forms they do because of the nature of ontological energy. Water waves take on only the shapes that water can manifest but the forms of ontological energy can manifest all possible things that can exist. The forms of ontological energy can actualize any of the inherent virtual possibilities that exist in the nature of the formless ontological energy.

The forms include not just the forms of things in external observer independent reality but observers themselves are complex forms within that reality. And even the models of reality that exist in observer minds are also entirely forms encoding the interactions and relationships of observer forms with the forms of external reality.

195

In particular even all the apparent self-substances of things are only forms upon analysis, as well as all observers and all their feelings and the meanings they ascribe to things. The forms encoding all things *are* those things. Things are their forms, the information of themselves, and nothing else than that. Thus forms are not to be thought of as unreal in any sense. They are the true underlying reality of the world, the only reality of the world, other than the ontological energy in which they appear that gives them their reality and presence in the present moment.

All forms are information only. In-*form*-ation is literally what has form. All information is form and all forms are information only. Every shape, every form, of whatever type is pure information and information only. Forms must occur in some medium and in the case of the world of forms that 'medium' is ontological energy, the presence of realness and actuality. However ontological energy is not a medium in any physical sense. It is merely the living presence of reality, of existence in which all real things manifest and from which all real things acquire their reality. Ontological energy exists only in the present moment which it manifests as its presence. All the apparent media, such as water, in which the forms of the world seem to appear are themselves only associated forms upon careful analysis.

There is ultimately only one 'medium' in which all forms manifest, and that is the single medium of ontological energy, the present information space of actuality, of being, of reality. All the apparent media that support the apparent forms are themselves discriminable into the forms that define the qualities of those media as modeled in mind. Thus all that exists in the world, in the universe and in reality, are abstract information forms that all manifest the same reality of being of the underlying ontological energy of the present moment.

THE EMPTINESS OF FORMS

Because all forms are pure information in the underlying ontological energy all forms are 'empty'. That is they have none of their apparent qualities and self-substances that seem to make them what they are. Or more accurately these qualities and apparent self-substances are themselves additional associated information forms most often forms encoding the interaction of thing forms with observer forms. All forms

196

are empty in that they are diverse manifestations of the same single substance of ontological energy. Ontological energy is the 'water' in which the waves constituting all the forms of reality appear.

Forms consist of their abstract information content only. The forms of the world are all the things of the world without their apparent self-substances or qualities. What makes things things is their information content only. Under careful analysis all things are the information of themselves only. All of the apparent qualities and self-substances of things are additional forms that encode the computational interactions of the forms of external reality with the forms of observers in their internal models of external reality.

For example the apparent physical self-substance of stones is actually an association of information forms such as hardness, opaqueness, texture, heaviness and so forth which are all information describing the interactions of observer forms with the intrinsic informational structures of the chemical information of the stone. All such qualities and apparent self-substances are persistent associations of various types of forms only.

Thus the universe consists entirely of empty forms manifesting like waves, ripples and currents in the water of the possible, the formless ontological energy that fills and is reality. The universe consists only of evolving information forms. These are interpreted as the bright, colorful, dimensional, physical world of things in the minds of organismic observers. But these interpretations themselves, their meanings and feelings, are all also only empty information forms. However this reality is the true reality of our experience. It seems real and wonderful because it is real and wonderful. Nothing changes. Reality is as it always was. It just now reveals its true nature.

THE LAWS OF NATURE

By analogy with computers we can distinguish two categories of forms; data forms and code forms. Just as in computer software where code forms compute data forms these are both equally information forms whose function is in their context. The code forms are sequences of elemental operations called the laws of nature and thus all the laws of nature are an intrinsic part of nature rather than being forced to stand in some mysterious realm outside of nature as they must when nature is misrepresented as an exclusively physical world.

When all physical things are recognized as empty information forms and the world is recognized as consisting only of information then the laws of nature become a natural and intrinsic part of nature. **Only in a computational world of pure information forms do the laws of nature find their rightful place**.

The laws of nature are the computational rules of reality. They consist of a hierarchy of levels of which the most fundamental is the structural and operant laws of the extended fine tuning including the fundamental logical operators of reality which humans model as Boolean algebra. These logical operators can be considered the basic machine language code structures that are fixed and unchangeable in our universe.

At the level above that are elemental routines such as the particle property conservation law and the laws of quantum number and the other basic laws governing the structures of atoms and molecules. Above that various sequences and associations of these laws operate on increasingly complex aggregations of data forms to manifest emergent laws at greater levels of complexity. A fundamental question is whether these emergent laws consist only of sequences of lower level routines or are entirely separate laws.

At a higher level, organisms themselves are emergent self-modifying programs combining sequences of lower level machine language and callable subroutines and these are the information structures that observers experience as their existence and actions in the world. These organismic programs are *functionally* analogous to artificial intelligence systems that incorporate learning routines that modify not only their data structures but to some extent their code structures as well.

FORMS ARE DYNAMIC

All forms, even those that momentarily seem to remain the same, continually evolve. Happening is an intrinsic characteristic of the reality of the present moment and all forms are continually re-computed according to the law of nature forms in computational interaction with other forms. All forms must continually happen to remain in existence in the present moment, even those that appear to remain the same. The stone that remains more or less the same for thousands of years is continually happening to stay the same. If something does not continually happen it passes out of reality into the nonexistence of the past. Happening continuously pervades all reality and is responsible for the flow of clock time through the present moment which is the rate of its passage. Thus all forms are dynamic and evolve continually due to happening.

Only happening keeps the world alive and real and present. Without happening nothing would happen and there could be no xperience and thus reality could not manifest itself and would vanish. Happening is what gives life to the universe. Happening is the continuous presence of reality in the present moment. Without happening the present moment would collapse into the formless, back into its state of non-manifestation prior to the big bang.

FORMS ARE CONTINUOUS

Though mind conceptualizes the world as consisting of individual things undergoing individual events, the reality is that all forms exist together as a continuous dynamic computational whole. In an ocean of water, the totality of currents, waves and ripples at all scales exists as a single continuous structure in a single continuous medium of water that makes up a single ocean.

Likewise in the universe all forms exist together as one single enormously complex evolving form incorporating the continual interactions of all potentially discriminable individual forms. This is true because all forms interact and thus all forms are interconnected by the forms of their interactions. This single universal super-form consists of the continuous interaction and evolution of all individual forms. It is the complete information structure of the universe, of the totality of reality itself.

This is also very much the view of quantum theory which conceives of reality as a single enormously complex wavefunction that incorporates all individual wavefunctions (Hawking & Hartle, 1983).

MIND AS ANTENNA

Mind is like a surfer that focuses on the form of a single wave in the ocean because that is what is meaningful to its functioning. A single wave is a meaningful structure to mind but ignores the fact that the wave remains an undivided part of the continuously moving water of the entire ocean. Mind operates like this because it is computationally much simpler to compute small sets of discrete individual things and their relationships than the continuous reality of the entire interacting ocean of waves and ripples at every scale. One could say that the 'purpose' of mind is to extract forms meaningful to an organism from the entire ocean of forms.

Thus the mind's simulation of a world of discrete individual things is not the actual reality of the world but a very simplified digitalized representation. Minds have evolved to discriminate and isolate the very small subset of forms of possible importance to an organism. By necessity they are largely unconcerned with the total continuous reality in which the forms of interest are occurring. This ability to consider complex forms as discrete individual things vastly simplifies the computational load on an organism. Yes, it leaves out huge masses of data which may become relevant but if so mind can adapt to consider those individually as well. Organismic minds are very flexible computational systems. They have to be to facilitate the effective functioning of their organisms.

Thus an observer functions as an antenna tuned to pick out particular forms of interest to its functioning from the entire complex of continuous form. What is actually extracted is only the minutest fraction of what is actually going on in the very complex world of forms that constitutes an organism's environment. Organisms exhibit a near miraculous effectiveness in extracting forms important to their survival from the huge continuous flux of forms. Their perceptual antennae have been fine-tuned by billions of years of evolution to home in on information useful to their functioning.

They accomplish this by themselves having internal forms which are tuned to constructively interfere (in the sense of the interference of wave forms) with the continuous forms of their environments so as to bump up the amplitude of specific results of importance when they occur while other forms of little importance are filtered out. This is a common phenomenon in the world of forms which governs the interaction of forms in general. It is essentially the same thing that happens in a decoherence where two wavefunctions interfere to bump up an event into dimensional actuality.

THE NETWORK OF FORMS

The universe of forms is a single continuous form. Within this whole individual forms can be defined somewhat arbitrarily, though in actuality individual forms tend to be tuned on the basis of natural structural domain boundaries. Thus the single continuous form of reality can be discriminated into individual forms in a potentially uncountable number of overlapping ways. However there are many general rules by which observers discriminate individual forms from the whole such as degree of variation from background (information edges), utility, correspondence to inherent categorizations in the mental model, emotive valuations, ease of computability, discrimination of basic law of nature forms, etc. etc.

The single universal form continually evolves at what become local clock time rates in accordance with its underlying laws. From any observer perspective this can be considered as a whole dynamic network of all interconnected forms which continually evolves at local clock time rates in accordance with its law of nature forms and this includes the evolution of the forms of that observer as well. To a classical observer this network is incredibly vast and dense and includes every quantum event through all hierarchies of higher level emergent forms in one integrated logically consistent fabric of reality. As it evolves the data fabric of present moment reality is continually woven by the computations of all its forms.

All individual forms, however defined, are connected through the network to all other forms and all evolve according to self-consistent rule based law of nature sequences through clock time as a single structure in which happening acts as a ubiquitous processor that continually re-computes the entire system in the present moment.

THE UNIVERSE AS COMPUTER

The universe is a computational system that continually computes its own state of existence in the present moment. The law of nature forms are a toolbox from which higher level code sequences evolve and continually operate on the data forms to compute their evolution. Each p-time processor cycle of happening computes the current form state of the entire universe in the present moment at whatever relativistic clock time rates apply where the computations occur.

All this occurs not in dimensional spacetime but in the non-dimensional, non-physical logical computational space of reality that underlies it. This is a distributed system analogous to a ubiquitous multiprocessor system in which processing occurs at every elemental data point in the whole. For example the particle property conservation law exists inherently as part of every particle property information structure and in the nature of ontological energy itself so that every particle property packet in the universe 'knows' how to evolve at every clock cycle. This is the only way that nature could know how to behave according to the laws of nature.

The underlying process of the universe is entirely computational. It consists only of the evolution of information. New form states are continually computed from previous ones and whatever form states exist are interpreted by observers as physical things in a dimensional world in their simulations of reality by adding their own qualia to the information forms of the external data structures. But as observers are also only empty forms this whole process is actually just the additional computational evolution of forms within the observer as part of a computational universe and its interactions with the rest of that universe.

Though the underlying extended fine tuning code, and the elemental laws of nature remain fixed, new code sequences computing the occurrences of every event of the universe are continually being generated along with new data form states. Not only do the data form states evolve but so do increasingly complex emergent code structures that govern them. At the organismic level these codes structures become computationally intelligent in that they become able to self-organize to produce code designed to further instinctual imperatives through intelligent choices between mentally modeled alternatives. To at least that extent the computational structure of the universe incorporates intelligent code sequences and is programmed to learn.

REALITY AS PROGRAMS

Thus reality can be said to consist of innumerable programs analogous to a vast nexus of co-running software, all potentially discriminable aspects of the single continuously running program that is the world of forms. All individual programs exist as subroutines consistently integrated into the single program of the universe.

This is unlike individual silicon based programs with discrete processors in that each element of the whole is continually processed by happening simultaneously. The processor of happening cycles everywhere simultaneously in the present moment though always at the local clock time rate. The single processor of happening in the present moment drives the evolution of the entire system.

And unlike silicon based programs these are the living programs of reality that run in the actual here-nowness of reality and thus manifest their results as the reality of the world. They are what is actually real in the present moment and they are all that is real.

At the most elemental level are the basic logical operations analogous to the Boolean operations of silicon computers. In fact this basic logical structure must be quite similar to human logic for human logic to so well represent the logic of reality. Nevertheless there are likely some fundamental differences that must to be elucidated to arrive at a formal theory of everything.

Above that are the elemental structures and laws of nature such as the particle property conservation law which are fixed and analogous to firmware. These serve as the basic 'machine level' routines upon which the higher level programs of reality are based.

Above that are the largely automatic programs that generate the natural processes of the universe according to the aggregate operations of the laws of nature. These generate a natural universe in a statistical manner due to the probabilistic nature of quantum processes.

However at this point large scale programs begin to emerge and take on a life of their own. These expresses themselves as complex subsystems of the whole that operate as individual programs according to higher level laws they themselves generate through processes of self-organization. Though these laws all operate through complex sequences of lower level routines they exhibit higher level directives when considered in aggregate as individual systems.

This becomes quite clear at the level of organismic programs, the programs that actually are the various living organisms of the world. While each of these ultimately operates only through calls on basic processes invoking the elemental laws of nature, organisms clearly operate as intentional systems toward the fulfillment of the high level directives encoded in their instinctual software. And they clearly operate intelligently in the sense that they compute optimal actions from possible sets of actions in fulfillment of instinctual and other imperatives.

But emergence does not stop with the computational behavior of individual organisms. There are even more complex programs executing all the social and historical processes of organismic aggregates each of which has a life of its own and exists as an actual running program in the world of forms. These independently operating actual programs in the world of forms are responsible for the evolutionary history of life forms and the major flows of human history and compute and generate all social and cultural processes.

Thus the world of forms consists of all such programs at all levels simultaneously operating and interacting to compute the actual state of reality in the present moment. Each one of us and every other thing in the universe as well exists as a subsystem in this overall system and operates in tightly coupled interaction with it. These programs execute everywhere driven by the processor of happening continually cycling at the local clock time rates.

Because they are continually run by the processor of reality they are all living programs in the sense that they are real and actual and happening. Thus the entire universe, the entire world of forms is a living program consisting of innumerable living subprograms continually interacting together to compute the universe of the world of forms at every instant.

Reality is the present moment result of the interactive computations of myriads of discriminable programs operating simultaneously as a single system. These programs run in happening in the present moment and thus are the self-manifestation of reality. This is the true fundamental nature of the world of forms and of the universe it manifests in the xperience of observers. It is the self-manifestation of reality as the xperiences of all forms.

And all observers are themselves running programs, computational forms continually computing among all the other computational forms. In concert all these programs together weave the information fabric of reality, in concert together they all produce the information harmony of the Uni-Verse.

The world consists of information only. The re-computation of information at every instant constitutes the xperiences of generic observer forms. Thus it is more accurate to say that all that actually exists is the current computational results of all the living programs of reality, each computation of which manifests reality as xperience as the current state of forms.

FREE WILL

Unlike silicon based computers the computations of the world of forms are not entirely deterministic because they do not filter out quantum randomness as silicon computers are designed to do. Instead the probabilistic manner in which spacetime emerges from decoherence events is incorporated at the level of elemental computations. The result is that every bounded area of the entire universal computational system has some free will in the sense that its computations are not entirely determined by computations either external to it or prior to it. This is why all organisms have some degree of free will because their microstructure consists of quantum processes and, depending on the details of their structures, the randomness of these processes percolates up through their computational hierarchy as it is organized into decision making at the scale of the whole organism.

The proper understanding of free will is that the information form computations occurring within any bounded system, in particular any organism, are not necessarily completely determined by either computations external to that bounded system or by prior computations within the bounded system.

Organisms certainly respond to external events and they operate in accordance with their instinctual needs to eat, drink, survive and procreate but they do this with computational intelligence and with a considerable degree of freedom from external causes. It is in this sense that all organisms exhibit free will, as in fact does any bounded area of the whole universal computational system. The fact that the computational structure of organisms is highly complex relative to inorganic systems means that organisms typically exhibit much greater free will simply because they have many more networks and hierarchies of 'moving parts' involved in their functioning for random processes to affect.

The popular notion of free will as the decision making independence of a small area of consciousness from the rest of an organism conceived of as deterministic is an illusion based on the mistaken notion of one's self being identical to one's ordinary consciousness rather than one's entire being. It is the entire being that is a computational system, certainly not just consciousness which at best serves mostly a quality control function and as a reward system.

ALL RANDOMNESS IS QUANTUM

There is no true randomness at the classical level. All actual randomness is the result of quantum randomness filtering up and manifesting at the classical level in the particular information structures in which it becomes amplified. But we must be careful here because there really is no independent classical level. In all respects the so called classical level is the emergent appearances of our familiar human scaled world from the interaction of quantum processes. The classical world is actually the transient emergence of the macro-scale appearance of physicality rather than any actual physical objects or processes.

Thus all apparent randomness at the classical level is quantum. There simply are no classical level laws of nature which are not deterministic. Therefore there can be no source of randomness at the classical level. In particular the classical statistical laws are generalizations describing random quantum processes in aggregate.

So the source of all apparent randomness at the classical level is actually amplification of quantum randomness. There is considerable confusion on this point because much of what is thought to be randomness at the classical level is actually non-computability, the inability to compute the information sequences involved due to their complexity. The weather is a good example of combined non-computability and quantum randomness in a very complex system.

The classic example of throwing dice is another illustrative example. The fall of dice is entirely deterministic down to the quantum level, but it is effectively non-computable due to the complexity of the calculations and the similarity of the faces of the dice. So again the apparent randomness at the classical level resolves into a combination of both classical non-computability and quantum randomness with no classical randomness at all.

We tend to think of the future as unpredictable but in fact it is almost entirely predictable. If the future state of reality was not almost entirely predictable from moment to moment it would be impossible to function or even exist. We live in a delicate and precise balance of predictability and randomness in which we are able to predict most of the future well enough to function while having just enough of the spice of randomness to make things interesting and allow free will. This exquisite balance is one more remarkable aspect of the extended fine tuning that makes human life as we know it possible.

THE CAUSAL NETWORK

The entire temporal network of forms in the universe is traditionally thought of as the causal network. It is conceived as a sequence in which temporally prior data form states 'cause' subsequent ones along their sequential connections from node to node in the positive time direction. While essential to organismic functioning this view is erroneous in several important respects.

First the proper view of the causal model itself is not the usual simplistic view that one single event causes another. The actual information and program network is enormously dense and complex and includes a huge hierarchy of nested levels and connections from the most elemental to the highest each of which constantly interacts with innumerable others and within which very complex feedback loops and other types of nonlinear structures can occur. Causality is never anywhere near the simplicity of event A causing event B, because there are always innumerable events along many interlinked causal chains to every event. Not only that, but the network stretches back not just to immediately prior events but back to the beginning of time in an unbroken computational chain. Insofar as causality holds the big bang can be thought of as the ultimate cause of every event.

Aristotle and others recognized this problem and identified various classes of causes such as proximate, necessary and sufficient (Aristotle, Vols. 17, 18, 1989). Proximate causes being events immediately antecedent to an effect; necessary causes referring to events without which the effect would not have occurred; and sufficient causes referring to events in themselves sufficient to produce the subsequent effect. While these classifications are useful they do not begin to capture the overall view of the enormous network of events linked to every effect.

FROM CAUSALITY TO CONSISTENCY

However there is far more serious problem with the usual view of causality. The traditional concept of causality comes from the common sense conception of a physical universe in which prior events impart little physical push-like effects to subsequent events thus bringing them into existence. However there are insurmountable problems with this model.

Causality is imagined as a mysterious universal mechanism of unspecified nature that is responsible for subsequent events appearing after previous events. However carefully thought through it is clear that causality is simply a name given to the fact that subsequent events follow previous events according to computational rules and there is actually no such universal physical mechanism. In fact **no such general physical mechanism of causality is actually described anywhere in any of the equations of science**. Thus causality turns out to be an interpretive categorization of temporal sequence rather than an actual physical aspect of nature. It stands outside of science itself and thus is a metaphysical concept rather than an actual physical mechanism.

Science does describe specific individual forces that are imagined to effect changes but never any general causal force. However all those particular forces actually boil down only to descriptions of subsequent states in terms of previous ones. Though they are considered 'physical' we have seen that all apparent physicality is an artifact of how reality is simulated in the minds of observers. What is simulated as a physically felt push is actually an internal feeling, an information form interpreted as a feeling, due to a change in the forms involved, or a displacement of the forms involved, rather than an actual physical mechanism in external reality. The apparent results of forces is actually the result of the computations on the information which is their actual reality rather than anything physical.

Science actually consists of its mathematical equations not the interpretations of those equations. The equations work because reality itself is a computational structure. Thus causality is simply a descriptive name for the general concept of temporal sequences of equations rather than anything actual. It is the projection of the apparent before and after sequences of mental representations of events to a world simulated as physical but which is actually computational.

Because the form network of reality is entirely informational rather than physical there can be no causality in the sense of physical things somehow pushing other physical things into existence. That is as illogical as saying that $2 + 2$ *causes* 4. Previous information states do not 'cause' subsequent states; rather they evolve into them in conformance with the laws of nature. Because there are no physical things there can be no physical causality. What actually happens is all forms continually evolve and interact according to their intrinsic logical rules. Change is a logical sequence or progression rather than a physical network of causality. There simply is no actual causal force, there are only forms continually evolving according to intrinsic computational rules.

So under analysis causality reduces to only temporal sequence. There is no physical motive power by which any form 'causes' any other form. There is only a rule based computational sequence of forms just as there is in running software. Thus we must abandon the notion of physical causality and replace it with that of abstract information structures consistently evolving according to natural logical rules. The idea of causality must be replaced by that of consistent evolution of forms; that is of information evolving according to consistent rules.

Consistency is the key here. What consistency means is that all form sequences always evolve by the consistent rules of nature and these rules are such as to form only internally consistent chains so that wherever they might converge in common events they are always logically compatible with each other. There will never be cases in which the form structures of converging chains no matter from how far apart in the universe they have converged are inconsistent when intersecting in common events. Thus all form chains are always able to interact without any logical contradiction. No part of the universe can be logically inconsistent with any other.

The internal self-consistency of forms is the fundamental rule of the world of forms. If the universe was not a logically consistent and logically complete system it would tear itself apart and could not exist.

HOW THE PRESENT DETERMINES THE PAST

The implications of this paradigm shift are profound. If causality evaporates into only temporal sequence and what is happening is just the logical evolution of forms then we cannot claim that the past 'causes' the present, at least in the usual sense. We can however say that the past determines or necessitates the present if we understand that these words are to be understood in a purely logical rather than physical sense. That is the forms of the past could have evolved only into the forms of the present as they actually are and not into any other forms so in that sense the past has determined the present. This determination was not absolute of course since it contained an element of constrained quantum randomness which we will consider shortly.

But the key insight is that if we accept the form world as a consistent logical structure through time there is an even stronger sense in which the *present* determines the *past*! Because the actual fact of the reality of the present form structure of the universe as it is absolutely requires that the past is/was absolutely as it was in every detail even down to every quantum event. With absolute certainty there could not have been any other past with even the slightest variation whatsoever that would have resulted in the present being exactly as it is! Therefore the current state of the present absolutely requires that the past be exactly as it was. Thus the present determines the past much more strongly than the past can be said to have determined the present. Because due to quantum randomness alternate variations in the present could have evolved from the same past, but given the actual present there can be only one single exact possible past that evolved into it.

However this raises the problem of how do we actually know what the past was? The problem is that the only way we actually know (or think we know) the past is not by direct experience of it which is clearly impossible but precisely by backward projection of the present state of the information structure of reality! So there is a circularity here since the past is always entirely an imaginary phantom constructed by projecting the current state of things backward to deduce what would have been necessary to evolve into the present. So there is really no sense in which there is any past at all other than our backward projection of it from the present.

Thus claiming that there was a past which evolved into the present comes full circle because we deduced that past only by imagining what would have evolved into the present from which we deduced that past! The whole exercise is a circular argument of questionable credibility. And it only makes sense because the logical rules by which we conduct this exercise seem to consistently work in all situations. But of course that whole argument depends on the same fact of its application to its seemingly successful *past* applications.

But since we actually do see the past at distance in the present doesn't that allow us to confirm our backward projection of the (local) past from the present? Certainly if so only to a limited extent. But there is a problem here since what we see at distance in the past we actually see only in the present. We have good reason to believe what we see in the present is the image of the actual past of distant forms but there is no absolute way to verify this since there is no possible way to actually be there in the past to confirm it.

The fact that the past does not exist and is not real adds another element of uncertainty. There is a fundamental sense in which it is meaningless to say anything about something which does not even exist! The whole meaning of past tense can only be a backwards projection from the present of what form states would have evolved into the actually existing current form states. In a very fundamental sense saying something 'was' is meaningless and is only another convenient artifact of our simulations. Memory after all is always only a present simulation of something that does not exist though we assume it once did but which we can never actually confirm.

So the fundamental insight here is that the form state in the present moment is all that exists; and that if we project a currently non-existent consistent rule based evolution of forms through clock time then we must accept that there must be (and have been) a mutual simultaneous

211

absolute bidirectional determining or necessitating of form evolution in both temporal directions. And this temporal structure is absolutely deterministic in both temporal directions in every last detail. It is entirely fixed and unalterable.

Thus there is (was), with one end in the present actually being the present information state of reality, a single evolved form structure which is the same (though backwards & forwards) in both directions, which is consistent in both directions, and absolutely determinative or necessitating in both directions simultaneously. The total computational history of forms is a consistent necessary temporally bidirectional structure. But of course it must be understood this entire conceptual model exists only as a fundamentally un-provable hypothesis and conceptual form *in the present*.

Saying there 'was' a past is not the same as saying there 'is' a past. Saying 'was' implies there is not actually a real extant past. The whole idea of the past turns out to be a present fiction impossible to actually verify by experience though logically consistent. The past does not actually exist. It is only a logical deductive sequence in the present by backwards extrapolation of logical temporal sequences to arrive at what we believe would have evolved forward in time to produce the present as we know it. In other words the past actually exists *only* as its information traces or information consequences in the present and it is these we use to deduce what we think it would have been in the past.

This raises the basic epistemological question of how do we actually 'know' anything at all since everything except immediate experience is in effect a past memory in this same sense and only the minutest fraction of what we consider our knowledge actually exists in the present except as selective and likely flawed representations in memory. There are so many ways in which knowledge seems illusory, and this is certainly one of them. The whole exercise is an analogy by extension of the short term memory mechanism of logical sequence in the perceived present moment extended as a general principle into the deeper past. But since the process does work sufficiently to allow organisms to function there must be some validity to it, at least in the short term scope of computing organismic actions.

BACKWARDS DETERMINATION FORWARD UNCERTAINTY

Consistent with this is the fact that all the laws of physics with few exceptions work equally well both backwards and forwards in time (Wikipedia: Time reversibility). This confirms our thesis that the logical determination of forms is temporally bidirectional. Quantum wavefunction 'collapse' was thought to be an exception but this interpretation has now been replaced by the theory of decoherence in which wavefunctions do not collapse but simply interact in a manner which seems equally valid in both temporal directions though again in the forward direction stochastically and in the backward direction deterministically.

The other exception was thought to be entropy but this appears not to be true either. Entropy is simply the aggregate measure of distribution states of elemental matter under the influence of prevailing forces. However as previously explained in Part II, this is not a fundamental principle of reality but an artificial measure dependent on the actual mix of prevailing forces. From this perspective there is nothing at all in the equations that govern the interactions of the elemental particles that cannot be run backward according to the same equations that governed their forward temporal motions.

With regards quantum randomness, the present determines the past absolutely but the past could theoretically have evolved into a different present. However it did not. The present as it exists is the only present that can exist because it is the only present that does exist and the fact of its existence therefore falsifies all other possible presents and pasts.

Presumably when the past was the present the stochastic nature of the evolution of the world of forms could have worked out differently to produce a different present. But this is a hypothetical view from a past which does not exist. In the view from the present which does exist things could not have been different coming forward from the past down to the results of every last random quantum process.

Some may raise a further objection here. Even if the present uniquely determines the past one could still imagine another possible present. But this leads us to a contradiction because that present would then of course determine another unique past! Therefore we must reject the possibility that the past could have led to any other possible future than it did. And of course the existence of the actual present immediately falsifies any other possible presents.

We must deal only with reality as it actually is and all other possibilities that do not exist are not reality and have nothing to do with reality. So in that respect there is no reason to assume that anything other than what does exist including other fine tunings could actually have existed. We must reject the view that the past could have produced alternate futures because it obviously did not.

The status of 'could have' is extremely questionable especially when falsified by the absolute of what is. The whole problem of giving 'could have beens' any validity may be due to an over extension of syntactical logic to situations to which it does not apply. It seems reasonable to say the key could have been under the mat but when we find it in our pocket then we know with certainty it could NOT have been under the mat. We must not let the innate assumptions of language evolved to describe the simple logic of daily things and events mislead us. Reality is always exactly and absolutely what it is and could be nothing else than it is even if we can imagine that it could be.

So the correct view seems to be that the world is exactly and absolutely as it is with no possibility of even the slightest variation, and the view that the past could possibly have evolved into a different present is nonsensical since only the actual present exists. In this way we arrive at a completely deterministic system in both temporal directions between the present and any point in the past. Syntactical logic, with its simplistic concepts of past tense, has a difficult time of accurately describing the temporal consistency of actual reality.

Thus it only makes strict logical sense to speak of quantum probability from the perspective of the present towards the future since the future does not actually exist and thus there can be no such contradiction. Thus the future is continually being determined probabilistically in the computations of the present, but the past into the present is entirely fixed and completely deterministic in both temporal directions.

Thus the logical structure of reality is logically consistent and completely deterministic in both temporal directions from past to present and from present to past, but subject to constrained randomness from the present towards an as yet undetermined and nonexistent future. However we must always remember this entire logical structure actually exists not in actual reality but entirely in the present in computational directedness and organismic mental models of the logic of temporal sequence from past to present to future.

BEYOND THE ANTHROPIC PRINCIPLE

This discussion applies directly to the problem of the fine tuning (and by extension our extended fine tuning) of the universe; that is why the particular values of the fundamental constants are so conducive to intelligent human life when only small variations in any of them would have produced a universe in which intelligent life could never have evolved (Davies, 2007).

It is immediately clear that if it is the present that actually determines the past then it is the very fact of our existence in the universe, as it is absolutely self-evident, that requires the fine tuning be exactly as it was, or more accurately as we think it had to have been to result in the exact actual present that includes us.

This takes us beyond the anthropic principle which states that the fine tuning must have been such as to result in intelligent life only because we intelligent life forms are here to ask the question. The problem with the anthropic principle theory is that its corollary is that the fine tuning in our universe is a statistical accident out of an immense set of equal possibilities which is actually quite an enormously unwarranted assumption which in turn leads to all sorts of convoluted multiverse sidetracks (Vilenkin, 2006). But there is a much more reasonable alternative for the fine tuning.

Stated in terms of consistency the past must by necessity be consistent with the present and therefore the fine tuning must be exactly as it is and could not have been otherwise. One might try to argue that the present could have been other than it is. But it actually couldn't be other than it is since that is conclusively falsified by the fact of its existence as it is. The syntactical logic of language has misled us because the present is and therefore must be absolutely as it is. Therefore the past as we conceive of it must be/have been exactly what is now consistent with what would have produced the present over time via the laws we impute to the evolution of forms. This uniquely determines the fine tuning exactly as it originally was and still is.

This in itself solves the problem of why the universe seems designed for intelligent life, specifically us, to exist. It must have been designed such because we do exist and our existence requires that the original fine tuning and the entire computational history of the universe must have been exactly such that the entirety of the universe, including us, exists exactly as it does, because the very fact of its and our existence falsifies all other possibilities.

The fact that this argument seems counter intuitive is only because we have a false interpretation called causality which we must discard in favor of the logical consistency of a computational reality, and the false notion of a real past when only the present moment is actually real and by its existence uniquely determines the past that led to it being thus.

Thus the fine tuning could only have been exactly as it is/was because it had to have been so to produce the actual present that actually exists. Since the actual present does exist, the past that resulted in it is the only one that could have existed. This solves one of the major questions bedeviling modern science and essentially eliminates the need for all varieties of multiverses.

THE CONSISTENCY CONJECTURE

There is an additional possible explanation for the extended fine tuning which is not an alternative but compatible. I suspect that when what I call the extended fine tuning, that is the total irreducible fundamental structure of reality, is clarified it will turn out that it is exactly as it is because that is the only possible fine tuning that produces a self-consistent and logically complete universe and thus it is the only possible fine tuning that can exist. Thus from this perspective as well there is only one possible fine tuning and that is the one our universe has.

I propose this as 'The Consistency Conjecture' and if it is confirmed it will help solve one of the most fundamental problems of reality; why what exists is what exists. I suspect the consistency conjecture can and will be demonstrated. The theory that the fundamental structure of our universe is the only one possible because any alteration would introduce fatal inconsistencies in its logical structure is certainly an elegantly simple and beautiful theory. Whether it is true or not remains to be determined.

If the Consistency Conjecture does turn out to be true it will revolutionize scientific thinking and eliminate most of the rationale for the current proliferation of theories requiring multiverses, pocket or bubble universes, and probably a lot of string and M theory as well because these are in large part all attempts to account for the assumed statistical unlikelihood of our particular fine tuning assuming all possible variations were equally possible. The assumption that all possible variations in the fine tuning are possible has no rationale behind it whatsoever and is raised only because no specific reasons for the fine tuning have been thought to exist. When such reasons are discovered, and I believe they will be as the extended fine tuning is explored, the universe will become a much simpler and more elegant place.

Consistency means that in any network of logical forms a contradiction between validly derived statements is never encountered. In other words one never encounters a statement that any x however defined is equal to not x. Of course this depends on the original logical premises of the system themselves being consistent so that they never result in such a contradiction. In the universe these original *a priori* irreducible premises are the complete set that composes the extended fine tuning, whatever that may include.

THE LOGIC OF REALITY VERSUS HUMAN LOGIC

Complicating the problem is correctly representing the actual computational logic of reality with human logic. Human logic and mathematics are clearly only generalized approximations of the actual world of forms logic that computes reality. There is only one single actual logico-mathematical system of reality but humans have devised a number of different human logics and mathematics. The actual logic of a fully consistent reality can include none of the contradictions and paradoxes that human logical systems can. It can only compute what is actually real.

The actual logic of reality is the complete set of computational rules of the laws of nature and their underlying logic. It is the complete logico-mathematical system of reality that governs the structure and evolution of the world of forms. Human logic and mathematics includes a number of generalizations that do not apply to the physical world. These include infinities and infinitesimals which do not occur in our finite universe whose elemental structure is granular rather than continuous.

Other possible aspects of human mathematics that may not exist in the actual mathematics of reality are zero and null sets, various types of self-reference and recursion (e.g. Gödel numbers), and likely some other inconsistent or unnecessary assumptions.

AN ULTIMATE THEORY REQUIRES A NEW FORMAL LANGUAGE

Because of the differences between the logico-mathematical system of reality and human logic and mathematics it is almost certain that the ultimate theory of everything will have to be expressed in a new symbolic structure that more accurately maps the actual computational structure of reality.

Human mathematics and logic are fundamentally just games with rules. When one knows the rules and the often purposely arcane abbreviated symbol structure it is fairly easy to understand because it all follows the stepwise rules of logic which are in essence quite simple. The problem is coming up with software that is based on a logico-mathematical system that accurately describes all aspects of the actual world of forms.

There is also the fundamental problem of the structural nature of forms themselves that the logic operates upon. Human logic assumes discrete things, properties and relationships upon which its rules operate but it is not at all clear that the actual forms of reality are discrete or whether discrete things are only a characteristic of the interference of the intrinsically continuous forms of observers with the intrinsically continuous forms of external reality in a sort of decoherence of discretenesses.

We need to clarify what we mean here. At the finest elemental logical level of reality it is likely that reality is indeed discrete or digital, however at the level of our experience it is pretty clear that instead of being composed of interactions of discrete classical things and their relationships, it is composed of a continuous flux of highly interacting elemental aspects of things which is fundamentally granular but which manifests more as continuous functions than individual interacting things.

Consider again the analogy of an ocean of water. At the atomic and molecular level it is granular and at the macro level behaves as a continuous body of water. However the surfer thinks of it in terms of individual waves and their relationships because these individual things 'decohere' out of the continuous ocean as it interferes with his model of the reality of what an ocean is. His wave antenna isolates wave forms out of a continuous flux of water. All these views are proper and must be included in the ultimate theory of the reality of the ocean of reality.

The validity of ordinary logic depends entirely on the discrimination of stable well defined things and relationships. In the real world of forms, from which discrete things are tuned from huge fluxes of sensory data forms and then organized by minds, things are inherently fuzzy and often difficult or impossible to exactly define so it is not at all clear how well a logic based only on exact discrete things can represent the actual logic of reality. One cannot easily or consistently apply human logic to A if A is continually changing its stripes. Thingness at least aggregate thingness is always changing. Human logic itself may be valid but how applicable it is to the real world of forms remains to be seen. Even the usual discrimination of forms into things, properties, relationships, laws etc. may not accurately represent the true underlying structure of forms.

In our wonderfully flexible syntactical logic the definitional descriptions of things often vary according to context. A thing originally identified as ice cream may soon be considered a mess. Things regularly transform to other things and while formal logic finds it difficult to cope the syntactical logic of English copes quite well however it does not always produce a tightly valid logical sequence when it does so. In general syntactical logic works fairly well on limited form sets within which the basics of form structure can be assumed constant but not across such limits where one must continually redefine things in the middle of logical sequences. That inherently limits the scope of logical description of a reality that is always in flux. So clearly both formal logic and syntactical logic are ill-suited to exactly describing the true continually changing definitional complexities of reality. Formal logic works only on small temporary sets where definitions are artificially held constant and fails at the points they alter.

There has been some recognition of some aspects of this problem even by mathematicians and attempts to generate mathematical systems that more accurately represent the actual structure of reality for example by Gregory Chaitin in his attempt to define numbers that accurately map a granular universe without infinitesimals (Chaitin, 2006).

Numbers in human mathematics can have any degree of precision, but actual physical numbers are necessarily limited in precision because there are minimum and maximum size limits to things in the universe. The actual number system of reality is not the same as the human number system's idealized generalization of that physical number system. For example it appears that counted numbers have a different status in this respect than descriptive numbers. The number of atoms in an aggregate may be exact at any time but the numeric descriptors of say sizes of atoms have inherent limits of precision. The exact characteristics of the number systems used in the computational system of reality need to be clarified, if in fact numbers in themselves divorced from specific data forms actually exist.

GÖDEL'S THEOREM DOES NOT APPLY

Gödel's Incompleteness Theorem is an example of how human logic and mathematics need not apply to the logico-mathematical system of reality. Gödel showed that there will always be true statements in arithmetic whose correctness can never be demonstrated from the axioms of arithmetic and thus that arithmetic is logically incomplete. Gödel's theorem is a proof that in human logico-mathematical systems of the complexity of simple arithmetic that is it is always possible to have true statements that cannot be proved by valid logical sequences from their axioms.

However the logic of reality is computational, that is all current states are the computed results of prior states. Thus it is impossible that any actual current logical state cannot be derived from prior states because that is the only way they are produced. If Gödel's proof did apply to the logico-mathematical system of reality there would be actual events which existed but could never be generated which is a contradiction and thus impossible. Therefore Gödel's proof cannot apply to the logical structure of reality. Therefore the logical structure of human mathematics does not accurately represent that of reality. Thus Gödel's proof proves not only what it sets out to prove, but also that human mathematics does not accurately represent the mathematics of reality.

Also Gödel's proof of his theorem depends on the existence of a particular type of recursion that allows metalanguage statements in which an arithmetic proof are formulated to be treated as statements in that same arithmetic in the form of what are called Gödel numbers (Hofstadter, 1980). Thus it seems obvious for starters that this type of recursion is not part of the actual logic or mathematics of reality and applies if at all only to human mathematical systems.

Thus while human mathematical systems under certain assumptions are provably incomplete the logico-mathematical system of reality is necessarily complete and internally consistent. Since the universe must be entirely consistent to exist we would expect that it would be possible to construct a consistent human logico-mathematical system to accurately model the mathematical logic of reality but to accomplish this basic changes in our ideas about mathematics and logic will be required. A logico-mathematical system must be specifically designed to accurately model that of reality, and it must be computational since the logic of reality is a computational system.

Gödel's theorem certainly does not invalidate the primacy of logic as the fundamental principle of the world of forms. In fact he proves his theorem with logic. His proof would never have been accepted if he had not used logic and not used it rigorously.

The main issue here is the implication of Gödel's theorem for the logical structure of reality. If Gödel's theorem were true and human logic was an accurate representation of the physical logic of reality then there is something wrong with the universe. We would have to conclude that there are things that occur in the universe which have no well-defined logical antecedents. And that the logical structure of the universal logical network has discontinuities, areas which do not connect to other areas. And that the entire logical network cannot be traversed, including both backwards and forwards in time, from some arbitrary event A to another arbitrary event B. But in a computational universe as we have proposed it this is impossible. This is one more strong additional line of reasoning that the universe is indeed a computational system as we have described it.

Turing's halting problem deals with the same issue from a computational perspective (Penrose, Chap. 2, 1990). A computational system which cannot logically reach B from A will run forever trying every possible computational path to do so. If the system halts having found B from A, we know the system is consistent and complete through that path at least, but if it has not halted in some specified time does it just need more time or is the system actually incomplete? Turing was able to prove that for a general definition of a computer (Turing machine) and program state it is impossible to decide whether it will ever halt or not. In other words the Halting Problem is undecidable in general. The only way to tell for sure is to determine whether all possible paths have been tried. In the actual universe of course such an experiment is impossible and completely unnecessary.

Again the Halting Problem does not apply to the running programs of a computational universe since all states actually are computed directly from prior states. Therefore such a universe is automatically consistent and complete. What the Halting Problem might tell us, assuming the logic of reality is the same as the logic of Turing machines, is that it is impossible to predict whether any given hypothetical future state of reality could or could not ever be computed in all possible cases. In other words there might be some seemingly reasonable and possible hypothetical future state of reality that could never be computed by reality even if it seems a state consistent with the current state of reality. For any particular hypothetical state this might be undecidable.

In any case as we have previously stated, the world of forms must be entirely consistent and complete because if it were not it would tear itself apart at the inconsistencies and pause not knowing what to compute at the incompletenesses and thus could not exist.

SCIENCE AS SIMULATION

Reality is a self-contained computational system thus to effectively model it science should be as well. Science should be entirely reformulated as a self-contained simulation of reality implemented in software.

Reality is a computational structure similar to running software. Thus the best scientific model of reality must be software as well, ultimately a single simulation software that works on any data state entered to correctly predict subsequent states in any situation. A shortcoming of current science is that it exists as scattered equations divorced from their natural logical computational framework. Only a software program that actually computes science puts those equations in their natural logical framework and so completes the structure of a scientific model of reality.

In comparison current science conceived as equations scattered among language sentences is imprecise and inactive. It does not compute reality by itself but necessarily depends on fallible human involvement to set up computations. A true scientific model would remove humans from the computational process and operate entirely on its own. Only then could science be considered a complete system.

A single program that computes it would be the best possible model of reality, because that must incorporate the logical framework as well as the mathematics that exists within it. A collaborative wiki type program starting with the complete extended fine tuning and the basic laws of nature that anyone qualified could update and exhaustively tested for accuracy across the largest scope of reality; this will be the science of the future.

In a universe that consists only of information and programs there don't need to be physical mechanisms to explain things. We need only a self-consistent computational system in accord with observations. This greatly frees up the range of possible explanations and allows us to break free of many interpretations and lets the software speak for itself about what constitutes reality. This is a new paradigm for science.

The criterion of true knowledge then becomes maximum consistency across the entire range of information in a system with the minimal number of independent axioms, those irreducible information forms which constitute the extended fine tuning of the universe.

This is what we seek in a TOE, a theory of everything, encompassing the whole of science as a description of reality and upon which all human knowledge is based through consistency with it. Current science exists as mathematical fragments each describing some aspect of physical reality and this exists in a largely unrecognized and unstated intuitive logical framework necessary for the mathematics to make sense.

The very fact that science currently consists of mathematical descriptions is clear though unrecognized evidence that reality itself is a computational system rather than the usually imagined physical material world. Science best describes reality *with* a logico-mathematical system thus reality *must itself be* a logico-mathematical system. This is self-evident when it is clearly understood. How else could a logico-mathematical system correctly represent a physical universe if that physical universe was not actually a logico-mathematical system itself? Again we have another convincing line of proof that reality is a computational information system rather than a physical one.

Of course there are disparities between science's logico-mathematical system and that of reality. Human science is a selective approximation and its form and medium are not completely up to the whole task. Thus science also requires a new formal language which more accurately models the actual language of forms of reality itself.

The complete TOE will consist not of science in its current form but of a simulation model of the actual logico-mathematical system of reality based on the actual logico-mathematical structure of reality rather than the current human logico-mathematical structure. This will be a single computer model which when input with any possible actual data state will accurately evolve that data state in accordance with how it would evolve in the computational system of the universe itself. Only thus can we achieve the next level of accuracy of our TOE.

Fundamental scientific progress will consist of attempting to model the entire logico-mathematical system of reality as outlined in this book with a simulation model based in a new logico-mathematical language of reality. Such a simulation model can be the only acceptable TOE.

And that TOE must incorporate all the insights of this book recognizing that not all of reality is mathematical but all of reality is logical and thus subject to encoding in software. To be complete a TOE must incorporate the logic of consciousness and the present moment, and all the other non-mathematical aspects of reality science currently ignores as 'philosophical' but it must also incorporate mathematics as needed.

THE EXTENDED FINE TUNING

What I call the extended fine tuning is the set of all the fundamental irreducible information forms and code structures of the universe, and more generally of reality, that cannot be derived from any others. Since they don't appear to be the consequences of anything else, there appears to be no particular reason for the extended fine tuning being as it is so why is it what it is and not something else? This is the fundamental unanswered question about why reality is what it is. What presumably small set of facts about the universe is fundamental and why? It is these alone that will be sufficient to logically derive the entire rest of reality.

Though not a complete listing the extended fine tuning includes the usually accepted fine tuning of science plus all the fundamental characteristics of reality detailed in this book and no doubt others as yet undiscovered as well.

The standard fine tuning of science consists of the 25 freely adjustable parameters of the Standard Model plus one for gravity though there are other versions favored by some (Wikipedia: Fine tuning). These are the fundamental constants whose values seem to be completely independent and arbitrary with no known reasons for why they are what they are in our universe. These typically include the values for the speed of light, the gravitational constant, the Planck constant, the fine structure constant and other independent constants that determine much but certainly not all of the structure of our universe.

However it is clear that this standard fine tuning is not all that is necessary to produce the universe as we know it. These standard lists omit many additional fundamental aspects of reality that also seem arbitrary and irreducible, many of which we have described in this book.

There are a number of other fairly obvious components of the extended fine tuning. For example the very fact that the specific elementary particles that exist are the ones that do exist. It is certainly possible to imagine a theoretical universe without electrons, or protons, or any other particle. Why this exact particular set with all of their exact characteristics? And why are they all composed of the same small particular set of particle properties? Why is it that it takes a little bit of particle type, charge, mass-energy, spin and so on to make something real in this universe and nothing else?

The fact that the universe has 4 and only 4-dimensions is another example. That its overall geometric structure is a hypersphere; the fact that the randomness of the quantum world is constrained just sufficiently to allow an element of freedom while those constraints produce sufficient predictability for organisms to exist and function is another example of another just right balance that produces the universe we observe as a universe favorable for intelligent life.

Another is the 'size' and more importantly the details of the big bang. Why the specific amount of actualization that took place? The fine tuning question asks if what did actualize in the big bang could have been any different. It is unlikely that its basic characteristics could have been. The general characteristics of the waves that arise in water are always the same and depend on the nature of the water in which they arise. The specific forms can vary but not the fundamental structure.

Thus it is reasonable to assume that the nature of ontological energy from which all forms arose in the big bang necessarily limits the fundamental structure of forms to only what actually exists. Part of that will be their logical self-consistency across the entire universe. The fact that all levels must be consistent with all others throughout the entire universe must impose severe restrictions on the basic logical structures of forms.

The essential core of the extended fine tuning is the existence and structure of logic itself. The basic logical structure of reality which is likely fairly similar to the basic structures of human logic such as Boolean algebra, the prepositional calculus, set theory, basic mathematics, and so on is clearly what determines the structure of reality. In a computational universe we need all the logical operators and operations it takes to actually compute that universe.

The single most important fundamental structural fact of reality is its logical consistency and completeness. This is the fact that a set of logico-mathematical rules can even exist which are able to compose a consistent and complete logico-mathematical system of sufficient richness and scope to encompass the reality that does actually exist. This is a central aspect of the miracle.

Our Consistency Conjecture posits that there is only one single logically consistent form structure possible and it is that single fact of existence that generates all the components of the extended fine tuning. In that case all the components of the extended fine tuning are derived from this single axiom of reality. In this case the internal logical self-consistency of the universe becomes its single fundamental defining characteristic.

If this is true then the extended fine tuning becomes the Consistency Conjecture alone since all other aspects of the extended fine tuning are then consequences of it. The fact that all forms are compatible aspects of a single complete consistent structure across the entirety of reality and all levels of emergence, including the observer forms and their simulations of the whole consistent structure which includes these forms in its consistency is quite amazing when one considers it.

Since reality is a computational system it must be consistent and complete otherwise it would tear itself apart at the inconsistencies and pause at the incompletenesses and thus could not exist. Thus there is apparently an absolute necessity that reality be one complete internally consistent form structure and the Consistency Conjecture states that there is only one such possible consistent system that can exist and that is the one that does exist and that is the reality of our universe. If this is true then the Consistency Conjecture becomes the second fundamental axiom of reality after the Axiom of Existence, that existence must exist because non-existence cannot exist.

The Existence Exists axiom is the self-necessitating axiom that demonstrates why something must exist. The Consistency Conjecture, if true, tells us why what exists is what must exist. Upon these two axioms of reality, and the Axiom of the Necessity of Logic, all else depends.

The Consistency Conjecture, if confirmed, requires every aspect of the extended fine tuning to be exactly as it is. In other words the extended fine tuning is not arbitrary and fundamental but a consequence of the Consistency Conjecture. However it is clear this needs to be confirmed along with how and why any variation in the extended fine tuning would violate consistency and completeness.

The key is to reveal the actual underlying logic of the forms of reality to better understand their connections with what fundamental forms are compatible with them. This is not trivial since the logic of reality is clearly not completely isomorphic to human logic though human logic does appear to be largely compatible when some of its inapplicable generalizations are removed. But we need to understand the complete structure including its dynamic networked mathematical nature as well.

When the fundamental structure is understood with the necessary requirements for its existence we will be in a better position to also understand how this logical structure relates to the fundamental forms that exist within it. There is a single consistent form structure that includes both its logic and its fundamental data forms in a single integrated consistent structure that consists of forms in the act of happening. At that point the necessity of the extended fine tuning in terms of logical consistency should become clear.

Perhaps something as simple as understanding the extended fine tuning constraints that result in a universe that still exists and is able to manifest in the consciousness of an observer narrows it down considerably. Certainly if a universe cannot manifest it cannot be considered logically complete or consistent. However there must be much more to it than just this.

Somehow this consistency structure must incorporate not only human digitally based logic but continuous logical structures such as that of an entire ocean of water which can be consistently discriminated as the motions of currents, waves and ripples at all scales. And it also must include the consistent logic of general purpose computational systems in which unlimited levels of routines all exist in one consistent system based in sequences of simple machine level logical operations if that in fact is the case.

It is clear that the extended fine tuning must be exactly as it is for the whole universe to be exactly as it is. Therefore since the universe is exactly as it is the extended fine tuning must also be exactly as it is. Since everything else derives from the extended fine tuning the self-evident and exclusive fact of reality's existence as it is absolutely requires the extended fine tuning to be exactly as it is because that and only that is its source.

It is however important to review the extended fine tuning to determine what is truly irreducible and what aspects might be the logical consequences of something else.

We have already shown that the very fact of existence is a logical necessity, but why at the fundamental level is what exists that which does exist? Certainly the basic characteristics of reality seem necessary for existence to exist. It is hard to imagine anything existing that was not actual, present and absolutely what it is. It is perhaps possible to imagine a timeless virtual formless existence without happening however, and thus the emergence of happening and clock time likely coincided with the big bang.

And certainly the fundamental fact of the nature of ontological energy, the fundamental substance of reality that manifests the characteristics of being real and actual and present and that happening exists are central elements of the extended fine tuning. And the very fact that the world of forms arises within ontological energy as its manifestation in the form of xperience. Also the very fact that reality does manifest itself as xperience in all forms as generic observers, and so is knowable to consciousness is another requirement both for reality to be as it is and for organismic life to exist. It is aspects of the extended fine tuning like these which all taken together are required for the existence of organismic life and for ourselves to exist as we are and for the universe to exist as it is.

This is only a beginning that hints of much to come but it does seem to be on the right track…

EMERGENCE

Emergence refers to the fact that the behavior of aggregates of more elemental constituents tend toward distinct higher level forms of their own that are more effectively described by laws different than those that describe the constituents themselves. However in all cases emergent laws are consistent with the elemental laws and in many though possibly not all cases can be derived from them. Understood in this way there is no doubt at all that emergence is a general characteristic of the world of forms.

For example the emergent laws that best describe chemistry are not those describing the constituent elementary particles of chemicals even though they seem to be entirely determined by them. And in turn the laws of geology and biology may be consequences of the laws of chemistry and physics but are very much different in form. And of course humans are biological systems but the rules by which humans operate seem far removed from the laws of chemistry and particle physics.

The Principle of Emergence is the assumption that underlies the fine tuning question, that there is a universe fine-tuned to evolve from elementary particles to chemistry, from chemistry to life, and from life to intelligence, and that all this 'direction' to the evolution of the universe is with high probability a natural consequence of the fundamental extended fine tuning and not the operation of complete chance or any independent higher level laws.

So progressively higher level systems tend to emerge from those of lower levels and the innate structure of the elemental laws leads to the self-organization of elemental processes into independently meaningful higher level processes at aggregate scales. Instead of forming random homogeneous aggregates, aggregate elemental processes tend to cohere into discrete meaningful assemblages that operate by their own laws which are not meaningful and do not apply at the elemental level from which they emerged. These are the characteristics of emergence which are responsible for all the higher level structures and laws of the universe.

THE PRINCIPLE OF AGGREGATE EFFECT

Most if not all elemental structures are such as to automatically produce higher level emergent structures in their aggregates. A core example is the various binding strengths of chemical bonds which determine all the properties of the different chemical substances. These in turn determine the forms chemical substances take from water drops, the shapes of crystals, to the strengths of wood and stone. And these emergent structures in turn automatically lead to even higher level emergent structures such as the forms of all the things that are composed of wood or steel, or the forms of higher level aggregates of water such as streams, rivers and oceans. And the compressive and tensile properties of various minerals in turn is determinative for the forms of mountains and continents and so on up through the forms of planets, stars and galaxies to the form of the entire cosmos.

I call this the Principle of Aggregate Effect, that elemental structures are such as to automatically produce higher level emergent structures in aggregate rather than just random or homogeneous assemblages of their components. Of course there are many variations on this theme. Gas molecules do form relatively uniform aggregates but even they too form emergent structures such as atmospheres, winds and rising helium balloons in their interactions with other aggregate effects under the influence of forces such as the strength of gravity.

So the Principle of Aggregate Effect is a very general principle inherent in the very structure of the world of forms. It is even difficult to imagine elemental laws that would not lead to emergence of some type of higher level structures in aggregate.

230

And this is a hierarchical principle. The emergent structures that arise at any level themselves are such as to automatically produce even higher level emergent structures in their aggregates. The very structure of forms at all levels tends to lead to emergent structures in the aggregate. This is an inherent principle of the world of forms.

THE PRINCIPLE OF INTERACTIVE EMERGENCE

In general emergent structures emerge not just as simple isolated aggregates but in computational interactions with other programs. Crystal forms for example emerge not just as isolated aggregates of molecules but in interaction with environmental variables such as temperature, pressure and the presence of other chemistry. This is how crystals of any given chemical acquire so many different variations on a single form, why snowflakes come in innumerable variations.

And in general aggregates are not uniform, that is they incorporate elemental structures of diverse types whose aggregate interaction results in additional variation in higher level structures. Most of the discriminable constituents of the world of forms consist of mixed emergent structures with complex interaction histories.

The entire world of forms, the single structure of the entire universe, can be considered to have emerged up from the elemental laws up through many levels of emergent hierarchies, and ultimately from the structure and laws of the extended fine tuning. It is implicit in the very nature of the extended fine tuning that it does produce the emergence of the universe as we know it through multiple levels of aggregation. This is of course not a deterministically exact but a stochastic process subject to constrained quantum randomness.

Though the general principles of emergence are simple, the actual details of emergence are enormously complex as they essentially encompass the interactions of all the actual structures of the universe at all levels. All this evolving structure is the complex computational result of all the individual programs in the universe continually interacting at all emergent levels to produce the actual universe as it is.

This can also be thought of as a kind of symmetry breaking where at each stage of emergence the range of possible forms any material could theoretically take gets pruned by its emergent laws but then simultaneously those reduced forms are given a broad range of variation in their interactions with other forms.

THE UNIVERSAL LAW OF EVOLUTION

All forms, not just biological forms, are subject to a Universal Law of Evolution in that all forms are continually selected by their interactions with the other forms that constitute their environments. This is the general process that determines which forms persist, which alter and how, and which transform into other forms. This evolution of forms is a complex interactive process in which all other forms constitute the active environment of every particular form.

Darwinian evolution is just a special case of this Universal Law of Evolution which applies specifically to living forms which have the characteristic property of the ability to propagate their kind. In this respect Darwinian evolution applies over lineages of forms rather than just to individual forms themselves. In other respects Darwinian evolution is a subset of the Universal Law of Evolution.

Thus individual information forms or programs may seem to have a life of their own in which they become increasingly adapted to their form environments or fade away. The result of the operation of the Universal Law of Evolution is that the world of forms continually operates to compute form states or programs that are more and more well adapted to their form environments.

All forms evolve under the interactive computational influence of other forms. Their environment is an environment of forms and all forms are the environments of other forms. This ensures that all forms continually tend to evolve towards increased adaptation to each other. Thus it can be said that the current form state of the universe is in some sense the best adapted state possible in the present moment. Its totality is characterized by being in a state of optimal self-adaptation. This is related to its absoluteness, in that it is exactly as it is and thus could be nothing else than it actually is.

This process tends to produce increasing emergent complexity of new programs and new forms with new higher level laws governing them. The interaction of forms constitutes a continual computation which computes the information of their interactions and this results in altered forms better adapted to their environments which in turn consist only of the forms of each other.

SELF-ORGANIZATION

The world of forms is enormously complex. It doesn't just consist of static aggregate built upon aggregate built upon aggregate. It is a dynamic computational system in which all sorts of subsidiary structures spontaneously arise as the results of the complexity of the computations involved. These include all sorts of nonlinearities, multi-level feedback loops, chaotic subsystems, fractal systems (Mandelbrot, 1983) and others. Presumably any dynamic forms and subsystems that are consistent with the whole can eventually occur as the result of computations.

Since this whole computational system of the world of forms is dynamic it is best considered as an enormous complex of interacting programs each of which computes its particular form in interaction with all the other programs in its computational environment. Again just as forms themselves are somewhat arbitrarily discriminated from the single universal form so programs also are somewhat arbitrarily discriminated as subsystems of a single universal program depending on their meaningfulness to the discriminating organisms.

Self-organizing systems are of especial interest. Self-organizing systems are discrete programs that arise computationally out of the form flux like standing waves or eddies and tend to self-perpetuate themselves over time rather than quickly dissolving back into the background. They achieve this by incorporating subroutines which protect their forms against external degradation by other forms. In this way they are able to persist through time as discriminable quasi-stable information structures.

Self-organizing systems of many types are common. They include rock formations, individual stones, mountains, planets, rivers flowing in riverbeds, and of course all living beings. Self-organizing programs are

233

all programs like other programs. They just are forms that tend to perpetuate themselves in their form environments. Self-organizing systems always arise in interaction with other programs and their form structures and are always computed in interaction with their form environments.

There are many other types of forms and types of interactions of forms that can be classified as well.

ORGANISMIC PROGRAMS

The programs we call living organisms are a special subset of self-organizing systems. These are the programs that encode the information of and operate as the total existence and behaviors of all living organisms from viruses to humans. They are all characterized by the ability to reproduce copies of their kind. Thus they are self-reproducing programs which encode their software and hardware instructions in their special information forms of DNA and pass them from generation to generation.

All life forms are the evolving computations of organismic programs and every living being can be considered an organismic program. Life forms are self-organizing systems with the additional characteristic of computational intelligence, purposeful action and the ability to propagate their kind. They incorporate an internal computational subprogram that intelligently computes actions designed to preserve and procreate themselves on the basis of an internal model of their environment.

This is true of all life forms from the simplest to the most complex though of course there are innumerable variations in functionality among species in this respect. But all can be considered as computational information systems or programs whose functioning is driven by instinctual imperatives such as self-preservation and procreation.

Life is a major step in emergence. No longer do the programs of reality operate automatically according to fixed laws of nature but they now incorporate volition and functional intelligence. However in a fundamental sense organismic programs are not distinct from other

234

types of programs but are just programs with particular structures which tend to self-perpetuate their forms. Thus they tend to persist and function more effectively than other programs.

However from a computational perspective the essential characteristic of organismic programs is that they are able to modify their own code to varying degrees. Rather than automatically operating only in accord with laws common to all of inanimate reality they have gained the ability to internally generate varying degrees of animate action based on a simulation of themselves as a separate entity whose interests are to be furthered.

Life initially arose as various forms of simple carbon chemistry due to the unique ability of carbon to form very complex bonds with both itself and other elements. It is likely that these original precursors to life were fairly common events and likely still are in certain environments. However today when these precursors arise they are all quickly eaten by existing life forms before they can organize themselves into life whereas originally in an environment devoid of life they would have been able to persist and further organize into the original life forms. This would explain the apparent absence of life still originating today. The precursors, which naturally would be nutritional to life, are just eaten by existing life as soon as they appear before they are able to self-organize into new life. Thus the precursors have not yet developed any defensive abilities against their progeny.

The chemistry of the self-organization of these precursors into the original life forms is not clear but certainly involves a protective packaging around a simple RNA type information structure able to self-replicate in the presence of nutrients in the form of additional amounts of its chemical components as with viruses. Once these simple life forms originated they would have evolved via selection of natural variants of themselves, those more successful surviving in greater numbers. And from this point the evolution of all life on earth proceeds as revealed by science.

A key element to the success of organismic programs is their ability to procreate their type. By encoding plans for themselves in DNA sub-forms they manage to transcend the limits of degradation of the chemical and biological forms of which they are composed and pass on both their hardware and software to copies of themselves in the form of that DNA (Owen, 2009). Thus life forms or organismic programs are the prime example of self-organizing emergent structures. But nevertheless they are fundamentally just programs among all the other programs running in reality which in interactive association compute the current state of reality in the present moment. Organisms are just programs of a specialized and rather successful type that have arisen naturally through emergence from the innate form structures of lower levels.

In turn some organisms, especially humans, but other organisms as well, have sufficiently developed internal models of reality that they are able to understand and manipulate the details of emergence with their technologies to build dens, nests, homes and other structures which are additional form programs in the world of forms and consistent with it. These of course include some of the most complexly designed and precisely discriminable forms in existence.

Organismic programs are characterized by sub-forms consisting of recursive models of their environments on the basis of which they compute their actions. Because these mental models can model non-existent temporal duration and 'what if' states they allow organismic programs to direct the evolution of reality to the extent of their abilities. Thus, as programs within the world of forms, they give the universe some ability to direct its evolution as well.

THE NATURE OF THE LAWS OF NATURE

Up to this point this is just a novel interpretation of the usual view of the structure of nature as described by the physical and biological sciences which do a remarkably good job of explaining how most of the known structures of the universe emerge and evolve in interaction with others. However there are some additional subtleties with respect to forms, programs and laws that need to be clarified before emergence can be fully understood.

What we call the laws of nature are just similarities between similar programs. Only programs actually run in the world of forms and the laws of nature are the structural rules which govern how programs can form. Because these rules restrict the structures of programs that arise they produce similarities between programs of similar types and these in turn govern the computation of forms in similar ways. It is these actual structural rules of programs that are called the laws of nature.

So the laws of nature do not exist computationally in the sense that programs do but are the underlying virtual structure of ontological energy which determines what kind of programs and forms can arise and how they interact. They are similar to the nature of water which determines what types of wave forms can arise in water. These underlying laws of nature are an essential aspect of the extended fine tuning of reality.

The basic laws of nature are the extended fine tuning. They include the basic logical structure that the world of forms must obey from the existence of the basic logical operators and their consistent and complete logical structure to the other basic rules by which programs form and incorporate structure. Many of these are still unclear though others have been hinted at in this book.

So the laws of nature are an additional even more fundamental level to reality. They stand between the pure formless presence of ontological energy that gives reality to the world and the world of forms that evolves within it. They are the virtual structure intrinsic in the very nature of ontological energy that controls what form types may arise within it.

This is not the same as the usual mistaken view of modern science of laws of nature existing independently and somehow magically controlling the execution of all the multiple programs to which they apply because it defines the actual laws of nature differently. Most of what current science considers laws of nature are actually programs. The actual laws of nature are the structural rules of those programs. And in turn it is these programs that directly manifest as forms in the process of happening.

Most of what current science considers laws of nature are just similarities extracted from similar programs and encoded in the mental models of observers. These are considerably different than the actual laws of nature though they are ultimately derived from them.

THE UNITY OF FORMS AND PROGRAMS

Because reality exists only as an instantaneous present moment, we must abandon the distinction between programs and forms and realize that what exists at all levels of emergence are forms in the process of happening. That is forms consist not just of static forms that are re-computed from moment to moment but are also the information of how they are changing. Forms are the instantaneous forms of their programs as well as their data state in one single structure.

Forms are not movies or TV programs in which the appearance of motion is derived from a sequences of still frames. The motion is actually part of the form itself. The program is part of the form. It is the aspect of the form that gives it its directedness and therefore its reality.

This view is consistent with the nature of reality as xperience which is the continual re-computation and alteration of forms in the actual process of changing. The reality of forms is not static video frames but actually changing or happening forms, because only change manifests because only happening is real. It is this happeningness of reality that self-manifests it and makes it real.

Thus the actual reality of the world of forms is that forms and programs are a single unity best characterized as happening forms, or forms of happening. The forms that exist in the present moment are not static data states but are the actual present moment happening of those forms. Forms include their changing nature as well as what is changing. What is is always what is happening. Thus happening forms combine the notions of both forms and programs which are just two incomplete perspectives on the same thing.

Thus the world of forms does not consist of separate programs and data as silicon based software does but is a unified structure in which every part contains both what humans would call the data and code in a single structure, and this true of whatever form structure one may choose to identify across all levels of emergence. These changing forms are roughly analogous to the processors of silicon computers where code and data intersect in actual change.

This is inherently difficult to conceptualize because humans automatically think of reality in terms of nouns and verbs, of objects and actions. But that is an artificial dualism that exists primarily in human mental models of reality as a computational aid rather than in the world of forms itself. The world of forms actually consists of instantaneously self-evolving forms at all levels of emergence in a single super-consistent structure.

And the world of forms doesn't consist of individual code and data streams intersecting in one or a few processors as it does in silicon computers. The evolution of the world of forms is completely different in this respect because its entirety exists in the single processor of happening and so the entirety is recomputed in every instant. The processor of happening is a ubiquitous aspect of reality itself and thus is coterminous with every form in the universe at all levels of emergence simultaneously, the whole of which is thus recomputed at every instant of happening.

THE STRUCTURE OF EMERGENCE

The key to understanding emergence is to understand that all the intrinsic form evolutions in the world of form are all continually simultaneously recomputed at once in interaction with each other at all levels of aggregation. Everything is its continual happening, but those computations are always happening not as individual forms but as interactions of forms at all levels of emergence in a single super-consistent form structure.

The happening of forms is the computational interaction of forms and this consists not of individual forms but as a single logically complete structure. All individual forms are observer dependent discriminations from what is actually a continuous single whole form that is the entire evolving information structure of the universe.

This single form is enormously rich, dense and complex. It consists of the underlying structural domains of every one of its overlapping forms, hierarchies, and sub and super sets, all of which exist as their instantaneous form of happening. Any one of these can be considered as the xperience of a generic observer by which reality self-manifests itself. And every one of these can be considered the xperience of the other forms it is interacting with or has interacted with. This single form consists of all possible forms from the most elemental through all levels of emergence up to the single emergent form of the whole form. And all this exists as its instantaneous form of happening.

Though individual forms within the whole are arbitrary, there are to some extent natural boundaries of structure that tend to emerge as individual forms amenable to observer discrimination, but these are

239

always dependent on emergent level. The form of a stone emerges at its level, but at the level of its mineral constituents or a landscape hardly exists. Thus ultimately all individual forms are arbitrary discriminations meaningful to observers.

This includes not just apparently static forms such as stones but forms of interaction as well. In this case forms tend to discriminate along interactions meaningful to observers.

What are called emergent programs and forms are just programs discriminated over greater scope recognized as aggregates of constituents. Individual forms and programs are to a great extent an arbitrary concept dependent on how an observer discriminates the forms in question.

The world of forms exists naturally as multiple hierarchies of forms in which the very structure of lower level forms automatically generates higher level structures in aggregate. Because this hierarchical structure is inherent to the entire world of forms the world of forms can be consistently viewed at any level as the instantaneous happening of the forms at that level and since the world of forms is a single super-consistent whole that level view will always be consistent with the whole and all its other levels.

This is because emergent forms and processes consist of lower level ones and lower level ones automatically produce higher level ones through the principle of aggregate effect. There is no sense in which any one level 'causes' another level since they all happen simultaneously as different level effects of the whole system. Whatever is at all levels happens simultaneously and super-consistently.

From this super-consistent whole organismic observers can extract what they think of as laws, programs and forms at any level from the information histories of the world of forms. This separation actually exists only in observer simulations of reality though it is based on an implicit structure of the world of forms over temporal sequence.

So observers can view emergent forms equally well at all levels. This is what allows observers of different scales to exist and function by discriminating emergences meaningful at their level and scope of existence.

The actual individual structures of emergence are in many cases well understood by science but they should be interpreted in this light as the

240

inherent computational information forms they are. Most aspects of emergence become clear with this approach.

MORE ON EMERGENCE

An ocean of water continuously evolves as a single structure in which every part at every level of aggregation is instantaneously recomputed at every instant in interaction with others. The human mind can extract data forms such as water molecules, waves and currents; laws which can describe the rules of evolution at each level; and programs that evolve data states according to those rules in any particular bounded volumes of the ocean but what actually exists in even our direct experience is simply a unified complex of super-consistently evolving forms that is then subject to conceptualization in terms of individual things and actions.

It is always the happening of form complexes that is the primary reality. It may be this can only be formulated in a new language of reality since its fundamental structure doesn't seem easily expressible in human language.

The world of forms consists of a complex of innumerable processes of which many are of similar type. For example the same or similar computations exist in the computational evolution of every leaf on a tree of any particular species, and only slightly less similar in the developing leaves of all trees of that species. Thus the laws and programs governing the form evolution of every leaf exist as an intrinsic part of the form of each evolving leaf. It is quite clear that most biological forms are the result of computational processes (Rashevsky, 1960). But in a computational reality in which everything is its continuously evolving form these computational processes are the things themselves.

The evolution of forms must then be both elemental and emergent simultaneously across all levels of hierarchy. Both the individual chemical reactions and the overall emergent pattern must be computed simultaneously in terms of each other. It will be bi-causal in both directions between top and bottom. The emergent programs operate through ordered elemental sequences and complexes which all evolve simultaneously in parallel rather than sequentially (though of course forms themselves evolve sequentially in clock time).

Thus emergent level programs actually consist of ordered complexes of elemental programs just as the elemental programs exist as part of all higher level complexes of which they are elements. They both are aspects of each other and evolve simultaneously. They are just different observer perspectives on the same thing depending on what level of emergence is being discriminated. And all emerge ultimately from the extended fine tuning and the original form state of reality at the big bang.

Ocean, wave, tree, forest, ecosystem, human, societies, history, all are just different observer perspectives on different levels of the program complex that is the total evolving world of forms.

In this view all higher level emergent laws are just naturally evolving commonalities among similar programs that are identified by organismic observers by a process of pattern recognition (Uhr, 1973). They are the structural constraints on evolving forms. They can be modeled as independent entities in observer mental models of reality but in the evolving forms themselves they are just the common constraints on structure of similar forms. Thus the laws of nature at all levels are just similarities among the program structures of similar emergent programs. The evolving forms of leaves on a tree will have similar computational structure and it is those similarities that are the laws of nature that govern the growth, function, and death of leaves.

What we have previously called forms are just video frames of continuously evolving forms in the present moment. And what we have previously thought of as programs are the evolving nature of those forms, the form of their evolution in interaction with other forms which is part of their form. The true nature of form is the information of its instantaneous evolution. This is the information of itself and the information of itself includes both what humans discriminate as form frames and form evolution.

Forms are intrinsically dynamic. The happening of a form is its data, all of its data. Not just the static form of itself we would imagine at any particular frame but how that form is changing in that moment. Forms can't just be their data forms because then they wouldn't actually exist. What actually exists is the continuing change, the continual re-computation which is the actual manifestation of form and the xperience of the form. Forms that are not in a state of continual re-computation are lost from the present moment and cannot exist. They

242

are no longer happening and thus they no longer exist. This is the being and actuality of the totality of the form in the present moment.

For example we ourselves are certainly not a sequence of snapshots of our form, but the actual continual dynamic changes of all parts of our form in the present moment. We are the continual happening of ourselves. We, like all things are a continual process rather than a sequence of states. The sequential video frame view of things is a convenient digital fiction in our mental model of reality and thus easier to compute with the limited resources of the human brain than the actual continuous nature of reality. This again is a major difference between our mental model of reality and reality itself.

The information of a form is not what it is but how it is happening. Things are not their static forms but their continual changes and everything without exception from the most elemental to the highest level is continually changing as it is recomputed by happening. Static forms, static states of forms, simply do not exist, except as modeled in mental models of reality, and even then the actual reality of the mental model itself is always its continuous happening.

This approach solves the problem of where emergent programs and emergent laws reside in the world of forms. Forms, laws and programs are aspects of a single reality of xperience, manifestation and happening. Emergent structures are just sequences and complexes of elemental, and elemental just parts of emergent. All levels evolve together super-consistently as a single unity across the entire world of forms.

Emergent laws are just commonalities of program structure across similar emergent programs in observer reality models. All three aspects, forms, programs and laws, are observer perspectives on a single structure that is the reality of every individual form of the world of forms and the totality of interactions of all discriminable forms.

The reality of the world of forms is happening which manifests as xperience, the single unity underlying forms, programs and laws. This view has some similarities with what is called process philosophy but in the context of our whole theory is quite different (Wikipedia: Process philosophy) (Whitehead, 1929).

And it is not really individual forms that are changing because forms continuously flow into and out of other forms. Forms inherently transform. Forms are not stable entities that change but things that can

243

be arbitrarily discriminated from the form flux at particular moments by observers. Only observer discriminated snapshots of this process are modeled as individual forms that change. The process itself occurs not as changing and interacting individual forms but as a universal flux of interactive happening from which individual forms and programs can be observer discriminated at any given instant. Thus the identification of individual forms and programs is dependent on those of observers.

Observers are forms that extract or discriminate individual forms or programs of interest from the total form flux. And observers themselves are among the forms discriminated by themselves and other observers. The flux is inherently indeterminate in that individual forms emerge arbitrarily as xperience in the xperience of other forms. And all forms are the interactions of forms in which forms form and dissolve into other forms. All such forms act as generic observers of their interactions and thus manifest reality as xperience in the forms of themselves. All individual forms are the xperiences of themselves and reality manifests itself as those xperiences and this is a somewhat arbitrary organization dependent on interactions with other somewhat arbitrary forms.

Elemental forms and programs automatically aggregate as emergent forms and programs. That is their intrinsic nature. Emergence exists as aggregates of elementals and elementals exist as components of aggregates. All exist as a single super-consistent multiply overlapping whole up and down the entire hierarchy of form from the most elemental to the entire universe of form. The world of forms, the universe, is the continual manifestation of form in the form of xperience which is the continual happening of itself in the present moment in which reality self-manifests itself.

This is not an easy thing to understand because human mental models are designed to encode simplistic discrete temporal digital models instead of this continuously shifting instantaneous process. But hopefully it is now clearer.

THE TEMPORAL STRUCTURE OF PROGRAMS

Since reality and the world of forms exists only in the present moment programs with temporal duration sequences cannot exist. The programs of the world of forms can't exist as extended code sequences that are sequentially processed. It must consist only of the inherent instantaneous directedness of the instantaneous current interactions of forms and that instantaneous information in the forms themselves must be sufficient to compute the whole of reality.

The existence of programs consisting of as yet unprocessed code sequences like silicon based software is self-contradictory and thus impossible. First, these code sequences correspond to future events and the future does not exist so they cannot exist. Second, they would exist as exact deterministic sequences which would disallow any step to be stochastic since that would make the next step impossible to exactly express in code. Third, there would have to be innumerable different program code sequences each governing particular forms and since reality is the continuous interaction of all transforming forms there would be no way for each of these independent sequences to know what the others were so as to be compatible with them and mutually compute an interactive future in a consistent manner. They would inevitably clash.

Thus programs in the form of code sequences governing future events cannot exist and thus programs with any temporal duration or sequence cannot exist. The appearances of programs with meaningful temporal sequences exists only in retrospect as inferred past sequences of what produced the instantaneous changing states of forms. In this sense programs are fictions that exist in the mental models of observers or more leniently in the past information histories of the world of forms as modeled by observers.

Thus it is only the actual process of change in the continual instant of happening that exists. This carries an intrinsic directedness towards the next state of being but that is only realized through the interaction and realization of all such processes. This is the only model that does not lead to contradiction and thus must be the correct model.

Imputed information histories is all that exists of programs. The instantaneous intercomputation of all interacting form states produces the appearance of a coherent program in its past information trace as it progresses. The only thing that actually exists in the reality of the present moment is the complex evolving form structure of the moment.

The laws of nature exist only as the actual rules governing the underlying structure of that change in the single instant of reality and programs exist as the information histories of the actual complexes of interacting changes that the laws govern the structure of.

Thus it is clear that the actual form structure of instantaneously changing forms is considerably more complex than what we usually think of as the structural forms of things. It contains both that and its instantaneous changingness which directs or evolves every form and form complex towards the future.

Thus the meaningfulness of reality associated with patterns with temporal duration exists only as the past information traces of the instantaneous change structure of the moment. Forms self-evolve in such a way as to produce the semblance of meaningful programs with duration in the mental models of observers. This is because the rules of instantaneous change are themselves consistent and meaningful. In reality all law and all programs exist and manifest only as the computational directedness of the instantaneous present moment.

How all this information is structurally combined in single instantaneously changing form structures requires further clarification. However even in silicon computers data and code are both identically bit sequences that are distinguished by different contexts in the structure of the processor so somehow the context and structure of happening itself may be determinative here.

THE TEMPORAL PROGRAMS OF ORGANISMS

It is clear that form structures or programs with temporal duration do exist in the mental models of organisms. And it is precisely such structures with temporal duration that make organismic forms unique. The existence of these forms raises some interesting questions. What is their structure and since mental models of reality are also part of the form structure of reality why don't similar forms with duration exist in external reality as well? And how can a program sequence with temporal duration work in a mental model if all form computations everywhere exist only instantaneously? How does a mental model of reality with temporal duration even exist in a durationless reality?

The key to understanding these questions is that the current form states of all forms *are* their information histories and thus contain implicit information about their temporal sequences. So the temporal sequences we can think of as programs do exist implicitly in all currently evolving form structures. This is because all current forms are the computational results of their past interactions with other forms.

What characterizes organismic forms is their ability to incorporate this aspect of reality to encode specific simulations of form states of interest in mental models which can be further organized and referred back to in any present moment. This is how organisms are able to act as programs with computational intelligence and volition. In particular it requires the existence of short term memories in which comparisons of ongoing sequences of form states opens reality to temporal meaning which is absolutely essential for intelligence and volition. Without this capability to one degree or another there could be no organismic forms, no effective life forms.

The ability to hold copies of form states in short term memory and compare them to determine and encode their relationships is the basis of all meaning. Nearly every type of meaning depends of temporal comparison of some sort. Without it there could be no music or any comparative meaning at all. There would just be the instantaneous current states of things without any context whatsoever.

Every form is the xperience of the other forms it has interacted with. From this arises a computational basis for temporal duration because forms are their interaction histories. There just needs to be a mechanism that uses this to encode specific copies of the transient processes of reality for future organization and reference. This is achieved through the sensory and neural mechanisms of organisms which is what they do. They form internal copies of forms which are then stored in memory.

This is how organisms have gained temporal duration models of reality because all forms are duration models of their interaction histories at the level of xperience of generic observers. Such referential forms exist in all organisms in primitive fashion but in more precise symbolic forms in advanced organisms.

Thus organisms are programs with models of temporal duration that allow them to compute intelligent actions toward an imagined future. This gives organisms the directedness that enables them to manipulate an actually durationless reality to their own advantage. Organisms are forms that that have acquired the ability to direct the future toward desirable predicted outcomes.

Organisms are forms like other forms. They are just forms with specific substructures that open the instantaneous happening of reality into a simulated reality with temporal duration. Though that reality is entirely imaginary it is computationally sound to a sufficient degree that functionality is possible and thus effectiveness is greatly improved. It is only this ability that allows any of the non-random abilities of organisms to sustain themselves including all functionality down to basics such as eating, drinking and avoiding predation. All organismic functionality is computational and it all depends on the ability to predict a non-existent future which requires them to seem to exist in a present moment with temporal duration.

Of course organisms actually exist and operate in the same instantaneous present as all forms do. It is the ability of organisms' computational forms to generate instantaneous forms directed towards specific ends rather than just as the result of blind natural processes that produces forms in the present moment with volitional directedness rather than just directedness.

This gives organisms some degree of free choice since the directedness is the result of internal computations which though often in response to external forms are not fully determined by those external forms. It is free will even though most of these computations are made at the unconscious rather than the conscious level. In most cases the conscious level just goes along for the ride exercising some minimal quality control and reward function after decisions have already been made.

HIERARCHICAL SYSTEMS

There is another interesting question and that is whether there are other forms that exhibit intelligence and volition besides those of individual organisms, in particular the forms of superorganisms such as termite colonies, but other forms as well such as other animal and human societies, the vast sweeps of history and perhaps even higher level emergent structures than those such as the Gaia of the biosphere (Lovelock, 1995). This is vast subject which will only be touched on here.

Organisms can be considered as programs that to some extent write or modify their own code. Is this something that other higher level programs do as well, and if so only programs that operate through organized collections of organismic forms or are there others as well?

Do the great processes of history and social movements also operate as independent super-programs generating their own direction or are they only the aggregate results of the organisms they operate through? To what extent are men's actions controlled by the fates or the greater processes of history and to what extent are they free?

How about evolution itself? As we have earlier seen all processes and the entire evolution of the universe is strongly though stochastically determined by the extended fine tuning. The history of the universe tends to converge towards certain forms of emergence though to what and to what degree is not entirely clear.

Since self-directing organismic programs such as humans do exist there seems no inherent reason to believe self-directing non-organismic or superorganismic programs couldn't evolve as well. This is essential just a matter of the internal structure of the program rather than any biological necessity. It seems reasonable that programs of other types could potentially evolve into self-directing programs at any higher level. It seems likely that many higher level program structures naturally evolve from the extended fine tuning and many of these will exhibit various homeostatic and self-directing mechanisms. This seems implicit in the very form structure of reality.

The behavior of superorganisms such as termite, ant and bee colonies and swarming behaviors are instructive. Though both colonies and swarms act as independent entities exhibiting behaviors and problem solving capacities superior to those of their component organisms they seem to be pretty successfully modeled by interactions amongst their individual organisms. Emergent behaviors do seem to emerge naturally from the aggregate behavior of individual organisms but there is then downward feedback back to individual behavior. So once again it is the whole system at all levels that is determinative and super-consistent.

For example the greater processes of history strongly influence the behavior of individual humans. Of course the processes of history are in turn the aggregate behaviors of individuals but there are certainly very strong feedbacks on individual behavior. So again higher and lower levels both influence each other and thus exist as a super-consistent whole as is typical.

And it is clear that the great programs of history include not just aggregates of individual humans but of natural processes such as climate as well in a consistent directed whole. In general everything is computationally connected with everything else.

In human societies we do clearly see both processes in action as individual human interactions clearly generate emergent social movements and memes while at the same time society itself in the form of its legislators, moral authorities, role models and memes influences the behavior of its members.

Because it is all levels that operate together in a super-consistent manner to generate the behavior of the whole 'hierarchical systems' is a better descriptor than emergence which only describes the operations of the higher level. Hierarchical systems can be more or less loosely structured and determinative. The behavior of both termite colony and individual termites is much more closely coupled than human societies in which top down rules though often very broad and powerful are not tightly the results of individual decisions of the general population. There are many variants and certainly neither level completely determines the evolution of the other.

It is likely in all hierarchical structures that individual interactions and higher level programs exist in a super-consistent whole where neither level necessarily determines the action of the other but it is the overall super-consistency that governs the whole. This is consistent with the view we arrived at in terms of the past and present forming a deterministic super-consistent temporally bi-directional system. In fact it seems to be just another aspect of that same structure. This is to be expected because the totality of all levels is processed simultaneously by happening.

We can extend this thinking up and down all levels of emergence. In this view the entire hierarchical structure of the world of forms is best understood as a single super-consistent system in which every level acts upon all other levels to compute and guide its evolution. Within the entire system there are innumerable types of form structures some of which exhibit the capacity to self-organize and self-direct their evolution.

Organisms are notable among these but there are likely many other types as well of which many are currently unrecognized. To what extent the universe as a whole can be characterized as an intelligent self-directing system is uncertain but it certainly incorporates intelligent self-directing subsystems and to that extent, at least, it can be.

The standard view of science is that ultimately all emergent laws are completely determined by a small set of elemental laws of physics. Though upon reflection many scientists would probably not apply that strictly to human behavior, perhaps positing some degree of free will operating there in the form of higher level laws at least partially independent of the elemental level. So even science is ambivalent on this question.

If there were any independent higher level emergent processes they would have to act by determining the execution of lower level processes in some manner. But then they would be functionally identical to those sequences and one could equally say that the higher level laws actually *were* those sequences. So the only reasonable model is a bi-directional view in which emergent processes are structured aggregates of lower level processes and the question of which level controls which is meaningless. As long as aggregates exist super-consistent hierarchies automatically form. All levels exist and function simultaneously as a single super-consistent whole.

Super-consistent hierarchical systems seem to emerge naturally from the extended fine tuning and the multiplicity of aggregates. How and why this is so, and what aspects of the basic logical structure of the world of forms facilitates it is fairly well explained by science with the exception of the initial origin of life itself. Are there any other possible logical systems than that of our universe that would also allow the emergence of quasi-independent intelligent self-aware programs? The answer to that question would shed light on how it occurs in our universe.

The basic rules of logic are so fundamental it is hard to imagine any other set that might actually exist and be functional. However it may just be that the actual logico-mathematical structure of reality deals not just with the discrete variables of human logic and syntax but also, at least at emergent levels, with continuous forms that can be tuned from a single continuous form and encoded as discrete variables in the mental models of organismic observers all at the same time in a single super-consistent system. At least it seems that is what would be required to effectively model the actual logic of reality.

The world of forms is single enormously complex evolving hierarchical form. From this whole individual forms and their interactions can be discriminated at innumerable levels which are always consistent with any others even when all forms are essentially arbitrary bounded areas and perspectives of the whole. Thus the whole system exhibits an amazing super-consistency and completeness. It seems hard to believe that any other logical structure than that of our universe could possibly result in such a structure. Remembering that the basic logical structure, the very existence of logic itself, of the universe is the core of the extended fine tuning it is clearly what determines the structure of reality.

Thus our Consistency Conjecture, that our extended fine tuning is the only one that could exist because it is the only one that leads to a logically complete and super-consistent universe seems eminently reasonable. A computational universe which was not super-consistent and logically complete would tear itself apart at the inconsistencies and pause at the incompletenesses and could not exist.

The proper description of this structure is fraught with difficulties. Though science does a generally excellent job at describing its individual aspects once discriminated there is no science that describes the underlying structure especially when observers are included as discriminating forms themselves. It seems the superposition of a huge number of overlapping individual evolving forms at innumerable levels of hierarchy whose interferences discriminate individual forms. Perhaps a method similar to Fourier analysis, which describes complex waves as superpositions of many types of simple sine waves, but in terms of all fundamental wave types of the world of forms, would be applicable (Wikipedia: Fourier analysis).

ARE THERE HIDDEN QUANTUM LAWS?

Another theoretical possibility is that independent emergent laws might exist and operate by imposing hidden variable influences on quantum randomness. It seems this could occur without violating any of the known laws of nature. All quantum processes that appear random could actually be being determined by hidden laws so long as the aggregate results obeyed the usual probabilistic constraints.

For example the individual particles in a collection of radioactive particles can decay in an enormous number of different ways and still generate the same half-life. And the same is true with respect to the constrained randomness of all quantum processes. And of course it is obvious that classical level results depend heavily on which random results actually occur. So it is certainly theoretically possible that some hidden laws could be determining which particle decays at any given time while still ensuring that in aggregate all particles decay with the same half-life. This could lead to wildly different real world events without violating any known laws of physics.

Though this is certainly a theoretical possibility I know of no evidence that the sequences of quantum events are in any way affected by higher level emergent laws or that any such higher level laws exist though many people obviously do believe in extra-natural causes and this would be a theoretical causative mechanism. Nevertheless it should not be discounted out of hand because it would not seem to violate any known physical law since there are no laws describing how quantum randomness is chosen. This mechanism should certainly be considered if there is any evidence that the structure and evolution of the universe cannot be explained by the operation of elemental laws only.

I suppose the best evidence for this would consist of some sort of statistical studies of coincidence or synchronicity that demonstrated non-random effects but even if the phenomenon were real it would be inherently difficult to know how it might manifest itself and thus how to design experiments to detect it.

INTERNAL AND EXTERNAL FORMS

Another important question is to what extent emergent patterns and laws exist in external reality and to what extent only in the reality models of observers. It is clear that many if not most of the meaningful patterns observers see in the world of forms are products of their internal models of reality rather than the external world of forms. However it is certainly true that the logical structure of reality must contain the information structures that can be given those meanings. Thus the actual mix is not always easy to tease apart.

Take the game of Go for example in which extremely complex and even profound strategic forms can arise from sequences of very simple rules (Takagawa, 1972). The rules of Go themselves are invented by

253

humans and thus exist only in human reality models and in human sharable media. However the underlying information structure of ruled board and black and white stones is a human constructed emergent form in external reality that the human generated and stored rules of Go are overlaid upon.

To win at Go one must deal with both external and internal emergent laws that govern complex patterns of individual stones rather than just randomly executing valid moves. It is the emergent strategic forms that are important and control the sequences of elementary operations. The possible emergent forms are determined by the valid elementary operations, but which strategic forms are followed determines the elementary sequences executed which in turn manifests the emergent forms that determine the progress towards a human defined 'win'.

Go is a good analogy for how various levels in the hierarchy of forms of any type play out in reality as a complex mix of internal and external forms. It is certainly true that the reality is the entire hierarchy of forms at every level though any particular form at any level may be what is important to a particular observer in terms of winning. Higher level laws may manifest through both temporal sequences and spatial patterns of lower level events and certainly there must be a mutual up and down determination for consistency.

The entire form structure of Go including the complete hierarchy of laws of both the simulations of Go players and those of external reality exists as superimposed forms in the world of forms of which both Go boards and players are a part. Since Go players and their mental models are part of the world of forms the total hierarchical form of Go in itself in its complete complexity is what exists in reality even if much of that is particular to specific observer forms and thus stored in mental models rather than external reality.

All of these aspects and levels must work together super-consistently for the game of Go to exist and proceed. The emergent patterns of individual games are stored as the actual patterns of their manifestations both as transient external forms and as modeled in the players' simulations. Both external reality and observer forms are logical domains of a single world of forms.

The rules and strategies of Go are independent of the state of any particular game and exist only in the simulations of players who understand them. These are imposed over the mental models of the external patterns of stones on wood. In the mental models of observers individual game patterns emerge from the rules and external forms as a consistent complex of internal and external forms.

Thus many emergent structures exist only as mental forms in the form structure of observers. But they are typically overlaid over mental models of form structures in external reality. Many types of such forms exist as organismic minds tend to lushly populate their realities with internal structures. And these are also stored in shared human media and communicated in speech. So to a great extent observer reality models serve as sources and repositories for many of emergent forms of reality which exist and are executed only through observers.

It is not always clear which forms are internal and which external. Take the status of numbers in the world of forms. The cardinal numbers used for counting are characteristics of collections of multiple things (Wikipedia: Natural numbers). But it is unclear whether a computational reality needs to count things numerically or whether it just operates directly on individual forms.

Thus it is possible that cardinal number forms are stored only in observer models of reality if counting is exclusively an organismic observer function. But this is not certain. For example the particle property conservation law needs to keep track of the total amounts of particle properties. Is this done by counting them or merely by allocating all that exist? And if so in what sense does that constitute counting? And it is clear that since there can be no physical infinities or infinitesimals that these and many other human mathematical concepts exist only as form structures in the minds of observers. When the nature of numbers in the formal structure of reality itself is better understood this should become clear.

Questions like these are probably best explored by computational simulations of the operational structure of the world of forms on silicon or quantum computers. If we can effectively model the operation of the world of forms on silicon we will be that much closer to deciphering its actual structure in reality and to what extent numbers and other form structures are necessary.

FORMS AND XPERIENCE

Xperience itself is the only indisputably self-evident manifestation of reality which is exactly as it is taken prior to any interpretation including any discrimination into individual xperiences. Even all subsequent interpretations of *experience* are themselves only the direct xperience of those interpretations. An xperience is never a thing, however things as constructs are themselves xperienced as that is ultimately their only reality. But the true nature of an *experience* is the *xperience* of the construct rather than the thing itself. Thus individual things are always constructs in the minds of observers rather than actual inhabitants of some other external observer independent area of reality.

Thus there are some basic points with regards to the nature and identity of individual forms and how they relate to xperience that must be clarified. It is clear that the entire world of forms is a single program or a single computationally evolving form but it is also clear that the identification or discrimination of individual forms and programs from it is to a great degree organismic observer dependent, arbitrary and inexact.

Thus any discussion of xperience as the continual re-computation of 'individual' forms must be carefully considered. And we must consider the difference in how 'individual' forms are defined or identified at the generic and organismic levels.

The world of forms is computational so it must be exact in the sense that it consists of precise unambiguous information forms and computations. It could not be computed if it wasn't exact in form and computation. This exactness includes constrained quantum randomness. It excludes the notion that the world of forms actually consists only of the various contradictory views of observers and that there is no single external reality common to all.

Thus the world of forms must exist as a single complete self-consistent computational system actually 'out there' in an actual reality external to and independent of any particular observer's xperience. However this single external reality does consist entirely of xperience as it consists only of the continual re-computation of forms which is defined as xperience.

The fact that multiple observers each observe similar structures in the world of forms is good evidence that something responsible for those structures actually exists external to particular observers. There is for example little doubt that actual living sentient entities such as the fox sleeping in my garden actually do exist in the world of forms independent of their experience by other organisms such as myself though what their actual forms or program structures are will be very much different than its representation in either my mental model or those of other organismic observers.

Though a consistent solipsism in which everything exists only in the mind of this (whoever this is) observer is theoretically possible *if that mind is taken as the whole of reality* there seems to be no evidence for it at all it and much against it. For one thing the fact that it behaves like it's based on consistent laws external to the observer rather than being entirely under the control of the observer and is populated by other similar observers who appear as objects within it and who each claim it is their mind instead all strongly weigh against it.

As with computer software all computations actually execute only at an elemental level analogous to machine language operations. However enormously complex emergent forms and programs simultaneously compute in terms of aggregate sequences and clusters of such elemental computations. Therefore there is a single real independent world of actual forms, independent of any particular observer, containing many levels of emergent hierarchy that continually re-computes its current state of existence through elemental level operations.

Emergent forms and programs at many levels automatically emerge from elemental and lower level computational structures such as binding energies for example. These include all emergent structures up to and including organisms and beyond. Thus *the structural basis* of all individual forms or programs, both elemental and emergent, must actually exist in a single external reality independent of any particular observer.

However what identifies individual forms or programs is not as clearly defined in the actual world of forms as it seems to be in our organismic models or as it seems to actually be at its elemental level. First there is a computational continuity between all forms which are continually re-computed in terms of their interactions with other forms and thus their instantaneously evolving form state is a combination of the computational evolution of the form and the snapshot of the form at that present moment in one more complex and subtle type of form.

The difficulty of isolating individual forms becomes quite clear when the world of forms is considered as running programs. Take the actions of some organism considered as a running program. What constitutes the actual computational nexus? It clearly includes all the 'external' circumstances, including the actions of other organisms, influencing those actions. So these are all clearly part of a single overall computational nexus that is actually computing the state and actions of the organism. So the overall 'program' computing individual actions becomes enormously extended and complex and actually includes the entire relevant consistency network of the organism as a single computational system. Therefore the entire notion of individual programs becomes virtually meaningless, or at least quite vague and arbitrary, in the actual external world of forms even though it certainly is functionally meaningful in the mental models of organismic observers.

Take the example of a cheetah chasing a gazelle. Though it can be meaningfully simplified in a simulation as separate programs of cheetah, gazelle, and environmental details, the actual computational nexus that determines the action is the single system of interaction of the ongoing computations of all of these actors in a tightly integrated computational system that can be best considered as a single program.

This system includes an enormous number of simultaneous computations down to the cellular energy mobilizations of both organisms, their dynamic musculature, their mental model computational systems, and the interactions of their feet with the details of the terrain. The actual computational nexus of this system as it actually plays out in the world of forms includes every last detail of this consistency system theoretically back through the birth and development of both organisms to the big bang. All of these are parts of the single consistency network that constitutes the entire world of forms. Therefore the notion of 'single programs' and 'individual forms' is inherently ambiguous and arbitrary in the actual external world of forms.

Thus the intrinsic forms of reality are always part of the single continuous computational structure of the entire world of forms and best considered as 'domains' within it rather than separate independent entities. Emergent forms or programs self-differentiate within the whole on the basis of natural boundaries between types of structure. These are not absolute set boundaries but general often overlapping areas of difference across which particular types of structures tend to vary.

There is also the problem of the temporal continuity of individual forms. The notion of the continual re-computation of an individual form assumes the continuing existence of that individual form. But it is not at all clear when it is a single form that is changing or when that form becomes a new form or even splits into several new forms or even vanishes, and at what point in the process on what criteria is that distinction to be made? Clearly particular individual forms continually lose their identities in other new forms.

Thus in the actual external world of forms the definitions of individual forms or programs is tenuous at best except possibly at the most elemental level. At the most elemental level the identity of individual forms is somewhat clearer, but even at the level of elementary particles their forms are often recomputed into other particles and so are transient at best as are all forms other than the most elemental such as those of the particle properties.

Thus we can clearly state that the continual re-computation of all forms constitutes xperience but we cannot as clearly and unambiguously ascribe that xperience to particular individual forms moment by moment. What we have to say is that whatever the individual forms of the moment may be and however they are identified, their continual re-computation does constitute xperience. Thus individual xperiences, like forms and programs themselves, are not fixed and unambiguous but dependent on how observers identify them. They are what they are to themselves in a world prior to discrimination and without context and their discrimination into individual xperiences or forms or programs seems observer dependent in large part.

The world consists only of evolving information, but since all that actually manifests is the continual re-computation of all forms in a continuous creation event of happening in the form of xperience, it is more accurate to say that all that actually exists is the current computational results of all the living programs of reality, each computation of which manifests reality as xperience.

The apple itself exists as a first approximation as an actual information structure in the external world of forms that acts as a framework or scaffolding for the information of itself in the experience of various organismic observers. But since some of the past information of the apple is distributed in the information of all forms that have interacted with it the true complete information of the apple consists both of the information of itself and the past information of itself distributed among other forms it has interacted with. But the latter is its past self as opposed to its current self but even its current self will consist of its current interactive computations with all other computationally impinging forms. And when multiple forms computationally interact which part belongs to which? Individual forms are never as simple to identify and isolate as they appear in our mental models and thus their true nature becomes inherently elusive.

There is certainly a sense in which the apple manifests as its own experience of itself as its forms are continually re-computed. But without an external observer to impose its own boundaries to isolate the form of the apple from the continuous world of forms how are we external observers to define the apple which self-xperiences? In our mental models of reality individual things are defined on the basis of individual characteristics such as colors, shapes, locations, behaviors, and so forth but these too are inherently difficult to isolate and define and in general do not necessarily even exist in external reality in the present moment as they are often duration based characteristics which do not exist in the reality of the present moment.

All we actually seem to have is a continuous virtual sea of self-xperience inherently undefinable in terms of individual forms until discriminated by some organismic observer. At the non-organismic level forms only xperience, and actually are, their own continual re-computations and have no models of individual forms or programs other than that implicit in their own form structures. Only in an implicit or virtual sense do non-organismic forms tune and thus identify other forms in the form of their own form content. Thus individual forms cannot be even said to exist *to each other* at the non-organismic level even though they do in the view of organismic observers. This is characteristic of the inherently logical space of the world of forms which plays by its own rules rather than those of organismic observers.

However to some extent forms in the world of forms are self-defining on the basis of domains. Certainly this must be true of organismic forms which self-organize themselves into separate volitional entities albeit with inherently indistinct boundaries at the elemental level.

But however they are defined either by self-definition or in the mental models of other observers their continual re-computation constitutes the xperience of that form or program. Since the world of forms itself is single it cannot consist of overlapping individual forms except in the mental models of organismic observers. However it can and does consist of overlapping domains of various types of structural variation.

Thus it seems that the actual definition of discrete individual forms is something that occurs only in the mental models of organismic observers, and perhaps at the level of the most elemental forms. Though there are naturally self-differentiating overlapping emergent domain structures in the external world of forms they do not self-identify as such but remain part of the computational whole until individual forms are discriminated by organismic observers generally on the basis of natural domain boundaries.

Thus at the non-organismic level the world of forms is best considered as continuous forms and continuous xperience with natural but implicit or virtual overlapping domains of emergence in terms of which organismic observers tend to discriminate individual forms or programs. Thus at the non-organismic level nothing more about individual forms or xperiences can really be said since while natural form domain structures do exist they are implicit and only organismic identifications of individual forms and programs in their mental models are explicit and discrete since individual things properly arise only as concepts in the mental models of organismic observers.

So the world of forms external to any particular observer is an intrinsically continuous structure because it does not consist of discrete forms but of the continuous interacting computations that maintain its reality. Thus it is an essentially continuous computational whole because it is all computationally connected not just its forms connected. Individual forms are based on domains of form distinction within a continuous whole. Science could be said to agree with this view in considering the totality of reality as a single wavefunction composed of the interactions of all elemental wavefunctions and this is consistent with our analogy of reality as a single ocean of continuous form.

The forms that organismic observers generate in their mental models of reality tend to be unitary forms with enormously simplified structure. And they are often seen as static or evolving in discrete steps unlike the actual forms of the world of forms. In the simulation a tree is a tree, with leaves and trunks but the form of the real tree is every last twig, leaf, cell, elementary particle and particle property as a complete hierarchical structure in a state of continual evolving computation in interaction with other forms. The individual forms in simulations can be any individual aspect of the whole and these can be individually modeled as needed, as individual leaves, branches or the whole tree. But the actual external reality is the domain structure that is amenable to the extraction of these individual views.

So reality consists of a real single external computational world of forms executing at the most elemental level which automatically generates naturally emergent structures. However the form boundaries of these emergent structures are not precise since the world of forms operates as a single computational structure in which emergent structures are always being computed in interaction with their environments as well as themselves. Thus their evolving form states inherently include interactions with external form states and thus from a computational perspective are a continuous whole while from the perspective of mental models it is conceptualized as sequences of video frames consisting of individual static form states.

Since individual forms in the moment are their computational changes rather than a sequence of snapshots of form states, their xperience consists of their *changing states* rather than their *changed states*, their change rather than what they are at any given moment. Thus it becomes more difficult to conceptualize what constitutes individual forms. However they are defined their continual re-computations constitute their xperiences.

Because emergent structures and programs are the automatic expression of their aggregate elemental operations, rather than being computed or caused by them, they change simultaneously with those elemental operations. This across level simultaneity should not be confused with emergent form structures which themselves take time to re-compute new forms. The point being that forms at all levels of emergence evolve as a single simultaneous structure as the elemental operations occur expressing as simultaneous computational changes at all levels.

However the continual re-computations of all forms at all levels of emergence of the single external world of forms can be considered the xperiences of each of those forms and thus each of those forms can be considered as a generic observer 'having' those experiences however the individual generic observer may be defined.

Thus the entire world of forms, considered as a single entity, can be clearly considered as a single precisely identifiable form consisting of all individual forms however individually identified from the whole. And the continual re-computation of this single form is the total xperience of the entire world of forms, and by extension of the universe of itself. And it is this whole world of forms that is the single precise external reality we have sought. It is characterized by being exact as it must be to be computed and it does have an implicit structure consisting of overlapping domains, however it does not explicitly exist as discrete individual forms except as modeled in the simulations of organismic observers.

This single form is thus the self-manifestation of the reality of the world of forms to itself in the form of the xperience of itself. And within it individual forms can be identified at all levels of emergence whose continual re-computation of their forms constitutes their xperience of themselves which is the self-manifestation of their own individual reality.

Every individual observer xperiences this single world of forms in its own terms as its own xperience. Its xperience is always that of the continual re-computation of its own form only. Xperience is always and only of itself as the re-computation of itself into continuing existence by happening in the present moment.

Thus while there is a single world of forms external to any particular observer, every observer however defined xperiences reality only in terms of, or as, the continual re-computation of its own form. Thus in the view of every individual observer reality consists only of the continual re-computations of its own form.

However since every form is the information of its interaction history with other forms this self-experience contains information about other forms and in this way observers of all types experience other forms or programs as well though in the case of generic observers this xperience of other forms is implicit consisting only of the re-computations of its own forms with no explicit knowledge of the other forms as separate entities whose information is contained in their own forms.

At the organismic level surfers, oceanographers and smelt variously identify the individual forms of waves, currents, and tides from a single continuous ocean. In general organismic observers tend to tune forms or programs from the entire continuous world of forms which are meaningful to them and then compute on these as discrete individual objects when in fact they are very complex forms with imprecise boundaries. Only thus are organismic observers able to simplify their reality models sufficiently to function.

Thus organismic observers may often compute in terms of a dog as a single object when the dog is actually an enormously complex form or program including every sub form down to its elementary particles and at that level most certainly does not have clearly defined boundaries.

And consider again individual waves, currents or clouds continuously evolving into other forms. And as ever more complex hierarchies and sets of forms are defined their definitions become more and more likely to be arbitrary and volatile. In fact part of the progress of science is the discovery or new and more useful and meaningful ways to define individual forms from the whole.

And since these internal simulation programs and form structures are part of reality as are the programs and forms of the organisms of which they are part, reality itself obviously has the intrinsic capability to generate and accommodate such forms. However at an overall level all the local inconsistencies and inaccuracies become consistent and accurate in the context of the organismic forms which generate them.

Organismic observers including humans are forms or programs within the world of forms characterized by sub-forms which consist of internal mental models of their realities which cannot be completely accurate representations of actual forms in external reality. The only completely accurate representation of a form is the form itself or perhaps a digital copy of a digital form.

Organismic *experience* consists of the continual re-computation of an organism's own internal forms. As with *xperience*, organisms *experience* external forms only because, as with all forms, the internal forms of the mental model are their form histories and thus contain information about other (including external) forms they have interacted with even if indirectly through their form history networks.

There are many levels of xperience occurring within the total form of an organism. At the level of its constituent cells through most of its internal biological processes each individual form xperiences its environment in its own form re-computations, though even at this level we might speak of *experience* rather than *xperience* in the many feedback mechanisms designed to maintain homeostasis. However at the level of the mental model the organism experiences its environment in re-computations specifically designed to convey maximum information about the forms of the external world in its interaction history.

Experiences are loosely defined as *xperiences* that occur in the field of consciousness. The consciousness of the individual contents, or experiences, of consciousness is just a particular type of form or program of a biological structure within organismic observers that contains a recursive element of information that tells the observer that *xperiences* are being *experienced*. The code not only registers the experience but also tells the organism it has been registered. It is functionally similar to the monitoring systems that provide the status of various systems in an automobile or aircraft. It is essentially additional code that tells the program what it is doing. There is no essential difference between xperience and experience other than the structural type of form or program of the biological structure that it occurs within that contains this additional level of self-notification.

Both xperience and experience occur as self-manifestations of reality within various types of forms within reality. There is no essential difference in that they are all real and actual xperience and therefore would be conscious if there were only the necessary biological program structure that provides the additional recursive information to inform itself it is happening.

The underlying structure of the human mental model is the structure of language and is revealed by it. This is a further more efficient development of the representational mental models of other organisms.

The mental model forms or programs have an innate internal structure designed to model reality in a simplified manner that is easier and more efficient to compute. This internal structure is encoded and passed in DNA from generation to generation as part of the organismic software. For humans this structure is revealed in the underlying logical structure of the syntax of language.

Though it is inherently difficult to exactly isolate individual forms from the continuous single form of the world of forms, this is what organisms do on the fly to create an *ad hoc* digital simulacrum of reality that is much easier to compute. Basically this model consists of loosely defined individual 'things' characterized by properties and relationships in an internally computable structure. This structure can be characterized as 'the logic of things'.

Though inherently highly simplified and incomplete these mental models are flexible enough to accommodate acceptable levels of inconsistency and still generate useful predictive results. The organism's ability to computationally accommodate some inconsistency by continually modifying the definitions of individual elements is the key to its success.

The underlying structure of mental models is a generalization of the logical structure of reality capable of modeling forms that do not exist. It is also capable of modeling inconsistent forms, as well as very simplified representations of actual external forms. In particular mental models are capable of modeling 'what if' forms and imagined future forms that do not actually exist in the real world of forms. Mental models can generate forms pretty much at will but in general they do it meaningfully in ways that enable effective functioning in terms of likely future states.

The forms organismic observers conceptualize the world of forms in terms of are all based on the intrinsic logical structure of reality as modeled in their internal syntactical or representational structures but are different for each organism and type of organism. And they are each fleshed out by how the particular organism perceives and interacts with the intrinsic external logical structure.

So every organismic observer has its own view of reality but there is enough consistency to confirm there is something common out there they all view somewhat differently. Thus the process of determining what reality actually is is a matter of teasing out what is really out there from what each observer adds to it in its internal representation of it.

There are real domain structures out there in the world of forms independent of the xperience or experience of any particular observer. Every form xperiences its own existence as it is continually recomputed however individual forms may be defined. This is how reality manifests itself as the xperience of generic observers and the experience of organismic observers. In the case of organismic observers it is the overall structural content of their internal mental models of reality that constitutes the knowledge of the organism involved, be it human or otherwise.

THE PRINCIPLE OF CONVERGENT EMERGENCE

A fundamental question with respect to emergence is how tightly is it directed? There clearly is a lot of directedness and pre-determination in the extended fine tuning but since it also incorporates quantum randomness what is the nature and extent of that directedness? And is the directedness due only to the natural operation of the elemental laws playing out or is there any sense in which higher level emergent laws also contribute to or guide the direction of the whole?

Without doubt the extended fine tuning strongly determines the evolution of the universe as it first determines the gross structure of the

266

physical universe and the actual chemistry of it which likely in turn naturally leads to the appearance of life on habitable planets, which in its turn evolves by pre-determined emergent rules towards intelligent life. Thus in this sense the current state of the universe was pre-determined within stochastic constraints by the original extended fine tuning. Thus emergence seems to necessarily converge stochastically towards pre-determined outcomes, but to what extent?

The Principle of Convergent Emergence is the fact that the evolution and emergence of forms necessarily self-selects pre-determined subsets of all possible alternatives. Reality tends to converge towards specific end states pre-determined by the extended fine tuning. For example it seems clear that the laws of chemistry as they exist in our universe are an exact convergence emerging from the laws of particle physics. However the actual chemistry that exists at any particular location is not just a direct consequence of the original fine tuning but obviously the result of plenty of quantum randomness as well. That depends on the stochastic interactions of all sorts of forms and laws.

The emergence of life is probably quite certain given proper circumstances as chemistry seems so well designed to manifest a wonderfully rich variety of life. In turn the emergence of intelligent life seems a very likely outcome given life and a conducive environment because in general intelligence conveys adaptive advantage. This convergence is of course not going to be exact because quantum processes always interject a degree of randomness that ultimately expresses in the selection mechanisms of biological evolution. So convergent emergence might always eventually trend towards intelligent life forms though not necessarily in human form.

Nevertheless the intelligent life that does emerge will likely tend to have grasping appendages capable of forming and manipulating objects; will likely be social and have speech and culture since all these are pretty much required for cultural intelligence and most of the success of humans is due to cultural rather than individual intelligence. The intelligent life that emerges will also probably tend to be an aggressive predator since predatory species tend to be more intelligent and capable.

Perhaps the tendency to destroy the planet upon which intelligence emerges is another likely end point of convergent emergence as well since the very characteristics that made our species so successful seem to be those that may lead to its destruction as well.

Emergence is a phenomenon that tends to be simultaneously up the scale of complexity as well as forward in time. The emergence of increasingly complex forms of life through evolution is the prime example and has its source in the emergence of more and more complex chemistry over time.

An open question is what other higher level processes might be directing emergence and evolution. Emergence is clearly exponential. The emergence of intelligent technological beings themselves generates much greater direction to subsequent emergence and evolution so that the process continually builds upon itself. Are there other similar higher level emergences guiding evolution? I would suspect there are many as yet unrecognized by humans.

Humans after all have pretty limited brain power. Human brains are pathetically small computational devices considering the amount of information that makes up the entire world of forms. It is inevitable that there must be numerous large scale emergent patterns that simply are beyond registration by such limited devices. And the larger these unrecognized emergent forces are the more global their effects are likely to be and the less likely they are to be recognized by human minds.

Many such patterns have already been discovered by the vast extension of human computing power available through data collection and scientific data analysis (Wikipedia: Data analysis) so there obviously must be others as well. Another problem is humans making sense of it all. Humans tend to recognized such large scale patterns individually when they do at all but rarely grasp how they operate in interaction. The more variables in any study the more difficult it is to isolated the effects of any particular variable so there seem to be limits to human understanding.

Even large scale predictive models of economies for example currently seem beyond reach though without a doubt such large scale systems do operate according to their own emergent laws. Discovering and modeling such large scale emergent systems is one of the important future goals of human intelligence and will certainly itself help guide future evolution.

THE ULTIMATE CONVERGENCE CONJECTURE

If we extrapolate convergent emergence to its ultimate conclusion we can postulate an Ultimate Convergence Conjecture, namely that the form structure of the universe is statistically evolving towards an intelligent self-awareness in which all local generic observers and intelligences become networked in a single universal intelligence that tends to maximize its self-awareness, intelligence and functionality.

This process could be thought of as an originally unconscious universe gradually awakening to its own existence through the evolution of intelligent subsystems. Or, defining God as the universe itself, even the gradual awakening of a previously unconsciously functioning God. We certainly see this trend locally here on earth in the exponential networking of information into unified systems with the exponential increase in networking vast arrays of scientific instruments into a global communication network linking more and more humans towards a single intelligent(?) information system.

To what extent this can continue to evolve as a broader trend across the universe in the future remains to be seen. One might expect so absent catastrophic interference events. How long into the far distant future this might last in the face of the gradual increase in entropy remains to be seen though the final entropy death of the universe may not be as certain as it seems as we saw in Part II.

THE SHERLOCK HOLMES PRINCIPLE

All forms are information and information only. Every form is the exact result of its entire transformation history going back to the beginning. And since every form is determined by its interactions with other forms it is not only the information of itself but also information about other forms it had interactions with and by extension information about the forms those forms had previous interactions with. This information is potentially available to observers who experience those forms by understanding the logic of forms and their interactions.

Thus every form carries as part of its form information about other associated forms. This is a fundamental principle of the world of forms. I call this The Sherlock Holmes Principle. **The Sherlock Holmes**

Principle states that every form is entirely the information of itself, and the information of itself is the information of its form interaction history and thus includes information about other forms it has interacted with computationally.

Every form is information only, and this information is the information of itself, of what it is, which is the information of the computational results of its interactions with all other forms going back to the beginning. Every form *is* the information result of its entire history and that history includes information about the entire history of reality.

Because every thing in the world is a form and forms are information only, every thing in the world is just the information of itself and that only. This information is not just the thing itself but is the history of the result of its interactions with all other forms. At a profound level the current form that anything is is the information history of that form. All things are the information of their complete computational histories and that is all they are. What every thing is now is exactly the result of what happened to it through its entire past evolutionary history.

All things are the information of their computational histories and that is all they are. And things without exception are information only. They are the information of what they are now which is the information of their computational interactions with other forms which contains information about those other forms.

However the information form history of any particular form about other forms is necessarily incomplete as it does not contain all information about all forms in its interaction history. The information of every interaction is distributed through the subsequent network of all its resultant forms and is not complete in any, and later events continually dilute the information of earlier. Nevertheless the total information of all forms considered as a single form is the entirety of the past as it currently exists in the present. But this information is distributed through interaction networks of forms rather than existing in individual forms.

Thus information of past events exists not just in individual forms but in networks of forms and in forms of forms of forms at all scales and hierarchies which each encode additional overlapping information. Since events are the nodes of entire networks of events the information of every event exists in a distributed manner across all current forms whose networks trace back to that event. In essence the entirety of information of every event exists distributed across all current forms

270

networked back to that event. But since event networks tend to be complexly cross linked the information of all past events now exists in its entirety distributed among many current forms.

Thus every current form and superset and hierarchy of forms contains clues in the form of partial information to the nature of many past events. So the entire information of the past history of the universe presumably exists fragmented and redistributed across all current forms. Thus presumably an omniscient observer could in fact know the entire past history of forms by combining the information available in all current forms.

It appears that none of the information of the entire history of the universe is ever overtly lost. Information is never lost because the forms that carry it always evolve into other forms. Forms themselves never just disappear, they are always transformed. Like waves in an ocean they all continually merge into other waves to form new waves. The individual identities of waves are submerged in new waves but their information content persists forever in the form of the subsequent waves as part of the total ocean of information. Thus the universe itself as a superorganism can be said to remember, and actually xperience, its entire past computational history in its total current form structure. Because the current form structure of the universe is the information history of its entire past.

The form of a fallen leaf is the fallen leaf itself, but its shape and DNA forms encode the information of its species and its genetic history going back millions of years and beyond. It's individual form contains information of all of the events of its particular growth and growth environment. The result is that every leaf is its complete information history *and that is all it is*.

The pattern of fallen leaves on the lawn encodes the fact of Autumn and the exact history of all the breezes that placed them there as well as the types of surfaces on which they fell. So every little thing and pattern of things in the world is the information of itself and the information of itself is the information history of all the computations that resulted in it being what it is. There is absolutely no speck of form which does not carry hidden information because it consists entirely of the hidden information of its past waiting to be revealed. The entire history of the morning backyard going back to the dawn of time lies in its current state this morning. This dawn and everything in it is that information and is only that information.

Everything is information only. The world of forms consists entirely of information and that information is incredibly dense and potentially informative. Few can read more than the slightest amount of what is there, but some, like Sherlock Holmes, much more than others. Science can be understood as the decipherment of the information that constitutes forms. This is detective work and science is essentially good detective work. But there is certainly far more information in forms than science has yet deciphered or any observer can ever know. Organisms are tuned by their evolution to extract basic information relevant to their functioning and survival but by default that excludes all the rest. The proper purview of science is the hidden information of the world of forms. The universe is the information of what it is and how it came to be that way and science is the study of that information.

Every form except the most elemental consists of many integrated levels and types of subsidiary forms. Forms are not just the forms of what we call things, but of every complex of associations and relationships between any forms we care to consider. Every individual thing in the universe is a form and every grouping of forms from whatever observer perspective is always another form. The universe of forms is the set of all forms and all sets and subsets of forms including itself as the single form that includes all others.

INFORMATION

A better understanding of information is in order. Currently information is roughly defined as the amount of 'meaning' a form has in terms of a human observer (Wikipedia: Information). For example a million bits of Shakespeare contains a large amount of information but a million random bits is considered to carry no information. But this is really not information itself but human meaningful information and should be understood as such. Information itself should be objectively defined as the amount of variation in form because this is what information is in the context of understanding the universe as a computational information system.

When this is understood both current information theory and the concept of information entropy become suspect (Wikipedia: Information entropy). A million bits of Shakespeare and the same million bits in a completely random sequence actually carry exactly the

272

same amount of information in the world of forms. It takes that million random bits to completely represent that particular randomness. The amount of information is the same in both sequences though subjectively the amount of meaningfulness in the first state is much more to a human observer. But if the observer knows nothing about Shakespeare or English the amount of meaning becomes the same in both sequences. Obviously the actual amount of inherent information has not changed but only the observer. There is no difference in the amount of variation between the two states so the amount of inherent information independent of any observer must be the same.

Information entropy posits that as the distribution of matter becomes more and more randomly homogeneous with energy entropy the amount of information in the universe approaches zero. However this applies only to observer meaningfulness rather than information in our definition. The amount of real information remains the same because the amount of form variation remains the same. That variation just now describes every last detail of the entropy state. And additionally we have previously seen that energy entropy itself is also suspect because it depends on the prevailing forces at any given time.

There is a caveat here though as emergent structures tend to collapse as entropy increases so it does appear that the hierarchical information stored in emergent structures as additional layers of forms would be lost. Thus information may not be conserved currently as higher level structures increase and diminish over time.

The amount of information depends on the variable form structure of the universe. In the general local interaction of forms information is not lost so much as redistributed even if the ability to recover it is limited. It all depends on the total amount of variation encoded in the information in the world of forms and how it is distributed. Since the world of forms, like a self-contained frictionless ocean, consists of forms continually sloshing about and transforming into other forms with no damping effect the forms theoretically slosh about forever continually transforming into other forms. Locally information is generally conserved in the transformation of forms as they interact.

Thus the universe always contains most if not all its entire past information history distributed through the entire network of information forms within it. The amount of information in the universe continually grows as more and more complex structures emerge. In fact emergence can be considered the result of the increase of information resulting from the information all the increasing number of events in the universe. Only through emergence of new information structures can that additional information be retained. This is possible because information is stored not only in individual forms but in hierarchies of forms and relational networks of forms which emerge over time to store that information. In a sense the increase in emergence is a mechanism to store the increasing information of the history of the universe. Thus the universe continually tends to become information richer.

However this is subject to the limits on information at the elemental level. Eventually information gets diluted to the point that it is lost to the granularity of reality. For example the information of any given wave is distributed among all subsequent waves it interacts with but eventually is lost within the molecular structure of water.

Not only does this process include data forms but also new code forms as well as emergent laws emerge as sequences and organizations of elemental laws. So the universe can become more and more 'intelligent' and more and more filled with knowledge. While individual observers have extremely limited access to this knowledge and intelligence it is most certainly there. At what point can the universe as a single superobserver be said to become self-aware of itself and in what respects?

THE INTELLIGENCE OF DESIGN

The world of forms as an information system containing all code and data sequences encoding its past history incorporates an enormous intelligence and amount of knowledge even in its individual forms. This level of intelligence can be quantified by comparison to what it would take for a human to design and produce the same universe including all its constituent organisms down to the last detail and much less even the complete design of a simple gnat.

Viewed from this perspective the intelligence of the universe is many many orders of magnitude greater than that of the finest human intelligence or even the totality of human intelligence. The total knowledge and intelligence incorporated in the entire world of forms including the entire history of the universe down to the most insignificant quantum event is incomprehensible. The fact that the design of the universe is intelligent of course does not require or imply an intelligent designer. It does however raise the universe itself to a God-like level.

THE LOGIC OF THINGS

Organisms relate to the world and organize their simulations on the basis of what can be called the logic of things. The logic of things is the basic rules that organisms experience as governing their simulations of reality. It is any particular organism's internal model of the laws of nature and includes the common sense rules of functional intelligence at the level of organismic functioning. An organism's model of the logic of things will be based on how things function in terms of its experience and will typically be tight at an unconscious fundamental level and looser and more *ad hoc* at a conscious level.

For example 'events have causes' is a fundamental rule with many corollaries such as material things persist as they are unless something moves or changes them. Things of the type that don't disappear don't disappear. Sharp objects may cut; lions are dangerous when hungry; things must move continuously through space to get from one point to another are other examples. In many organisms it also includes basic concepts of number such as if there were three birds and there are now two visible the other one must be somewhere else.

The basic logic of things is quite similar across species of the same level but there are considerable differences as well. It even varies considerably among humans. There are many more obvious but implicit rules that form the basis of effective understanding and functioning in the world. These are the classical level functional rules that both organisms and intelligent robots must use to function successfully in their environments.

These basic logical rules of an organism's relationship to reality begin to develop in humans as infants and they are shared in one form or another by all organisms. Though the proper study of cognitive science since Piaget (Piaget, 1956, 1960) first studied them, there has been remarkably little in the way of an systematic exposition of what these logical rules are that govern the behavior of humans and other organisms. Artificial intelligence and robotics have made significant progress in specific areas but to my knowledge no one has provided a comprehensive listing or computational simulation of any set for any organism. No one seems to have effectively modeled the functional structure of any organism in terms of its logic of things computationally, an effort that seems long overdue.

LANGUAGE

Natural languages such as English are quasi-logical structures designed to encode and express the logic of things including the forms of observer feelings about reality. Rather than the strict self-consistency of formal languages natural languages enable shifting observer views of reality to exist within a single world view. This is essential in human simulation models of reality which typically are not completely self-consistent but *ad hoc* over specific areas of discourse. This enables meaningful comprehension of areas of discussion as definitions and context change to accommodate the fluid continuous nature of the world of forms.

Observer models of reality tend to be specific and focused and much more static and fixed than the continuously changing forms of external reality. They tend to impose fixed logical structures on specific aspects of reality useful in the moment to the understanding and functioning of organisms. These are somewhat similar to the differences in world views between different persons or species each of which organizes reality in ways appropriate to it individually in its internal model.

The point here is that the logic of the world of forms, while entirely self-consistent in itself, is so in a manner that is amenable to shifting quasi-consistent models which are not necessarily completely inter-consistent because they incorporate different definitions and working assumptions about shifting aspects of reality. They tend to momentarily freeze and consider snapshots or video frames of a continuously changing reality. And they address different sets of simulated reality structures from different points of view of the same areas of reality. In fact mental models of reality tend to exist as discrete quasi-consistent areas that are often blissfully ignorant of each other. It is this capability that enables humans to frequently hold clearly inconsistent views in their internal models of reality without being aware of the inconsistencies.

For example a surfer will simulate waves differently than a physicist. They are both imposing different models of reality on the same general area of external reality but from entirely different perspectives. Because different models with different scales and logical structures can be imposed on the same area of the world of forms there will likely be some inconsistencies between simulations even though in general the views may be locally self-consistent.

And they will always be reconcilable when the observer itself is taken into consideration just as the varying views of relativistic observers always are. It all depends on what particular forms are extracted from the world of forms at what levels, and how they are then reformulated in the mental model of that area of reality. When the extraction and modeling is observer dependent as it always is there is no guarantee of complete consistency between observer models of reality. They will always be relative to the observer.

Language, and the communications of non-human organisms, are media designed to encode and facilitate these quasi-consistent world views based on the logic of things from particular observer perspectives in the moment. They are generally locally self-consistent to enable understanding and functioning in particular limited and often transient environments of reality, but are not designed to be strictly consistent with the logic of reality itself.

These mechanisms of thought and language have evolved precisely to allow inconsistency within quasi-consistency rather than to strictly enforce consistency, because that is the way in which observer models of reality operate due to the inherent limitations of observer models of reality. And this must be the case to allow language and mental representation to simulate the non-existent what if scenarios upon which computational intelligence depends.

Nevertheless, as part of the world of forms and its entirely self-consistent computational reality, all such systems themselves are entirely consistent with the totality of reality when the local nature of the assumptions, sources and errors of the mental models of observers are taken into consideration. All those inconsistencies and errors in observer mental models of reality become consistent when the observer contexts are understood and they are understood as relative to the observers involved.

CONCLUSION

Reality consists of ontological energy and the world of forms that arises within it. That is the totality of reality. Because forms arise in the ontological energy of reality they become real and actual as well.

The world of forms is an evolving computational system that is self-consistent and logically complete. It is continually re-computed to create the current form state of reality in the present moment and thereby bring it into existence.

All forms are their information only and all information is form. Form and information are two words for the exact same thing.

All the discriminable, namable 'things' of the world without exception are forms and thus are only the information of themselves and the information of themselves only. The world of forms is the actual logical substrate of all the apparent 'things' of the world in which everything actually happens.

The world of forms is a single continuous computational structure in which every part is computationally connected to the whole and the whole is continually re-computed in every instant by the ubiquitous 'processor' of happening which pervades the whole.

The world of forms is a single exact structure independent of any particular observer. It must be exact in form to be computable. This exactness includes the exact probabilistic computations of quantum randomness. It cannot consist of multiple overlapping individual things and still be consistently computable for a number of reasons explained above.

The world of forms is exact but it does not consist of discrete individual things, except possibly at the most elemental level. Instead it is a continuous self-consistent interconnected whole characterized by *overlapping domains* of structural similarities of many various types and forms of information.

Within this whole, lower level forms automatically tend to produce emergent structures in their aggregates due to the inherent nature of their elemental structures. For example binding energies of particles in atoms automatically manifest as the higher level emergent structures of materials in their aggregates and so on up the scale of emergence.

All forms other than the most elemental are emergent and they come in innumerable varieties, types and levels. They include the forms of all inanimate structures, of all organisms and even higher level structures such as superorganisms, societies and historical processes.

There are many levels of emergent structures and all exist as super-consistent *aspects* of hierarchical systems in which all levels evolve simultaneously as a single unified system in which no level can be generally said to 'produce' any other level. All levels are just aspects of the whole hierarchy. All higher levels manifest through their components and all components manifest as their aggregates.

Living organisms such as humans are specialized types of forms which construct internal simulation models of their form environments on the basis of which they intelligently compute volitional actions.

All the individual 'things' of the world are internal forms which are models based on external form domains. Thus discrete individual forms exist only in the simulations of organismic observers. These individual 'things' do not exist in the actual external world of forms but organismic observers tend to discriminate them on the basis of the information domains that do exist in the external world of forms.

This much simplified digitalized internal simulation of reality enables organismic observers to compute their functioning much more efficiently and effectively than having to deal with the actual continuous and enormously complex forms of reality.

For example in the actual external world of forms what observers would identify individually as a tree, a leaf, or a branch would all be domains of a single exact structure that included every detail of form down to the individual cells and elementary particles and would be part of a continual computational nexus including every aspect of its environment and thus computationally connected with the entire world of forms in a single tightly integrated system.

Observers tend to identify and extract individual 'things' on the basis of imprecise overlapping form domains in the whole continuous computational nexus. These are individually identified on an *ad hoc* basis.

This process occurs as internal observer forms acting as antennae 'tune' individual forms from the domain structure of the external world of forms. These tuning forms are themselves finely tuned by evolution to extract meaningful individual forms and relationships from the world of forms that are useful to the functioning of the organism. Thus organisms very effectively tune prey and predator forms from the continuous computational whole.

These information samples are then fleshed out in their simulations with additional forms consisting of information encoding the organism's perceptions of them, interactions with them, and feelings about them. It is these qualia forms combined with the external form sample that are represented in the simulation as the apparently physical things in an apparently material world. However all the apparent 'things' of the world are all actually only the information of themselves as are all forms without exception.

Organismic observers themselves are also only complex forms of evolving information within the single observer independent world of forms. Objectively they are individually discriminated as such in the simulations of other observers and themselves. Subjectively they exist as their *xperience* and their *experience* only depending on whether unconscious or conscious types of forms are being computed.

All forms are continually re-computed in interaction with other forms in the present moment by happening. This continual re-computation is what continually re-computes them into existence in the present moment. If they were not continually re-computed into existence they would vanish from the present moment and thus from reality.

All the experiences of organismic observers consist of re-computations of their own internal forms only. Thus **all experience is always actually only of itself**. An experience of something external actually consists of the computation of a change to an internal simulation of it. For example seeing an external object actually consists of computational changes *to the internal forms* of the retina and visual system.

We can extend the concept of *experience* as the re-computation of forms in an observer simulation to all forms and define *xperience* as the re-computation of any form without exception. Thus *xperience* is the exact same process as *experience* in the generic sense of every form that exists.

Thus the re-computation of any form constitutes the xperience of that form of itself and its reality because the xperience *actually is* the self-manifestation of reality in the form of that form. Nothing unwarranted should be read into this. It is exactly what it is, the re-computation of a form without context or conceptualization.

However we can then interpret the world of forms as consisting of xperience only. And we can say that xperience is the self-manifestation of reality in the continual re-computation of all form. Thus reality self-manifests only as xperience and xperience is precisely the xperience of the self-manifestation of reality in a form. In this way reality continually self-manifests itself into existence in the re-computation of forms, and continually xperiences its reality as xperience.

This is true both of the *xperiences* of inanimate generic forms and of the *experiences* of organismic forms. Thus the interpretation of the fundamental process of reality as xperience neatly integrates the necessity of the observer, at both generic and organismic levels, as an essential component of the reality of reality because it is only through the xperience of observers that reality self-manifests itself.

Experience is a special type or subset of *xperience*. Experience is the re-computation of specialized forms in the simulations of organisms which contain not only the information of the experience but information informing the organism that it is having that experience. Experience is functionally similar to the monitoring systems of automobiles that inform it of the states of its various forms but occurring in biological systems with much more detailed internal representations of themselves.

The actual forms of the external world of forms are not static video frames that are computed sequentially moment to moment but actually the information of how they are instantaneously changing. It is only this active nature that can constitute xperience. Thus forms are the forms of their actual changingnesses, rather than static video frames that are computed sequentially from moment to moment. Thus they are actually a complex and subtle amalgam of both their form states and how they are changing in the moment. In this sense they continually self-compute their evolution in interaction with other forms. This is their xperience of themselves.

At the inanimate level of actual forms in the external world of forms xperience cannot be assigned to individual forms because there is no context or conceptualization at the inanimate level. It is just raw xperience in itself devoid of context or assignment to individual forms.

However the xperience of the entire world of forms is properly the xperience of the single form of the entire universe of its continual self-manifestation of itself in the form of xperience. In this way the entire world of forms, and thus the universe itself, continually xperiences its own existence as the xperience of its self-manifestation, and self-manifests its existence as its xperience of itself.

Though the actual reality of the world of forms exists only in the present moment, its temporal trace forms a logical structure we interpret as the past history of the universe back to its beginning. This past has no *actual* present reality except in its information traces in present forms. The past as a logical structure exists entirely as a self-consistent backward extrapolation from the present of what prior states would have necessarily evolved into the present state of the world of forms according to our current knowledge of the laws of nature.

Thus since only the present actually exists the present exactly determines a past that would have exactly determined the present. The whole of present and past exists as a single super-consistent bi-directional information structure that is completely deterministic in every respect.

From the perspective of temporal duration the evolving world of forms can be considered as innumerable individual interacting programs which again are discriminated individually only in organismic simulations of them.

The operation of these programs creates what is usual considered the 'causal network' of reality. However there is no such thing as actual physical causality. This is because the world is a computational information structure rather than a physical structure. 2+2 does not 'cause' 4, it computes it. And this is actually confirmed by science since there simply are no actual variables of causality in any equation of science whatsoever. Causality is simply an interpretation or meta-principle that denotes the existence of reproducible temporal sequence. Causality does not actually exist in reality itself.

Thus the true nature of the information history of the world of forms is a consistency structure rather than a causal structure and this structure is consistent both backwards and forwards in time.

Because only the present actually exists the present is what actually determines the past. The past is entirely a projection from the present information state of reality of what, at any given point of past time, would have computationally evolved into the actual present form state to produce the present exactly as it actually is. Thus past and present exist as a single completely deterministic information structure exact in every last possible detail.

Thus, given the self-evident undeniable actuality of the present as it actually is, the past could not have been different than it actually was in any slightest detail whatsoever. It must have been exactly as it was in every detail to have produced the actual present that self-evidently exists. The self-evident existence of the present as it actually is conclusively falsifies all other possible pasts.

Thus the original extended fine tuning could only have been exactly as it was with no possibility whatsoever of any difference at all. Given the actual existence of the present as it actually is there simply could not have been any other extended fine tuning. By the Consistency Conjecture it is also likely that the exact extended fine tuning that did and still does exist is also likely the only possible one that would produce a self-consistent and logically complete world of forms and thus the only one that could exist. Thus there seems to be no need at all for any of the various multi-verse theories premised on the possibility of innumerable other fine tunings which now turn out not to be possible after all.

However the future is probabilistic as it does not exist and so is undefined. The future is always in the actual process of being computed, and thus is subject to constrained quantum randomness in how events unfold. The future is probabilistic because it has never existed and thus is still uncertain within the constraints of quantum probability.

Because the computation of reality in the present moment is probabilistic there is free will. Free will is the fact that the computations of form complexes are not completely determined by either their external forms or their own past forms. This is due only to the probabilistic nature of quantum processes within form complexes that are able to be amplified up to the level of overall action. This is consistent with the fact that organisms exhibit free will in the intelligence of their internal computations as expressed in their actions.

Thus all true randomness is quantum. There is no true randomness at the classical level other than what percolates up from the quantum level. Most of what is mistaken for classical randomness is actually non-computability. And all quantum randomness occurs only as individual spacetimes are linked and aligned because it is only then that nature has no rules to tell it what to do and so is forced to align them randomly. See Part III, Elementals, for the details.

All things without exception are only the information of themselves and that is all they are. However this information that they are is also the information of their interaction histories. Forms are continuously being altered in their interactions with other forms and this leaves traces of those other forms in their own forms. Thus the information that all things actually are is actually the information of their information histories. Thus all things are the information of their information histories which includes their interactions with other forms back to the beginning.

Thus all the xperience of forms, which is actually the xperience of their own re-computations only, is also the xperience of other forms they interacted with in the past even if indirectly. This is how forms are able to xperience not only themselves but to xperience other forms as well. Because all forms actually are the distributed information of other forms they are able to xperience other forms in the xperiences of the re-computations of their own form.

This is the Sherlock Holmes Principle which is the basis of all knowledge and science. It states that all things are their information only and this information is the information of other forms they have computationally interacted with and that information is retrievable through additional interactions with observer forms.

Everything is its information only and that information is its information history. Each individual leaf, in every aspect of its shape and its DNA, and the pattern of leaves on the lawn, each are only the information of exactly what they are and this information is also the information of their past interaction histories with innumerable other forms and thus contains information about those other forms. Thus the entire world and everything in it consists only of information about themselves and all the other things they have interacted with. All is information only.

All of us, all organisms without exception, live entirely within our own private simulation of external reality and that simulation is in turn its information only. All our experiences, feeling and meanings are ultimately only the information of those experiences, feelings and meanings.

The super-consistency of the world of forms includes the mental models of all observers including ourselves. Our models of this reality are accurate, and thus constitute knowledge, to the extent they are consistent with the inherent logic and structure of the external forms they simulate. Because we can have no direct knowledge of that external observer independent reality, and because it must be a self-consistent system to exist, the only test of accurate knowledge of reality is its own internal self-consistency across as wide a scope as possible. True knowledge consists of a maximally self-consistent internal model of reality across its entire scope.

The apparent bright, colorful, material, dimensional world with all its feelings and meanings is actually only the information that makes up and represents that world to us and conveys its experience in our mental model of reality. Like all forms it is all empty forms of information given its reality by existing in the ontological energy of the present moment. The information of the experience is the experience itself given reality by existing within the present moment of reality.

Though both we and the world of our experience are only information this is what the real world actually is. It is real because it exists in reality and it is what it is because it is the information of itself. This includes all our feelings and experiences of the bright wonderful world around us which are actually just the information encoding these experiences. This understanding does not diminish the reality of the world in any respect whatsoever. Instead it enhances its reality to understand its true nature. The question then becomes how to experience this reality as it actually is and how to live within it as it actually is. This leads us to consider the nature of realization…

PART VI: REALIZATION

APPROACH

In this part of the book we take what we have learned so far about the nature of reality and integrate it into our personal experience. We define 'realization' simply and explicitly as the clear understanding and direct experience of the true nature of reality. Realization is simply realizing reality as it actually is. In our usage it has no religious or metaphysical connotation whatsoever. However the realization of the actual presence of reality as it actually is is truly an awesome and profoundly transforming experience!

We have attempted to describe a comprehensive view of the true nature of reality. But can this view also be verified by direct experience and can we then live in a state of realization of it? And if so to what extent since many of the aspects of our illusory mental model of reality seem intrinsic to the human condition? To what extent can they be transcended to directly reveal the reality they conceal?

Though our mental model of reality clearly misrepresents reality's true nature we must remember that since reality includes everything that exists and excludes nothing, we are all already continually experiencing and living within reality as it actually is. So realization is not a matter of searching for reality elsewhere but finding it right here and now in the true nature of everything within and around us.

Thus reality is not to be found outside of the things and experiences of our daily life but in seeing the true nature of these things. If everything without exception is part of reality then even the illusions inherent in our mind's simulation of reality are part of that reality and just need to be experienced as they actually are. If we believe the world is as it appears that is illusion because it is actually our internal mental model of the world, but if we see the world of our mental model for what it really is that is reality. **Illusions taken for reality are illusions, but illusions seen as illusions are reality.** The realization of the reality of the magician's trick is not what it appears to be but in understanding how it fools us, and this is equally true of all aspects of reality.

There are many approaches to the direct experience of reality. All involve directly tuning consciousness to the fundamental presence and nature of the formless ontological energy that underlies the world of forms. But we must also recognize and reengage with the world of forms as the manifestation of this fundamental reality. And then insofar as possible in human form we must seek out and act in accordance with the deeper actual logic and forms and flows of reality that lie hidden within mind's simulation of them. What we discover when we succeed is in accordance with not only the deep logic of reality and modern science but with some of the deepest insights of ancient philosophy as well.

This part of the book describes the experience and fundamental principles of realization but not any practices or techniques to achieve it. That will be reserved for a possible subsequent publication.

DIRECTLY EXPERIENCING COSMOLOGICAL REALITY

Our consciousness in the present moment is the direct experience of the fundamental processes of the cosmos. Our personal experience, and the xperience of everything in the universe, actually is the direct experience of the fundamental reality of the universe precisely because it is the direct presence of reality in these processes. The fundamental cosmological processes are not just happening out there somewhere in intergalactic space but right here and now inside all of us as well. This is an amazing insight when we realize how profoundly true it actually is.

The most basic aspect of our existence is that of our consciousness in a present moment of reality in which happening happens and clock time flows, and we see past time as distance. This fundamental structure of our existence is the direct experience of the fundamental structure and process of the universe because it is the direct self-manifesting presence of that fundamental structure and process.

Our consciousness itself is the immanent presence of the self-manifesting actuality and existence of reality itself. Reality self-manifests as our experience of it. And our existence in the present moment of reality is our existence within the surface of the cosmological hypersphere of the universe which is the locus of reality.

Our experience of the continual self-manifestation of happening as consciousness itself is our direct experience of the continual extension of the radial p-time dimension of the cosmological hypersphere which is the fundamental process of the universe and the source of that happening. This continually happens throughout the entire cosmos and within our own being as well. It is this cosmological process that gives all things, including ourselves, their existence and reality in the present moment.

Happening is the source of the STc Principle underlying special relativity which continuously propels all of us through time at the speed of light as the radial p-time dimension of the universe extends. The experience of happening is our direct experience of continuously moving through time at the speed of light.

This is also the reason that we experience an arrow of time. Our experience of the arrow of time is our experience of the unidirectional extension of the radial p-time dimension of the universe. And the fact that the STc Principle requires us to be at one and only one position in time is why there is only a single moment of time called the present moment in which everything exists including ourselves.

Because of this cosmological structure we directly see all 4-dimensions of our hyperspherical universe. The radial past dimension of time is seen in all directions with distance which directly confirms our universe is a 4-dimensional hypersphere. We actually see and confirm the hyperspherical geometry of the universe with our own eyes.

When we truly realize that the fundamental structure and process of the universe exists within us as the fundamental nature of our own existence this is truly an amazing and awesome experience. At every moment we are continually hurtling through time at the speed of light riding the continually extending surface of the universe in the present moment which that surface is.

This is what the experience of happening in the present moment actually is. And in every direction we look we see the radial past time dimension of the universe falling away behind us at the speed of light. Truly we are right in the middle of everything important with the best seat in the house! The fundamental structure of the universe lies clear before our eyes and all we have to do is look and see it as it actually is!

This is the realization of the fundamental structure and process of the universe in our own direct experience of it.

CONSCIOUSNESS ITSELF IS THE PRESENCE OF REALITY ITSELF

Consciousness itself is the direct experience of reality itself. When consciousness turns attention away from the individual thoughts, perceptions and feelings which normally occupy it then the underlying presence of consciousness itself is revealed. And this is precisely the self-manifesting presence of the fundamental nature of reality itself. The actual existence, presence and happening of consciousness itself is actually the self-manifesting existence, presence and happening of reality itself within ourselves as ourselves.

When consciousness turns away from all the individual contents of consciousness what remains is the presence of pure consciousness itself which is the living presence of reality itself within us. This is the single presence of reality and consciousness together within which all the individual forms of consciousness and our experience of all the individual forms of reality arise and by doing so become real.

Consciousness itself, and thus reality itself, can be conceptualized by analogy to a perfectly still pool of bright water. It is initially formless, completely real and actual, and is actually present in the present moment, and it is perfectly and absolutely exactly what it is. It is complete in that it is all that exists, and it is has life in the sense that happening continually happens within it. It is in itself perfectly formless so that at any moment the mental representations of the forms of the world arise and pass across its exquisitely sensitive surface as fleeting ripples.

This is the direct experience of the fundamental presence and nature of reality in human terms. The still pool is what we call ontological energy and others may refer to as Tao or Buddha Nature. It is also consciousness itself, which is the direct self-manifestation of reality within the human observer as consciousness. This is simply the human variety of the universal self-manifestation of reality in the form of the xperiences of all things that exist.

289

Reality consists of the fundamental immaterial presence of ontological energy and all forms which arise within it. This is the totality of reality. The most direct method of experiencing ontological energy is to minimize the appearance of forms so that the formless ontological energy that underlies them and in which they arise becomes clearer. Normally mind is preoccupied with all sorts of individual forms such as particular thoughts, feelings, and things. Thus consciousness tends to see the world in terms of these things and their relationships. But the deeper reality of consciousness is the consciousness itself in which all these individual forms arise to become conscious, and that is the self-manifesting presence of reality itself.

Through the mental exercise of emptying consciousness of its individual contents the fundamental substance of consciousness itself that remains is revealed. This is a traditional form of meditation and is an easily reproducible mental exercise accessible to anyone with practice. It is an easily demonstrated fact and there is nothing supernatural or esoteric about it at all. When this state is achieved it becomes clear that consciousness doesn't consist of the individual thoughts, feelings and perceptions that flow through it but is the fundamental real and actual presence of reality in which these forms become conscious. This is clear because consciousness itself remains even stronger and brighter as its individual contents diminish.

This consciousness itself that supports all forms is essentially formless and immaterial. It has a being or immanence like an internal brightness or radiance which is not so much light as the intrinsic presence and aliveness of realness. It is the energetic presence of being and actuality. Consciousness is the immediate actual presence of reality itself self-manifesting its presence as the experience of itself. These are its characteristics put into words but it itself is nameless and without characteristics or forms whatsoever.

Consciousness is not something produced by the human brain. Consciousness is simply the self-manifesting presence of reality in the form of an observer as its experience. The aspect of consciousness we call awareness is nothing more than the self-manifesting presence of reality in the present moment. Consciousness itself is the living presence of reality and not something manufactured by the human brain, though the particular forms of its contents are clearly constructs of the cognitive models of human observers.

This is clear because all the characteristics of consciousness itself are precisely the characteristics of reality itself. Thus consciousness itself is the actual manifestation and presence of the ontological energy of reality itself rather than something created by the human mind. It is the particular forms of *the contents of consciousness* that are products of the human mind. Consciousness itself in which these forms appear as contents is the self-manifesting presence of reality itself within a human form.

Thus the fundamental nature of reality itself is directly accessible to human consciousness because what we call consciousness itself is the direct manifestation of reality itself within an observer. Consciousness itself is simply the participation in the presence of reality, as a part of that reality, by an observer. Just as seeing is due to the presence of light *from* things rather than the eyes shining light *on* things, so consciousness is due to the presence of reality itself *in* an observer rather than something generated *by* an observer.

Thus we can say that consciousness is conscious because reality is real. Consciousness is simply the self-manifestation of the realness of reality within an observer. It is the fundamental presence of reality that manifests itself to all observers according to the nature of their forms. Consciousness is just the fact that observers necessarily participate in the self-manifestation of reality because they are part of reality. The only thing the observer brings to consciousness is its experience of it from its particular locus and the particular details of the forms of its contents which is modeled in terms of its particular simulation structure.

Thus consciousness itself is common to all observers but the details of how its contents are formulated depend on the structure of the particular observer. All forms in the universe act as generic observers in their xperiences of themselves which are the continual happening of their own forms in interactive evolution with other forms.

Happening and alteration of form is the manifestation of form which we call xperience. Thus the xperience of all forms is the self-manifestation of the fundamental nature of reality in the forms of generic observers. What we call consciousness is simply this exact same self-manifestation of reality in the form of human and other organismic observers which have recursively sentient form structures. Human consciousness is human xperience, the self-manifesting presence of reality within a human observer with a recursively sentient form structure that tells itself it is experiencing what it experiences.

Thus it is possible to directly experience the fundamental nature of reality because reality self-manifests as consciousness itself. Consciousness is the actual presence of reality within an observer. Consciousness itself is the direct experience of the living self-manifesting presence of ontological energy, the fundamental reality in which all the things of the world arise as forms and all thoughts and perceptions likewise arise as forms. Consciousness itself is reality itself in the form of an observer.

Because consciousness itself is essentially formless it is the presence of the formlessness of ontological energy and not just another of the forms that arise within it. Because it is formless and a non-dimensional experience it transcends the observer singularity.

Of course even consciousness itself is an observer experience to some extent as it does manifest in the form of an observer so the way an observer experiences it is somewhat particular to that observer especially so when it is described in language. But it is a very direct experience because of its formlessness and is as close as we can get to the direct experience of reality so long as we are in human form. Without some observer, generic or organismic, ontological energy could not be experienced at all; there would be no experience and reality could not manifest itself in any form because there would be no form in which it could manifest as xperience.

So by allowing the individual forms of the world as the contents of consciousness to fade away, and by tuning in to consciousness itself,, we directly experience the fundamental nature of reality itself because consciousness itself is the direct self-manifestation of the living happening presence of ontological energy itself in the forms of ourselves.

Whatever we choose to call ontological energy we confirm its presence and nature by the direct experience of its existence within us. This is the realization of the fundamental nature of reality which is available to all of us by directly experiencing our own fundamental nature which is that of reality itself.

THE ENLIGHTENMENT EXPERIENCE

Because reality is absolutely absolute and absolutely present its direct realization often occurs with sudden profound intensity. It has been compared to the sudden shock of confronting a tiger on the road or suddenly looking into the eyes of God and seeing God looking back. An enlightenment experience is the sudden realization of the actual awesome presence of the absolute realness of reality in all its immanence.

What was previously understood only as an abstract concept is suddenly realized as the living here now presence of reality itself directly within and around one. Zen calls this experience 'satori' but a similar experience is common to many religions (Suzuki, chap. 4, 1956). It can come as a sudden profound shock to consciousness as the veils of illusion suddenly drop away, the scales fall from one's eyes, and reality is suddenly revealed right here and now in all its awesome absolute realness as the living essence of all things. This is the direct experience of what we call ontological energy which is the underlying reality and presence of the existence of all things.

Because reality is *absolutely real and present* the effective intensity of its presence is unlimited and dependent only on the capacity of the observer to experience it. Normally mind operates at a mundane level preoccupied with a continual procession of mundane forms and tasks and doesn't allow consciousness to experience the truly awesome intense absolute realness of reality that is possible. Allowing consciousness to experience something of the true intensity of reality is normally reserved for sudden emergencies where maximum attention and engagement are required. This is because extreme situations mobilize intense fight or flight energy levels in both mind and body that cannot be sustained.

The enlightenment experience is somewhat similar in its intense clarity of mind but rather than extreme fight or flight adrenaline surges there is instead a strong, clear, healthy relaxed readiness of life energy that vitalizes rather than drains. This is a state of balance and refreshment rather than a continual dissipation of energy. One is continually aware of the awesome absolute presence of reality but there is a complete and total ease and acceptance and a perfect easy equilibrium in resting within it as if one had finally found one's true home (Wilhelm, 8, 1931).

Because the intensity of the actuality and presence of reality is absolute the only limit on the intensity of realization is the capacity of the realizer. By letting go of the natural tendency of mind to damp down the intensity of the experience of reality one naturally experiences that intensity at the level of one's capacity. To do that one must open oneself completely to the presence of reality and embrace it. Though sometimes frightening this becomes easy when it is realized there is actually no alternative to existing in reality as it actually is in the present moment even if we might attempt to escape it in our imagination.

Mind normally makes us wary of reality and the dangers it may hold but while it is certainly true there are many programs running in reality which may pose significant dangers to our individual existence, the actual presence of reality itself is completely benign and in fact embracing it more fully and intensely actually enables us to detect and deter hostile forms more effectively. Thus a major impediment to the intense realization of reality is the fear of the forms within it and the illusion that if mind damps the intensity of our experience of reality we somehow are protected from those dangers when the opposite is actually true.

Thus completely opening oneself and embracing reality and dropping the illusory fear of its presence is essential to its realization and simultaneously allows us to live more effectively within it.

This is the mind of the samurai which abandons individual self and accepts the total and absolute presence of reality, even including the ever present possibility of personal death, and in so doing is able to exist at ease in the present moment with maximum effectiveness (Harris, 1974). The ultimate bravery in abandoning the forms of self that seek to insulate self from reality gains maximum realization of reality and maximum effectiveness within it.

EXPERIENCING THE TRUE NATURE OF THOUGHTS

The forms that appear within consciousness become conscious only because they appear within consciousness itself. These contents of consciousness, our thoughts, perceptions and feelings are clearly the empty information forms of what they are experienced to be rather than physical things. Thus their only real 'substance' is that of consciousness itself. They are simply information forms passing through consciousness itself in which they become conscious.

This is easy to understand because thoughts clearly have no physical substance. Their nature as information is fairly easy to experience because these contents of consciousness are clearly not material things and thus must be just information in our minds. The problem is that their presence often elicits reactions from us that occupy our attention and interfere with this understanding. However all these reactions are themselves just further mental forms that arise and thus they too are also just the information they carry. Thus if we maintain a state of mindfulness in which we observe all the contents of consciousness as the forms of information they are we succeed in realizing their true nature fairly quickly.

There are further advantages to this in terms of realization, because when the forms of mind are recognized as just information passing through consciousness it becomes easier to mindfully recognize the unnecessary attachments and desires that lead to the appearance of subsequent forms of feelings of emotional suffering. These too are simply additional empty information forms that arise in consciousness as contents of consciousness. By recognizing the contents of consciousness as the information forms they are and how their sequences arise we gain the ability to break the sequences that lead to emotional suffering.

There are natural flows of these forms through consciousness depending on the state of our realization and our situation. But they are all only empty information forms that become conscious by appearing in consciousness. When mindfulness is maintained attachments and desires may still arise within consciousness but by recognizing them as empty forms that arise naturally in human minds *one is no longer attached to one's attachments* and desires and they gradually subside.

Thus the true nature of all the contents of consciousness is that they are empty information forms flowing through consciousness. The information they carry is all they are. They have no other reality and they can be recognized as such, as simply carriers of information that by becoming conscious in consciousness manifest themselves.

The empty information forms of the mind exist as forms within consciousness itself which is the self-manifesting presence of reality itself. Thus their true nature is information manifestations of the ontological energy of reality. Thus the realization of the true nature of the forms of mind is to understand and experience them as forms of ontological energy that all manifest the formless ontological energy of reality in which they arise. When they diminish and even vanish, it is pure formless consciousness itself that remains, but even if they remain realization is seeing them as forms of that formless consciousness itself which is reality itself. Realization is the direct experience of the presence of the reality of ontological energy both directly as formless consciousness itself and formless reality itself and as the true nature of all the forms that arise within it as manifestations of it.

All forms are manifestations of ontological energy and that only. Thus realization is directly experiencing the immanent presence of reality in all forms as well as in the formless. All forms of mind carry the information they are but because they are real and present because they exist as forms within the presence of consciousness itself and reality itself they automatically manifest that underlying reality. When we recognize the underlying formless reality within all the information forms we realize the true nature of forms.

EXPERIENCING THE TRUE NATURE OF THINGS

The key to understanding the true nature of the apparently physical things of the world is to understand they are all constructs of our simulations that arise in consciousness as information forms just as thoughts do. All the apparent material things of the world are all actually only their representations as contents of consciousness just as thoughts, feelings and meanings are. When this is realized all becomes clear, and the true nature of the apparently material world is realized as actually just various types of qualia overlaid on information structures sampled from external reality.

What appear to be the material things of the world are actually only associations of information forms in consciousness. A material thing is really just an association of co-located color, texture, resistance to movement, hardness, beauty, value etc. and every one of these things is itself an information form in our simulation of reality. And further every one of these attributes is information not just about the thing itself but of our interactions with it.

Thus things themselves exist only as bare information frameworks in the external world which in concert with the information structures of

296

the observer results in associated information forms in consciousness which are only forms of information empty of any substance other than consciousness and reality itself. All that exists in external reality of things is their bare empty information scaffolding.

The apparently material world in which we appear to exist is a construct of our simulation. It consists of associations of the information forms of our interactions with those external forms and the additional information forms that carry our feelings and meanings with regards those structures. The material world is just a very convenient illusion that enables us to function more effectively by fleshing out bare information structures with qualities, feelings and meanings, themselves additional information, that give them valuations to the observer. Realization of the true nature of things consists in actually recognizing and seeing these apparently material things of the world as the information forms they actually are by progressively deconstructing their form structures into the various forms of information that compose them.

With practice the things of the world can be recognized as the associated forms of information they actually are. The forms of things in consciousness are nearly identical to the thought forms that arise there also. Both are empty information structures, the only difference is that the basic scaffolding of thing forms is more closely based on logical information structures in external reality which are sampled and then extensively overlaid and embellished with forms added by mind. But those external forms are also only information forms devoid of any material substance. They just follow consistent computational rules that allow mind to effectively represent them as things.

Pick up a stone and study it mindfully picking apart each of its attributes individually into the information that it actually is. Eventually it will be realized as a combination of various types of information only, an association of qualities that arise as information forms in consciousness. It is not that the stone suddenly changes in anyway at all, it is just suddenly realized for what it actually is and has always been. In every respect it is associated forms of information only that takes on its realness to us simply by appearing in the self-manifestation of reality as consciousness within the form of a human observer.

Thus every seemingly material thing in the world is its information only and with practice can be realized as such. All its qualities and attributes are just the information of those qualities and attributes. All qualities are information that our mental model combines into the information structure it represents to itself as a material thing.

And thus the actual reality of every material thing, its very existence and presence and actuality of being, is the direct self-manifestation of the formless ontological energy of reality itself in the information form of that thing. Every seemingly material thing is its information and that information manifests the true nature and presence of reality. And that is what is realized in consciousness as the true nature of the thing as an association of empty forms filled with pure consciousness itself, which again is the presence of reality itself self-manifesting in the form of our consciousness itself.

The trick leading to the realization of the true nature of things is to understand and then to actually see that all things without exception are the information of those things and that information only, and that this information is actually real because it is the self-manifestation of reality. When this is understood and taken to heart the true nature of things becomes clear.

Some will insist that this analysis applies to the experience of things rather than to things themselves. That it is true that our experiences of things are indeed information forms in our minds, but that things themselves might actually have real material existences in a physical world. However there simply is no evidence for that at all. It is merely an unwarranted projection of our materialistic simulation of reality back onto the false external reality it assumes. Ultimately all knowledge of reality including that of our notion of an external material world exists only as internal information forms within consciousness. Our notion of an external material world exists only as information forms in our consciousness. Everything without exception is the information of itself only.

LIVING IN THE RETINAL WORLD

Once we understand and experience the true nature of individual things as information constructs we can expand that realization to the entire world around us.

The world of our experience consists of apparent things and their evolving interactions with ourselves and with each other in an apparently dimensional framework 'out there' external to us of which we are a part. But as with things taken individually all these things together are all only forms of information, the information of themselves and their relationships.

As a first approximation this apparently dimensional world populated by physical things is entirely in our head because it is actually our mental model of external reality rather than external reality itself. We know that what we see is not actually the sky but two combined 2-dimensional images on our retinas extensively post processed by our cognitive system into a 3-dimensional model inhabited by individual things including our self. This the bright wonderful world we seem to inhabit is actually inside our own mind which tricks us into experiencing it as external to us.

Thus we live under what can be called the Retinal Sky. What we see in all directions is not an external reality but post processed images from our retinas. And the same is true of our other senses as well. The world that we actually live in is an enormously complex information construct in our mind rather than the actual external world it appears to be. It consists of some basic information scaffolding filtered from the external world overlaid with the information structures encoding our interactions with it, all post processed into the simulated world we experience ourselves living within.

Thus when we look out into the world we are actually looking more into the information structure of our own mind than the external world itself. The external world contributes only the bare scaffolding of logical structure and all the rest is painted over that logical structure by our own minds. All the apparent qualities and individual self-substances of that world are all qualia and products of our own mind and exist only inside our own minds. This includes even the illusory dimensionality and spatiality of the world as well as we saw in Part III.

Thus the actual external world is completely unlike we imagine it. It is an evolving logical structure only. It has no size, position, orientation, or any other physical or material attribute as we discovered in Part IV. It is simply a logical structure in an non-dimensional information space that can be endowed with those attributes relative to an observer in that observer's simulation of it.

It is inherently difficult to see this illusion for what it is because our minds are programmed to see it as it appears rather than as it actually is. And this illusion is very convincing because it is the product of a long evolutionary development which has helped us and other organisms survive. Nevertheless it is possible to progressively realize the true nature of the world beginning with the illusory nature of individual things and stepwise progressing to the whole.

We do this by gradually teasing apart the many types of information that compose the illusion progressively recognizing each for what it is and what it contributes to the illusion. We see into the retinal world as if we were looking into a double sided mirror from both sides at once. Because the illusory world of our everyday experience is in fact a mirror that combines both the external and internal worlds in a single image[2]. Thus reality becomes our simulation and our simulation becomes reality. Together they combine in the single reality that includes both consciousness and external reality as a single reality and the structural forms of both external and internal reality in a single reality including both.

The realization of the true nature of the retinal world has many levels because there are many levels that make it up. Each level is another veil of illusion that must be progressively identified and analyzed into its information to determine how it distorts the reality it veils. Finally we begin to see both the reality behind and how it is distorted by each veil simultaneously. We have identified a long list of these veils throughout this book and how they each distort the reality they veil. It is ultimately up to the reader to realize them in action in his own experience of reality.

Another approach is to start from the nature of formless reality itself and work outwards progressively adding each of the aspects that mind adds while keeping the reality at the center always clearly in mind. Either way we finally discover layer upon layer of continually interacting information forms surrounding the living presence of the ontological energy of reality within. And at last we come to realize that it is this whole structure that is the whole of reality, because reality by definition includes everything without exception.

When we look out into the world we look into the depths of external reality and the depths of our own minds simultaneously. To understand the whole we tease it apart form by form and layer by layer into its information and see what emerges. The whole is an immensely complex information structure and it is that structure that constitutes the whole of reality. This is the realization of the retinal world.

MOUNTAINS ARE MOUNTAINS AGAIN

To the extent we realize the true information nature of the world as a manifestation of ontological energy we realize its reality. But the illusion of its apparent physicality does exist and since all that exists is part of reality that illusion is also part of reality. Not only is ontological energy and the deep information structure underlying apparent reality part of reality but the illusion of apparent reality that exists as our mental model of reality is also part of actual reality. And that mental model will be different for every organism and every one of those mental models of reality will also be part of reality.

Everything that exists is part of reality and that includes its illusory simulations in the mental models of observers. Those mental models too are additional information forms that exist in reality, and the information content of those forms is the apparent physical reality of an illusory world of forms. Reality is recursive in the sense that it contains mental models of itself in the simulations of organismic observers.

When this is realized it is clear that nothing has changed whatsoever. With realization all things are exactly as they always were. They are now just realized for what they actually are, as illusory observer information structures that manifest the information of an apparent physical reality for the convenience of those observers to facilitate their functioning in reality.

The goal is not to have the wonderfully rich and useful illusory world we thought we lived in disappear into some colorless invisible abstract pure information structure. Realization is continuing to live in the world of forms as it always was while understanding what it actually is. Realization is not to withdraw from the world of forms but to better understand and more fully experience the total world of reality as it actually is. Though our internal simulation of reality is an illusion in the sense it is not the reality of the actual external observer independent world it appears to be, it is also a part of the reality of that external observer independent world of forms when understood as the simulation it actually is. Both the observer itself and its simulation model of reality are themselves forms in the real external world of forms.

The illusion of the mental model exists as actual real information forms as part of reality. Realization is just a matter of perspective. Illusion taken for reality is illusion but illusion understood as illusion *is* reality. In terms of the world of forms the illusions of our mental models of reality are the evolved natural reality of our human form. By experiencing the usual reality of the world of our experience as a simulation of reality we add a whole new world of richness to the reality we inhabit.

This is expressed by the Zen saying that "mountains become mountains again" after they were previously seen as illusions of mountains rather than the real physical mountains they first naively appeared to be (Watts, p. 126, 1957). They are mountains again because that's what mountains really are – information structures that mind naïvely simulates as physical mountains with all the wonderful illusory qualities of mountains we know so well. Mountains are first seen simply as the physical mountains they appear to be. Then they are recognized as illusory constructs of our simulations of reality. But then finally it is realized that what mountains really are is the illusions they appear to be. They are the same information structures they always were, but it is now realized that their reality actually consists of the illusions of themselves recognized as the illusions they are.

Because everything is part of reality, illusion is also part of reality. But only when illusion is seen as illusion is its reality experienced. When illusion is mistaken for reality it is illusion rather than reality. Thus realization is realizing that illusion as illusion is the true nature of illusion. That is the realization of reality, of things as they are. It is to be maximally engaged in the world of illusion while realizing it for what it actually is. It is experiencing that both things as they are and as they appear to be simultaneously combined is their complete true nature. It is seeing both the distorting mirror and the image that it distorts simultaneously so that the true nature of the whole is realized. In this way we realize the true nature of mountains and of ourselves simultaneously because the true nature of mountains is how they are represented in our simulations of them.

But beyond this is the realization that all the forms of the world and thus the entire world we live in is the direct self-manifestation of the underlying reality of ontological energy. All forms arise in ontological energy and become real by arising therein. Ontological energy is the underlying reality of everything including ourselves, and all things are forms that arise within ontological energy thus becoming real themselves. But their reality always consists of their underlying ontological energy rather than what they appear to be. Buddhism expresses this by saying, "all forms are empty", meaning that things are empty of their apparent self-substances and their only true substance is the formless presence of what we call ontological energy (Conze, Heart Sutra translation, 1974),

This is the deep experience of the true nature of reality. It is realizing all things as forms of ontological energy as they arise as forms in mind's simulation of reality which like all things is itself an information complex within ontological energy thereby becoming real.

By experiencing our simulation as the simulation of reality it actually is we experience the true nature of the reality it simulates which includes itself. Only in this way do we realize the true complexity and the true simplicity of the totality of reality and experience things as they actually are, as abstract information forms fleshed out in our simulations as the familiar things of the world. By realizing the complete true nature of things they become even more wonderful and amazing than we thought they were. They are all realized as reality itself self-manifesting as the contents of a real actual present moment rich with interacting forms. It is ultimately the beautiful and useful illusions of these forms that is their reality.

REALIZING THE TRUE SELF

Because we live under the retinal sky within a mirror world combining both external reality and our simulation of it in a single world of experience our true self is coterminous with that entire world of experience and our individual self as it is usually imagined is an illusion.

Every aspect of the world we believe we live in is actually our own experience of that world as formulated in our simulation of it. So in a very real and profound sense every aspect of the world of our experience, including what we usually consider to be our experience of 'external' objects, is part of our self since it all actually exists entirely within our simulation of reality. So we are actually the totality of

303

everything that we experience without exception including all the things 'out there' in the external world. When we experience the world we are experiencing ourselves. Thus this experience is always prior to the usual distinction of self and not-self.

So realization is that experience itself is what is actually real since experience is all that we experience. The fundamental reality of experience is just raw experience antecedent to the dualism of ourselves as experiencer and things experienced, whether they are subsequently categorized as internal or external. This means that the usual distinction between self and not-self is an illusion that occurs subsequent to experience itself as experience becomes organized in our simulation of reality. And then even that mental model itself, in which the forms of self and not-self are stored, exists only as the direct experience of itself. Thus all is experience only, and generically all is *xperience* only, and all notions of experiencer and experienced, of self and not-self are themselves only subsequent experiences also themselves prior to any dualism of experiencer and experienced.

Thus there is no individual self that experiences both self and not-self things. The individual self is an illusory subsequent categorization of experience. If we even want a notion of self we must speak of a 'true self' which consists of all experience without exception and thus includes all the things of the world we experience as well as the illusory experiences of an individual self.

So all the forms in our experience are aspects of this true self. However we also directly experience the fundamental reality in which these forms arise as our consciousness itself, the presence of reality in which all the forms of experience manifest. Together this can be called our true self because it is the entirety of 'our' experience. The totality of experience itself prior to any dualism or categorization is our true self, or more concisely the totality of experience is true self.

Of course our individual self does exist as a convenient illusion in our mental model of reality which usually functions in terms of self and not-self. This aspect of our mental model has evolved to make it easier for us to act in such a way as to function and survive as an individual self so it does certainly make sense in the world of forms. Thus again realization is realizing both the true nature of the individual self as a convenient and very effective illusion and simultaneously the fact that all experience itself, antecedent of any distinction of self and not-self, is the true whole self because all experience, even the experience of seemingly external things actually occurs within the mental model of the individual self, or more accurately as raw experience itself prior to the categorization of an individual self.

The realization is that the totality of what we call 'our' experience, which is all that exists in our experience, exists as a single mind filled with the consciousness of all this experience, of everything that happens, that combines what we think of as 'our' consciousness and external reality together considered as a single mind or realm of experience. Fundamentally these experiences do not belong to any experiencer, nor are they of anything, they exist fundamentally just as pure experience itself manifesting as mind, again not a mind of anyone but just mind itself.

This realization is what the Diamond Sutra calls 'Awakening the mind while dwelling nowhere' (Wu, p. 62, 2005). There is no focus to consciousness because consciousness simultaneous pervades the entirety of this reality that includes all experience rather than being focused on any particular individual forms. Instead there is a total mental openness to everything as forms flow freely through consciousness itself as experiences. In this state all forms exist as pure raw uncategorized experience, antecedent to any notion of self or not-self or anything at all. They are just pure raw forms of experience with no meaning or reference because they as yet are not being categorized and structured in the mental model. They are exactly and only what they are in themselves as opposed to being interpreted or related to anything else at all.

There is no center to being with this realization because being pervades all experience. There is no center to being because this is an experience antecedent to the imposition of dimensionality and thus without dimension.

Though this realization is not the typical state of organismic consciousness it is the natural state of inanimate form which always exists as pure raw xperience itself devoid of any context or categorization or assignment to individual observers.

But then again the organized contents of organismic simulations also exist as further direct experiences. So once again self and not-self appear but not as the absolute entities they appeared to be but as additional direct experiences of themselves. Thus reality consists only of pure experience prior to self and not-self but self and not-self do exist as part of that direct experience, along with all the other individual forms with which the mental model populates reality.

What is directly experienced at this level is not just a mental state but the fundamental ontological energy of all things. While it is true this experience is objectively that of a human and must be in human terms to some extent this is only how it appears from the outside in the mental model of an external objective observer where every mental model of reality stands as a separate reality within the whole.

From the 'inside', subjectively, or more accurately directly, it is experience only which is the raw information forms of reality arising in a single reality of experience prior to the dualism of experiencer and experienced. It is the direct unmediated arising of the presence of the reality of primal forms. All else arises from the organization of this direct immediate experience in the simulation, and then that too is experienced itself only as direct experience prior to experiencer or experienced and so it goes.

Consciousness, and the experiences within it, fills the entire space of any observer's experience of reality. Thus consciousness and reality are one in the experience of the observer and this is the experience of the extended true self. In a very real sense all is consciousness only because all is reality only. To the opened mind consciousness and reality are one and the same and always awesomely real, present and absolute.

THE FUNDAMENTAL REALIZATION OF FORM

Any notion of the 'rest of the world' beyond the current scope of consciousness is only a thought form within consciousness and exists only as that thought in the experience of that observer. To any observer, the rest of the world that is not here and now exists only as imagined forms in the observer's consciousness. Thus consciousness itself rests in the real rather than the what might be and thus it is the presence of reality itself.

Reality manifests only in the consciousness of observers, and at the non-organismic level as the xperience of generic observers. Thus the *experience* of consciousness is a specialized subset of the *xperience* of inanimate and unconscious forms. Other than in its particular manifestations reality cannot even be said to exist in the most fundamental sense because reality exists only as its manifestations.

Manifestation is reality, and reality is manifestation. The notion that there is a single reality that manifests variously in the xperience of all generic observers is itself only a form structure manifesting in the simulation of some organismic observer. And since everything in the universe functions as a generic observer reality exists only in its manifestations of itself to itself.

Everything in the universe xperiences other things in the universe as its own xperience, and it is this xperiencing of everything by everything that is reality itself. More accurately reality exists only as xperience because only as xperience does it self-manifest and without manifesting it cannot be said to exist. Thus xperience exists. Some of this *xperience* includes the conscious *experience* of myself 'having' this experience of other not-self 'things'. But if I apply this model to myself as an observer I must also apply it to all the other observers that appear as experiences in my experience. Thus I must assume all other observers which I conceptualize objectively also experience only raw experience as I do subjectively in their own experience or more accurately *are* that experience as I myself am 'my' experience.

Thus the totality of reality itself must consist only of xperience, but that xperience exists as separate domains of xperience in which each organismic observer sees all other observers in terms of its private experience which is not actually properly its 'own' until organized in its mental model of reality and self-assigns itself to a 'self', and each of these is then modeled in the mental models of all others.

Thus reality exists as fragmentary domains of experience each private from all the others, and each modeling the others as objects in its own experience. And this entire system constitutes reality as it self-manifests itself as these domains.

And as a further complication these observer domains are intrinsically arbitrary in that each is an information construct in the simulation of one or more others, each of which may categorize it differently.

So finally, at the conscious level, reality consists of experience only but who or what that experience belongs to is intrinsically arbitrary, itself existing as experience as the contents of some other experience or experiences. Not an easy realization!

The point is that it is experience itself that is the only primary reality. All that exists exists as experience and this experience is prior to its categorization into the experience of some observer of something. It is just raw experience only. Even the experience of the categorization into experiencer and experienced is itself only a direct experience. So no matter what the apparent contents of experience it is always and only just raw experience which is the self-manifestation of reality in form.

It is certainly very difficult to even describe this in English as its logical structure is so different from the structures English is designed to formulate. Think of a multitude of completely separate domains of pure raw experience with no overlap. Now think of each of these domains self-organizing its experience into coherent structures which include models of themselves experiencing other things. These domains then begin to self-structure their experiences and conceive of themselves as observers 'having' these experiences. However all this structure also actually exists only as the raw immediate experience of itself so the true nature of every domain always consists only of raw experience in one form or another.

And though these domains are completely separate with no overlap of actual experience, part of the experience of each domain consists of objective models of other domains but these structures also themselves exist only as additional direct experiences of themselves as modeled in other domains.

Now back up and understand that every one of these domains is an intrinsically arbitrary structure in the experience of some other domain that could potentially bound any set of experiences as modeled in the experience of the experiencing domain. Thus all that actually exists is pure domainless experience that is neither bounded nor unbounded but just is itself and nothing more. It is pure experience with no external or contextual structure. It is nether separate spaces or a single space, it just is what it is as pure experience with no external context because its reality is only in what it actually is rather than in context which it lacks except of course as simulated in other domains.

Thus what we end up with is that the existence of reality is its self-manifestation as experience but it is impossible to inherently assign experience to observers, or more accurately experiences are assigned to observers all the time but only in the experiences of those assignments.

All there is is experience itself as it actually appears as experience in the present moment. This experience then self-organizes into the further experience of this observer and the other things of reality. This observer presumes that there are other domains of experience in which the same thing is happening but that presumption exists only as a further experience modeled as another experience of this observer, and this observer is 'himself' just another raw experience in the midst of experience.

All that can properly be said to exist is reality self-manifesting as experience to this observer, but this observer is actually just one of those experiences. Thus all that exists is pure experience, and this pure experience is the self-manifestation of reality. All organization of that experience is itself just further raw direct experience.

The only way this can be realized is simply to realize raw pure experience itself as the fundamental accessible reality, including the raw pure experience of all the structures of the simulation realized as the raw experience they actually are. All is experience only in the experience of what is experienced as this observer. All subsequent models of reality themselves exist only as their raw direct experience. Ultimately this is all that exists and this is the true self which is the self-manifestation of reality itself as true self. This is the realization of the fundamental form structure of reality.

REALIZING CHI AND THE ENERGY BODY

The presence of reality or ontological energy within an organismic being is called 'chi'. Chi in this proper definition is a completely natural and obvious self-evident phenomenon and not in the least unscientific. Chi is simply the ontological energy within our own form that gives us our being and reality and our actual presence and reality in the present moment. We experience it directly as the combined internal and external feelings of all parts of our body as a single energy body. This is our chi and our energy body and we all feel it all the time though amazingly most of us don't recognize it as the single unified entity that it self-evidently is.

Everyone is aware of the feelings of the individual parts of their bodies especially when they feel unexpected sensations. These feelings of all parts of one's body are the feelings of one's chi pure and simple and chi is just the name given to the self-evident fact of these feelings and nothing more than that is implied. Now take the feelings of every part of one's body and feel how they actually all together form an entire single body of feeling. This is the realization of one's energy body and it is a realization anyone can have in a minute or two. All the feelings of all parts of one's body are the feelings of chi in all those parts, and these feelings of chi all together form a whole continuous body which roughly mirrors the physical body and is called the energy body.

So properly understood chi and the energy body are not unscientific esoteric concepts but direct experiences everyone has all the time. Of course that doesn't mean we should accept without question the many questionable claims made about them.

Most of us tend to think of ourselves as our physical body but actually in our direct experience we are our energy body. Our physical body is a construct in our mental model of reality but our energy body is our direct experience of our self from the inside. It is strange that we tend to think of ourselves as our physical bodies when after all our physical body doesn't even have a complete head or back in its visual representation but our energy body certainly does have a head and a back. Our physical body lives without a visible face but our energy body is complete and is our direct experience of our self. Our energy body is the direct self-manifestation of reality itself within our form. Therefore it is our real body and our real being.

Like all aspects of the physical world our physical body is an illusory mental construct laboriously cobbled together from the actually real experiences of our energy body. It is likely that most other species exist more as their actual energy bodies than humans do, and many in fact seem to have little concept of even having a physical body.

As we have just seen our 'true' self is the combined direct experience of not only our internal bodily feelings but of the feelings or experiences of all of our senses and energetic activities and all our mental processes as well. So our complete energy body includes the totality of all these experiences. It includes all the experiences of all the feelings of both 'internal' and 'external' worlds. If we touch ourselves it includes both the feelings of touching and being touched. It also includes the feelings of touching supposedly external things, and it includes the 'feelings' of all other types of sensation and perception as well.

Our energy body also includes all our thoughts, emotions and perceived meanings as these also are all forms of chi since all experiences are forms of chi, since all forms are forms of ontological energy and chi is the experience of ontological energy within us. Thus our true self is the total combined experience of all the energetic processes of both our selves and the world, and all these are 'our' chi and the energy body of 'our' true self as they all occur within 'our' mind which is actually the mind of our total experience which includes all the experiences of things we categorize as both internal and external to us. These are all experienced flows of ontological energy in the forms of experience. Taken all together they constitute true actual being which is the energy body which includes all 'our' experiences without exception.

Thus the energy body is not dimensionally localized within our physical body because the dimensional localization of the physical body is a construct in our mental model of reality. It is a categorization after the fact of the direct experience of the energy body which is the actual reality of experience. However the internal feelings aspect of the energy body does tend to be simulated as roughly collocated with the physical body even though its experience is actually prior to the internal model of dimensionality constructed by mind.

Our strange dualistic notion of ourselves as mental processes within a physical body is an illusion because our physical body is an abstract concept constructed from multiple sensations over time whereas our chi and energy body are the direct immediate experience of our existence. And that chi and energy body includes the totality of every experience without exception including the experiences of our thoughts.

Our energy body is the combined forms of all aspects of our ontological energy or chi but the direct experience of the pure ontological energy itself is the fundamental aspect of this experience. This experience is special because it is very easy to directly experience the reality of ontological energy in its presence in the various forms of experience though in general the simpler the form the more easily the underlying ontological energy is recognized. It is easy because the reality of ontological energy is simply the self-evident reality of experience. Ontological energy is simply a name for the self-evident reality of experience.

One finds unending detail in the forms of experience of chi if one looks for it. On the other hand one can also let all or most of the individual forms dissolve away into the direct experience of the formless ontological energy itself or very nearly so. This more nearly formless state of the energy body is typically experienced as a glowing radiant energetic life force. Here one enters a meditative state where one opens oneself primarily to the formless direct experience of chi, the living presence of reality 'within', or more accurately as the direct experience of chi prior to any notion of within or without.

Since chi is the feelings of all parts of the energy body the feelings of chi obviously convey information as to the state of one's being. Once chi is experienced as a single energy body we become aware of the state of the various glows and flows of chi within it and with practice we begin to experience and understand how our physical and mental health correspond to these flows, specifically whether the flows feel strong and free and fresh or are blocked, cramped and stagnated by uncomfortable obstructing forms.

Chi and the energy body can be affected, guided, strengthened and purified to some extent by mind, breath, movements and other techniques. By learning these techniques it is possible to improve both health and the effectiveness of actions in the world. Traditional oriental medicine, yoga and other oriental disciplines are all based on this understanding though it is unfortunately often carried to unrealistic and unscientific lengths. While there are real beneficial effects they should not be mistaken for a panacea. One can improve one's own energy flows within natural limits but there are inevitably many other energy flows in the environment that continually interact with and affect our own. All other natural processes and beings, including those that would harm us such as enemies and disease organisms, all have their own agendas and chi forces as well.

Because the surrounding ontological energy flows of the universe continually flow through our form manifesting in our energy body as our chi the universe continually permeates and refreshes our being with its life force in every one of our forms. If happening did not continually flow through us we would simply vanish from the reality of the present moment and cease to exist. It is the flow of ontological energy through us that maintains our reality and being and life in the present moment. We are alive and real and have being because the universe is alive and real and has being within us and we are a part of its reality. To realize chi and our energy body we need only to turn consciousness to the whole flow of chi to directly experience it and participate in it more fully and effectively.

We are the empty information forms of ourselves in the all-encompassing space of ontological energy which creates and fills the universe. Our true substance is ontological energy only which continually glows and flows within us as our chi. This energy body is the true self of direct experience. We are an impermanent standing wave of information in the ongoing flow of ontological energy that maintains our being.

Happening continually refreshes our being and maintains our reality within the present moment. We experience this as the chi that continually glows and flows through our energy body. This is our direct experience of the self-manifestation of reality within us and the reality of us. This is the realization of our true being and the reality of our existence,

REALIZING BUDDHA NATURE

Buddha nature, like chi and energy body, is another oriental term which often draws scorn among Western thinkers, and often for legitimate reasons due to the many unrealistic and flaky associations attached to it. But again when defined rationally in terms of established concepts, Buddha nature can be a useful aid in understanding and promoting realization because it enables a more personal perspective on more abstract concepts such as ontological energy and chi.

In our definition Buddha nature is simply another name for chi or internal ontological energy from a more personal and individual perspective connoting the possibility of personal realization. Thus Buddha nature is simply another term describing the realization of the true nature of the reality of individual things but from a more personal approach.

Again in our usage it has no religious or esoteric context whatsoever and the use of the term does not imply acceptance of the many unreasonable beliefs sometimes associated with it. Though some Buddhist schools use a more restrictive definition, limiting Buddha nature to sentient beings only, in our definition all things have chi or Buddha nature because all things are forms of ontological energy. This definition enables a simpler and more consistent view of reality as it is just another name for what we have already established.

Thus from this perspective realization can be considered the direct awareness or experience of the Buddha nature of all things as the true fundamental actuality that fills the emptiness of their forms with the reality of being. This is consistent with the views of the more reason based and philosophical forms of Buddhism such as Zen (Watts, p. 68, 1957).

In this view all the things and beings of the world share the same presence and self-manifestation of reality as their fundamental nature in common and realization is the realization of precisely this. All things share this same common nature and this is true no matter whether their forms interact in harmony or conflict with one's own form.

Realization involves seeing the Buddha Nature in all things and beings no matter what or who they are. As another name for reality itself the Buddha lives at the center of all beings, within the forms of all beings. Buddha bum, Buddha whore, Buddha killer, Buddha next door. All forms are manifestations of Buddha because all forms have Buddha Nature because the fundamental nature of all things is ontological energy and when we realize this and actually experience it we experience all things and beings as Buddhas whether they know they are or not, whether they have attained this realization or not.

This includes all animals and other organisms as well as people. Buddha bear, Buddha fox, Buddha bird, Buddha dog, Buddha cow, Buddha worm, Buddha flower, Buddha bacteria. In the form of chi the Buddha dwells in all beings waiting to be awakened to its true nature. And Buddha nature is the true nature of every non-living thing as well. Every stone, every drop of water and speck of dust is a form filled with the Buddha nature of ontological energy. In this view the entire universe of forms consists of Buddhas only.

Thus we ourselves also have Buddha nature and are Buddha. Buddha lives within us all and we can consciously choose to realize and express our Buddha nature in a clearer, purer more realized form. We can abandon the unnecessary and unhealthy forms of our personal self and become our Buddhas and move through every aspect of our lives as Buddha. We can be Buddha walking down the street recognized or unrecognized through the world of forms. We can choose to let our Buddha guide our actions as we go about our daily routines as Buddha. By realizing and becoming our Buddha, Buddha guides our actions. By surrendering our personal desires and attachments and prejudices to our Buddha nature we become our Buddha and let our Buddha guide our actions, our lives, our work, our destiny. We walk down the road as empty forms filled with the living ontological energy of Buddha being. In any case we are doing that already whether realized or not. It is just a matter of realizing it.

Of course much of this borders on personal myth, a personal perspective on reality, and we must be careful not to stray too far into fantasy. After all the Buddha within things can express only through the actual forms of those things. There are no super-heroes here. But there is nothing wrong with personal myth so long as it is recognized for what it is and does not lead us into delusional thinking but instead is used to inform and enhance realization.

With that caveat in mind then by becoming the Buddha we already are we become our true realized being in the disguise of our old self moving through the world of forms among other Buddha beings most of whom do not realize their Buddha nature.

Our old personal self was an illusion of internal mental forms programmed into us since our childhood. By becoming our Buddha our personal forms are transformed and purified by the flows of purer less mediated chi energy that naturally tends to manifest as a loving healthy life force. We swim like fish through the surrounding sea of living ontological energy, warm, loving and supporting. As our Buddha we realize we are but empty forms within a warm loving sea of chi which continually fills us with being and reality and we become better able to release and dissolve away all our stagnant unhealthy personal forms and blockages to allow chi to flow more smoothly and strongly and peacefully through us helping keep us vital, fresh and healthy. In this way, as our Buddha, our forms become more pure and balanced and strong.

By becoming our Buddha and living as our Buddha nature we discard the illusory shells of our old personal being that concealed it from us. We see the world as it is with Buddha's eyes and manifest Buddha's realization of his own Buddha nature as our true selves. In this way we commune directly with the fundamental nature of reality itself as it self-manifests within us as our Buddha nature.

LIVING IN THE WORLD OF FORMS

By becoming our Buddha, by understanding and realizing the world as a world of information forms, and the evolving flows of those forms as the operation of the many interacting programs computing them, we gain insight into how to better live in harmony with the ongoing programs of the world as we act as our own program among them.

This is the underlying principle of oriental martial arts applied not just to self-defense but to all aspects of life. Books such as The Book of Five Rings (Harris, 1974) and The Art of War (Giles, 2005) as well as the game of Go (Takagawa, 1972) are studies in the fundamental principles of the world of forms. And the various schools of martial arts, most notably Aikido (Saotome, 1989), also exemplify these principles to greater or lesser degrees.

In general the more one recognizes Buddha nature the more one's distracting personal forms drop away as unnecessary and thus the more one is able to recognize and tune into the underlying flows of the world of forms and synchronize one's own chi flows with them. And thus the more effective and at home in the world of forms and in life one becomes.

The key is tuning into the underlying forms of things not only at the level of individual things but as the continuous flows and interactions of forms at multiple levels including the forms of motions and thoughts and actions of people and the dynamics of social forms as well. It is studying how chi forms flow and interact by becoming directly sensitive to and aware of those flows. This is achieved not just through intellectual analysis of forms but by clarifying one's own forms and tuning one's own chi flows to become more sensitive and open to the greater chi flows of the world around one. And of course by practicing interacting with them with realized mind. To the degree this is successful one becomes more effective and at home in the world.

Because the total reality of the true self includes all experience the flows of 'our' chi forms include the forms of interactions of self and external world and thus provide information about the programs running around us. To the extent it is accurate and complete we are able to directly sense the flows of chi not only in what we think of as our self but in forms external to us as well as they become part of our extended energy body, and we sense the flows of external chi in our internal chi flows as they are all actually a continuous sea of inter-responsive interconnected flows.

This is the direct use of chi in oriental martial arts and more generally for acting effectively in the world. Aikido in particular emphasizes recognizing and engaging an opponent's moving chi forms and then redirecting them with gentle force instead of opposing them directly.

316

The key is to empty oneself of personal forms that interfere with the realization of more important external forms which is done by emptying one's own chi so that the flow of chi of your opponent, or more generally of whatever external forces you are engaging, is clearly sensed in your own chi. Thus the external chi flow is directly sensed in one's own chi. Then rather than just forcefully opposing external flows, to automatically sense how to engage and redirect them with minimal effort to desired effect. Thus rather than blocking an attack with force one engages and continues the sweep of its flow while efficiently redirecting it away from harm. One's strength is thus concentrated on the weakness of the engaging force. This is the principle but of course one needs to practice the possible forms till they are automatically activated as needed.

And there is nothing magical or superhuman about this as no matter how effectively this is done it is not always possible to achieve a particular effect as the laws of nature always apply and other organisms also have their own chi agendas. But when necessary the wise man knows when to remove himself from the field of insurmountable forces to await more auspicious circumstances. As Sun Tzu says, "One picks battles one can win", (Giles, 2005). This too is part of realization, the realization of the fundamental principles of form interactions and the enhanced ability to sense them that comes from emptying oneself of interfering personal forms by realizing one's Buddha nature.

REALIZING COMPASSION

When the common Buddha Nature of all things and beings is recognized it naturally elicits understanding and compassion towards them no matter how antagonistic or distorted their forms may seem to be. And in turn compassion tends to help resolve and harmonize conflicts between forms.

Though all clashes among programs follow the natural computational laws of the interaction and evolution of forms many can be avoided through realization and compassion and a deeper and clearer understanding of the ways forms flow and interact and thus may be harmonized. Many of the conflicts among forms derive from superficial incompatibilities that are often resolved in the recognition of some mutual commonality of interests as well as their common underlying nature.

While all forms have Buddha nature and thus everything that happens is an expression of the laws of nature and is an expression of Buddha nature it is also true that some forms are more naturally harmonious than others and more conducive to the realization of their common nature. Often this involves the reduction of the personal forms that support individual self-identities that lead to personal attachments and ignorance and thus to unnecessary conflicts and suffering. Excessive concern with individual forms always tends to obscure the greater realization of the true common nature of reality that all forms share.

In Buddhist terminology a realized being who acts with compassion to aid the realization of others is called a Bodhisattva. The actions of a Bodhisattva can take many forms depending on the circumstances of the forms encountered. In general it involves working in the world of forms to reduce the forms of ignorance, attachments and suffering of others that impedes their own realization. This can be done by direct action, by teaching or just by the example of manifesting realization in the world. Hopefully it includes publishing books such as this one as well!

Though certainly anyone can act to help alleviate suffering it is most effectively done with realization because then the actual forms in play are better understood and more effectively managed and unintended negative consequences are minimized. Thus better to work on realizing one's own Buddha nature and then work in the world as Buddha insofar as possible. Ideally helping all beings to realize Buddha nature would better harmonize conflicting forms and achieve a significantly more peaceful world where all beings lived more in balance and harmony in a beautiful, peaceful new Garden of Eden in a sustainable balance with the natural systems of the Earth. One can dream....

Though currently impractical due to the evolved nature of humans as short sighted self-interested beings any progress towards this ideal is admirable. But effective action depends on a deep understanding of the large scale programs at work and the consistency structure of the world of forms. Compassion is not always simple. For example saving the lives of millions of starving children will likely lead to even more starving children in the future. Thus wiser and more compassionate in the long term to concentrate on reducing human overpopulation to a sustainable balance with earth's limited resources. Depending on available resources doing both would be even more compassionate.

There is a vast amount of unnecessary suffering in the world that could be eliminated by wise global and individual actions and policies. Much of this unnecessary suffering is the result of limited short term awareness of the world of forms in which humans tend to act for their own immediate personal gain. With realization and better understanding of the large scale long term implications of the historical programs at play it is potentially possible that human war and violence and excessive greed will become things of the past or at least greatly diminished.

The core problem in achieving this is that altruistic action by one party tends to put that party at a competitive disadvantage with respect to those who continue to act in their own personal self-interest. However it is clear that if all parties acted altruistically for the common good that would in fact in general improve the lot of all. The problem is being able to break out of the old dynamic that seems to be best for each party individually, but is less good for all parties together, to a new altruistic dynamic equilibrium which might initially seem less good for each party individually but maximizes the total good of all and thus eventually the wellbeing of each individually. The form structures here imply that wise top down rules equitably applied to all would be the most effective approach.

In the long run this depends on all children being raised and educated to understand and identify with their common natures as both earthlings and Buddhas rather than identifying with their ethnic, religious, national and other group affiliations and personal status as most do today. That depends on everyone being educated with a deep understanding of the planet wide ecological forces that are necessary to sustain us all. It depends on the realization of a natural compassion towards all beings including humans, other animals, and natural environments and the earth itself, becoming a common guiding principle. This tends to come naturally when the common Buddha nature of all things is realized.

Hopefully the result will be a world in which enlightened men and women work together to purify and heal the environment rather than pollute and destroy it. Where an enlightened optimal balance of positive technology sustains and improves nature rather than degrading it. And all this is informed by a universal free intelligent information system that itself functions as an enlightened, super-wise intelligent being that provides not a million hits of mostly irrelevant information to every query but the single few most useful and informative answers.

The ideal government to manage this would be a worldwide meritocracy where there are no competing individual governments or politics and everything is managed by the wisest public servants as determined by an educational system designed specifically to produce them for the true common good on the basis of their proven superior abilities to properly conceptualize and solve real world problems.

Where the mission of a global just government is to serve the entire Earth, and its people and other creatures for the good of all and the whole system as an optimally sustainable system. A single planetary government that provides free education, health care, rescue and disaster services, and public works projects and to which all contribute equitably for the optimum good of all. All in a single global planet-wide system without country borders with lasting peace, freedom, justice, happiness and prosperity.

This will represent the realization not just of individual humans but of humankind and the planet as well. Humans as a species must transcend the outmoded dysfunctional aspects of their evolved natures to survive as a species and for the natural world to survive as well. The very aspects of human nature that resulted in humans taking dominion over the planet; their intelligent self-centered ruthlessness, competitiveness and propensity to exploit and destroy to maximize their own personal short term success; are the same forces that now accelerate the destruction of the natural systems of the earth and that will eventually also lead to their own destruction as well when they exceed the carrying capacity of the biosphere as they evidently already have.

KRISHNA DANCING

Krishna dancing is an archetypal image of joyous expression of ecstatically free flowing chi in human form that is another form of realization. It is the celebration of the experience of the Buddha within functioning not in daily life but in a special spontaneous celebration of the wonder and divinity of reality and of being alive within it. Like Buddha nature we all have the dancing Krishna within us and he wants to dance!

By becoming Krishna and dancing spontaneously we express the joy of being alive in the universe back into the universe. We thank reality for giving us our life and existence and vitality which we express in celebration and praise in a direct manifestation of our own divinity as part of a divine reality. We express our joy to celebrate and reinforce the divinity and joy of reality with positive feedback.

By expressing our divinity and joy in a free and spontaneous celebratory ritual of song and music and dance we feed the universe with divinity and joy and so add to its own. We become the universal joy of existence expressing itself back to itself. We surrender the forms of our personal selves and let our internal Krishna take over and let loose our flows of chi in whatever spontaneous forms of movement come naturally of themselves. We move in celebration of and to maximize the healthy vitality of our energy body. And thus joy overwhelms our being and moves our chi and endows it with the divinity of the youthful God. And there are always others around to dance with be they humans, animals, clouds or breezes. And the birds and the breezes and the flowing water and other natural rhythms of the world of forms help provide the music Krishna dances to.

As Krishna dancing we realize and dance with the flowing forms of reality and join them in ecstatic harmony. We align our program with the surrounding programs of reality and become a single joyous celebration for the direct expression and experience of ontological energy as the life force that gives us and all things together their reality and existence.

Another variation on Krishna dancing is a spontaneous free style Tai chi in which one realizes and becomes one's energy body and lets one's energy body move of its own accord however it will. By allowing the energy body to move freely and spontaneously one's physical body follows and one's chi flows freely through one's whole energy body and refreshes and harmonizes one's life force. It is thus an ideal exercise for all body systems. By so doing we free ourselves from the usual restrictive forms of being an ordinary domesticated human being in our daily lives. We transcend these ordinary forms of ourselves so they no longer constrain us as they usually do in maintaining the cramped artificial personal images, postures and movements of ourselves that our true being and our true long repressed animal so longs to escape from.

This is the spontaneous play of children and baby animals that is so full of the natural joy of being alive and real and free. Returning to this is one of the healthiest natural yogas one can do. In general society greatly restricts such natural joyful playful action but it can be recovered without running afoul of society's rules when done with proper realization.

When done correctly the movement, action and vocalizations originate directly from the energy body rather than the physical body and the energy body moves the physical body rather than vice versa. One does not think about moving the physical body. One forgets the physical body, becomes the energy body, and lets the energy body move, act and vocalize of its own accord as it wishes to enjoy and enhance its chi, and the physical body follows.

A similar approach can be taken to all actions in the world of forms. All one's actions and movements in daily life can become a dance of life in expression of the flows of chi through one's energy body. All actions then become an expression of the joy of existence. Every movement made is a movement of dance, the movement of the divine dancer within, even in the placing of every object.

Of course Buddha nature and Krishna nature are just particular expressions of chi which itself is just the pure life force of reality. Thus chi is automatically expressed in all the different forms of which humans and more generally organisms are capable. It is just that its expression as Buddha nature and Krishna dancing is an inherently free expression which is optimally healthful and vitalizing for one's being, much more so than our usually very socially and psychologically restricted movements and personas.

Unhealthy conditions are often associated with particular socially programmed internalized blocking forms that trap chi and express themselves as unhealthy stagnations of one's vital force. These forms that block the free flow of chi are not conducive to a whole and healthy being. They generally arise as the result of psychological and social programming due to our sub-optimal personal histories and they typically express themselves as the particular habitual movements and postures that express our personal psychologies and personas. By realizing and freeing our chi one becomes directly aware of these chi blockages and expressing chi in free open flows helps purify and dissolve these unhealthy stagnant forms. And it enhances the realization of what chi and energy body really are and thus the realization of the true nature of reality itself.

MEDITATING BUDDHA

Perhaps the most direct and deepest experience of reality is becoming one's meditating Buddha sitting in a state of enlightenment, and we all have this meditating Buddha within us. In this state all forms dissipate and vanish insofar as is humanly possible and all that remains is the direct experience of the presence of the fundamental reality of ontological energy as pure consciousness itself. This is a state of detachment from the world of forms with only the intense experience of pure near formless ontological energy self-manifesting its intrinsic brightness of being real and actual and the pure life force of happening. This is reality itself manifesting as consciousness itself devoid of any obscuring forms so that the essence of reality shines forth clear, present and absolute.

In this state we enter the center of being within all forms. At the center is the golden glow of living reality which then radiates outward fragmenting into all the forms of being. This is the experience of, "Being at the center of Nothingness rather than Nothingness at the center of Being", as described in *The Secret of the Golden Flower* (Wilhelm, 1931).

At the center of being is the perfectly still immanent presence of consciousness and reality itself undisturbed by forms. In this state consciousness turns inward to its source at the center of being, the center of reality and dwells there in perfect harmonious equilibrium self-manifesting as the pure experience of nothing at all but its essence. Consciousness floats there in eternal free fall untethered and perfectly centered and balanced of its own accord, in pure brightness with nowhere to go.

Forms fall away like type from a bright white page and vanish. All ripples vanish from the surface of the still bright pool. All thoughts, attachments and suffering are released and dissipate. All the things of the world vanish as well. One seems no longer tied to space or time and exists only in the eternal timelessness of the present moment. One continually falls like a waterfall never going anywhere because there is nowhere to go. In this state one exists in a perfect radiance of brilliant warm light ever fresh in a state of eternal creation. This is the experience and realization of being one's ultimate true self. It is the direct experience of the self-manifesting presence of reality itself as pure consciousness itself. It is the direct realization of what we really are in our innermost being.

But of course as a living human being, a form in the world of forms, we must eventually return to the world of forms. The trick when we return is to continually experience that same center of being in the midst of the world of forms by retaining the realization of the center of being deep within the layers upon layers of swirling empty information forms that radiating in fragments from the center of being. A computational web continually weaving the current state of the universe surrounds the center. The pure formless energy of being fractures into the million forms which each reflect it like shards of a mirror thus revealing their own forms. But always at the center the essence of being remains formless and pure even while it shines forth in the countless forms of the world.

DEFINING GOD

If we choose to have a God then defining God as the universe itself, as reality itself, is the only reasonable choice. The immediate advantage to this definition is there can be no doubt at all that God exists since reality exists. And the interminable useless theological arguments over the attributes of God now become simply the exploration of the nature of reality by reason and science.

By this definition God automatically assumes the most basic of its usual attributes. God is ubiquitous and omnipresent by definition since reality is so. God is omnipotent as the universe is the source of all action. God is omniscient in that reality contains and actually is all knowledge.

And the experience of God becomes the direct experience of the true nature of reality which is certainly the experience of divinity if anything is. And not only that but this divinity is our own true nature as well so that one can now truly say that God dwells within us, that we are God.

By this definition God manifests personally within all of us as life and consciousness and is the true self of all personal beings. By this definition we and all things all participate in and manifest the divinity of reality. By this definition God is equivalent to and another name for

Buddha Nature though with a more Western connotation of perhaps broader scope.

Again, just as with Buddha nature and Krishna dancing, defining God as the universe is just a way of conceptualizing and relating to reality in a more personal manner. As such it is another form of personal myth. Personal myths can be useful aids and comforts and are not inconsistent with reality so long as they are realized as myth and not confused with actual reality. Only when they are mistaken for reality do they become delusional and hamper realization, otherwise they can be perfectly consistent with it and even aid it.

From this perspective God, being the true nature of all things, looks at us through every eye and looks out of our eyes at the world as well. There God sees itself looking back at itself looking at itself in recognition of itself. In this way God recognizes and knows itself and the universe and reality and we and all organisms become the sense organs of God that allow God the universe to experience and know itself.

This is true not just of looking and seeing but of the experiences of all our senses and our consciousness as well. All the organisms in the universe are the means through which the universe as God manifesting in those personalized forms is able to experience and know itself and thus to begin to become self-aware. We and all beings are the individual sense organs and minds of God through which God knows and experiences itself and the universe gains self-awareness.

Properly realized there is nothing supernatural about this realization. God as the ontological energy of the universe exists in every form but is only expressed through the actual form of that form. God sees only out of forms with eyes and cannot see out of forms without eyes but since all forms are xperience God xperiences through all forms and is xperience itself, but only in whatever form that xperience comes in. This is entirely consistent with the theory of this book if we just define God as another perspective on ontological energy.

Because xperience is the self-manifestation of reality, God can be said to create and self-manifest itself as the xperiences of all things. This is the universe xperiencing, and in some forms knowing itself, and this is how God manifests and knows itself and becomes self-aware.

Thus the universe and God is its own self-awareness of itself self-manifesting as xperience. In a fundamental sense it is not even clear we can meaningfully speak of the existence of a world of forms absent its xperience of itself because there is no way to confirm its existence or structure if it does not manifest itself.

Thus reality is reality xperiencing itself. And all of us and all organisms and all things and forms are part of this process of the self-realization of the universe and thus the self-realization of God as xperience.

This notion of God has both a non-personal ubiquitous aspect and innumerable personal manifestations as the essence of all individual things and personal beings. We may sense the presence of God in the meadow but God remains unseen and formless other than in the actual forms in the meadow that God actually manifests as. We may realize the presence of God in the form of every being and thing but God is always limited by the forms within which it manifests. It is like feeling God's presence in everything all around us but God never appears except in the actual forms of the world manifesting only through those individual forms and their Buddha Natures.

Man may long for God to appear as a personal caring and protective being in full divinity with supernatural attributes but this never occurs because God manifests only in actual forms and all actual forms are natural and obey natural law. The actual reality of God is much much more profound than any supernatural being.

This is an entirely rational view of God insofar as it goes but one must always be wary of the danger of imputing any of the traditional delusional supernatural characteristics of the Gods of traditional religions to this God. This God is more akin to the rational scientific God of Einstein (Wikipedia: Religious views of Albert Einstein) and is simply another name for the immanent self-manifestation of reality in which the universe of forms arises.

In addition God by this definition is the formless ontological energy or Buddha Nature of reality that is the reality in which all forms manifest. We as forms within that reality partake of that reality directly and thus are forms of God. The non-personal presence of the divinity of reality is the living presence of God because this is the living presence of reality and reality itself is the true divinity. Because it has all the traditional characteristics of divinity such as omnipotence and omnipresence, and is the creative and motive force of reality it can be considered divine.

In a very real sense we are this God or at least some of the individual sense organs of God because as we move through the world it is only through our eyes and selves that the universe and thus God experiences itself in our particular experiences of itself. One could reasonably say that God created us as the sense organs and consciousnesses of itself that it might better experience and know itself through us. From this perspective that could even be considered our purpose for existing. The universe creates intelligent beings that it may know itself and become conscious of itself.

And the universe incorporates realization that it may itself realize its true nature and divinity. And that is equally true of all of us and of all life forms that exist or have existed to the limit of the capabilities of their forms. We are all together bound in the web of universal xperience and consciousness through which the universe knows itself. May that be an enlightened and compassionate xperience!

The direct experience of reality itself as consciousness itself is the living presence of this God in a non-personalized form. It is waking into a world where the presence of God is tangible but being formless remains unseen. But then some person or even some animal opens its eyes and looks at you and God suddenly manifests in that personal form looking out through those eyes. And all the while you were looking in vain for God with your own eyes it was actually God that was looking through your eyes! God manifests in both personal and impersonal form because there is nothing that is not God, defined as reality, and there are both personal and non-personal forms in the world.

If our true destiny is to function within God as a sense organ of God then the more accurate and compassionate and enlightened that sense organ is the better is God's experience of the reality of itself. Each of us is a little fragmentary bit of God, a little bit of God's total mind and body, by which God knows itself and with realization becomes enlightened through us as we become simultaneously enlightened through God. And this realization is its own reward. Perhaps the progress and purpose of evolution is to evolve better, wiser and more enlightened sense organs of God so that the universal God can become wiser and more enlightened through us as part of it.

Thus God is then the totality of all forms including all of us simultaneously acting as its innumerable sense organs and consciousnesses and is the combined xperiences of all things of itself. It is all its forms xperiencing itself and thus continually self-manifesting its formless nature to itself in the present moment of its presence.

REALIZING LOVE

Chi is experienced as the internal feelings of our existence and life force that are always felt within us all. It can be experienced tinted with many moods from eroticism to depression to anger to fear and anxiety. Biologically these correlate to hormonal flows and energetic flows in our bodies. Though these feelings may be more concentrated in some areas than others they tend to flood our entire energy body. One aspect of realization is allowing chi to manifest within us as the pure divine love of the universe filling our being and becoming our being.

This love is not the worldly 'love' for particular things we might be attached to, though chi also expresses in those forms, but the pure energetic essence of the love of simply existing and being real devoid of any attachments or objects of love. In this form chi manifests as pure unconditional and undirected love and fills our being with joy. This is a health enhancing and rejuvenating power that furthers our realization of all aspects of reality. And there is an objective reason why this particular form of manifestation of chi within us is the natural state of our energy body.

It is because the very fact that we actually exist and are alive here and now in the present moment is the greatest possible blessing imaginable no matter what the condition of our form may be. There is nothing more wonderful than existence itself. An essential aspect of realization is to experience existence as the blessing it is. In a sense our very existence is the ultimate act of love of the universe or the universal God for us. The simple enormously improbable fact of our existence is the ultimate blessing of the universe and of God for us. It is the ultimate act of love and thus we by necessity dwell within that love that is the act of our existence!

This is realized even more profoundly when we understand how enormously improbable our existence actually is. From the millions of other sperm that didn't make it in our conception, the millions of other sperm that didn't make it in the conceptions of each of our billions of different ancestors back to the beginning of life and beyond to everything else that had to go exactly right for us to exist today even for the brief time that we do. What an enormous coincidence that we are alive today! What an enormous act of love of the God universe for us that we do exist! Existence is the ultimate blessing and our existence is the ultimate act of love of the universe for us to bring us into being. Thus it is entirely natural that we experience our existence as love, as the pure unconditional love of the universe for us. By experiencing the reality of the universe that manifests within us as divine love we merely realize the divinity of our own existence.

By extension the very existence of the universe itself, or God if you prefer, is an act of love and thus is the existence of love itself. Ontological energy itself is the energy not just of being but since being itself is love, it is also the energy of love. Thus the presence of ontological energy within us as chi which constitutes our true nature and our energy body, and our consciousness, is very naturally experienced as the experience of pure perfect divine love absent attachments to any form. Love is the very essence of being.

When we realize this we experience the love of the universe for us in every aspect of itself and we love the universe back in every breath full of pure love we take and in every action we perform because the chi of both our being and the universe is experienced as love itself. This is experienced directly as our energy body filled with a glowing radiating fluid energy of the pure essence of love that encompasses and completes our being so that we feel completely whole and need and want nothing else at all.

When we experience chi and consciousness as love it helps heal and purify and cleanse the forms of our being and it radiates back from us into the forms of the world as chi flows back out of us into the world as love. Thus it helps purify and heal the other forms of the world as well. By realizing our being as love itself we introduce the realization of divine love back into the universe as well, both because we ourselves are part of the universe and because love then freely flows out of our form into other surrounding forms.

Since the act of creation is an energetic act of love and happening is a continual creation we are all being continually recreated and sustained by the love of the universe for us. Thus our existence is a continuing act of love and can be experienced as love. Love is the creative life force of ontological energy that powers existence forward through time because love is the energy of happening and the continual creation of the universe. Our very existence and continued recreation in every moment is the universe actively loving us and confirming and validating our being. It is God's ultimate affirmation of and caring for our being. This is not something made up absent reason but an actual experience of reality. It is the power of a personal myth that is entirely consistent with reality.

When our own existence is experienced as love this love naturally flow back out into other forms. These can be the forms of lovers and friends and any forms to the extent they are receptive. By sharing our experience of God's love we help spread the experience of the pure divine love of reality back out into the universe. In this way God experiences its own divine love of itself and for itself in all the possible forms of itself.

There are many possible varieties of personal myth that may aid in experiencing this realization so long as they are recognized as myth. I know of some that imagine themselves wrapped in the loving arms of a great mother goddess being flooded with intense unconditional glowing love without a care in the world, or even back within the womb of the goddess in total and absolutely safety. Personal myth has no limits other than one's imagination. So long as it is useful and understood as personal myth rather than as objective fact it is entirely consistent with reality. There is no reason realization can't be fun!

REALITY IS ALWAYS ENOUGH

Because reality is absolute in the sense that it is all that is or can be exactly as it is in the present moment it is always enough. This is always true no matter where you are or what your situation. There is after all nothing else possible in the present moment than what actually exists.

When this is realized there is never the need for anything else or any sense of loss, incompleteness or anything lacking. Because reality is the very substance of our being it is all that is ever needed because it is all that we can ever have or be. The ever present formless essence of reality is all that can be and thus its direct experience is all that one could ever want or need. It is our very essence and our only true self and there can never be anything else. Forms come and go but the essence of reality always remains and that is always enough. This is always true; even as one works in the world of forms to effect changes in the forms, our own inner nature, our own true self, never changes. Forms come and go but Buddha Nature always remains and our thus our true reality always remains. God never leaves our presence.

Forms continually change and come and go but the common reality within all forms is always present, its presence self-manifesting as the present moment. All forms are empty, it is the essence of being in all forms that is permanent and always present and always available to us if we just open ourselves to its realization.

ACCEPTANCE

Because reality is what is and absolutely so and cannot be otherwise than it is it must be accepted as such to be in accordance with reality. The necessity and inescapability of absolute acceptance of what is is an essential part of realization. This is true not just of the formless essence of reality but of the current state of all forms in the present moment. Once the forms appear they absolutely are as they are and absolutely must be accepted exactly as they are if reality is to be realized. Otherwise we deny the reality upon which we depend.

That need not keep us from working to effect change, it just means accepting that the forms we are working to change are the ones that actually exist. By accepting things exactly as they are we increase our ability to change them.

There is also another more mundane aspect to acceptance. It is the acceptance of things as they are by releasing our desires and attachments for things that are likely beyond our attainment. By releasing unreasonable desires and attachments and by accepting our situation in life as it is we release many of the forms that lead to suffering and come closer to realizing our true self as it actually is in the present moment. Our true self is the one thing that is always attainable and within our grasp should we just open ourselves to it and embrace it because it is what we actually are.

There is an ultimate bravery in the total acceptance of reality as it is and confronting its awesome absoluteness directly and completely. It is also the total acceptance of our complete and total aloneness in the eternal presence of God the universe. We are completely and totally alone in a personal sense because our personal forms are inherently distinct from all other personal forms, and yet we are always completely and absolutely in the presence of God because we share the ontological energy essence of reality that is the actual presence of God within our personal form with all other forms.

In absolute acceptance of what is we dwell at peace in pure love in the present moment. In this state of completeness there is nothing that is needed. Reality is always enough. It is always eternally fresh and real and alive and is always immediately available to us because it is us our fundamental nature.

REALIZING THE ILLUSION OF TIME

The present moment is all that exists and it has no effective duration on human time scales. And the reality of the present moment is continually happening. All other aspects of time are ultimately illusory. There is no past and there is no future. One can imagine the bright reality of the present moment surrounded on all sides by darkness but in reality there is no other side, there is only and always the bright reality of the present moment which corresponds in cosmological terms to the surface of the hypersphere of the universe in which all existence exists. And the geometry of this universe is a logically complete space in itself that has no outside. Only as an illusory projection from the present do the past and future hide unseen incalculably near behind the retinal surfaces of the world.

The apparent duration of the present moment exists not in reality but only in our mind's simulation of reality in its short term memory. The actual duration of the present moment in the world of forms is vanishingly small and far below the temporal resolution of the human observer. Only in our internal simulation of the present moment is it opened and given duration by our short term memory sufficiently for forms to be held and compared and only thus are we able to extract and temporally compare forms and thus to generate additional relational forms in our simulations. Without an illusory present moment held open by short term memory our experience would consist only of unrelated instantaneous form after form after form with no relationships whatsoever. It would revert to the *xperience* that characterizes all inanimate forms.

There would be no music or even any sounds or anything else meaningful at all since all perception and comprehension depends on temporal comparison of forms. Our experience would be precisely the xperiences that inanimate objects have with no short term memory or internal models of reality. They would simply be happening forms with no context whatsoever to even know they were changing. Thus even the present moment we appear to experience is a complete illusion and this once again demonstrates the totally illusory nature of our internal model of reality.

This can be realized to some extent by intently focusing consciousness ever more precisely and narrowly on the exact moment of becoming into being, on the exact razor's edge of happening and letting everything else disappear. This is best done with closed eyes concentrating on the exact moment of becoming into being and vanishing of smoothly continuous sound or music. With practice the present moment collapses into instantaneousness and with it the experience of music and even sound itself begins to disappear. This is a truly profound and even frightening experience as the awareness of reality itself seems to collapse towards non-being and the true computational nature of reality threatens to emerge directly into consciousness.

At the instantaneous actual level of becoming into being and vanishing, xperience of course goes on as it always did. At this level it seems fuzzy and incomplete and riddled and raveled with the loose ends of entanglement and decoherence. Thus the actual edge of our cosmological hypersphere is vanishingly thin and ill-defined. Instead of the seemingly intact and continuous surface of a soap bubble or balloon it resolves into a vast web of decohering quantum processes. This is the level of actual happening in the computational world of forms, the actual processor cycle of happening that is far below our capacity for direct realization. It is a simple fact of existence that many aspects of reality are fundamentally inaccessible to realization.

Thus the seemingly insignificant fact of our short term memory is absolutely essential to opening reality into the illusory world we imagine we are living within. It is only this little ability of mind that gives meaning to anything at all in our simulation of it and opens reality into an illusory world with enough present moment duration for us to meaningfully exist within it.

REALIZING THE ILLUSION OF DEATH

Confronting total naked unmediated reality face to face in realization of its actual nature is the ultimate bravery and the ultimate joy. Upon reflection the absolute awesomeness of existence and being real in the present moment may conjure the specter of non-existence. But death, our personal death, is an illusion that exists only in our mind's simulation of reality.

It is impossible to experience one's own death because there is no experience after death. So since reality is experience there is no personal death and personal death is an illusion. Just as the existence of reality must necessarily exist and nonbeing cannot exist, so personal death cannot exist in the experience of an observer. Of course we experience the deaths of others but we can never experience our own death because we are only our existence.

And anyway why should we suffer and worry about not being around after our death? Do we worry because we were not around before our birth? Do we worry that we are no longer around yesterday? Do we worry that we do not exist somewhere else? We are nonexistent in every moment of time but the present moment because only the present moment exists. Does that cause us to suffer? If not then why does the thought of our non-existence in a moment of time which does not even exist cause us concern? Certainly the future does not exist and it is only in the future that we might not exist. We are alive now and that and only that is all that is real. Our death simply does not exist. If you are reading this then only life and existence exists.

Worrying about death is an illusion because we are giving illusory reality to forms which do not exist in reality but only as attachments to imaginary forms in which we imagine our non-existence. Like all attachments to forms which do not actually exist we can reasonably use them to plan our actions in the world of forms to the extent that they are accurate projections. But the generic worry about death absent a real threat is dysfunctional because it robs us of the very enjoyment of life we so fear to lose and that is a worse threat to our existence than the more remote possibility of our death. The ultimate defeat of death is in the greatest enjoyment of life in the present moment because that is all that is actually real and that maximizes our total existence.

A compatible approach is the direct acceptance and even confrontation of death. This is the samurai code of accepting that death may come at any second and befriending that reality to maximally enhance our life and the intensity of its experience. It is the mentality of the martyr who willing gives his life for what he considers a higher cause (absent the usual delusional aspects of the cause). It is the acceptance of the inevitability of one's personal nonbeing and embracing it as a lover. It is leaping forward gladly to confront death and laugh in its face and perhaps defeat it once again this time but even if one dies trying a total acceptance of its ultimate inevitability that makes every moment of life precious.

All men die, it is just a matter of how and when. We are all empty forms in a world of forms. As Buddha said, "all compound entities must cease" (Tsunemitsu, p. 11, 1962). All forms eventually transform into other forms but the ontological energy, the underlying reality and life force, of all forms persists. Thus with death there is no afterlife or reincarnation of individual beings as our individual being is our forms and death is the disintegration of those forms. Without the forms of our being there is nothing to manifest our individual self.

It may seem as if one's chi spills out into the forms of our disintegration and from there back into the world to manifest in other forms. But the reality is that chi was never 'ours' in the first place. Because ontological energy is formless it is not localized or individualized. It is just the single formless medium in which all form appears. Forms come and go but in its essence ontological energy remains formless and forever unchanged.

Realization is using the intensity of this understanding of the transience of being to enhance the appreciation and enjoyment of our actual real being in the present moment even down to its smallest detail as in the scent of a single flower, whose brief beautiful existence is an apt metaphor for life itself. Every last detail of life is an absolute awesome wonder and the greatest blessing imaginable if it is just realized as such! Life is to enjoy!

GOOD AND EVIL

There are no absolute good and evil in the world of forms. These are human concepts, and by extension organismic concepts, which are always relative to some human standards. Whether effects are good or evil is always judged by someone at some time and what is good for one is often bad for another. However there are generally accepted social standards from culture to culture that have evolved primarily to facilitate stable societies. These social standards are the primary references for good and evil around which individual standards tend to cluster.

The idea of karma, that good ultimately begets good and evil begets evil is not consistent with the actual laws by which forms evolve. There may be a general tendency for like to beget like but there are numerous exceptions and by whose standards are ethical results to be judged, and at what point in the continuously evolving network of events? And there is certainly no reincarnation so there can be no karmic transmission from one lifetime to another.

However it is possible to outline some general ethical principles in the context of realization. Certainly the first is to seek realization itself. While Zen correctly points out that enlightenment is not something to be found by seeking it, that is the view from enlightenment rather than from the path towards it. The corollary is to promote realization among all beings and to minimize suffering. This can be done by example, by teaching and hopefully by writing books such as this one.

Another very reasonable core ethical standard is protecting and fostering the sustainable health and viability of Earth's biosphere. This is arguably the single most important ethical principle in that it sustains and maximizes the health and existence of all known life. Earth's biosphere is the only known cradle of the convergent emergence that seems to be in the process of bring self-awareness to the universe. For this to flourish human society must become sustainably integrated with nature, and man must begin to tend the earth as a natural Garden of Eden. It would be an enormous, perhaps irreversible, setback to the apparent direction of the evolution of the universe if man was allowed to destroy the viability of the earth itself with all that implies.

While there can be little argument with this principle the difficulty is in the details. The earth is such an enormous complex system that it is easy to be led astray as to the relative importance of individual situations by the emotionally charged arguments of special interests. Clearly one should first ensure the viability of systems at the global level and then work downwards to local decisions made in light of the global. It is clear that at the local level there are always tradeoffs because what is good for one species or constituent will likely be less good for others. Nevertheless there are accepted principles such as maximizing diversity and the health of interacting systems rather than that of particular organisms that serve as a guide.

Another fundamental ethical principle is compassion and the recognition of the Buddha nature of all beings, a realization of our fundamental empathy with all other sentient beings and active compassion to minimize their sufferings as well as concern for their realization.

This has profound consequences for how one relates to other beings including the question of eating meat. One recognizes the living sentient spirit within all animals and their capacity for suffering but at the same time one recognizes that predation fills an essential natural ecological function; that all individual organisms must die and that death both supports life by providing food for other life and also makes room for new life and thus eventually for better adapted life.

And as life itself can be considered the ultimate good is it better for an animal to have lived a good and happy life till it is humanely slaughtered for meat or is it better for that animal to have never had the joy of existing at all? And if animals are to be killed for meat is it better to kill thousands of small creatures such as shrimp or one large cow of equivalent nutritional weight? These are profound questions that should always be approached with compassionate empathy for the beings involved.

Good and evil are not simple and are always human valuated momentary snapshots of isolated events in an enormous web of ever changing forms. And these judgments are always relative to each other in complex interacting processes playing out over various time scales. In general enlightenment and compassion for all beings including oneself and for the sustainable environment of the Earth are the great universal goods our actions should attempt to foster.

REALIZING PURPOSE AND THE MEANING OF LIFE

What is the meaning of life and what is life's purpose? As human concepts the answers to these questions are necessarily relative to human belief systems. There are no absolute meanings in the world of forms. Objectively with respect to the world of forms purpose and meaning are simply what individuals make of them. They are clearly human terms and therefore relative to human actions and their effects on oneself, others and the world. But is there some deeper purpose perhaps?

If we accept that the evolution of the universe is or might be based on a convergent emergence towards the universe becoming self-aware and thus possibly more self-compassionate and peaceful the purpose and meaning of life might be found simply in contributing to that process. There are innumerable ways in which this could be done but certainly realizing one's Buddha nature and becoming an enlightened sense organ and consciousness of the universe as a means for its greater self-awareness and manifestation of its true nature is probably as close as one can get to a universal purpose or meaning in life.

Zen has a compatible approach that purpose is acting in accordance with the underlying principles of reality and flows of Tao or ontological energy. It is to act not so much from one's personal desires, attachments and programming but in concert with the greater programs driving the world of forms. In so doing one gives up much of one's personal agenda and acts as one's realized self, one's Buddha within. In this view our ultimate freedom consists in giving up our personal freedom to align with the flows of greater reality, and thus our own realization and service is an example to others helping liberate them from suffering.

The traditional Buddhist notion of the Bodhisattva who upon realization returns to the world to spread realization by example is the prototype of this principle. The notion is that by teaching, working with the poor and needy, or simply manifesting realization in the world one furthers realization and ultimately helps release sentient beings from suffering.

THE GATELESS GATE

Realization is not to be found within the gates of any sect or temple. Realization is the direct experience of reality and thus is to be found anywhere and everywhere. Reality is everywhere and all one has to do is look with realized eyes to see it. No technique or path or teaching is intrinsically better than any other or even necessary. Sitting can be useful but realization is not just found in sitting. Realization is to be found anywhere in the entire world around us at every moment of our existence because realization is the recognition of reality and everything is part of reality.

There is no transmission of realization or enlightenment. Teachers can be useful in demonstrating and guiding along a path towards realization but they cannot transmit any realization at all. There is nothing to transmit when everything is already present. Reality continually self-manifests itself and reality itself is the only true teacher. All one needs to do is open oneself to the continuous presence of reality and see it for what it actually is.

Realization is not to be found just in some koan. The study of reality itself is the ultimate koan in whose solution is found realization. The quantum koan and many others have been the subject of this book. Reality is the only master and it presents itself as a koan every second of our existence. Reality is the ultimate unanswerable question, the ultimate unsolvable koan. The solution is not in the answer but in the vanishing of the question in the realization of the presence of reality as it actually is. The ever present living presence of reality itself unmediated by illusion is the only possible answer. The answer lies not in words but in direct experience.

This is the meaning of the Japanese Zen expression, 'Mu Mon', which can be variously translated as 'no gate', 'the gateless gate', or 'the gate to emptiness' (Blythe, 1966). 'Mu' does not mean nothingness in the usual western sense, but refers to the emptiness of forms in which is found the true presence of being. Mu Mon means there is no gate that must be passed through to achieve enlightenment. It specifically implies it is unnecessary to pass through the gated entrance to any Zen temple to achieve realization. Wherever you are you are already in the reality you seek.

YOU ARE ALREADY ENLIGHTENED

There is really no trick or effort to realization or enlightenment. You are already enlightened. Everyone is already enlightened and always has been. Enlightenment is simply a matter of realizing you are already enlightened and always have been because there is nothing that is not the real and actual presence of reality lying completely clear and visible before you. Of course realization can be refined, but enlightenment is just seeing reality as it actually is and it is always exactly as it appears.

Everything in the world, every experience is exactly what it is. Yes, it has a deep structure, and yes it carries hidden secrets which are also part of reality, but nevertheless what we experience is exactly what we experience and that constitutes reality because reality is exactly what is in the present moment and even if it is illusion experienced as illusion that is the reality of the present moment. However the deeper realization is experiencing that illusion as the illusion that it actually is and thus its deeper reality. That then becomes the reality of the present moment realized more clearly.

Realization is simply whatever experience exists in the present moment as it is with or without any cognitive interpretation in the mental model because those interpretations also appear only the direct experiences of themselves. And so on it goes. So direct experience includes even the direct experience of cognitive interpretations as well, whether or not realized as such. Illusion taken for reality is illusion, but illusion seen as illusion is reality. Everything is illusion but everything is reality because reality consists entirely of illusion when it comes to forms. The empty illusory nature of forms is their reality, and their reality is the manifestation of the nameless fundamental presence of reality in which all forms arise and manifest which is the true nature of the universe and all things in the universe including ourselves.

With insight, study and practice more and more of the true nature of things is realized but what we do experience now exactly as we experience it, realized as such, that is the true reality of the present moment. Thus we are all already enlightened and it is just a matter of waking up and realizing we are already here and always have been!

Greetings!

PART VII: THE FUNDAMENTAL PRINCIPLES OF REALITY

Here we attempt to summarize the nature of reality as clearly and concisely as possible in a somewhat more formal manner.

EXISTENCE

The first fundamental question of reality is why does something other than nothing exist?

The Existence Axiom: Existence exists because non-existence cannot exist. This is the fundamental self-necessitating axiom of reality upon which all else stands. Thus there never was a nothingness out of which something arose. Thus there is no need for a creator or creation event. Something has always existed.

Something has always existed however the universe itself clearly came into being ~13.7 billion years ago in the big bang. This was not a creation event out of nothing but an actualization event out of a previously existing virtual state of reality which already contained all possible possibilities, a state similar to a generalized quantum vacuum, what we will shortly define as ontological energy.

Definition: The totality of what exists is reality. That something does exist is self-evident and we define reality as everything that does exist.

THE LOGICAL NECESSITY OF REALITY

The validity of the Existence Axiom presupposes that reality at its fundamental level is a consistent logical structure in which a contradiction cannot exist. In fact if reality were not a logical structure it would be impossible to even conceive or speak meaningfully about it, especially from within it, and one can only speak of it from within it. If reality were not a consistent logical structure it would be impossible for organisms to function within it which they self-evidently do. Therefore reality must be a consistent logical structure.

The Axiom of Logic: Reality is a self-consistent and logically complete system.

The Computational Nature of Reality: Because reality is a self-consistent logical system, and it is self-evident that reality is happening, then reality must be a logical rule based *computational* system.

The Axiom of Information: Because reality is a logical computational system it must consist only of information at its fundamental computational level because computations compute only in terms of information.

The Equivalence of Forms and Information: We use the terms 'information' and 'forms' interchangeably throughout. They are the exact same thing in our usage; forms from the perspective of structure, and information from the perspective of content, but these are actually exactly the same. All forms are information and all information is form.

The Axiom of a Self-Consistent and Logically Complete Computational Reality: Reality is a self-consistent and logically complete computational structure that evolves according to logical rules defined as the laws of nature. If it were not it would tear itself apart at the inconsistencies and pause at the incompletenesses and could not exist. Again this axiom assumes itself and is self-necessitating.

Definition: The Laws of Nature are the computational rules, including the rules of logic, by which reality operates.

The Principle of Knowledge: Because of the Axiom of Logic reality is a knowable structure because it can be logically, and thus accurately, described in terms of its own logical structure. Thus it can be meaningfully described in books such as this, and organisms can function meaningfully and effectively within it.

ONTOLOGICAL ENERGY

Reality self-evidently consists of the fundamental presence and actuality of reality itself and the forms which exist within it and thus have reality and existence themselves. We define around the nature of this self-evident structure.

Definition: All that exists is reality and we call its fundamental nature 'ontological energy'. Ontological energy, the energy or actuality of being, is simply a term we define to usefully denote the self-evident existence and nature of reality in terms of its self-evident attributes.

The Attributes of Reality: In human terms reality is characterized by its fundamental attributes:

1. It is real and actual and the locus of all being.
2. It is absolute in that it is exactly and completely what it is.
3. It is present and its presence manifests as a single common universal present moment which encompasses all of reality.
4. It is continually happening. Happening is the processor that drives the computational evolution of forms.
5. It can be considered a living system in the sense that it is self-motivating since there is nothing external to it that moves it.
6. Devoid of forms its underlying nature is formless but all individual forms exist within it thereby becoming real and actual.
7. It self-manifests as the reality of all individual forms.

Ontological energy is a name for the self-evident presence and actuality of reality which itself is formless but in which all forms arise thus themselves becoming real and actual and present in the present moment.

All of reality consists entirely of ontological energy. Ontological energy is the one single 'substance' and locus of reality. It is existence itself. Ontological energy is simply a name for the self-evident nature of reality as the source and locus of everything that exists and the underlying nature of its reality.

Ontological energy is not a physical substance, or medium but an abstract dimensionless information space filled with the presence of reality and being in which all the information forms of the things of the world become real and actual and present in a present moment, and in which happening continually computes the state of existence of all forms.

Ontological energy can be conceptualized by analogy to an ocean of intrinsically formless water in which all the waves and other forms of water arise thus becoming real. As the nature of the forms that arise within water are determined by the nature of the water they arise in so the forms of reality are determined by the virtual nature of reality. Ontological energy is somewhat similar to the ancient concept of Tao.

THE EXTENDED FINE TUNING

The second fundamental question of reality is why what actually exists is what exists rather than something else. Why is the extended fine tuning that determines the basic structure of reality what it is and not something else? The Consistency Conjecture provides a likely answer and we provide a definitive other reason below.

Definition: The Extended Fine Tuning is the complete basic irreducible structure of reality from which the information structure of all the rest of reality is computed in a consistent manner. The extended fine tuning is the virtual nature of ontological energy that determines what actual forms can exist in reality. It includes the irreducible laws of nature including the fundamental laws of logic as well as the irreducible form structure and values of constants of nature.

The Consistency Conjecture: The extended fine tuning that exists is the only one that can exist because it is the only one that results in a logically consistent and complete computational reality. If the Consistency Conjecture is verified it, the Axiom of Logic, and the Existence Axiom would constitute the three fundamental axioms of reality upon which all else is based.

The basic logical rules and operators by which reality computes are themselves part of the extended fine tuning. Thus they themselves necessitate that reality is a logical computational structure. This is a necessary consequence of the Axiom of Logic. The question then becomes whether all other aspects of the extended fine tuning are also

344

necessary to ensure this or whether they could be otherwise and still be consistent with a logical structure. In any case it is clear that all components of the extended fine tuning must be self-consistent with each other and the logic of reality for reality to exist.

THE WORLD OF FORMS

Definition: The World of Forms is the totality of all forms and thus of all information that exists. It is the entire information structure of reality and the fundamental computational structure that actually underlies all the things and events of an apparently physical universe. It is an abstract logical space or structure in which all forms exist in continuous interactive computation. This fundamental computational level of reality is neither dimensional, material nor physical but logical.

Definition: Forms are all the discriminable information structures of whatever type that arise in ontological energy without exception. A form is the information of anything that has structure or can be discriminated or named. Forms include not just all individual forms at any level but all possible sets and subsets of forms, all hierarchies of forms, and all emergent forms. The entirety of all forms constitutes a single universal form called the world of forms.

Definition: Things are the interpretations of specific types of information forms in the minds of organismic observers. Though they are interpreted as material things in a physical universe, all things are actually only their information only. The underlying structure of all 'physical' things is actually their information being computed in the world of forms. Information forms are the true fundamental structures of all the apparent 'things' of the world without exception. How this works will be explained shortly.

The Emptiness of Forms: Since all forms are actually only information they have no individual self-substances other than that of the reality in which they arise. Reality consists entirely of ontological energy and the actively evolving forms of information that exist within it in the present moment. Like waves that arise in water whose substance is always water, the substance of all the forms that arise in ontological energy is ontological energy only. All forms are information forms of ontological energy only without exception.

Thus all the 'things' of the world, that are actually only organismic interpretations of forms, are also empty of any self-substances other than ontological energy.

The Reality of Forms: Forms are abstract information forms of ontological energy. Thus they are real and actual because they exist in the reality of the present moment. They are all the actually real things of the world. Because they are actually information only does not mean they are less real in the least. Their computations have real effects in the real world and constitute the real events of the world. The computations of forms are the manifestations of reality.

The Single Form of Reality: All forms together constitute the world of forms and all forms together exist as a single unified form which can be discriminated into individual forms in innumerable different overlapping ways by various organismic observers.

The Continuity of Forms: The world of forms exists as a single complete continuous form in that all its parts are computationally connected with all others back to the beginning and across the whole in a continuous and logically complete consistency network.

The Exactitude of Forms: The world of forms is computational so it must be exact in the sense that it consists of precise unique unambiguous information forms and computations. It could not be consistently computed if it was not exact in form and computation. This exactness incorporates constrained quantum randomness. It excludes the notion that the world of forms actually consists only of the various contradictory views of observers and that there is no single external reality common to all.

The Actuality of a Single World of Forms External to any Particular Observer: Thus the world of forms must exist as a single complete self-consistent computational system actually 'out there' in an actual reality external to and independent of any particular observer. The fact that multiple observers each observe similar structures in the world of forms is strong evidence that something responsible for those structures actually exists external to particular observers.

Definition: Form Domains are natural structures that emerge computationally in the single form of the world of forms. They consist of areas of similarity of various types of information structures within the single continuous form. Form domains are multiply *overlapping* structural distinctions. They do not define individual forms but organismic observers tend to define individual forms in terms of them. Domains are the emergent structures of the world of forms.

For example currents and waves are overlapping structures isolated from a single continuous body of water differently by oceanographers and surfers. Trees, leaves and acorns are individual observer identified forms based on overlapping information domains in a forest. Domains actually exist as information structures in the world of forms, but, with possible exceptions at the elemental level, individual forms exist only in observer models of reality.

ORGANISMIC OBSERVERS

Definition: Organismic observers are individual forms based on form domains within the world of forms that are characterized by having internal models of their realities. Thus all organisms including humans are themselves specialized form domains within the world of forms.

In general organismic observers correspond to human and other biological life forms though they could also include robotic systems. They all have some degree of internal simulation model of their environments in which they experience their existence and on the basis of which they more effectively compute their functioning.

Organismic Simulations of reality. The reality that organisms experience their existence within is actually their own internal mental simulation of that reality. The simulation exists as specialized internal forms that model, interpret and embellish the actual external forms of an organism's environment in the observer independent world of forms. However this simulation is also a part of that external world of forms. More on this and its implications shortly.

COMPUTATIONAL REALITY

The world of forms is an active computational system. It continually re-computes its current information form state in the present moment and thus the current state of the universe as viewed by human observers. It is a rule based internally consistent and logically complete computational system that continually evolves in accordance with the laws of nature.

Happening is the ubiquitous processor of reality. Happening continually drives the simultaneous re-computation of all forms in the present moment and thus maintains their existence in the reality of the present moment. Though analogous to the sequential processors of computers it is different in that it computes all forms simultaneously.

Forms are the forms of their instantaneous happening. Since reality exists only in the present moment the true nature of forms is not static forms being re-computed into new static forms but of forms in the actual process of continuous change. Thus every form itself contains the information that can be extracted as its static form plus the information of how that form is actually changing. Every form contains both the data of itself and the code that is changing that data.

This is at least true at the level of organismic perception which is far above the resolution of any granularity of actual happening.

Reality as a single running program: Though the world of forms actually exists only in the present moment, from a temporal perspective it can be usefully thought of as a single running program which continually computes the current form state of reality and thus the current information state of the universe.

Reality as multiple interacting programs. From a temporal and organismic perspective the world of forms can be conceptualized as innumerable individual running programs. Each of these programs continually computes its current state in the present moment in interaction with all the other programs that constitute its program environment.

The world of forms is a continuous computational whole. However since all forms are continually computed in interaction with the other forms of their environment they all actually exist as a single computational nexus that extends across the entire world of forms rather than as individual programs. All individual programs, like all individual forms, exist as overlapping domains on the basis of which organismic observers discriminate individual programs from the whole.

The software analogy. By analogy the world of forms can be thought of as code forms operating on data forms driven by the ubiquitous processor of simultaneous happening in the present moment. The data forms encode the current state of nature, and the code forms are the laws of nature and programs based upon them that compute the data states. However as with computer programs data and code are both forms of information with different contexts. Though running programs computing data states are a useful way to think of the world of forms from a temporal perspective reality actually exists only as instantaneously changing forms in the present moment.

Computations occur only at the elemental level. As with computer software all computations of the world of forms actually execute only at an elemental level analogous to machine language operations. All the other programs of reality exist as sequences and complexes of these elemental operations. Simultaneous computations of the same domains at multiple levels could not be consistent.

The extended fine tuning level. At the level of the extended fine tuning the programs consist of the basic logical operations of reality, its fixed 'machine language' operations, upon which all else is based. These are functionally rather similar to the basic Boolean algebra of silicon computers since the basic logic of reality must be common to both for reality to be comprehensible to humans. However there are some important differences. The extended fine tuning also includes the basic structures of nature and the values of the basic constants of nature as elements of its computational structure.

The elemental level. At the elemental level are the basic laws of nature such as the particle property conservation law and other fundamental laws that are responsible for the elemental material structures of nature. These are apparently fixed and thus analogous to the 'firmware' of reality.

Inanimate programs. Above that are the largely automatic programs that generate the natural 'inanimate' processes of the universe according to the aggregate operations of the laws of nature. These are enormously complex programs consisting of innumerable computations governing the aggregate interactions of countless particles and all the levels of emergence therefrom.

These programs continually compute the underlying information structure of what organismic observers view as the material universe. These programs are not completely deterministic but have an element of quantum randomness as will be explained shortly.

Organismic programs. Above this level organismic programs begin to emerge and take on lives of their own. These programs to varying degrees incorporate internal models of their environments in terms of which they intelligently compute volitional actions toward instinctual ends of survival, procreation and pleasure versus pain. Though these programs all operate through complex sequences of lower level routines they exhibit higher level directives when considered in aggregate as individual systems.

These programs are what are interpreted as the various living organisms of the world in the mental models of humans and other organisms. While each ultimately operates only through calls on basic processes invoking the elemental laws of nature, organisms clearly operate as intentional systems towards the fulfillment of the instinctual imperatives encoded in their software. And they clearly operate intelligently in the sense that they compute effective actions from possible alternatives.

We are programs running in the world of forms. Each of us is a organismic program continually computing our own life and history in interaction with an environment consisting of innumerable other programs, each of us part of the single computational whole which is the single program of reality.

Superorganismic programs. Emergence does not stop with the computational behavior of individual organisms. There are even more complex programs computing all the social and historical processes of organismic aggregates each of which has a life of its own and can be isolated as an actual program in the world of forms. These independently operating actual programs in the world of forms are responsible for the great flows of the evolution of life forms and the major flows of human history as well as the computational evolution of individual lives and families, all in interaction with the programs that constitute their environments.

The realness of programs. Because these programs are the real processes that compute the world of forms from the perspective of organismic observers they compute what is real and actual into existence because they generate the actual information that constitutes reality. This information is what we and all the other things of the world actually are. These programs are real and actual and happening and have real effects. Thus the entire universe, the entire world of forms, can be thought of as a living happening program consisting of innumerable living subprograms that continually interactively compute the reality of the universe of the world of forms.

Reality is the present moment result of the interactive computations of myriads of discriminable programs operating simultaneously as a single system. These programs run in happening in the present moment and thus are the actual self-manifestations of reality. This is the true nature of the world of forms and of the universe it manifests in the xperience of observers.

And all observers are themselves computational forms continually computing themselves in interaction with other computational forms all of which they compute in their simulations of themselves within their view of reality. In concert all these programs together weave the information fabric of reality, in concert together they all produce the consistent information harmony of the Uni-Verse.

The General Principle of Evolution: The general principle of evolution states that all things are forms and the evolution of all forms is determined by their interactions with their environments which consist of other forms. Thus the subsequent forms of all forms is selected by their interactions with the forms that constitute their environments. Darwinian evolution is a special case of this more general principle specifically applicable to the survival of organismic form species rather than individual forms. It applies to species of organismic forms which are a specialized subset of forms which reproduce their kind.

EMERGENCE

Definition: Emergent forms are aggregate form structures that exhibit forms and obey rules that are not the simple additive results of their constituent forms. For example elemental forms are emergent from the extended fine tuning; the laws of chemistry emerge from these elemental laws; the laws of biology from those of chemistry and so forth. All forms but the most elemental are emergent.

Definition: Form Domains are the multiply overlapping structures that result from emergence. Emergent structures and domains are identical concepts and effectively synonyms. Organismic observers tend to discriminate individual things on the basis of domains from what is a single continuous world of forms. Leaves, branches, trees and forests are all overlapping emergent form domains in a single continuous exact world of forms that observers discriminate as individual things on an *ad hoc* basis.

The Principle of Aggregate Effect: The inherent structures of forms at all levels naturally results in emergent level structures at higher levels with associated emergent laws operating at those levels. For example the binding strengths of elemental particles naturally results in the structures of materials at aggregate levels and these in turn result in the structures of even larger scale objects composed of those materials.

The super-simultaneity of emergence. The entire hierarchy of emergence all operates simultaneously as a super-consistent whole. All levels are simply *aspects* of the same hierarchical structure. No level inherently computes other levels thus levels are not consequences of other levels but *aspects* of the whole hierarchical system. The entire hierarchy of emergence is the simultaneous consequences of its computational structure of reality in the instant.

For example the elemental laws do not compute the laws of biology. The laws of biology are natural *manifestations* of the operation of elemental laws in aggregate. Therefore they manifest simultaneously with the elemental levels.

This simultaneity of expression should not be confused with the actual relationships between specific processes across different levels and how they are computed in any given case which depends on the details of computational structure involved. Processes at all levels can compute those at other levels through various feedback mechanisms depending on the structures involved. The point is that lower levels do not automatically compute higher emergent levels since all levels are natural expressions of the same underlying computations.

Hierarchical super-consistency. The world of forms is a logically consistent and complete information structure across all levels, scopes, sets, sequences, and redundancies (in mental models) of forms. This self-consistency encompasses the whole universe of forms and simultaneously up and down all the innumerable emergent hierarchies of form and within and importantly across and between all individual generic observer form xperiences and models of reality.

This is true because all levels other than the most elemental are all aspects of the actual computations of reality which take place only at the most elemental level. Actual multiple computations at multiple levels of the same hierarchy could not be consistent.

However programs at higher than elemental levels consists of complex sequences of elemental level 'machine language' operations and these can operate as independent intelligent volitional processes.

Proof: If the computational world of forms were not logically consistent and complete it would tear itself apart at the inconsistencies and pause at the incompletenesses and could not exist. Because the world of forms does exist it must be logically complete and self-consistent and cannot contain a single inconsistency or incompleteness. However it does consistently include inconsistent systems on the basis of their false premises as in many mental models of reality.

Corollary: Since all actual forms in the world of forms are computationally generated there can be no Gödelian incompleteness in the world of forms as by definition incompletenesses cannot be computed. Gödel's Proof applies only to human logico-mathematical generalizations of the actual logico-mathematical structure of reality which differ in certain significant ways, and not to the computational structure of reality itself.

The consistency of the extended fine tuning. Principle of Extended Fine Tuning Consistency: The extended fine tuning must itself be a self-consistent structure since it leads computationally to a self-consistent and logically complete world of forms. This is significant with respect to our Consistency Conjecture.

The Principle of Convergent Emergence: Emergence tends to stochastically converge on general outcomes pre-determined by the original extended fine tuning. Atomic structure, chemistry, biology, intelligent life, language and manipulative appendages are progressive examples, though not necessarily leading to the exact form of human beings.

The Ultimate Emergence Conjecture: There may be a single ultimate emergent law of universal scope of which humans are not yet aware which may even drive the direction of the universe as a whole. It may be driving the evolution of the universe towards some end pre-determined by the extended fine tuning. The original extended fine tuning may in effect function as such a top down law as it was and is the governing form structure of reality. At the top-most level it may express as a single governing principle rather than a set of seemingly unrelated elemental rules and constants. It is reasonable to assume this ultimate principle is guiding the evolution of the universe towards an increasing state of self-awareness.

'PHYSICAL' REALITY

Definition: The Universe is a name for the world of forms from the usual organismic perspective of a material world. However its actual fundamental structure is the evolving information structure of the world of forms and its apparent physical, material, and dimensional nature is an interpretation that arises in the minds of organismic observers in their interactions with it.

Premise: all the 'things' of the world without exception are their information only.

Evidence: There is overwhelming evidence that all things are their information only.

1. To be comprehensible, which it self-evidently is, reality must be a logical structure. To be logical and self-evidently happen it must be computable. To be computable it must consist of information because only information is computable. Therefore reality must consist of information only.
2. The laws of science which best describe reality are themselves logico-mathematical structures. Why would the equations of science be the best description of reality if reality itself did not consist of similar structures? This explains the so called "unreasonable effectiveness of mathematics".
3. By recognizing that reality is a logico-mathematical structure the laws of nature immediately assume a natural place as an intrinsic part of reality. No longer do they somehow stand outside a physical world while mysteriously controlling it.
4. Physical mechanisms to produce effects become unnecessary in a purely computational world. It is enough to have a consistent

logico-mathematical model that is in accord with experimental evidence.

5. When everything that mind adds to reality is recognized and subtracted from mind's internal model of reality we find that all that remains is this information structure. This can be verified by carefully analyzed direct experience.

6. This view of reality is tightly consistent with the other insights of this book which I believe are themselves also consistent with modern science though not with many of its interpretations. Total consistency across maximum scope is the test of validity.

7. This view of reality leads to simple elegant solutions of many of the perennial problems of the fundamental nature of reality and leads directly to many new insights.

8. In particular it leads to a new understanding of spacetime which allows a conceptual unification of quantum theory and general relativity and solves the paradoxical nature of the quantum world.

Thus we must conclude that all the apparently material and physical things of the world are the experiences and interpretations of certain types of information forms in the mental models of organismic observers and by extension in the science they create.

The Actuality of the Laws of Nature states that the laws of nature, being forms of information in a reality consisting only of information forms, are an integral part of nature as real as the data forms that encode the information of things, and thus are as real as the things of the world. Thus the laws of nature do not stand apart from nature in some mysterious metaphysical realm while controlling it as in the current mistaken interpretation of science. That the laws of nature find a natural place in our model of reality is additional strong evidence of its validity.

ELEMENTALS

The elemental structure of the world of forms consists of the particle 'properties' and the rules that govern them.

Definition: The particle 'properties' are the unchanging elemental bits of reality that make up all elementary particles and thus everything in the universe. These are properly understood not as 'properties' of particles but as the actual *components* of reality that in valid combinations make elementary particles.

The particle properties. The particle properties include identity, (the various particle 'numbers'), mass-energy, the charges, spin, parity and intrinsic time direction. There are some questions about how these are to be defined but our definition is they are whatever the unchanging separate components of all elementary particles are.

The laws of nature that govern particle properties include the rules that govern which combinations of particle properties combine to produce actual particles, and the strengths of their values which are components of the extended fine tuning. There are other elemental laws of which we will mention the two most important.

The particle property conservation law states that the amounts of all particle properties remains the same through all particle interactions. Because the total amounts of particle properties stays the same even when they are redistributed to make up different particles it is the particle properties rather than the elementary particles that are the true unchanging elemental constituents of reality.

The laws governing the structure of atoms and molecules, such as the law of quantum numbers which governs the orbital structure of electrons in atoms, are other basic laws of nature. This elemental structure and the laws which govern it are responsible for most of the structure of the universe.

These laws are either part of the extended fine tuning or immediately reducible to it. They are near if not part of the complete set of irreducible components of computational reality and are the elemental code and data forms that compute the structure of the universe at all scales.

Definition: 'Entanglement' is the necessary arithmetic relationships imposed on the particle properties of interacting particles by these elemental laws. Interacting particles whose particle properties are interrelated by these laws are said to be entangled on those particle properties.

Thus in general all particles in the universe are entangled with other particles with which they have interacted on the particle properties specified in those interactions.

Definition: 'Decoherence' is an entanglement of particle properties with dimensional characteristics such as mass-energy or spin. A decoherence interrelates dimensional attributes of particles to particular dimensional values. Decoherence establishes specific dimensional relationships between particles, but only with respect to each other. Dimensional particle properties are conserved in decoherences.

*The Principle of the Relativity of Entanglement and Decoherence: Because they are relationships specified only between individual interacting particles, decoherences and entanglements occur only in the frames of the particles involved with respect to each other only with no intrinsic immediate relationship to other observer frames. Therefore every decoherence network will have its own view of dimensionalization consisting of the dimensional relationships determined by its decoherence history.

The Principle of the Relativity of Entanglement and Decoherence is the key insight for understanding the material structure of reality because of its profound consequences.

Bound Decoherence. Individual particles bound into the atoms and molecules of matter can be interpreted as bound decoherences because they result in persistent entanglement and decoherence relationships between the bound particles.

THE EMERGENCE OF SPACETIME

Premise: There is not a single fixed pre-existing spacetime common to all forms within which things exist and events play out. On the contrary individual fragmentary spacetimes emerge as connected networks of decoherence events.

Evidence: This view is based on the actual establishment of dimensional relationships by the elemental laws of nature and leads to the conceptual unification of quantum theory and general relativity and the resolution of all quantum paradox. It is also based on the fact that the only observation of spacetime possible is in the form of dimensional events rather than actual measurements of spacetime itself.

The apparent incompatibility between quantum theory and general relativity is because quantum theory mistakenly assumes a fixed pre-existing spacetime within which quantum events occur while in general relativity events and spacetime are part of an integrated structure in which each influences the other. By understanding how spacetime actually emerges from quantum events these theories can be conceptually unified in a single consistent theory.

The source of quantum paradox. Likewise the apparent quantum paradoxes are all with respect to that same mistakenly assumed pre-existing spacetime and are resolved when the emergent nature of spacetime is understood.

Definition: An 'Entanglement or Decoherence Network' is the network formed by successive sequences of entanglement and/or decoherence events. The successive interactions of all particles in the network imposes arithmetic relationships among all particles in the network on those particle properties specified in the successive events.

Definition: A spacetime manifold is the view of the dimensional relationships determined in a decoherence network from the perspective of a particle, or object composed of particle, in the network. Every particle in an entanglement network functions as a generic observer of the entanglement relationships of the rest of the network from the perspective of its entanglement relationships to other particles.

Definition: By extension every object composed of particles has its own manifold which is the view of its entanglement decoherence network from its own frame.

Definition: A spacetime, or individual spacetime, is another term for a manifold. It is the view of any observer of the dimensional relationships that constitute its decoherence network. Thus every observer has its own individual spacetime which is its manifold.

The Principle of Spacetime Independence: The spacetime of every observer exists as a completely separate spacetime with no dimensional alignment or relationship to that of any other observer unless or until those spacetimes have been linked and aligned through common decoherence events. It is only through shared decoherence events that spacetimes combine and align.

The Principle of Spacetime Incompleteness: Individual spacetimes are always partial and incomplete. They are limited in scope as they do not include all events in the world of forms. And they are limited in the particle properties that are specified since not all particle properties are specified in every particle interaction.

The Principle of Spacetime Alignment: When separate spacetimes link via a common decoherence event all the specified entanglement and decoherence relationships of their separate networks become aligned in a single common spacetime because that common decoherence event establishes a dimensional relationship between the networks.

The Principle of Free Choice: When separate spacetimes link and align in shared decoherence events that alignment occurs probabilistically because there can be no rules governing the alignment of separate spacetimes because there is no common background spacetime of reference. Nothing actually changes in the two spacetimes, their dimensionality is just now aligned with respect to each other.

The Principle of Free Choice is the source of all probabilistic quantum randomness and thus of all randomness since all true randomness is quantum. Whenever there are no rules governing a computation in the world of forms it must occur randomly within its possible constraints. This is why all true randomness has to do only with dimensional aspects of reality. The alignment of separate unlinked spacetimes by a decoherence linkage event demonstrates this.

Example of the spin non-locality 'paradox'. The spin non-locality 'paradox' is a good example of how our theory resolves quantum paradox. In the usual example the spin orientations of the two particles exiting an interaction are already aligned opposite to each other by the conservation law but the orientation alignment of that partial spacetime is as yet unaligned to the spacetime of the laboratory and observer.

When the observer measures the spin alignment of either particle the whole two particle spacetime becomes aligned with that of the laboratory, and thus the other particle will be immediately found with equal and opposite spin alignment in the frame of the laboratory. There is no 'non-locality' paradox and no 'faster than light' transmission of spin alignment. There is simply the alignment of two previously unaligned individual spacetimes. Because there can be no rules governing how separate spacetimes align nature is forced to align them randomly.

The resolution of quantum paradox: All the apparent quantum paradoxes are paradoxical only with respect to a mistakenly assumed fixed, common, pre-existing spacetime which does not exist. Spacetimes are actually constructed piecewise as the dimensional relationships established by networks of decoherence events due to the operation of the particle property conservation and other elemental laws governing the interaction of particles.

These individual spacetimes seem paradoxical with respect to each other because the dimensionality of separate spacetimes is not aligned with respect to each other until they are linked and aligned by a common decoherence event such as a measurement. Prior to such linking their dimensionalities are undefined with respect to each other and thus describable as the probabilities of how they can become aligned.

This is why particles are described as wavefunctions prior to a measurement decoherence event. Wavefunctions actually describe how the spacetimes of separate quantum systems can become aligned with respect to each other rather than the dimensionality of particles with respect to a non-existent pre-existing classical spacetime.

Spacetime transience: Because all spacetimes are generated on the fly by decoherence events they exist only as decoherence relations in the present moment and must be maintained by continual decoherence events or fade back into the logical space from which they emerge. However the current state of their entanglement and decoherence relationships incorporates the history of their past entanglement and decoherence events. Their current state is the computational result of all their past decoherence and entanglement histories.

There is no pre-existing, fixed spacetime common to all observers. Spacetime is not a single fixed background to all events but consists of individual spacetime structures that are generated piece-wise on the fly by decoherence events.

The emergence of classical spacetime. Classical spacetime as we imagine it in our mental models of reality simply does not exist. It is a convenient mental fiction constructed of the dimensional aspects of a remembered framework of actually observed events with the imaginary intermediate spaces interpolated between them. This works only

360

because the elemental laws of nature generate dimensional relationships that tend to emerge as consistent overall structures. However there are always some loose ends at the elemental level and these are where the so-called quantum paradoxes appear in the form of unlinked independent spacetime fragments.

However in areas of continuous dense decoherence events such as the familiar world we live in, large scale classical type spacetimes tend to emerge as enormous networks of decoherences human observers link into via the decoherences of their senses with the environment.

An essential part of this spacetime is all the individual quasi-stable spacetimes generated by the bound decoherences of matter. All material structures are mini-spacetimes which form an essential aspect of the overall classical spacetime we appear to inhabit.

Cosmological spacetime. Due to the structure of the elemental laws of nature all individual spacetimes do tend to converge towards the spacetime structure of general relativity at large scales and thus of familiar Newtonian spacetime at ordinary scales of experience. Thus what we consider to be the classical spacetime of our experience can be considered the logico-mathematical structure inherent in the way that dimensionality emerges from decoherence events as determined by the conservation laws and the structural laws of matter. Spacetime is a logico-mathematical structure inherent in the elemental laws of nature rather than an actual extant physical structure in which the events of the world occur.

General relativistic spacetime. The spacetimes that emerge from decoherence events are naturally the curved spacetimes of general relativity when the mass-energy particle property is taken as the scale of the dimensionality that emerges. This causes spacetime to be dilated around mass-energy concentrations and thus generates the correctly curved spacetime of general relativity.

The conceptual unification of quantum theory and general relativity. Thus there is a conceptual unification of quantum theory and general relativity that emerges naturally from the recognition that spacetime is something that emerges from decoherence events rather than being a fixed pre-existing common background within which events occur.

Thus the understanding of the true nature of spacetime and how it emerges piecewise from decoherence events conceptually unifies quantum theory and general relativity while simultaneously resolving all quantum paradox and providing an explicit reason why nature must behave probabilistically at the quantum level when individual spacetimes link and align.

The genesis of relative motion. As forms dimensionalize the particle property conservation law requires them to do so with relative motion with respect to each other. This is because the rest masses of particles are not exact multiples of each other and thus cannot be conserved in interactions except with the discrepancies in rest masses being expressed in kinetic or wave energy. This requires the interactions of particles to produce relative motions between them. This requires dimensional spacetimes in which that relative motion can occur and this is the genesis of those spacetimes.

All forms of mass and energy are different forms of relative motion between forms as they become dimensionalized as individual spacetimes are generated. They are numeric information in the world of forms as to how dimensionality emerges as relative motions in the xperience of generic observers.

Rest masses consist of vibratory motion. Because rest masses continually vibrate very rapidly relative to all observers their motion appears to be absolute and the rest masses fixed. All other forms of energy are also either linear or wave relative motion. This is consistent with string theory which considers material particles to consist of vibrating strings.

Potential energy is a convenient accounting trick. It is not really the energy of a system itself but the equivalent blocking energy of another system.

The conservation of mass and energy. The conservation of mass and energy consists of the conversion of equivalent amounts of relative motion from one form to another. How else could something be conserved if were not actually different forms of the same thing?

COSMOLOGY

The big bang. Though ontological energy has always existed in its formless state, the world of forms that manifests as the universe to human observers began in an actualization event called the big bang. Ontological energy in its formless state may be said to 'contain' all possible virtual possibilities in an unactualized state. It is a more comprehensive version of the quantum vacuum containing the extended fine tuning in an implicit or virtual state.

The STc Principle: Everything without exception continually moves through spacetime at the speed of light. That is the combined velocity of everything without exception through space and through time is always the speed of light. The STc Principle underlies the Theory of Special Relativity which can be derived from it[1].

Since observers by definition do not move relative to themselves in space all their STc velocity is through time. Thus everything is always moving at the speed of light through time according to its own comoving clock. Thus each one of us is continually traveling through time at the speed of light.

The speed of light is actually the speed of time. It just so happens that electromagnetic radiation has no time velocity in its own frame and so always travels at the speed of light in space relative to every observer clock.

The STc Principle is the source of both the arrow of time and the fact of a privileged present moment of time because it requires the continuous movement through spacetime and a particular location in spacetime for everything that exists. The STc Principle puts both the arrow of time and a privileged present moment on a firm physical basis. It falsifies the notion of 'block time', that all moments of time exist simultaneously.

The arrow of time. The arrow of time is a consequence of the STc Principle because it requires the continuous unidirectional movement of everything through time.

The present moment. The present moment is a consequence of the STc Principle because it requires everything to be at only one particular point of time.

There is only one cosmological geometry consistent with the STc Principle. That is the universe as a 4-dimensional hypersphere with its surface the 3-dimensions of space, and time its radial dimension converging back to the big bang at its origin.

The cosmological hypersphere. At large scales the individual spacetimes generated as networks of decoherence events tend to converge towards the structure described by general relativity in the form of a cosmological 4-dimensional hypersphere though always from the perspective of individual observers. This is the result of taking mass-energy as the relative scale of decoherence dimensionalizations which leads to individual spacetimes being dilated around mass-energy concentrations.

There are two kinds of time. This is conclusively demonstrated by the time traveling twins in which the twins meet up again with different clock times *but always in the exact same present moment*. Thus clock time is different than the p-time defined by the present moment.

Definition: P-time is the time associated with the present moment which is the current locus of the continual extension of the radial dimension of the cosmological hypersphere. The present moment is the surface of the cosmological hypersphere.

Definition: Clock time is the rate of happening in the present moment which varies according to relativistic conditions. Thus clock rates can vary but all clocks, whatever their rates, are carried along together in the present moment by the continual extension of the p-time surface of the universe.

There is a single universal present moment common to all observers. This present moment is the p-time of the surface of the cosmological hypersphere. It is the same for all observers and everything in the universe because it is the only locus of reality.

The surface of the cosmological hypersphere is the locus of reality. Thus our cosmological geometry is only the surface of the 4-dimensional hypersphere because the interior corresponds to the past which no longer exists. This 4-dimensional surface is all that exists. Properly speaking there is nothing other than it. It is the intrinsic dimensional result that the elemental dimensional emergences of individual spacetimes tend to converge towards on the largest cosmological scale.

Thus the universe is finite and has a positive curvature. The amount of curvature is a measure of the p-time dimension back to the big bang.

This is a measurable prediction of this part of the theory, which states that Ω, the 'flatness' of the universe, should be very slightly >1 the value for a flat universe. It appears that only *clock time rates* are directly measurable by clocks. However Ω is a measure of p-time.

The Hubble Expansion. It is possible that this hypersphere is not exactly spherical. It could have wobbles like a giant soap bubble which could help explain variations in the Hubble rate of expansion of the 3-dimensional space of the surface. However the Hubble rate of expansion is measured in clock time which is not the same as p-time. Since the clock time rates and p-time extension rates need not be proportional this could also explain the varying rates of Hubble expansion over time including that of the inflationary period.

Proof: The 4-dimensional hyperspherical geometry of the universe is directly observable and thus verifiable. We directly observe that we live in a 3-dimensional space and we directly view time at distance in every direction from every point in that space. That is direct observation of the radial time dimension that extends backward in all directions from every 3-dimensional spatial point. Thus we all see all 4-dimensions all the time. This view of our 4-dimensional universe is called our light cone which is a visual slice through all 4-dimensions from our observer singularity.

Definition: The 'Observer Singularity' refers to the fact that every observer exists in the present moment but to it everything else at any distance exists in the past to at least some slight degree due to the finite speed of light. Thus every observer constitutes a spacetime singularity through which the future comes into being as the present moment and flows outward in every direction into the past at the speed of light.

Time travel: We all continuously travel through time at the speed of light all the time. However nothing can ever leave the universal common present moment since it is the only locus of reality. So there can be no actual time travel to the past or future because neither actually exists. It is however possible to travel at different clock time rates relative to each other's clocks as we all stay within the present moment. This is a real difference in the rate at which physical processes and happening occur but they still occur only in the present moment. These are the only senses in which time travel is possible.

Presumably all clocks can only run forward though at different relative rates. Though cosmologically it seems theoretically possible that some part of the cosmological surface could temporarily fluctuate backwards along the radial time dimension that would seem to be inconsistent with the STc Principle.

INFORMATION COSMOLOGY

As stated previously forms are information. Thus the world of forms consists entirely of evolving information. The world of forms can equivalently be called the information world or the information substrate of reality. This fundamental level of reality consists entirely of computationally evolving information which continually computes the current information state of reality and thus of the universe which is the manifestation of the world of forms in the mental models of human observers.

The Principle of Information: Since all 'things' are forms, and all forms are information, every 'thing' in the universe is its information only. All is information only in the ontological energy of reality.

The nonexistence of causality. Causality does not exist as a physical process. It is simply a description of the general fact that predictable temporal sequences exist in the world of forms. The world of forms is normally interpreted as a vast complex causal network. However there is actually no such thing as causality. No law of nature incorporates any variable of causality whatsoever. Causality turns out to be simply the general fact that predictable temporal sequences exist in the world of forms. Causality is entirely an imaginary meta-concept that has no actual existence in the world of forms or even the universe of 'things'. The world of forms is an information structure, not a physical structure. Calling it causal is as nonsensical as saying $2 + 2$ *causes* 4.

Consistency not causality. What actually exists in the world of forms is consistent computational relationships rather than causality. This insight that there is no cause and effect but only consistent computational relationships has major implications and frees us from the illusion that the past 'causes' the present.

The present determines the past. When the non-existence of causality and the fact that reality exists only in the present moment are understood then it becomes clear that it is the present that determines the past. The present exactly determines a unique past, at any point in past time, which is precisely that information state which would uniquely determine the exact present that actually exists.

Of course in actuality the past does not exist except in organismic understandings of what it would have had to have been to result in the present to the limits of understanding of the organism in question. However the past can be said to actually exist in the present in the forms of things that encode their precursor states.

Bidirectional present-past temporal consistency. Thus the present and past form structure exists together as a uniquely determined self-consistent temporally bidirectional structure, exact in every possible detail, that could not be other than it actually is. But the actual reality of that past exists only in the actual form structure of the present.

The complete determination of past and present. Thus both the present and past are exactly determined and are exactly as they are and could not be otherwise in any single detail no matter how insignificant. However only the present moment actually exists and the past exists only as the logical implications of the information structure of the world of forms in the present.

This analysis assumes the present is a fixed form state, however it is actually a computational evolution in the process of happening rather than a static fixed state. So this must be factored into the analysis.

The Super-Anthropic Principle: Since the present uniquely determines the past the original extended fine tuning must have been exactly as it was with not the slightest possibility of being different. The original fine tuning of the universe must have been exactly as it was because only that fine tuning could have produced the universe exactly as it is today in the present moment. That original fine tuning is uniquely determined by the actual extant state of the universe in the present moment. The extended fine tuning of the universe is the only one possible given the self-evident fact of the current state of the universe. The existence of the present as it actually is falsifies all other possible pasts.

The Consistency Conjecture: There is another compatible explanation for the extended fine tuning, the complete list of irreducible facts of reality. The Consistency Conjecture states that the extended fine tuning must be exactly as it was and is because that is the only one that results in a logically complete and self-consistent computational information structure for the universe. This is a conjecture that requires proof, but I suspect it is likely to be true. Certainly the fact that the basic logical rules of the universe, which require the universe to be a self-consistent computational system, are themselves a part of the extended fine tuning leads us to believe that the rest of the extended fine tuning may be necessary as well.

Together these make a strong case for the actual extended fine tuning being the only one possible. In either case the extended fine tuning must be exactly as it is which seems to completely eliminate the need for any multiverses, bubble universes or parallel realities which are all theories primarily to explain why our particular fine tuning was chosen out of an immense set of presumed possible alternatives which now turn out to be impossible after all.

The Single Universe Conjecture: If in fact the extended fine tuning is the only one possible then it is likely that the single universe that we observe is the only universe that exists. Most varieties of multiverse theories are based on the enormously un-parsimonious assumption that all possible variations of extended fine tuning are not only possible but necessarily exist giving rise to separate universes. This assumption is conclusively falsified by the Super Anthropic Principle.

Only the future is probabilistic. Past and present are completely fixed and determined, thus only the future is probabilistic and not exactly determined because it does not yet exist. What the future will be when it becomes the present is continually being computed in the present moment in a process of constrained randomness in which most of what happens is predictable but with enough randomness to make things interesting and enable free will.

Definition: Free will means that the evolution of all forms, including those of organismic observers, is not completely determined by their histories or by forms external to them because all forms incorporate quantum randomness to greater or lesser degrees.

The usual misunderstanding of free will as the independence of a 'self' from the rest of an organism mistakenly ignores the fact that the actual 'selves' of organisms are their entire computational systems which includes every aspect of their entire form structures as a single system. Thus human and other organisms' free will consists of their ability to generate actions not entirely determined by their external environments due to the amplification of the internal quantum randomness of their constituent computations.

The ability to make intelligent choices among imagined alternatives is not itself free will as it could be deterministic. Free will is the degree to which choices are made randomly. In general most decisions are computed at the unconscious level and the conscious self merely serves as a top level quality control mechanism with little actual decision making function.

All randomness is quantum. There is no true classical randomness. All apparent randomness at the classical level is either the effects of quantum randomness amplified up to the classical level or often simply non-computability due to the complexity of the processes involved. Weather is a classical level emergent phenomenon combining both processes.

This is clear because there are no true probabilistic equations describing classical level phenomena. There are statistical equations such as those for the behavior of large aggregates of particles such as for heat, pressure, and turbulence but these are all based on predicting averages of quantum level processes.

In general the more complex the form the more opportunity for quantum randomness to be amplified up to the level of overall action though how this is expressed depends on the actual form structures involved. All true randomness derives from the manner in which individual spacetimes link and align at the quantum level via decoherences as described above.

Some forms, especially manmade digital forms are specifically designed to reduce their random 'free will' to the absolute minimum. But even digital media are eventually subject to quantum randomness. And even many natural forms one can identify such as the stability of protons maintain themselves as well. Everything depends on the details of the individual form structures.

All things are their information only and the information of themselves is their information history. Every form, and thus every 'thing', is precisely and only the information of itself, of what it is, and that information is the current result of its entire past computational information history. All the things of the world are their information content only and that information is not just the current information of themselves in the present moment but consists entirely of their information histories dating back to the beginning. Thus all current things are not just only the information of what they are now but that information of what they are now is their information histories as well. All things are the information of their information histories only.

Look at any 'thing' at all of whatever type. Its actuality is its information only. It is the information of itself, of what it actually is to the last detail, and that is all it is. And that includes the information of the particular observing observer's interaction with it as well. Not only that but that information is not just the information of the thing itself, but that information actually is the current computational result of that thing's entire past interaction history including the information of its currently being observed.

The self-evidence of information. Under careful observation everything without exception is self-evidently its information only. The information of what it is without exception is actually what it is and that only. This is a directly observable insight, though one that involves a major paradigm shift in the way we look at and conceptualize the world. We tend to think of the majority of things as the things they appear to be but this is actually in all cases just the information of what we perceive them as mixed with the information of how we relate to them. With understanding and practice this is directly observable and self-evident. Understanding and directly perceiving that all feelings, meanings, qualities and relationships of things are simply and exactly the information of those things is the first step towards realizing this insight.

The Sherlock Holmes Principle: All information forms contain extractable information about other forms they have interacted with. All forms and sets of forms are not only the information that is themselves but this same information is also information about other forms in their past interaction history. All forms are simultaneously the form of themselves, and also the computational result of their entire past form history of interactions with other forms.

All forms are the distributed information of prior forms. The information histories of all forms are composed of the distributed information of the other forms they have interacted with.

Thus the present 'thingness' of every form is precisely and exactly its past computational history. All things *are* the information of their histories of interactions with other forms and only that. This applies to all forms and all sets of forms at all levels in the hierarchy of forms. All things are the information of their information histories which is the reassembled information of their interactions with other things.

Thus all current forms and sets of forms contain retrievable information about other forms in their computational network both past and present and a vast amount of information about the entire history of forms is contained distributed across the totality of all current forms whether or not it is effectively retrievable. This information is retrievable to the extent the current form states and the logical rules of the world of forms are understood and tuning forms are available to retrieve it. The Sherlock Holmes Principle is the principle upon which all knowledge and science are based.

Imagine that everything in the world was an image and that image consists of the torn up and reassembled pieces of all previous images in its interaction history. Now imagine this as an unending repetitive process. That is what 'things' actually are. All things are puzzles constructed of pieces of previous puzzles.

The computational history of the entire world of forms is a consistent network through time in which all current forms are only and exactly the precise result of their entire past computational histories. Thus all things are not things in the usual sense but instead are the information of other things back to the beginning of time. All things are information that consists of the information of other things. This is what all things actually are and what the entire world of forms actually is.

The Principle of Exponential Information: Thus the information content of forms is not just that of some set number of forms considered singly but of all possible combinations of forms at all levels, including the recognition that forms are discriminated from the world of forms differently by different observers in overlapping ways.

For example the leaf is not just the exact complete information of that particular leaf but also contains multitudes of additional information about the history of the species, the health and environment of its individual tree and the history of that particular leaf, the principles of biology and chemistry and all manner of other things, much of it in tandem with the information content of its combined forms with other things.

And every set of forms such as the pattern of leaves on the lawn also contains multitudes of additional information about the seasons, the winds, the temperatures and so on. This is true because that is actually what the leaf and the pattern of leaves on the lawn are. They are only the information of themselves which is only the information of their interaction histories. All things are their information only and that information, especially in combination, is enormously complex and informative. **The notion that things are just individual separate things is an illusion.**

Thus the true amount of information in forms is immensely greater than a simple bit count of the amount of variation in individual forms because it is an exponential sum across all possible combinations of forms.

Definition: The proper measure of information in any particularly defined form is the quantity of discriminable variability rather than the amount of meaning to a particular (human) observer which is the implicit usage in standard information theory. A million random bits actually has the same information content as a million bits of Shakespeare. It is the precisely the number of bits necessary to express that particular amount of randomness. Thus the concept of information entropy is also suspect.

There is a useful sense in which information can be defined as the quantity of meaning to a particular observer but this is not the same as the intrinsic possible information in a bounded area of the world of forms. However since forms are discriminated only by observers and differently according to the observer we must be careful when trying to quantify information.

The Principle of Information Distribution: The total information of every form interaction event is distributed among all the resultant forms, and thus among all subsequent interacting forms in the resulting interaction network no matter how complex. Thus for example the information of the original extended fine tuning is distributed through all past forms into all present forms, and the information of all past events is distributed through all subsequent events in the event network originating from that event into the present. Thus all current forms are packets of distributed past information about previous forms.

The Non-Conservation of Information: All past information of all prior form states is implicitly preserved in the current form states

proceeding from those states and this implies that the total information content of reality should be increasing. It is theoretically possible given the current data form state and the complete set of laws of nature to run the present backwards and know the entire past which implies all information about all past states is contained distributed among the present states of forms. That would imply the total amount of information in the world of forms is continually increasing as the past becomes more and more extensive and its information is added to the world of forms. However there are practical questions as to what observer form(s) this information would be available to.

Increasing information might be true to the extent that the computations of forms was deterministic but it is not completely so. Thus information about the past may be being lost in the randomness of quantum processes over time. Another consideration is that information about the past is progressively submerged in that of the present and gradually becomes weaker and weaker to the point of being lost in the granular structure of the elemental level below which information cannot be encoded.

The Principle of the Theoretical Conservation of Information. From moment to moment no information is ever theoretically lost because like waves in a *frictionless* ocean forms of information are merely transformed and redistributed into other forms. No information is ever lost theoretically; it is just continually redistributed through the network of forms. However depending on its dynamics, previous information is gradually submerged beneath the randomness and granularity of the elemental level.

All waves that ever existed in the ocean are theoretically still there redistributed across the entire ocean, but to far below the level of ever being observable or their information recoverable. Nevertheless, as science continually demonstrates, an amazing amount of past information is retrievably distributed through current form states. Everything we know or think we know about the past is extracted from the information of those past form states distributed through the information of current form states.

XPERIENCE

Definition: Xperience is any computation of form without exception. *Xperience* is defined by analogy as a generalization of the *experience* of organismic observers. Xperience is the computation or re-computation of any form whatsoever, whether that of inanimate or organismic forms.

Experience **is a specialized subset of** *xperience.* Experience is the subset of xperience that consists of the re-computations of self-referential forms of consciousness in the simulation of an organismic observer.

Xperience is always only of itself. Since xperience is the re-computation of the form itself it is always of itself only, of its own change or re-computation.

Experience is always only of itself. Experience, as a subset of xperience, is also only of itself, of its own change or re-computation.

All the experiences 'of' other things are always a re-computation of the experiencing form itself. For example the experiences an observer seems to have of external things are actually only re-computations of its own internal forms in its simulation of those external things.

Forms xperience other forms as their xperience of their computational interactions with them. Because re-computations of forms tend to be in interaction with other forms those other forms can be experienced in the computational changes to the experiencing forms. This will be explained in more detail shortly. Thus forms do experience other forms but only as their own experience.

Xperience is implicit. This is true both of the xperience of inanimate forms and the experience of organismic forms. However the xperiences of inanimate forms are just their re-computations themselves without any context or explicit concept of the other forms they are experiencing. Therefore they are implicit and unconscious though they are real and actual xperiences.

Experience is explicit. Organismic observers, on the other hand, explicitly experience other forms in the re-computations of the self-referential forms of their simulation of them because they are able to experience that they are being experienced and because they are able to put them into context in terms of comparison with other experiences.

Generic Observers. All forms without exception can be considered to be generic observers as all forms continually xperience the reality of the existence of their form in its continual re-computation.

Organismic observers are a subset of generic observers. All organismic observer forms also continually experience the reality of the existence of their forms in their continual re-computations.

Like individual forms and programs, observers, both generic and organismic, exist in the world of forms as domains of emergence and are discriminated as *individual* observers only in the simulations of organismic observers.

The Xperience Principle: Reality consists entirely of xperience. The re-computation of forms is all that happens and thus is all that exists. Thus all that exists is xperience which is the continual re-computation of all form into continuing existence in the present moment by happening. If forms are not continually re-computed into existence they vanish from the present moment of reality and do not exist.

The Principle of Self-Manifestation: Reality continually self-manifests itself only in the continual re-computation or xperience of all form. Only through this self-manifestation of itself does reality become actual. Thus only observers xperience reality. Reality is known only through its manifestations as xperience.

The primacy of xperience. Reality exists only in its manifestations as xperience. Reality cannot be said to actually exist except as it manifests itself.

Thus the universe exists only in its observations of itself by the observers that constitute it which includes the re-computational happening of all its forms. The universe can be said to exist only as it manifests itself to itself. Reality is xperience only. Forms manifest only in their re-computations as xperience. An observation requires an xperience and only as things are xperienced do they manifest. The present moment contains only xperience of manifestation and manifestation of xperience. Thus xperience and manifestation are two sides of a single process.

The xperience of the single unified form of the world of forms can be considered the xperience of the universe self-manifesting itself to itself and by doing so becoming real and actual.

The necessity of the observer. Because reality exists only in its manifestations as the xperiences of observers, the observer is an intrinsic aspect of reality through which reality manifests its reality. Thus without generic observers to xperience it reality cannot manifest itself and cannot manifest its reality, and a reality that cannot manifest itself cannot have its reality confirmed and thus cannot be said to be real.

The world of forms consists only of forms. And the continual re-computations of forms is xperience, and only through xperience can reality manifest itself and become real and actual. Thus reality cannot exist except through the forms in which it does exist and without whose continuing xperience it would not exist. Thus the existence of forms and their xperience of their existence is required for reality to become actual. Thus the observer is an essential and necessary aspect of reality for reality to become real and actually exist.

CONSCIOUSNESS AND EXPERIENCE

Definition: *Experience* **is a specialized type of** *xperience* **that occurs consciously in the simulations of organismic observers.** Like *xperience*, *experience* is simply the continual re-computation of its own forms, however these forms are self-referential in nature. They are the information that other forms in the simulation are being unconsciously *xperienced*. They are forms that monitor the xperiences of other forms and encode the fact that they are happening and by doing so they constitute the *experience* of that *xperience* and so bring it to consciousness.

Experience occurs in a specialized area of consciousness in the simulation. This process occurs in the specialized area of consciousness within the simulation that many people mistakenly consider their self. This area is characterized by attention and the focusing of attention on various aspects of *xperience* to monitor it and thus bring it into conscious *experience*.

The evolutionary function of consciousness. This area of consciousness emerges naturally in the simulation as it provides a high level overall view of the essential elements of the simulation as a single computable structure. It can only do that by effectively simulating essential unconscious portions of the simulation while also encoding the information they are being xperienced. Thus it brings unconscious *xperience* into conscious *experience* by encoding it in an overall context in which the xperiences both happen and are known to be happening. This enables organisms to better compute their functioning at the highest possible level of the whole organism which can only be done if the organism actually knows and experiences what is being computed which it does because the forms of experience contain that information.

Xperience is real but implicit and virtual. The nature of *experience* can be better understood by comparison with *xperience*. Xperience is actual and immanently manifests itself as itself, but it is implicit and virtual because there is no context or conceptualization of xperience in itself. It is being xperienced but it does not know it is being xperienced because it has no conceptual context that tells it that it is. There is no associated information of an 'it' that is having the xperience, there is only the reality of the xperience itself. Thus it is actually xperienced, but it is xperienced unconsciously. It does not xperience *itself*, because there is no encoded concept of self. It just is pure raw xperience.

Xperience in organismic forms. It may be difficult to grasp that all inanimate forms, all inanimate matter, is continually xperiencing its own existence unconsciously. But it becomes easier to understand when we extend xperience to biological processes. The vast majority of the biological processes of the body also continually xperience their re-computations unconsciously. It is easier to understand that organs might xperience hormone flows for example in the sense that they react to them, but this is precisely how all inanimate forms xperience their environments as well by reacting to them. Both are simply the continual interactive re-computations of their forms in which they react to other forms and thus xperience them.

Experiencing xperience. Experience, on the other hand, consists of specialized information forms that monitor and simulate the xperiences of other forms and thus make them conscious in those simulations. Forms of all types are first simulated unconsciously as xperience in their mental simulations. Consciousness then further selectively simulates some of these simulation forms in self-referential forms that combines the information of what they are with the information that they are happening. This constitutes the *experience* of the *xperience* of the originally simulated forms. And because these forms include the information that they are being simulated they have knowledge of themselves and become conscious experience.

Anything can be simulated. It is just a matter of encoding the information in an information form. Thus it is easy to convince us we are conscious with information that tells us we are, and it is those forms that actually are our conscious experiences. They are our conscious experiences because they tell us they are.

Experience monitors xperience. Experience is similar to the detailed monitoring systems of a Mars rover that provide information about what the actual operational systems are doing. Extend this concept to a biological robot in exact human form with enormously more detailed monitoring systems and you automatically arrive at conscious experience. It is unreasonable to think that such an exact human biological robot would not be automatically conscious, that some mysterious immaterial thing called consciousness would have to be added to make it conscious. Therefore, since the robot would consist only of information forms, it is obvious that it is some specialized type of form in organisms that is responsible for the knowing what is happening that constitutes the form structure of consciousness.

The area of consciousness monitors the happening of other forms and encodes the fact of that happening in its own forms as experiences of them. Because this is contextualized self-referential information about other information it allows the organism to know it is experiencing that information. Knowing it is experiencing something is itself just a specialized self-referential form of information and thus can be represented as the forms of experience.

Consciousness versus experience. Thus it is the specialized self-referential forms of experience that allow organisms to experience that they are experiencing things. However without the additional element of ontological energy experience would just be dead static non-existent forms without actuality. What really makes the forms of experience real and actual and therefore conscious is they are happening in the ontological energy of reality. This is what gives them their actual existence in reality which is the essence of their consciousness as opposed to their self-knowledge.

Thus the fact that experience knows about itself is due to its self-referential forms, but the fact that this experience really pops into the reality of consciousness is due to the fact that it actually happens in the self-manifesting reality of the present moment. It is this self-manifestation of experiencing itself into reality that makes it conscious.

The reality of xperience. All *xperience* as well as all *experience* actually pops into reality. Thus all xperience is just as real and happening as all experience is. Both are absolutely real in the exact same sense of manifesting the actual reality of ontological energy. Thus the *xperience* of a stone is just as real as the *experience* of a human but the xperience of the stone is not known to itself objectively because its forms are not self-referential. It remains only a subjective xperience. Both types of forms are absolutely real and actual because both occur in reality, thus it is just a matter of the different actual structures of the forms involved. The forms of *xperience* don't include information that they are being xperienced, but the forms of *experience* do.

Xperience is always only that of the actual forms involved. When a stone is smashed it does xperience the smashing but it xperiences no pain because there are no forms that encode pain, but when a worm is smashed it does xperience pain because there are information structures that encode pain involved as these are necessary for the functioning and survival of living organisms.

The forms of experience are observer dependent. Conscious experience includes both specialized forms whose structural details are functions of the structures of individual organisms, and the self-manifesting reality they become conscious within by happening within. The self-referential forms carry both the information of the happening forms themselves and the fact they are happening. This makes them known to themselves. And then the fact that this happens in reality is what adds all the characteristics of consciousness that makes this self-knowledge conscious.

Individual experiences are *contents* of consciousness *itself*. All experiences become conscious by appearing in consciousness itself. All thoughts, feelings, meanings and everything else that becomes conscious by appearing in consciousness itself is a type of experience. Experiences are the self-referential form contents of consciousness itself.

Definition: Consciousness *itself* (as opposed to its contents) is the self-manifesting living presence of reality in an organismic observer such as a human. Consciousness itself is not something added by mind or generated by the brain. It is the living self-manifesting presence of reality in mind and the participation of mind in reality as part of reality.

Consciousness itself is that specialized area of the simulation in which experience occurs.

Evidence for consciousness *itself*: The existence of consciousness itself can be clearly demonstrated through the mental exercise of emptying consciousness of its contents. When the individual contents of consciousness are allowed to fade away then the continuing presence of consciousness itself is realized. Consciousness itself then clearly remains as a bright empty awareness. This is the actual presence of reality itself, the direct experience of the self-manifesting presence of ontological energy. This is the specialized monitoring function waiting for forms to monitor and finding only the presence and experience of itself.

Consciousness itself is intrinsically devoid of contents and the contents of consciousness become conscious by appearing within it just as the forms of the world become real by appearing within reality. If fact both processes are different perspectives on the same self-manifestation of reality. Both are the appearances of types of forms within the ontological energy of reality. Reality self-manifests in general throughout the world of forms, and consciousness is the same process of the self-manifestation of reality but in the self-informing forms of an organismic observer.

Evidence that consciousness itself is reality itself: That consciousness is the self-manifesting presence of reality itself is demonstrated by the fact that all the characteristics of consciousness itself but one are actually the previously identified characteristics of reality itself. Specifically the presence, reality, actuality, and self-manifestation usually attributed to consciousness are actually the characteristics of reality itself. All that is added by mind is a particular computational locus for the forms that constitute the contents of that consciousness within the form of an individual observer and the structural details of experience.

The solution to the 'Hard Problem' of consciousness. How consciousness itself can arise from a 'physical' world has been called the 'Hard Problem' of consciousness. The short solution to the Hard Problem is that consciousness is conscious because reality is real. Consciousness itself is the self-manifesting presence of reality in a specialized area of mind that monitors and simulates *xperiences* in terms of self-referential forms of *experience*. This area of mind adds self-reference to organismic simulations of reality. Thus the Hard Problem is a false problem because it assumes a type of physical world

380

that does not exist. It assumes the standard view of a passive reality that waits to be manifested by consciousness rather than a reality which actively self-manifests itself as xperience, experience, and consciousness.

The traditional view is that consciousness manifests things rather than reality manifesting them. But this is an anthropomorphic prejudice and it is actually reality itself that self-manifests its presence as consciousness in certain specialized forms of an organismic observer just as it does as xperience in all forms.

Even if it were consciousness that manifested things ultimately that would require reality to do the manifesting since consciousness is part of reality and becomes real only by existing in reality. Thus the truth is that reality itself is doing the manifesting that is the essence of consciousness.

Just as we see because light enters our eyes rather than our eyes shining light on the world, so we are conscious because reality self-manifests as us and within us rather than our brain shining consciousness on reality. When reality is understood as a living self-manifesting presence this becomes clear.

Consciousness itself is the direct experience of the fundamental process of the universe. Consciousness is the actual living presence of reality itself in the present moment. This is also the direct experience of the continually extending hyperspherical surface of the universe which continually carries us through time at the speed of light. Thus consciousness itself is the direct experience of the fundamental process of the universe.

Though reality continually manifests itself in every one of our forms, consciousness is the area of mind in which reality manifests itself in a knowable manner as our mind simulates it and tells itself that it is being simulated.

MIND AND REALITY

Organisms, themselves evolving forms or programs, are discrete self-assembling computational systems whose hardware and

software designs are both encoded in their DNA and passed from generation to generation. Their software design includes the fundamental instinctual software which gives their actions volitional direction toward survival, procreation and valuations in terms of positive and negative feelings; the ability to construct mental models of their reality, and the learning abilities which enable them to intelligently and purposefully carry out their instinctual imperatives.

Organisms exist as integrated intelligent purposeful computational systems that include every last computation of all its forms down to the level of individual cells and even the elementary particles which compose them. They are a single integrated hierarchical computational system in which the vast majority of computations exist unconsciously as xperience. All living organisms are intelligent volitional computational systems or programs.

Organismic observers such as humans are a subclass of *generic* observers characterized by having internal computational mental models or simulations of reality. These models tune useful information from the logical structure of external reality, organize it in meaningful structures and compute actions against it which are effectuated in the external world through action systems.

The world we think we live in is actually our mental simulation of that world and exists only in our minds. It consists of a sampling of logical structure from the world of forms greatly embellished by our minds in ways that make it easier to compute and valuate so as to facilitate functioning. This is true for all organismic observers to varying degrees.

Definition: The Retinal Sky refers to the fact that when we observe the world around us we are actually looking into the structures of our own minds and perceptual systems. The sky we see is actually an image on our retinas and the structure we see in the world around us is mostly that of our own minds.

Our simulation consists of a continuous sampling of the logical structure of external reality organized and overlaid with additional information structures encoding our perceptions of, interactions with, and relationships to that logical structure.

The logical structure of this internal simulation is demonstrably accurate to the extent it enables organisms to function in reality on the basis of computations against it. However this simulation is a greatly simplified and embellished sampling of the actual logical structures of the world of forms as interpreted by a particular observer. Thus much is not included and what is included is heavily altered by the biological and cognitive forms of the observer.

Definition: All the differences between the actual form structure of the external world of forms and its simulation is defined as 'illusion'. Illusions are what prevent organisms from directly experiencing reality as it actually is or more accurately are the ways organisms experience reality which are not the actual true nature of external reality.

Definition: The 'Veils of Illusion' are the many different types of ways in which a simulation of reality differs from the actual structure of reality. There are a number of types of veils of illusion.

Method of discovered external reality. Thus the true nature of the observer independent external world can be discovered by progressively identifying and subtracting all that mind adds to its simulation of that world. We briefly review the veils of illusion and what they add to actual reality to discover what remains of reality itself.

Definition: Programmable Illusions are all the ways reality is distorted by individual personal, social and cultural programming. Because these are the result of personal programming they can theoretically be changed, though they often become habitual. These are generally what Buddhism speaks of as the ignorance, attachments and desires that often lead to suffering. They include all learned prejudices, psychological distortions, religious and other delusions, and in general all learned misrepresentations of reality.

Definition: The Illusions of Language are the distortions of reality due to its being conceptualized in the syntactical forms of human language. These are revealed by the underlying syntactical structure of language as consisting of subjects, objects, actions, properties and relationships which tends to be reflected in the underlying structure of the simulations of reality though not necessarily being true of reality itself. This also includes the representation of reality in terms of 'individual' things, situations and events in the simulations of both human and animal observers.

Definition: Perceptual Illusions are the distortions in reality introduced by organismic perceptual systems. These include the many ways reality is post-processed that aren't really there such as color changes with different backgrounds and those revealed by magic tricks and optical illusions. Large numbers of these are well documented. They all demonstrate not so much how mind can be fooled but how mind actually constructs its simulation of reality in terms of them.

Definition: Singularity Illusions are illusions stemming from the fact of the observer occupying a particular location in spacetime that the rest of reality is relative to. These provide important and profound insights into the true nature of reality. In particular external reality itself has no position, location, relative motion, size, orientation, or apparent clock rate because these are all relative to an observer and are thus characteristics of our simulations of reality that are not actual characteristics of reality itself.

A true view of reality would be no view of all because all views are from the perspective of some observer in all ways relative to itself. But the observer independent reality would exist not as the view of any observer, or even from all views at once. The whole idea of a view of it is contrary to its actual nature as independent of any particular observer. **Thus the true nature of observer independent reality can only be computational information which is all that can be observer independent.**

Definition: The Sensory Illusions are illusions stemming from the nature and limitations of the sensory process. For example reality does not consist of focused images of things because light waves in external reality are all unfocused. Also our simulation of reality cannot be true because it is based only on very limited sections of the whole spectrum of electromagnetic waves, sound waves and other types of information.

Definition: Illusions of Physics are illusions revealed by science about the nature of the world. For example physics tells us that reality actually consists of information in the form of interacting wavefunctions rather than discrete individual material objects at the classical scale. And it is well known that material objects are mostly empty space which is not how they are represented in our simulations of them. It is also clear that what we experience as all our sensations and thoughts actually consist only of information encoded as electrochemical impulses in our nerves and neurons.

Definition: Illusions of Quality refers to the fact that the objects we appear to experience are actually mostly made up of qualities that

reflect how we interact with them. These qualia are all added internally and are not attributes of objects in external reality. These include all apparent physical attributes of objects such as color, texture, hardness, and weight that are all actually information about how we experience things rather than innate characteristics of the things themselves. The qualia also include all the feelings and meanings we ascribe to reality which are not in reality itself.

Definition: The Illusion of Physicality is the fact that all the qualities and self-substances of things that appear to give them their physicality are actually all qualia in our simulation of them. Thus the apparent physicality of the world is clearly an illusion constructed in our minds.

Definition: The Illusion of Dimensionality refers to the fact that the actual world we live in does not exist in a dimensional spacetime. As we have seen dimensionality arises piecewise from decoherences and there is no pre-existing spacetime in the world of forms which exists only as a dimensionless computational information space.

Definition: The Illusion of Things refers to the fact that discrete individual things are simulations of reality rather than the actual structure of external reality. The structure of external observer independent reality consists of emergent domain structures which are overlapping structural variations in a single continuous world of forms. This is clarified by how infants and robotic systems learn to construct individual things from a continuous sensory environment.

Definition: The Illusion of Self refers to the fact that the self is a thing that is mentally constructed in the same way that other things are. There is no objective self in the external world of forms that is anything at all like it is represented in our simulation.

Definition: The Illusion of Historical Time is the fact reality only exists in the present moment. That contrary to our conception of a reality with historical duration all that actually exists is the instantaneously evolving form states of the present moment.

Definition: The Illusion of a Present Moment with Duration refers to the fact that the duration of the actual present moment is far below human perception but it is falsely represented in the mental model as having a few seconds duration. It is only this illusion of the persistence of things long enough to make temporal comparisons that is the basis of most of our ability to make sense out of reality. For example without this illusion there would be no sense of music which depends on the temporal relationship of notes. Without this there would be no conception of temporal comparisons or relationships of any kind possible and thus most if not all meaning would disappear.

Definition: The Illusion of Change is a related illusion due to the representation of before and after states in the simulation. All that actually exists in external reality itself is the single instantaneously happening state of the present moment rather than a sequence of video frames as it tends to be simulated.

Definition: The Illusion of The Present Future is an illusion produced in the mental model that things actually exist shortly before they actually happen. We live in an imaginary world slightly in the future of what actually exists which enhances our ability to act quickly to the extent it is accurate. In general the mental model continually presents us with what it expects and only modifies this as needed. This is well attested experimentally.

The reality that remains is evolving information only. When all these illusions are taken into account and subtracted from the simulation all that is left is the consistently evolving information our simulation is based upon. This is the world of forms which is the actual external observer independent reality we have sought beyond the veils of illusion. This method of revealing reality by subtracting illusions is strong evidence that reality actually is only a computational information system consisting of evolving forms.

All simulations are part of the world of forms. Because observers are also forms in the world of forms so are their simulations. Thus it is clear that all the illusory forms of all the simulations of all organismic observers are also additional forms in the external observer independent world of forms

The consistency of inconsistent simulations. Because all the forms of a simulation are part of a consistent world of forms they too must be a consistent part of that world of forms. However observer models of reality typically contain inconsistencies. This inconsistency is resolved by including the inevitably inaccurate premises they are based upon to the *ad hoc* methods by which the inconsistencies appear. When this is done overall consistency with the world of forms is preserved.

Thus the total world of forms remains a consistent computationally evolving information system. That complete system of the world of forms includes all the organismic mental models of itself that recursively encode how it is experienced and conceptualized by various observers.

This is how what is fundamentally a pure abstract computational information structure generates all the multitudinous views of itself as bright, colorful, physical worlds full of meanings and feelings in the simulations of observers though which reality experiences itself in innumerable different ways depending on the form structures of those observers.

Simulation is reality. Since the forms of our simulations are actual real forms in observer independent external reality then they are real, consistent, actual and true forms as well. Thus we as organismic observers do actually *directly experience* part of the reality of the world of forms as it actually exists in our simulations of other parts of it. Though our simulation is not an accurate representation of the external world of forms it simulates, it is an actual part of the real world of forms and it is direct experience of that part.

Thus escaping illusion does not consist of the impossible act of completely discarding our mental model of reality but of understanding it for what it really is and to the extent possible in realizing what the true nature of the entire world of forms actually is including the realization of the ontological energy in which all forms appear that gives them their reality.

KNOWLEDGE

Definition: Knowledge is the degree of correspondence across maximum scope of the computational structure of a simulation with that of the logical structure of the external world of forms.

The consistency theory of knowledge. The only test of knowledge is the completeness and internal consistency of an organismic observer's simulation of reality. Since it is impossible to directly compare the logical structure of the internal simulation with that of the external world of forms, this is the only possible test of the accuracy of knowledge.

It is an accurate test because the external world of forms is itself a logical structure. If it were not, simulations, which are themselves part of the external world of forms, could not be and reality would not be knowable and it would be impossible for organisms to exist within it. Since the world of forms is a self-consistent structure a mental model of reality must itself be self-consistent to be accurate and the degree of self-consistency is the degree of accurate knowledge.

Corollary: Because self-consistency is the test of accurate knowledge all inconsistencies in any mental model of reality indicate incorrect knowledge or lack of knowledge.

"The unreasonable effectiveness of mathematics." The fact that the universe is best described by the logico-mathematical structure of science demonstrates that it must be a rather similar logico-mathematical structure itself. How else could logic and mathematics best describe it if it were not a computational structure operating by logico-mathematical rules? This explains the so called "unreasonable effectiveness of mathematics", and more generally the effectiveness of logic and reason.

Good models of reality must be computational. Because the world of forms is a computational system the best scientific theories, including an ultimate theory of everything, should also be computational systems that actively compute results rather than consisting of isolated equations that require scientists to apply and compute them. That intelligence must be part of the theory itself.

Hopefully the model of reality presented in this book is itself internally self-consistent, consistent with modern science and with a careful analysis of personal direct experience as well across the entire span of human experience and thus represents the best current model and truest knowledge of reality. I believe it is.

Human logic and mathematics are generalized approximations of the actual logico-mathematical system of reality that computes its evolution. However there are some essential differences that must be addressed to more accurately model the logic of reality.

Differences between human and actual logic. Infinities and infinitesimals cannot exist in an actual reality which is finite. Reality is finite because anything actual must be finite. This is clear when the nature of infinity as an unactualizable and unrealizable *process* rather than a fixed state is understood. Also certain types of recursion such as that expressed as Gödel numbers and other inconsistencies of true (rather than quantum) logical paradoxes cannot exist in reality itself which is an entirely self-consistent system.

It is also likely that the concept of nothing, of zero, does not exist in reality. Nothing or zero may be only a comparative absence of something and likely a concept that exists only in observer models of reality. Reality itself can compute only what actually exists and likely has no need for zero. So these generalized conveniences of human logico-mathematics that allow the encoding of 'what ifs' and inconsistencies must likely be abandoned to achieve an accurate computational theory of everything.

Gödel's Incompleteness Theorem does not apply. The incompleteness theorem does not apply to the logical structure of reality since it is a computational system in which each state is computed directly from prior states rather than arising independently subject to proof. Thus the logico-mathematical system of reality can be and in fact must be logically complete.

Definition: Intelligence, specifically functional intelligence, is the ability to correctly construct and traverse valid logical sequences to act effectively in solving real world problems. This functional intelligence, common to all organisms to varying degrees, is used to compute optimal decisions in all aspects of daily life. It is only loosely correlated with IQ which is a measure of the ability to do well on IQ tests. For example a person with very high IQ could also make very poor life decisions. Every decision in life is an intellgence test of functional intelligence.

Definition: Wisdom is the combination of functional intelligence operating on large stores of pertinent knowledge including the ability to identify what is pertinent. Thus wisdom is the ability to optimally apply intelligence where it is most needed on the basis of the most pertinent knowledge.

Definition: Intuition is the operation of intelligence and wisdom at an unconscious level. Most of the actual computations of organisms occur at unconscious levels. Intuition is the emergence into consciousness of the results of such unconscious computations. Intuitions can be more or less accurate depending on the competence of the unconscious computations.

REALIZATION

Definition: Realization is understanding and directly experiencing the true nature of reality. It has no esoteric or religious connotations whatsoever.

The Here Now Presence of Realization: Because reality includes everything that exists it is not to be sought somewhere else but in the true nature of everything. With realization nothing changes, everything is as it always was, it is just now recognized for what it truly is.

The Realization of the Gateless Gate: Because realization is the experience of reality and reality is everywhere, realization is not to be found in any particular master, teaching, sect, temple, or path. Realization is not something transmitted from a master. The only true teacher is reality itself, and there is nowhere and in no form that reality cannot be found. Realization is not to be found in any particular teachings, but in the quantum koan and all the other riddles of reality discussed in this book.

The Realization of Existence: The realization of the actuality and necessity of existence and the impossibility of non-existence is perhaps the most subtle and profound realization of all. Yet it is self-evident and self-necessitating and impossible to deny.

Definition: The presence of reality is often realized suddenly and with great intensity in an Enlightenment Experience. Because reality is absolutely real, here and now there are no limits to the intensity of its experience other than the capacity of the experiencer.

The Realization of Fundamental Cosmological Processes: Our consciousness in the present moment, which is the core aspect of our existence, is the direct experience of the fundamental processes of the universe because it is the actual manifestation and presence of these processes within our own being.

The Realization of Happening: Our experience of the continual self-manifestation of happening is our direct experience of the continual extension of the radial p-time dimension of the cosmological hypersphere which is the fundamental process of the universe and the source of happening. It is this continual extension of the radial p-time dimension of the universe that is the motive force that continually re-computes all things, including ourselves, into continuing existence and reality in the present moment. Happening is the motive energy of existence that maintains the existence of the universe. It is the source of the manifestation of ontological energy in the forms of the world of forms.

The Realization of Living Reality: Happening is what gives the universe and everything in it life by continually recreating its existence in the present moment. The universe is a living system in the sense that it is self-motivating and its motion comes from within itself independent of any external force or cause.

The Realization of the STc Principle: The continual extension of the p-time radial dimension of the universe, which is happening, continually propels all of us through time at the speed of light. The self-evident experience of happening is our direct experience of continuously moving through time at the speed of light within the surface of the cosmological hypersphere as the radial time dimension of the universe continually extends.

The Realization of the Arrow of Time: Our experience of the arrow of time is our experience of the unidirectional extension of the radial p-time dimension of the universe.

The Realization of the Cosmological Basis of the Present Moment: The experience of us and everything else existing only in a single common present moment is our experience of existing in the extending surface of the cosmological hypersphere that is common to all of us.

The Realization of the Present Moment: This is the associated realization that the *presence* of reality manifests as the common *present* moment of reality in which all of reality exists.

The Realization of the 4-Dimensional Geometry of the Universe. We all continually actually see the 4-dimensional hyperspherical structure of our universe. The radial past dimension of time is seen in all directions with distance from every point which directly confirms our universe is a 4-dimensional hypersphere. We actually see the 4-dimensional hyperspherical geometry of the universe with our own two eyes all the time.

The direct experience of the fundamental structure and process of the universe manifests within us as the fundamental experience of our own existence. This is truly an amazing and awesome realization. Truly we are right in the middle of everything important with the best seat in the house! The fundamental structure of the universe lies clear before our eyes and all we have to do is look and see it and experience it as it actually is!

The Realization of the Singularity of Self: Because anything at any distance is experienced in the past, only we ourselves exist in the present moment in our experience. Thus we are a spacetime singularity through which a non-existent future is continually computed into existence in the present and thence flows out in every direction into the past.

The Realization of the True Nature of Consciousness: As consciousness itself is progressively emptied of all its contents it becomes clear that consciousness itself is not something generated by mind but the immanent self-manifesting presence and actuality of reality itself within us. The forms that reality manifests as within us are largely constructs of our own minds but the fact that it manifests at all is the living presence of reality itself within us. In this state we experience the formless presence of reality itself as consciousness itself.

The Realization of Ontological Energy: Take the self-evident presence and reality of all things and subtract the things. That which remains that gives all individual things that exist within it their reality is the actual real living presence of reality itself, what we call ontological energy. Tao is another name for ontological energy.

The Realization of the Emptiness of Thoughts: When the structural nature of all individual thoughts, feelings and meanings, and all other contents of consciousness is carefully examined it becomes clear that everything is only the information of itself. Thus thoughts have no individual self-substances other than the ontological energy manifesting as consciousness in which they all arise. Thus in this sense they are empty information forms only. This is the direct realization of the emptiness of mental forms.

The Realization of the Illusion of Attachments and Desires: When thoughts, feelings and meanings are realized as mere contents of consciousness rather than defining characteristics of self it becomes clear that one can alter or discard them. In this way delusional thoughts and dysfunctional attachments and desires can be recognized for what they are and replaced with 'right thought' thus reducing unnecessary suffering.

There are two kinds of people, those who realize they are programmed and who seek to recognize and transcend their programming, and those who think they are their programming.

The Realization of the Emptiness of Things: Because all the apparent things of the world are experienced only as contents of consciousness just as other thoughts are, they are all empty of physicality as all mental forms are. No matter how real apparently physical things seem this reality is only the information of themselves, their information framework in the external world combined with the information of how they are experienced in the simulation. This information is given its reality by arising in the reality of the present moment and is experienced as material things in a physical world. Nevertheless it is actually its information only.

When all that mind adds to the things of the world is subtracted all that remains is their pure information forms only. The true nature of all the supposedly material things of the world is their information only.

The Realization of the Retinal World: When we look out into the world we seem to exist within we are actually looking inward into the structures of our own mind. Reality is mind and external world intertwined as two sides of a mirror. This is the direct experience that the entire 'physical' world in which we seem to exist is simply a consistent computational information system of empty forms in our mind rather than what it appears to be. Because every aspect of the world we seem to live in, save snippets of logical structure, actually exists as logical constructs within our own simulation of reality, we realize it consists only of empty forms of information as all thought structures do.

The Realization that Mountains are Mountains Again: Though the true mountain exists as an empty information structure in the external world of forms independent of any particular observer, the internal mental model of that mountain also exists as a separate but related empty form structure in the world of forms since all forms are actual forms in the world of forms. Thus the true realization of the mountain is that it is as it appears in the mental model but only when that internal representation of the mountain is realized for what it actually is, the simulated information of its apparent self.

The Realization of Illusion: This is the realization that all things in the world are illusions, in the sense that they are not what they appear to be, but that they are also real because they are illusions that appear in reality. Thus the realization is that illusion mistaken for reality is illusion, but illusion recognized as illusion is reality.

The Realization of Reality: This is understanding and experiencing the world of forms as empty of any self-substances but absolutely full of the living realness and immanent presence of reality in the present moment. It is the direct experience of the reality of all things absent the things. It is understanding that all the information forms of the world directly manifest reality because they arise in the ontological energy of reality and this reality is directly realized in all the things of the world.

The Realization that things are their Information: This is understanding and actually seeing that all forms of whatever type are pure information only that together exist as a self-consistent computational structure that is given reality by existing within the ontological energy of reality. It is realizing that all 'things' without exception are their information only and all that exists is consistently evolving information in ontological energy. This can be actually experienced by successively picking apart the combined aspects of any individual thing and analyzing each into the information it actually is. Everything, including all the individual aspects that combine to give things their apparent physicality are actually the information of themselves only.

The realization that things are their Information Histories. And further it is the realization that the information that all things actually are is the current computational result of their entire information histories. Thus all things are their information histories and their information histories only.

The realization of the Sherlock Holmes Principle. This is the realization that the information histories of all things are the computational results of their interactions with other forms and thus their information histories include information about the other forms they have interacted with and thus that this is what they actually are. All things are the computational results of their entire information interactions with other things and thus are composed of the distributed information of other things. Thus information about other things can be read in the information that is every particular thing.

The Realization of Chi and Energy Body: Chi is the ontological energy within an organismic observer. It is directly experienced and realized as the combined internal feelings of all parts and aspects of body and mind as a total energy body. Both chi and the energy body are self-evident natural phenomena that everyone experiences all the time whether recognized or not and not supernatural or esoteric in the least.

When chi is recognized it can then be manipulated as an aid to health, wellbeing and effectiveness of action. However this is not a panacea or anything superhuman. Everything operates through natural forms and is limited by them and all other forms have their own chi as well which limits one's own.

Chi also includes all the internal feelings and perceptions of the apparently external things which are all actually part of one's internal simulation of the world and thus actually part of one's own self. Thus chi properly understood includes the total living experience of an observer.

The Realization of Experience: This is the realization that all that ultimately exists or is known to any organism is experience. However this experience is not initially 'it's' experience as experience itself is prior to the organization of that experience into the experience of a self and what it experiences. It is just raw primary experience without context or subsequent organization. Thus experience itself, raw and uncategorized, is the manifestation of reality itself.

And all subsequent organization of experience in any way whatsoever in the mental model is itself then experienced only as raw experience. So in all cases what actually exists is raw primary experience prior to any subsequent organization even if it is the experience of a previous subsequent organization. And in all cases experience is the self-manifestation of reality in the form of that experience.

The Realization of the True Self: Because experience includes every possible aspect of the manifestation of reality to any observer it actually includes both what that observer thinks of as its self and the entirety of the experience of the apparently external world. Thus experience includes all possible aspects without exception of both self and not-self in the totality of all that exists 'to that observer'. Thus the totality of experience, the totality of the energy body, is the true self of the observer because it all is part of its simulation. This is true both of an organismic observer's *experience* and the *xperience* of all forms as generic observers.

The Realization of the Self-Manifestation of Reality as Xperience.
Ultimately there is only xperience which is the self-manifestation of
reality as the continual re-computation of forms into existence in the
present moment. Reality consists of xperience only. Reality is its
continual self-manifestation as xperience.

The Realization of the Illusion of the Personal Self: This is the
realization that the individual personal self is a thing, and like all other
things is only an information construct in a simulation. This is a
corollary of the realization of the true self.

**Definition: Buddha Nature is a synonym for ontological energy
from a more personal perspective as an aid to realization.** It refers
to the fact that the ontological energy of reality is the only substance of
all things without exception. Thus Buddha Nature is the true nature of
all things including ourselves and all other beings.

The Realization of Buddha Nature: This is the realization that since
the energy body is the experience of reality 'within one' we can be
automatically considered a living enlightened being which can be called
Buddha Nature or the Buddha within. It is a personalization of the
energy body as an enlightened being as it is itself the presence of
reality.

Thus all things without exception have (more accurately are) Buddha
Nature. Buddha Nature is simply the living presence of reality in the
forms of all things. Then since 'we' are the Buddha Nature within our
particular human form, it can be experienced as the Buddha within.
This realization facilitates living and acting as a realized Buddha. Again
there are no religious or esoteric connotations. All things still act only
through their own actual forms and they manifest their Buddha Natures
only through their particular forms and the computational limits to
those forms.

The Realization of the Buddha Nature of All Things: From this
perspective all of reality ultimately consists only of Buddhas. Buddhas
looking at other Buddhas looking back at each other in realization of
their Buddhahood. And all Buddhas as empty forms manifesting the
single common underlying presence of the Buddha Nature of reality to
each other, and to themselves, and thus back to reality itself.

The Realization of Compassion: When one realizes the common
Buddha Nature of all things one recognizes the unity and brotherhood

of all beings and things and compassion towards them naturally arises. Most Buddhas are trapped in dysfunctional forms and situations that result in greater or lesser degrees of suffering. Compassion is aiding realization by helping other beings realize their Buddhahood; both by example and by helping remove the suffering and attachments and programming that impede realization.

Compassion includes compassion for one's own self. Compassion extends to all beings and includes taking the best possible care of oneself which also helps facilitate compassion for others. It is taking care of one's own mind and keeping it healthy and clear so as support one's realization. And it is treating one's own body with the utmost care and kindness as one would any being one loved. Our body is our always loyal long suffering beast of burden that carries us through reality for all the years of our lives, so treat it well and give it the thanks and care and love it deserves. And our mind is our closest most intimate and personal friend. Love it and care for it and cultivate its lasting health and friendship.

Defining God: If a God is needed we must define God as the universe or reality itself. This is the only rational definition of God because it ensures the self-evident existence of God. And then the attributes of God become a verifiable matter of science, reason and experience.

This understanding of God certainly doesn't diminish God in the least because it is the universe itself, if anything, that is miraculous and has divinity. The universe itself is certainly most worthy of our awe and adulation, and our religious and spiritual devotion. And this is a single common God all men can worship together in unifying peace rather than division.

The attributes of God. This definition of God is compatible with the fundamental attributes usually attributed to God. The universe is certainly omnipotent as the source of all power, omnipresent by definition, omniscient as all knowledge is contained within it, certainly divine if anything is, and most certainly miraculous. It also continually actively recreates itself in every moment in the present moment. And it is a living God in that it acts from within itself to move all things via happening.

The search to find God. From this perspective the search to know the true nature of reality becomes a search to find God. Only when the true nature of reality is understood and then directly experienced does the presence of God reveal itself in all its divinity.

When the world is finally directly experienced as an enormously dense complex of innumerable interacting forms all alive with the living actuality of reality of the present moment does the living presence of God appear manifested in all things and only then is God finally confronted and recognized in all its immanent glory.

We and all things are the living presence of God within. If God is the universe itself we then realize that God is the true nature of all beings and things and we recognize God in all beings and things in the forms that they are. Thus we see God looking back at us from every eye and listening to us with every ear. And God looks out through our eyes at God looking back at itself through all other eyes. In this manner God sees and realizes itself and we become the sense organs and distributed minds of God.

And this is true also of all other experience and consciousness. All forms are the forms of God experiencing itself in those forms. Again there is nothing supernatural here, only a new interpretation of reality. The experience of God is always restricted to actual existing forms acting according to natural law. For example God sees only through eyes, hears only through ears. We, and all things, are the sense organs of God by which it both manifests itself and xperiences itself and thus becomes real and actual.

The Realization of Love: The experience of our existence can be experienced as pure divine love; pure in the sense of an internal feeling of love without attachments to any object but simply the experience of our being, our chi, our energy body, as the feeling of love itself. There is an actual objective reason for this because the very fact of our existence is a proof that the universe loves us enough to have brought us into being in the face of enormous improbability and continues to sustain our being in this present moment in which we experience it. It is in this sense that the universal God of reality loves us and watches over us, and we are the presence of the living God within us manifesting us as we are the living life force of the universe within us.

The Realization of Personal Myth: Of course to some extent this is a personal myth because it is a personal interpretation of reality. We all have personal myths which may or may not be completely consistent with the logic of reality. These personal myths are largely ours to make up as we like and add those that most enhance us to our simulations of reality. Inconsistencies are not a problem so long as personal myths are recognized as myth rather than reality. Personal myths only become a problem if they are mistaken for objective reality and thereby become delusion.

The Realization of Realization: Because reality is all that exists everything we experience is part of reality exactly as it is and thus we experience only reality without exception. Thus we are all always already in a state of realization whether we realize it or not. It is impossible not to be. It is just a matter of understanding and experiencing this as it actually is. Thus realization is simply a matter of realizing we are all already here in the presence of reality and we are all already experiencing reality exactly as it actually is. And the understanding of what it actually is we are realizing is hopefully what we have achieved in this book…..

EPILOGUE

In this book I've done my best to present what I believe is the best and most comprehensive current view of reality as it actually is. It will be interesting to see what influence the book has on the general perception of the nature of reality if any. And even more interesting will be what other discoveries in the nature of reality will be made in the future though the author probably won't be around to see many of them. I only wish I could be around longer to experience for myself the surely astounding new insights that will be discovered, and eventually perhaps for a final theory of everything, if in fact that is even possible for such a limited intellect as man.

This book was written as the result of a lifetime of study of the deep nature of reality primarily to facilitate my own understanding and realization of reality. I feel it has succeeded to a remarkable extent much greater than I had first expected. I sincerely hope others will find something of similar value in it as well.

The model of reality presented in this book is the most consistent and complete across the whole of human knowledge and experience that I'm aware of and therefore, I believe, must represent the truest current knowledge of the nature of reality. I believe it is both internally self-consistent and also consistent with the established theories of modern science, though certainly not with most scientists' interpretations of those theories. And I believe it is also consistent with the deepest analysis of direct personal experience as well. Thus it hopefully stands as the most consistent model of reality across the broadest scope of reality which is the test of true knowledge. I'm pretty confident at this point it represents the best overall framework for understanding the nature of reality and that future advances will integrate naturally into its framework.

Nevertheless an immense amount of detail needs to be filled into its framework to fully flesh it out and confirm it and I sincerely hope others will follow up on that. And, as the product of the limited mind of a human observer it is of course necessarily incomplete and always subject to revision. It will be interesting to eventually see just how capable the minds of humans are of truly comprehending the mystery of the reality in which we exist. Or perhaps it will eventually be only the future computational systems that we humans create that will achieve the final breakthroughs in understanding. Ultimately only the universe itself can be said to truly understand and fully know itself because any theory must necessarily be only an imperfect part of the whole.

To some extent the mystery of the reality in which we find ourselves will always remain a mystery. Yet it is the ultimate mystery and the mystery that calls on the noblest aspects of the human mind to try and solve.

I apologize to the reader that this book is rather rough, and in many places not as clear and concise as I wish it could have been. It's still very much a work in progress that I hope to polish and expand as possible in future editions. So I hope the reader will excuse this and try to cut through the sometimes awkward and repetitive language to discern its message. It is not always easy to properly describe a reality which so often exceeds the inherent structures of language with language.

Thus I welcome all serious questions, comments and criticisms which should be directed to the author at EdgarOwen@att.net or look me up online. If the reader believes this model is incorrect in any respect please bring it to my attention with the reasons why. After all it is when errors are exposed that the truth is revealed.

NOTES

1.   For the mathematically inclined special relativity may be derived from the STc Principle as follows. To simplify the discussion we assume that any spatial velocity is directed parallel to the x axis. Then the STc Principle can be expressed mathematically as

$$\mathbf{v}_x + \mathbf{v}_T = \mathbf{c} \tag{1.1}$$

Where $\mathbf{v}_x$ is the velocity through space along the x axis, $\mathbf{v}_T$ is the velocity through time, and $\mathbf{c}$ is the velocity of light. Writing the quantities in bold indicates that they are vectors, that is they have both a magnitude and a direction.

Expressing the x velocity as a vector $\mathbf{v_x}$ is standard physics, however most physicists would probably recoil at expressing the velocity of time as a vector since it is normally considered to be a scalar, a quantity having a magnitude but no direction. In fact though, in a 4-dimensional universe, time clearly does have a direction which is always along the time axis, and thus it is most certainly a vector. The addition of two vectors always produces another vector, so that the result of Eq. (1.1) is a vector *velocity* in a particular direction and the magnitude of that velocity is always the scalar *speed* of light.

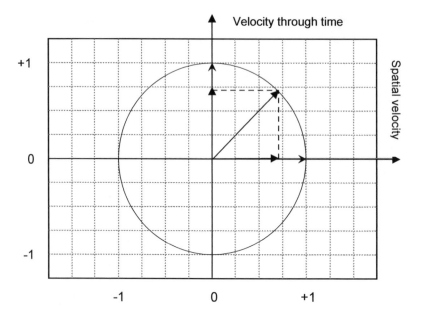

Fig. 1.1 The STc Principle. The vector sum of space and time velocities of every entity in the universe is always equal in magnitude to the speed of light c at every moment, as shown by the circle. Arrows show the three possible cases. When there is no relative velocity in space all of an object's spacetime velocity is through time at the speed of light as shown by the open-headed vertical arrow. In contrast, light itself always travels with relative space velocity $v_x = c$ as represented by the horizontal open-headed arrow. In the third case, when $0 < v_x < c$, the spacetime velocity is the vector sum of the space and time velocities along their respective axes as shown by the diagonal arrow. But in all cases the vector sum of space and time velocities is equal in magnitude to the speed of light as indicated by the circle.

Eq. (1.1) can be depicted graphically. In Fig. 1.1 the vertical axis is the velocity of time, and the horizontal axis is the space velocity along the x axis. When we plot Eq. (1.1), we get a circular arc of constant radius c = the speed of light. The graph shows an arbitrary example whose spacetime velocity vector extends from the origin to the circle along with the space and time velocity components of its vector sum. It also shows the cases in which the c spacetime velocity is directed either entirely along the time or the space axis.

The mathematical rules of vector addition are just the expressions of simple geometry and the Pythagorean theorem so that we can alternately express Eq. (1.1) as

$$v_x{}^2 + v_T{}^2 = c^2 \tag{1.2}$$

That is the sum of the squares of the x and time velocities is equal to the square of the speed of light. This is the more usual mathematical form equivalent to the vector form of (1.1).

From Newtonian physics we know that a velocity is the time rate of change of a distance so that the space velocity along the x axis could also have been written as dx/dt, the instantaneous rate of change of x distance with t time at any given moment.

Now what is meant by the velocity of time? The idea that we need to express, which we will understand more clearly in a moment, is that a moving clock runs at a slower rate than a stationary clock. So it makes sense to consider the rate at which the moving clock runs relative to the standard stationary clock as the relative velocity of the time displayed by the moving clock. We express this velocity as dT/dt, the time rate of change of the moving clock as measured by the stationary clock.

Another consideration is that distance in space is measured in spatial units such as meters, whereas distance along the time axis is measured in time units such as seconds. To have a meaningful equation in which both types of distances and their velocities can be compared they must be expressed in the same units. This can be done by expressing both in a unit such as light seconds, the distance that light travels in a second, $\approx 3 \times 10^8$ meters. This is easily accomplished by substituting cT for T to express the distance along the time axis measured by the moving clock. This gives the equivalent time distance (seconds) in units of spatial distance (light seconds). With these additions we can now rewrite Eq. (1.2) as

$$v_x^2 + \left(\frac{dcT}{dt} \right)^2 = c^2$$

and since for a constant c, dcT/dt = cdT/dt

$$v_x^2 + c^2 \left(\frac{dT}{dt} \right)^2 = c^2 \tag{1.3}$$

Rearranging and dividing both sides by c^2

$$\left(\frac{dT}{dt} \right)^2 = \frac{c^2 - v_x^2}{c^2} = 1 - \frac{v_x^2}{c^2}$$

and taking the square root of both sides we have

$$\frac{dT}{dt} = \sqrt{1 - \frac{v_x^2}{c^2}} \tag{1.4}$$

which gives the velocity of time (the relative slowing of its clock rate) for a clock moving at velocity v_x relative to a stationary observer's clock.

Now Eq. (1.4) is a fundamental equation of special relativity, an expression of the Lorentz transform, and from it all the standard effects of special relativity can be derived except for $E = mc^2$ which follows with the addition of the standard classical principles of conservation of energy and momentum. Thus we find that the theory of special relativity is in fact a consequence of the STc Principle.

2.   On a personal note the author's own mantra expressing the fact that the retinal world we live in is a mirror reality in which what we see around us combines both internal and external realities in a single unified structure is the palindrome, 'Ed is on no side'. I visualize it with a double faced mirror of reality in the middle of the palindrome reflecting each side back upon the other and thus creating two worlds each of which is the reflection of the other. Is it a mirror or is it a gate or is it a single reality? It is all simultaneously. My thanks to Susan at the NY Fed for bringing this to my attention back in the 1970's…..

BIBLIOGRAPHY

Aharony, Amron, et al. *Partial Decoherence in Mesoscopic systems.* http://arxiv.org/pdf/1205.5622v1.pdf, May 28, 2012.

Aristotle, trans. Hugh Tredennick. *Aristotle in 23 Volumes.* Harvard Press, 1983.

Berkeley, George. *Berkeley's Philosophical Writings.* Collier, 1974.

Blythe, R.H. *Mumonkan.* Hokuseido Press, 1966.

Budge, E.A. Wallis, trans. *The Egyptian Book of the Dead.* Penguin, 2008.

Chaitin, Gregory. *Meta Math, the Quest for Omega.* Vintage, 2006.

Chalmers, David. *Facing Up to the Problem of Consciousness.* Journal of Consciousness Studies. 2 (3) 1995 pp. 200-219.

Chomsky, Noam. *Aspects of the Theory of Syntax.* MIT Press, 1965.

Conze, Edward. *Buddhist Wisdom Books.* Thorsons, 1975.

Cornford, Francis. *Plato's Cosmology: The Timaeus of Plato.* Hackett, 1997.

Davies, Paul. *Cosmic Jackpot.* Houghton Mifflin, 2007.

Eddington, Arthur Stanley. *The Nature of the Physical World.* 1928.

Evans-Wentz, W.Y., ed. *The Tibetan Book of the Dead.* Oxford Univ. Press, 1957.

Feynman, Richard. *Lectures On Physics.* Pearson, Addison, Wesley, 2006.

Giles, Lionel. *The Art of War by Sun Tzu.* Special Edition Books, 2005.

Greene, Brian. *The Elegant Universe.* Norton, 1999.

Greene, Brian. *The Fabric of The Cosmos.* Vintage Books, 2005.

Halpern, Paul & Wesson, Paul. *Brave New Universe.* Joseph Henry, 2006.

Harris, Victor, trans. *A Book of Five Rings by Miyamoto Musashi.* Allison and Busby, 1974.

Hawking, Stephen W.; Hartle, James B. *The Wave Function of the Universe.* Physical Review D, vol 28, pp 2960-2975, 1983.

Hofstadter, Douglas R. *Gödel, Escher, Bach.* Vintage, 1980.

Johnson, George. *Strange Beauty: Murray Gell-Mann and the Revolution in Twentieth Century Physics.* Knopf, 2000.

Legge, James. *The Tao Te Ching of Lao Tzu (translation).* Commodius Vicus, 2010.

Lovelock, James. *The Ages of Gaia.* Norton, 1995.

Mandlebrot, Benoit B. *The Fractal Geometry of Nature.* Freeman, 1983.

Misner, Charles W.; Thorne, Kip S.; Wheeler, Archibald. *Gravitation.* Freeman, 1973.

NASA. *The Shape of the Universe*. WMAP website, 2013.

Owen, Edgar L. *Spacetime and Consciousness*. EdgarLOwen.info. 2007.

Owen, Edgar L. *Mind and Reality.* EdgarLOwen.info. 2009.

Penrose, Roger. *The Road to Reality*. Knopf, 2005.

Penrose, Roger. *The Emperor's New Mind.* Oxford University Press.1990.

Piaget, Jean, *Logic and Psychology*. Manchester University Press. 1956.

Piaget, Jean. *The Child's Conception of The World*. Littlefield, Adams & Co., 1960.

Popper, Karl. *The Logic of Scientific Discovery.* Basic Books, 1959.

Price, Huw. *Time's Arrow and Archimedes' Point*. Oxford, 1996.

Rashevsky, Nicolas. *Mathematical Biophysics.* Dover, 1960.

Saotome, Mitsugi. *The Principles of Aikido.* Shambala, 1989.

Smolin, Lee. *The Trouble with Physics.* Mariner Books, 2006.

Smolin, Lee. *Three Roads to Quantum Gravity.* Basic Books, 2001.

Susskind, Leonard. *The Cosmic Landscape.* Little Brown. 2006.

Suzuki, Daisetz. *Zen Buddhism*. Doubleday Anchor Books, 1956.

Takagawa, Shukaku. *The Vital Points of Go*. Nihon Ki-in, 1972.

Thorne, Kip S. *Black Holes & Time Warps.* Norton, 1994.

Tsunemitsu, ed. *The Teachings of Buddha.* Mitutoyo, 1962.

Uhr, Leonard, ed. *Pattern Recognition, Learning & Thought*. Prentice-Hall, 1973.

Vilenkin, Alex. *Many Worlds in One*. Hill and Wang, 2006.

Watts, Alan W. *The Way of Zen.* Pantheon, 1957.

Watts, Alan W. *Following the Middle Way #3*. Alanwatts.com, Podcast, 2008-08-03.

Whitehead, Alfred North. *Process and Reality.* Macmillan, 1929.

Wigner, Eugene. *The* Unreasonable *Effectiveness of Mathematics in the Natural Sciences.* John Wiley, 1960.

Wikipedia contributors. *Wikipedia, the Free Encyclopedia.* http://wikipedia.org

Wilhelm, Richard, Cary F. Baynes, trans. *The Secret of the Golden Flower*. Routledge & Kegan Paul, 1931.

Wu, John C.H. *The Golden Age of Zen*. Pentagon Press, 2005.

Edgar L. Owen was born April 1st, 1941 and quickly realized that reality is not as it first appears to be. A child prodigy, he entered the University of Tulsa at 15 and received a B.S. with honors in science and mathematics with a minor in philosophy at age 18 before completing several more years of graduate study in physics and philosophy.

In the early 60's he moved to the Haight-Ashbury in San Francisco where he hung out with notables from the Beat Generation, and conducted an intense personal study of the nature of mind and consciousness. From there he traveled to Japan where he lived for three years studying Zen and Buddhist philosophy and subsisting as a Ronin English teacher.

Upon returning to the US he began a career in computer science writing numerous programs in artificial intelligence, simulations, graphics and cellular automata while designing and managing advanced computer systems for the New York Federal Reserve Bank and AT&T. He then left the corporate world to start his own software business marketing his CAD programs which he ran for a number of years. Currently he owns a premier internet gallery of fine Ancient Art and Classical Numismatics.

Deeply immersed in nature since childhood, and always considering it the ultimate source of his inspiration and knowledge of reality, he has served as Chairman of his local Environmental Commission and organized several campaigns to protect the local environment and its wildlife.

Over the last several years he has worked to combine and organize the results of a lifetime of study of the various aspects of reality into a single coherent theory in this book. He now spends most of his time exploring how the wonderful awesome mystery of the presence of reality can be experienced more fully and deeply and enjoying his existence within it.

Edgar currently lives in Northern NJ in a big old house on top of a hill where he communes with nature and enjoys the company of his wild visitors including the occasional human. Edgar is currently single and looking for a younger housekeeper companion ☺. He can be contacted at EdgarOwen@att.net.